About the Author

Pierre-Antoine Donnet has degrees in Political Science and Chinese. After working for two years as a freelance journalist in Taiwan and Hong Kong, he spent five years in Peking as a press correspondent (1984–89). He has travelled extensively in Asia and is currently a correspondent in Tokyo. In addition to *Tibet: mort ou vif* (Editions Gallimard, 1990), he is also the author of *Le Japon achète le monde* (Editions Le Seuil, 1991) and *Tibet: des journalistes témoignent* (Editions l'Harmattan, 1992).

Tibet: Survival in Question

PIERRE-ANTOINE DONNET

Translated by Tica Broch

DELHI
Oxford University Press
BOMBAY CALCUTTA MADRAS

Zed Books Ltd
LONDON & NEW JERSEY

Tibet: Survival in Question is a revised and updated translation of *Tibet: mort ou vif*, first published in French by Editions Gallimard, 5 rue Sébastien-Bottin, 75328 Paris Cedex 07, France, in 1990. This English language edition was first published by Zed Books Ltd, 7 Cynthia Street, London N1 9JF and 165 First Avenue, Atlantic Highlands, New Jersey 07716, USA in 1994.

This English language edition was published in India, Pakistan, Bangladesh, Sri Lanka, Nepal and Bhutan (and not for export therefrom) by Oxford University Press, Delhi, in 1994.

Copyright © Pierre-Antoine Donnet, 1990

Translation copyright © Zed Books Ltd, 1994

Translated by Tica Broch

Cover designed by Andrew Corbett

Set in Monotype Baskerville by Ewan Smith, 48 Shacklewell Lane, London E8 2EY

Maps by Atelier Golok

Printed and bound in the United Kingdom by Biddles Ltd, Guildford and King's Lynn

A catalogue record for this book is available from the British Library.

US CIP is available from the Library of Congress.

ISBN 1 85649 129 3 cased
     1 85649 130 7 limp

In South Asia
ISBN 0 19 563573 6

Contents

Foreword

Tibetan civilisation has a long and rich history. The pervasive influence of Buddhism and the rigours of life amid the wide open spaces of an unspoilt environment resulted in a society dedicated to peace and harmony. We enjoyed freedom and contentment. Since the Chinese invasion in 1950, however, the Tibetan people as a whole have endured untold suffering and abuse. Tibetan religion and culture has been attacked, its artefacts destroyed and its proponents condemned.

Tibet's religious culture, its medical knowledge, peaceful outlook and respectful attitude to the environment contain a wealth of experience that can be of widespread benefit to others. It has lately become clear that no amount of technological development on its own leads to lasting happiness. What people need is that sense of inner peace and hope that many have remarked among Tibetans, even in the face of adversity. The source of this lies mostly in the Buddhist teachings of love, kindness, tolerance and especially the theory that all things are relative.

Our cultural traditions form a precious part of the world's common heritage. Humanity would be the poorer if they were to be lost. We have made every effort to preserve and promote them, but we will not succeed in isolation. We require help and support. That depends on the Tibetan people and their traditions being better understood and a greater awareness of the threat that confronts them both. This book, *Tibet: Survival in Question*, will make a valuable contribution to this.

In Tibet, as elsewhere, violence will not bring about peace. I remain convinced that peaceful negotiations are required if we are to reach a lasting solution to our conflict with China. However, as Tibetans become a minority in their own land, due to the Chinese policy of population transfer, the issue has taken on an undeniable feeling of urgency.

Pierre-Antoine Donnet recounts the Tibetan tragedy here on the basis of Tibetan, Western and Chinese sources. Citing recent changes in both Tibet and China, he is optimistic that a more honest and respectful relationship may one day emerge between the Tibetan and Chinese peoples. I can only add that I share that hope.

His Holiness the Dalai Lama, 1 December 1993

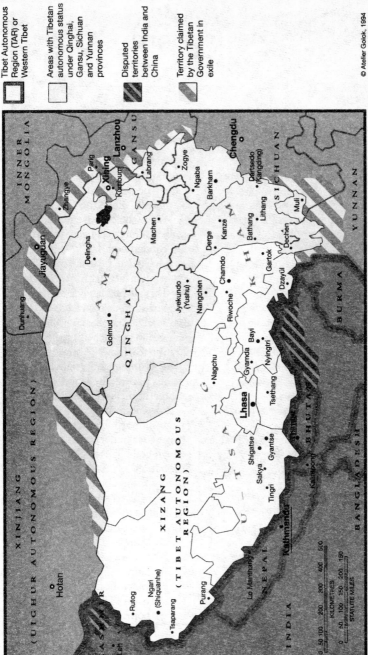

© Atelier Golok, 1994

Tibet Autonomous Region (TAR) or Western Tibet

Areas with Tibetan autonomous status under Qinghai, Gansu, Sichuan and Yunnan provinces

Disputed territories between India and China

Territory claimed by the Tibetan Government in exile

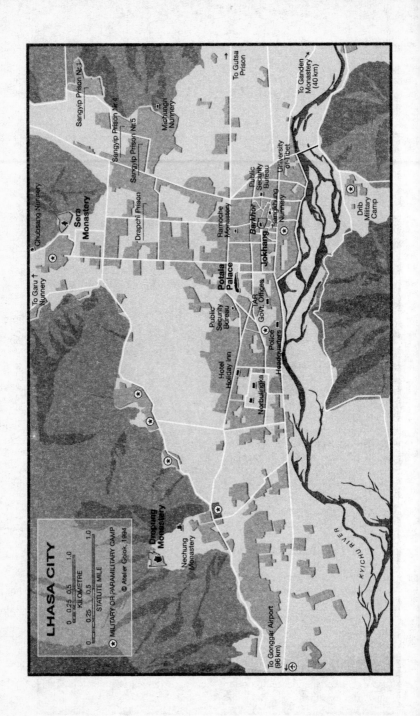

Chronology

Major events in Tibet's history

12000 to 6000 BC – Archaeologists date early settlements in Tibet to the Mesolithic era.

5000 BC – Neolithic bone fragments and pottery found in Chamdo in 1978.

416 BC – King Nyatri Tsenpo founds dynasty in Yarlung valley. Builds Yambul-hakang, first Tibetan fortress.

620–649 AD – Reign of King Songtsen Gampo, who unified Tibet. Written form of Tibetan language.

755–797 – Reign of Emperor Trisong Detsen. Apex of Tibetan empire, whose influence extends from the Pamirs to Turkestan and to Nepal. Buddhism takes root in Tibet: Indian master Padmasambhava.

791 – Completion of first monastery, Samye.

821 – First peace treaty between Tibet and China.

11th century – Second dissemination of Buddhism, many great monasteries are built. Decline of the imperial lineage.

1207 – Genghis Khan rules over China, Korea and territories reaching as far as Europe. Tibet falls under Mongolian domination.

1350 – Tibet throws off the Mongolian yoke, resumes independence; China follows in 1368, Ming (Han) dynasty.

1357–1419 – Je Tsongkhapa, founder of Gelugpa (Yellow Hat) school; founds Ganden monastery, Sera and Drepung.

1543–1588 – Sonam Gyatso, abbot of Drepung, third incarnation of Gedun Trupa (disciple of Tsongkhapa), conferred title of Dalai Lama by Mongolian prince Altan Khan (1578).

1652 – Fifth Dalai Lama visits Peking, invited by Shun Chih, first Qing dynasty (1644–1911) emperor.

1720 – Manchu army enters Lhasa to expel Mongolian invaders. The Manchu reorganize the Tibetan administration and impose a form of imperial 'super-vision'.

1723–1735 – Reign of Emperor Kangxi, who withdraws almost all imperial troops from Lhasa. From 1728 onwards, two Ambans in Lhasa act as representatives of the Manchu Emperor.

1788 – Nepal invades Tibet. Emperor Qianlong sends a large army to help the Tibetans. A peace treaty is signed in 1792. Tibetan administration loses a little more of its independence. Important decisions no longer taken without reference to the Ambans.

1795 – Death of Qianlong. Decline of Qing dynasty. Tibet seizes opportunity to recover its freedom.

1854 – Nepal invades Tibet again but Manchu army stays out. Treaty between Tibet and Nepal signed in 1856.

1910 – For the first time, a Manchu-Chinese army enters Tibet uninvited. It withdraws in 1911 after the fall of the Qing dynasty. Republic of China is founded.

1912 – Tibetan government orders the expulsion of all Chinese in Tibet. The last one leaves in January 1913.

1913 – The Thirteenth Dalai Lama and the Tibetan National Assembly proclaim Tibet's independence. Peking withholds recognition.

1914 – Simla Convention initialled: London recognizes Peking's 'suzerainty' over Tibet, not sovereignty. Tibet partitioned. China undertakes not to interfere in 'Outer Tibet'. Chinese government does not ratify the treaty.

1942 – Lhasa sets up a Foreign Affairs Bureau.

1 October 1949 – Mao Tse-tung proclaims the People's Republic of China.

7 October 1950 – 80,000 Chinese People's Liberation Army soldiers invade Tibet.

23 May 1951 – Signature in Peking of Seventeen-Point Agreement, to enshrine the integration of Tibet with China. China undertakes to respect Tibet's extensive autonomy.

26 October 1951 – Chinese army enters Lhasa.

10 March 1959 – A Tibetan uprising in Lhasa against the Chinese is brutally put down, thousands of Tibetans are killed. The Dalai Lama flees into exile in India. Thousands of Tibetans are jailed.

1 September 1965 – Peking proclaims the creation of 'Tibet Autonomous Region'. At least half of Tibet's ethnic area is annexed to the neighbouring Chinese provinces.

August 1966 – The cultural revolution comes to Lhasa. Temples and monasteries that were still standing are looted and razed. Thousands of Tibetans, lay and ordained, persecuted and sent to labour camps.

9 September 1976 – Death of Mao Tse-tung.

December 1978 – At Third Plenary of CCP Central Committee, ideology takes a sharp turn. For Tibet, dawn of limited religious tolerance.

January 1979 – First delegation sent by the Dalai Lama visits China and Tibet, followed by another three; no genuine dialogue emerges.

1 October 1987 – Hundreds of victims in violent aftermath of demonstration in Lhasa; official death toll is six deaths according to official Chinese figures but Western witnesses count thirteen or more.

5 March 1988 – Another demonstration in Lhasa put down with even greater brutality. Chinese Armed Police fire on the crowd. One death and 109 injured, say Chinese. Eight killed, say Tibetans. Hundreds arrested.

10 December 1988 – Police fire on demonstrators. Twelve fatalities and many injured, according to different sources.

5 March 1989 – Lhasa in flames. Rioting lasts several days. On March 7, imposition of martial law. Protests drowned in blood, hundreds of victims.

4 June 1989 – Tiananmen square massacre. Chinese army opens fire on thousands of demonstrators in the heart of Peking. Three hundred killed say Chinese officials; 1,000–3,000 butchered according to different sources. World discovers real face of Deng Xiaoping.

12 October 1989 – Paris. First meeting between representatives of Dalai Lama and Chinese dissidents (Federation for Democracy in China).

10 December 1989 – Nobel Peace Prize awarded to Dalai Lama.

1991 – 'Year of Tibet'; many events held to commemorate.

16 April 1991 – Dalai Lama meets US President Bush.

23 May 1991 – US Congress declares Tibet an occupied country.

23 August 1991 – UN Sub-Commission on Human Rights adopts resolution on Tibet: first for twenty-five years.

February 1992 – First UN document on 'The situation in Tibet' presents official PRC views contrasted with reports by seven recognized non-governmental organizations.

1992 – Peking declares Tibet a 'Special Economic Zone'.

November 1992 – Permanent Peoples' Tribunal on Tibet.

December 1992 – European Parliament adopts five-page resolution on Tibet.

January 1993 – London meeting of international jurists on Tibet.

27 April 1993 – Dalai Lama meets US President Clinton.

April 1993 – Government of Taiwan invites Dalai Lama with no preconditions, declares respect for Kashag Five-Point Peace Plan. On 14 May, first trip to Taiwan since 1950s for Kashag minister Gyalo Thondup.

24–25 May – Largest Tibetan demonstrations in Lhasa since 1989.

Preface

In Lhasa as elsewhere, a great deal of water has passed under the bridge since the first edition of this book came out in French in 1990. When I sat down to write it, I had just returned from almost five years spent in China, working as a correspondent for a press agency. My intention at the time was to produce a balanced account, to paint as honest a picture as I could of present-day Tibet. I allowed myself no prejudice nor indulgence with respect to any party. I felt that in order to better explain and convince, the different Chinese and Tibetan views would have to be described. Once these had been made clear and compared, the facts would speak for themselves. Polemics and partisanship would be unnecessary. I hoped that the book would serve as a tool to help the reader to reflect upon these events dispassionately, for ultimately, it is up to the reader to judge according to his or her own conscience, without any outside interference.

Now that the English edition is coming out, I have still not changed my mind. These principles have been respected. However, the considerable effort of updating the material compelled me to look closely again at the question of Tibet. I must confess that I was gripped by intense emotion at the feeling of extreme urgency that surrounds the fate of Tibet. With every year that passes, a far greater menace hangs over the Land of Snow. I am referring to the ominous operation to Sinocize its vast expanse with a human tidal wave that could wash away for ever its age-old civilization.

When that day comes, little will be left to differentiate Tibet from China. Only a few traces of folklore to entertain passing tourists. Returning foreigners who know the highlands well have been struck by the massive irruption of new Chinese settlers over the past few years. Wherever they go, they open restaurants, shops and hotels. A frenzy of new building projects has further disrupted the fragile equilibrium of the towns in Tibet. Recently, even casinos are being opened in Lhasa.

The return to a wholesale population transfer, after it had been given a lesser priority for a while by the authorities, seems to point to a new

official policy that is less overtly violent but ever so much more alarming: the worm in the apple. The Peking government seems to have finally understood that to tame rebellious Tibet, it is useless to fire weapons
that merely strengthen dissent and solidarity among the Tibetans: it is
enough to open the floodgates of China's teeming population. Since the
Chinese are so numerous and the Tibetans so few and widely scattered,
the outcome of this undeclared war is a foregone conclusion. How long
will it take for this stratagem to obliterate the Tibetan identity? Twenty
years? Ten? Even fewer? One thing however is not in doubt: despite the
great changes that have occurred all over the world, particularly the events
in the former Soviet Union, bringing renewed hope and courage to Tibet,
time is not on the side of the Tibetans.

Yet China has changed since the cultural revolution; far more radical
changes can be expected to occur in the coming decades. The fate of
Tibet rests in the hands of the future generations, who will be more
open-minded and more in tune with the contemporary world. No one
can predict the ultimate disappearance of Tibet, yet equally there is no
guarantee that it will indeed survive into the future.

The richness of the English edition of this book owes a great deal to
the translator, Tica Broch, who untiringly devoted an exceptional amount
of energy to the project. She is herself a recognized expert on the Tibetan
issue, and could probably have written the book herself. The thorough-
ness of the update has much to do with her efforts and I would like to
express my sincere gratitude to her.

Paris, 28 March 1993
Pierre-Antoine Donnet

In the Shadow
of Death

The memory of those first days in Tibet will remain as one of the great joys of my life. We spent our first night on the Roof of the World in a humble Tibetan inn where gamey odours hinted at low standards of cleanliness – but nothing bothered us. Owing to the altitude, my companion's lips had turned purple. Was it the lack of oxygen or the intense emotion that gripped us? Our hearts were beating so fast we felt our chests could burst. Standing under the midnight sky, at close to 12,000 feet, the feeling of being closer to the stars was very real. The stars seemed near at hand, floating in a sea of intense blue. I had never seen the Milky Way so clearly. Here we were at last in the Land of Snow, a land of myth and mystery, and tragedy too. It was long past dusk, but the nearby village echoed with chanting, songs and dancing. The villagers were celebrating a local festival in this tiny corner of Paradise. We felt exhausted and happy.

We had left Kathmandu at dawn the day before, packed into an overcrowded bus. As it slowly groaned and panted up the mountain road with its cargo of men, women, children, chickens, pigs and trunks, every snort threatened to be its last. It had rained enormously. From the big town of Tatopani to the border village of Kodari, we had squatted in the back of a large truck as it lurched painfully over a road badly damaged by the weather. The 'Friendship Bridge' over Sun Kosi river between Nepal and Tibet had been swept away by the torrential rain. So we continued on foot to Khassa, the first Tibetan border village, baptized Zhangmu by the Chinese. Perched high on a slope in the distance, a good twenty kilometres away, it took the better part of a day to get there, walking behind two Nepalese porters on the steep narrows paths that ran along the mountains. After several hours' struggle, often lagging far behind the barefoot Sherpas who nimbly picked their way among the rocks, we felt exhausted. But as we rounded a bend, the sudden vision of the first Tibetan village on its faraway, lofty perch, still at a respectable distance, gripped us with emotion. The pale mud walls of Khassa, almost completely cloaked by the mist, added an aura of poetry and mystery to the Tibetan land we had come to explore. It was a childhood dream come true. And yet, during those days of August and September 1985, we were not really ordinary tourists: I was visiting Tibet as a professional journalist, and I had been sent by a major news agency.

Before starting on our trip, first in Kathmandu and later in Pokhara, Nepal, we had spent hours with whole families of Tibetan refugees who had fled their country on foot and on horseback, after the failure of a bloody uprising against the Chinese in 1959. This exodus took place nine years after the victorious People's Liberation Army of Mao Tse-tung triumphantly marched through the streets of Lhasa. All of Tibet fell under the tight control of the Communist Chinese. With great simplicity, the refugees explained what they thought we would see in Tibet, where most of them still had relatives. I had already spent a year in Peking as a press correspondent and my job was to write regular dispatches on every aspect of Chinese society. I still had four years ahead of me in China. I had a fairly clear idea about the magnitude of the tragedy that had befallen Tibet as of 1950. But I resolved to see for myself, by visiting the place and talking to the people, putting into practice a slogan cherished by China's supreme leader Deng Xiaoping – although it was mostly honoured in the breach by his own government: 'Seek truth from facts'. In Lhasa, the authorities were preparing to celebrate the twentieth anniversary of the creation of the 'Tibet Autonomous Region'. This event had capped the 'normalization' of Chinese Tibet and the official integration of the high plateau into the giant web of the Peking administration.

On the day itself, 1 September 1985, the Chinese government had planned elaborate ceremonies in Lhasa that were to be graced by a high-level delegation of Peking's 'central authorities', including Hu Qili – then a rising star in the Party's Politburo – and Li Peng, a conservative Vice-Premier with big plans. For some time, the rumour had been going around that Tibetan 'splittists' who opposed the Chinese presence in Tibet were preparing a surprise, to draw attention to their rejection of the Chinese presence. Maximum security measures were to be taken to protect the ceremonies. For this reason, Tibet had been closed to Western journalists for several weeks, and despite our special visa to enter Tibet from Nepal, issued in Peking, I had to call on unsuspected reserves of patience to convince the Chinese border guards to let us in. We enjoyed the unusual privilege of being left alone, unrestrained by the hospitality team that the Chinese government provides for foreign journalists whenever they travel outside Peking. As we had no Chinese guide, we were theoretically free to plan our own moves, select our own itinerary and contact whom we wished. This meant we were among the first foreign visitors ever allowed to enter Tibet alone, without a tour group or a guide, since Peking decided to open the doors a crack in the early 1980s.

The road between Khassa and Lhasa, a strategic artery built for the

Chinese army in 1955 and 1956, is 800 kilometres long. High on the Tibetan plateau, in the middle of the Himalayas, it runs almost at the foot of the highest peak on our planet, Mount Everest or Chomolangma, the 'Mother Deity of the Earth' to the Tibetans. We travelled through this splendour for several days, first in a Jeep and then in a bus. We often halted near villages decorated with Tibetan prayer-flags. Above the white and ochre mud houses another flag was prominently displayed – the five-starred red banner of the People's Republic of China – as if to remind naive or absent-minded visitors that this was really China. One of the five stars is meant to symbolize that the Land of Snow joined the 'great Chinese family' in 1950. On the walls of some farmhouses, there were still slogans from the cultural revolution, often '10,000 years for the Chinese Communist Party'.

We had spent the night at Shekar, at the Dazzling Crystal Monastery. In times gone by, before the inappropriately named 'Cultural' Revolution, it sheltered 400 monks and lamas. Now almost a ghost town, Shekar is one of the staging-points for treks to the Mount Everest base-camp. The path runs through Rongbuk Monastery, the highest temple in the world, also entirely demolished by the Red Guards. Cold and trembling, we halted on the passes. From Lhakpa La, at 5,220 metres, we surveyed what must be one of the most beautiful panoramas our planet has to offer. This is the realm of the Eternal Snows, that burst into flames of scarlet and gold when the first rays of the sun touch the majestic peaks at dawn. Slowly the sky lights up with the purest blue imaginable. Here, far from the roaring cities, no trace of pollution, no sound besides the wind and the rustling of the prayer-flags that call upon the gods to protect those passing by. Transported by the beauty of the scenery, we are silent, enthralled by the profound harmony that surrounds us.

Soon after Lhakpa La we came upon the monasteries of Sakya, which rank among the most important sites in the history of Tibetan Buddhism. The oldest, built in 1073, had succumbed to the crass insanity of Mao's Red Guards, but one of the others had been partly rebuilt and restored. We saw our first ruins, met the first monks with their sad smiles, felt the first shrinking feeling in our hearts. We continued on our way to Shigatse, the capital of Tsang province and second largest town in Tibet. Nowadays its population is only slightly over 20,000, but for centuries, Shigatse was the seat of the Panchen Lamas, whose position at the summit of the religious hierarchy in Tibet was second only to the Dalai Lama's. In the seventeenth century, the Fifth Dalai Lama managed to reunite Tsang with the Lhasa area, called U, but the covert rivalry between Tibet's most highly venerated spiritual leaders – and particularly between the members of their respective households – never quite abated, to the great satisfaction of the Chinese authorities who cleverly turned it to their advantage.

Gigantic Tashilhumpo, one of the most prestigious monasteries of the Yellow Hat school, was also undergoing restoration at the time of our visit. Here again, the Red Guards had passed by and left the imprint of their fanatic ardour. In fact, it had been the soldiers of the People's Liberation Army who first initiated that shameful activity, well before the Red Guards. In Shigatse, we boarded an ancient bus to continue our trip to Lhasa. We sat on the wooden benches, surrounded by Tibetan nomads and traders. Their eyes round with curiosity, they gazed at us in silent amazement. Tibetans poke out their tongue in greeting. We tried to converse in Chinese. Many of the older monks speak almost fluent Chinese: they had all the time in the world to learn while they sat in China's jails. The roof of the bus had been piled high with a tremendous variety of packages, and our packs were lashed right on top. Along narrow stony roads that hugged the mountainside, skirting precipices that yawned for a thousand feet below, our Chinese driver displayed unusual ability in negotiating every curve, despite the visibly tired steering and a set of brakes that would not stand up to much investigation.

We also visited Gyantse, the third largest town. Our eyes took in the devastated temples and sanctuaries, the fallen *chortens*, the decapitated Buddhas and defaced frescos. The political cataclysm that descended upon Tibet had branded the entire landscape. We had not come to take stock of the destruction, but it was impossible to ignore. The road to Lhasa then runs along the Yamdrok Tso, the Turquoise Lake more than 250 kms wide. We still had to cross the Yarlung Tsangpo and leave the airport at Gonggar behind us in order to reach Lhasa, the city of the Gods. Walking or riding on bicycles, we tirelessly explored the defeated ancient capital.

I'm not too sure whether I am a believer or not, but a visit to a lovely Roman church or a mosque generally leaves me with an impression of inner peace. In Taiwan, Singapore, Hong Kong or even mainland China, dozens of Buddhist temples I have visited have left me with a similar feeling. In Lhasa however, in the monasteries and convents, in the holiest temple in Tibet, the Jokhang in the heart of the Tibetan part of the town, we gaped in dismay at the flaming new plaster Buddhas and the acrylic frescos on every wall. These places of worship left us with a bitter taste. We felt we were looking at theatre sets. During the cultural revolution, this had all been devastated. The hasty reconstructions, renovations and repairs revealed only too well the magnitude of the cyclone that had nearly consigned an entire civilization to the dustbin of history. We were looking at an injured, stricken, traumatized Tibet, after thirty years of a Maoism that no Tibetan old enough to remember will ever be able to forget.

As for us, we will also remember the passionate, feverish discussions we had in the dark, secret halls of the monasteries and in the privacy of Tibetan homes. Wherever we went, Tibetans anxious to tell their tragic tales of woe to a sympathetic soul took us to witness, unable to staunch the outpouring of distress. But their tears were mixed with the joy of welcome relief from a time of unspeakable suffering. Since 1979, Deng Xiaoping's China had allowed a current of greater tolerance and pragmatism. From the prisons and labour camps, many 'counter-revolutionaries' had returned. The sinister people's communes of Mao's time had been disbanded. When we mentioned the recently reopened monasteries, Tibetan faces broke into smiles. Let there be no mistake: Chinese officials had no intention of allowing the monasteries to become the Buddhist universities they had been prior to 1950. But Peking had indeed decided to scale down the ideological pressure. As a result, Lhasa no longer awoke to the strains of 'The East is Red', the Maoist hymn that had blasted uninterruptedly since 1959 from the loudspeakers dotted around the city. Quite simply, having recovered a small breathing space that had long been denied, the Tibetans had rediscovered a taste for living.

In later years, I visited other regions where several million Tibetans live, areas that were attached in the 1950s and 1960s to the neighbouring and very definitely Chinese provinces of Yunnan, Sichuan, Gansu and Qinghai. Several times I visited Dharamsala, a little mountain township in the northern Indian foothills of the Himalayas. Dharamsala has been nicknamed 'little Lhasa' since the Dalai Lama found refuge there after fleeing into exile in 1959. Only one hour's flight away are Ladakh and Zanskar, two valleys that border on western Tibet. At 10,000 feet in the northernmost corner of India, these arid valleys have also provided shelter to Tibetan refugees. In 1987 and 1988, when I was still based in Peking, Lhasa was in the grip of much ferment. A number of anti-Chinese riots broke out, and each time the Chinese authorities were taken by surprise. China thought that it could impose its will on Tibet by means of a novel approach, but just as in 1959, the Tibetans rose up and refused to be integrated. The bloodbath that followed revealed to public opinion in the West that in those distant regions, far away, a defiant people were confronting machine-guns with bare hands.

I wanted to go there and do my work as a journalist. As soon as the first news reached Peking, I flew to Chengdu, the capital of Sichuan and gateway to Tibet, only two-and-a-half hours' flight away. But it was not to be. I was never able to visit Lhasa again. Whenever I asked for permission, the Chinese authorities would refuse, politely but firmly. During all the years in Peking, I often wondered why Tibet was off limits to me. Had my reporting on Lhasa not found favour with the Chinese authorities? Was it from daring to write that Tibet had been invaded instead of 'liberated' by Mao Tse-tung's army in 1950? That statement had earned me a warning from the Ministry of Foreign Affairs in Peking. Or was it because the friendships I had made in Lhasa were felt to be a liability? Whatever the reason, it is conceivably out of that denial that the idea of this book was born. I decided that since I was *persona non grata* in Lhasa, it was my duty to carry through the investigation at any cost.

In March 1989, Lhasa was gripped by another outbreak of anger. Just like the previous ones, this latest outburst was brutally drowned in blood. For the next fourteen months, martial law held sway in Lhasa. Once again, Tibet sank into almost total isolation. Behind the wall of silence erected by Peking, the few stifled pleas that trickled out told of fear, arrests and torture, terror and death. Except for a few groups of well-off tourists travelling in compact groups, shepherded by trained official guides who kept them apart from the Tibetan population, Tibet in late 1987 reverted to being a forbidden land for us. Few were the free and independent journalists who could still do their job there with integrity. These additional developments served as further incentive for me to complete my project. In late 1992, confident that new surveillance and crowd-control policies would preserve 'stability', the Chinese authorities timidly reopened Tibet to individual travellers.

This book is not anti-Chinese. Nor is it anti-Tibetan, nor anti-Western. I have lived too many years in China and have too many dear friends in the People's Republic, in Taiwan and in Hong Kong not to love the country and the people. I have given almost ten years of my life to China. In the near future, I hope, the Chinese people will again make a unique contribution to the world. But I feel Tibet also deserves our attention, because if China is facing immense problems, as we all know, Tibet is facing the risk of death by violence. The obliteration of Tibet is one of the great tragedies of our century. We no longer have the right to close our eyes. This book is not partial, nor is it neutral. It is not an indictment, nor an essay on Tibetan Buddhism, nor a tourist brochure – neither is it the work of a Tibetologist. These pages have been written by a journalist free from any religious or political allegiance. My attempt to describe Tibet's odyssey since its 'peaceful liberation' by China is the fruit of much research that filled the intervening years – first in Peking, then in Europe and in India – based on multiple Chinese, Tibetan and other sources. Through the words of the great variety of actors and victims in the Tibetan drama, I have tried to present the causes and the consequences of the clash of two great civilizations. Despite the grievous outstanding claims that separate them, they may have to live together under the same roof for many years to come.

What is occurring on the Roof of the World is of relevance to us all. Situated at the intersection of the geographical and political interests of Asia's great powers, Tibet's value as a strategic pawn reaches far beyond its natural borders. Before 1950, Tibet was at peace. Until a satisfactory solution for the Tibetan people is found, Asia as a whole may well remain an area of conflict. Traditionally, Tibetans oppose violence, out of respect for the Buddha's teachings. Their spiritual leader, the Dalai Lama, offers the Chinese authorities the possibility of a dialogue. Yet among Tibetans in exile or in Lhasa, many voices are being raised in favour of recourse to terrorism. With a feeling of despair gnawing at their guts, some of the young are ready to fight to avoid genocide. But China does not seem willing to yield. Everything seems to indicate that it is prepared to use any means available to perpetuate its grasp on the Land of Snow. In particular, the ongoing population transfer policy threatens to drown Tibet under a tidal wave of Chinese. Eleven hundred million Chinese versus a maximum of six million Tibetans: the parties are ill matched. Foreign governments have consistently been very circumspect in their response to Tibetans' appeals for help, but the weight of world public opinion is finally beginning to make itself felt. The 1989 award of the Nobel Prize for Peace to the Dalai Lama was a further token of the emerging international awareness of the urgent need for a peaceful solution for Tibet. The award expressly provided recognition for the Dalai Lama's efforts over forty years in the service of peace, and it exhorted his people to be patient, for the transformation under way in the Communist world is so rapid and thorough that some day Tibet's time may come too.

Is there still time to save Tibet? Should it be saved? The Tibetan civilization seems moribund. Its vanishing traditions and culture have fallen victims to the forced Sinocization. While elderly Tibetans spin prayer-wheels and tirelessly chant *pujas*, absorbed in a world of abstruse incantations, the youth are dreaming of a society with no gods or Buddhas and whose common denominators are money, fashion and material comforts. After centuries of isolation, beyond the play of Sino-Tibetan rivalries, Tibet's options have run out: yesterday's Tibet is gone and if it wants to enjoy the future, the Land of Snow will have to adapt to contemporary realities. There are reasons to be optimistic – for several years now, a deeply rooted revival of Tibetan nationalistic feelings has swept across the lofty Himalayan plateau. For the several million Tibetans, is this the last hurrah? Or does it herald a new Tibet where spiritual and worldly realms finally coexist in harmony ?

Some of the events described in the following pages are atrocious. As I wrote, I occasionally wondered whether readers unfamiliar with this part of the world would believe me. Over the years, efficient Chinese propaganda has convinced a sector of the Western public to believe in a modernization and democratization of China. The more naive thought China had become a capitalist country. The Tiananmen massacre on the night of 3–4 June 1989, has at least had the salutary effect of exposing the realities of post-Maoist China. In a single night, the vision of people machine-gunned by their own army shattered the myth so patiently constructed over the years by Deng Xiaoping. Since that night, the Chinese themselves look at the horrors perpetrated in Tibet with very different eyes.

ONE

Red East versus Land of Snow

1

The Chinese Invasion

My country, Tibet, lived in a state of peace and harmony; my people had never seen modern police or armed forces before the Chinese invasion. Today, my hope and my dream are that the entire Tibetan plateau will one day become a genuine sanctuary of peace: a completely demilitarized zone, the largest national park or biosphere in the world; a place where all human beings will be able to live in perfect harmony with nature. (*The Dalai Lama, address of 26 June 1989, San José, Costa Rica*)

For most Westerners, the word Tibet conjures up mystery, magic, the occult and the unknown. The Land of Snow is so far from our world and it has been off limits for so long! Very few people have a clear picture of the extent of the tragedy that is being played out on the high plateau, the Roof of the World, where a whole civilization teeters on the verge of complete extinction. Ordinary Chinese citizens also tend to have only the vaguest notions about Tibet. Generally, their knowledge will not extend beyond the official story sanctioned by the propaganda department of the Chinese Communist Party, to wit that from 1950, the People's Liberation Army entered Tibet to carry out the 'peaceful liberation' of an inalienable part of the sacred territory of China. The Tibetan community in exile, its leader the Dalai Lama and a considerable number of Tibetans inside Tibet repudiate this version of the facts. As they see it, an independent country was attacked and invaded by a foreign army. Having recourse to the well-known methods of imperialism, a government decided to use force in order to subjugate a neighbour.

When the tramp of marching boots first shook the Tibetan towns in Kham, a region bordering on Chinese Sichuan to the east of the Himalayan plateau, the Tibetans' calls for help fell on deaf ears. The Chinese army's intrusion into Tibet was met with general indifference on the international scene. Foreign governments primly looked away in order not to see the violence of the Chinese. Tibet was left in complete isolation to face the rising tide of Chinese infantry that was sent, wave after wave, sweeping over its soil. The Western world's and India's pusillanimous attitude paved the way for the greater tragedy yet to come.

From 1966 onwards, to a much greater degree than any Chinese province or region, Tibet suffered agony from the horrors of the cultural revolution. The wholesale destruction of the monasteries and the inquisitorial persecution of the Tibetan clergy very nearly exterminated an entire people. To understand contemporary events in Tibet, it will be necessary first of all to examine the past.

Tibet: to be (Chinese) or not to be (at all)?

When the Chinese Communists came to power in Peking in 1949, radio broadcasts spread the news around the world like wildfire. But in Lhasa, a city hidden in the heart of the Land of Snow, dwelling in isolation at 11,830 feet in the high Himalayas, several weeks' trek from the valleys of China, there was no telephone and no radio station. And when the news finally reached the capital of Tibet, only a handful of Tibetan leaders were in any position to measure its tremendous consequences for their country.

It only took a few months for the threat from the East to materialize. It had been clearly spelled out from the very first day of January 1950, and it should have given pause to those who still wondered about Mao Tse-tung's intentions. Radio Peking had announced that: 'The task of the People's Liberation Army for 1950 is to liberate Taiwan, Hainan and Tibet'. Mao Tse-tung served notice on the world that he also intended to bring Tibet under his power. In Chinese, Tibet is known as *Xizang*, which translates as 'Western Treasure House'. The metaphor may have predestined Tibet to 'return' to the 'great Chinese family'. Playing his part as the new Emperor of formidable Communist China, the blazing Sun whose thought illuminated the four corners of its vast expanse, wearing a demi-god's halo of military glory after the triumph of the Long March and the decisive victory over the Nationalists, Mao waited less than one hundred days after the founding of the People's Republic before announcing his designs on Tibet.

Over the next few months, Chinese propaganda bureaux set to work to explain that Tibet was dominated by 'foreign imperialists'. The government in Peking issued warnings to any government that might consider thwarting its ambitions: support for the 'handful of reactionaries' and 'separatists' in Tibet would be seen as interference in China's internal affairs and it would be interpreted as an act of hostility against the Chinese people. India was the main target. Bordering on Tibet, it was the only country on earth that could counter the Chinese military offensive, for the Tibetan Himalayas served as a useful buffer zone between the two large rivals. It remained for Tibet to invoke the Indian origins of its religion and the particularly close historical links it had enjoyed with India, and hope for support in the ordeal that lay ahead. But to no avail. As soon as the first troop movements took place, faced with the invasion of Tibet by China, Nehru opted for a policy of non-intervention. In exchange for appeasement, he anticipated peaceful, good neighbourly relations with Mao Tse-tung. He had miscalculated, and India had every reason to feel betrayed in 1962, when China unleashed a brief but bloody border conflict on Indian soil.

In 1950, left to its own fate, Tibet could only call upon a disparate army of 8,500 men, who usually marched with their wives and children. Their modest arsenal boiled down to four dozen pieces of artillery, 250 mortars and 200 machine-guns. In the valley, over 750 miles from Lhasa, the enemy had lined up a considerable number of troops. Tens of thousands of soldiers were poised, waiting for the Great Helmsman's order to assault the Tibetan highlands. Well-trained and seasoned after several tough campaigns – the 'people's war' against the Japanese occupation and later the Nationalists under Chiang Kai-shek – Peking knew that its valiant Communist troops would make short shrift of the Tibetan resistance. For Mao, the vast expanse of Tibet was an easy, supine prey. How did China plan to justify a military invasion in a region where there had been virtually no Chinese for almost forty years? Peking explained to the world that the Tibetan people, as serfs and victims of a feudal regime, could wait no longer for their 'peaceful liberation'.

The official history of the Chinese Communist Party dwells at length on this painful period. A reference manual on the annals of the Chinese government claims that when the People's Republic of China was founded on 1 October 1949, 'the people of Tibet were longing for the arrival of the PLA to help bring an end to their sufferings, drive the imperialist forces out of their region and frustrate the scheme of the imperialists and separatists to sever Tibet from China … [T]he patriotic people of Tibetan nationality in the interior provinces, in gatherings or in the press voiced the desire for the central government's prompt dispatch of troops to liberate Tibet. They pinpointed the region as an integral part of Chinese territory and warned the imperialists to end all their aggressive designs on it.'[1] But who were these 'imperialists' about whom China was making such a fuss?

Some years later, in exile in India, the Dalai Lama was to specify that as far as 'imperialist domination' was concerned, in the late forties there were only six Europeans living in Tibet: one missionary and two radio operators from England, two Austrians and one White Russian. For decades, Tibet had been off limits to foreigners. The Lhasa government had managed to elude Britian's territorial ambitions. While the USSR had indeed cast greedy looks at the strategic plateau towering over China, India and all of Southern Asia, it had never seriously planned a military expedition. As for the fledgling Republic of India, it had more than enough problems on its plate, having just barely won its independence after throwing off the British yoke.

Undaunted by the prospect of ridicule, China's Communist scribes maintain that on 1 October 1949, the Panchen Lama, whose zone of influence as dictated by his position in the Tibetan religious hierarchy was confined to Shigatse, sent a telegram of congratulation to Mao Tse-tung and Zhu De, commander-in-chief of the Chinese army. He was only eleven at the time. But wisdom is not a prerogative of age; he reportedly expressed his 'eagerness for the achievement of the mother-land's unification and Tibet's liberation at an early date'.[2]

The attack began in earnest on 7 October 1950. Eighty-four thousand troops from the 1st and 2nd Field Armies of the People's Libera-tion Army penetrated into Tibet's eastern province of Kham, a zone lying in the foothills of the Himalayas east of Lhasa. The Chinese forces crossed the Yangtze river, the natural border with Tibet, and in the space of a few days advanced deeply into Tibetan territory. They met with unexpected resistance, when Tibetan units such as the Khampa riders fought back with swords, like heroes, against the advancing Chinese artillery. Taken by surprise, lacking a unified command, they were soon outnumbered and overrun by the assailants.

When the news of the invasion reached Chamdo, the provincial capital of Kham, it caused a panic. The Governor, Ngapo Ngawang Jigme, requested instructions from the government in Lhasa on the attitude he should adopt with the Chinese. There was no reply to his telegram. At this crucial moment, when the very existence of Tibet hung in the balance, the entire Tibetan administration was intent upon enjoying the annual picnic offered by the Kashag, the Tibetan Cabinet. A thousand miles away from the hostilities, the Tibetan aristocracy was socializing in the Norbulingka gardens. The inhabitants of Lhasa knew nothing about the Chinese advance. Those who did know had decided to keep it a secret for a while longer.

Alarmed by the approaching Chinese army, by now hardly one day's march away, Ngapo requested permission to surrender in a second desperate telegram, according to some versions of the story. It was denied. He lost his head, abandoned his post and fled. Yet he did not disappear from the Tibetan scene, for he joined the ranks of those who chose to collaborate with China, becoming one of its most faithful servants. He was so skilful in espousing the ever-changing political line of the Chi-nese Communist Party that he was one of the very few Tibetan leaders not to be affected by the cultural revolution.

Leaving aside any betrayals, of which there were few, the blame for the disconcerting ease with which Tibet fell into the Chinese fold must be placed squarely on the shoulders of the Tibetan government. Not once, between 1911 and 1949, did it succeed in obtaining the diplomatic recognition from abroad that was so desperately lacking – let alone starting to modernize the country. It must be said that the government faced unyielding obstruction and opposition from the leading monasteries in the Lhasa area, bent on keeping their influence and privileges intact. And this is how Tibet found itself entirely at the mercy of China in 1950.

On the battlefield, the Tibetan units that stood up to the Chinese advance were swept away in the blinking of an eye. A few days later, the Chinese government was in a position to announce that, '[t]o punish the reactionaries for their crime and remove obstructions to Tibet's peaceful liberation, the Central People's Government in October 1950 ordered the PLA to advance on Chab-mdo. After wiping out a Tibetan main force of 5,000 men, the PLA conquered Chab-mdo.'[3] Phase One of the Chinese campaign in Tibet had taken only eleven days!

A nation helpless and alone

For Peking, it was a success right down the line. Abroad, India's timid protests were futile – they were mere formalities, anyway. In confidence, a high-ranking Indian diplomat explained to me that Nehru hesitated, wanting to know the intentions of the Western powers if India decided to oppose China's *fait accompli* in Tibet. The response came loud and clear: 'This is your problem and we will not be intervening.' India was discouraged from undertaking any gesture likely to unleash a Chinese riposte. In hindsight, many Indian politicians now consider that his generous idealism and poor tactical skills led Nehru to commit an extremely serious mistake in letting Tibet go without demanding anything in return, at a time when China might well have been prepared to make concessions.

As for the United Nations, the less said the better. The Tibetans had placed their hopes in the United Kingdom, and it was precisely that country that moved the adjournment of the UN debate on the question of Tibet! The government in Lhasa, stunned and sobered, was petrified by the news. Faced with the imminent collapse of the nation, oracles were consulted, great lamas were solicited in despair, official trances were organized in the Tibetan capital. Appeals for help directed to the United Kingdom, the United States, India and Nepal elicited only the vaguest cluckings of sympathy. As the storm broke over its head, Tibet was left totally alone, brusquely abandoned by its old friends and protectors abroad.

Why was Tibet so badly prepared for what was basically a predictable occurrence? Why did Tibet fall with practically no resistance? The higher strata of the Tibetan government, paralysed by a long regency and the power vacuum that followed the death of the Thirteenth Dalai Lama, had been torn by unremitting dissension. They had squandered the precious years they could have dedicated to reorganizing the country and making ready to meet any attack. Drepung, Ganden and Sera, the three great monasteries near Lhasa that shared temporal power with the Dalai Lama and the Kashag, professed tolerance and non-violence, in keeping with the Buddha's teachings.

At another level, while the Tibetan aristocracy idled away the first half of the twentieth century in leisured splendour, making no effort to grasp the realities of the world around it, the great majority of Tibetans lived in a world that was light-years away from the revolution that had swept through China and was now knocking on their doors. Befuddled by the superstitions and religious practices of another age, Tibet's peasants and nomads were not ready to fight.

Finally and most grievously, when the country was poised on the brink in 1950, Tenzin Gyatso, the Fourteenth Dalai Lama – the only person who could have presumed to save it – was not even sixteen years old. The supreme temporal and religious leader of all the Tibetans and the undisputed focus of unlimited veneration was a frail adolescent who had seldom been allowed outside his palaces since early childhood. He had no experience of governing and knew nothing about the outside world, foreign policy or military strategy.

In the face of the approaching disaster, the full temporal and spiritual powers of a Dalai Lama were officially conferred upon him on 17 November 1950, three years before the required minimum age. He had been enthroned when still a child, but the power remained in the hands of a regent. Having been placed at the helm of a country about to go under, isolated internationally and with no armed forces worthy of the name, Tenzin Gyatso fled before the now inevitable arrival of the Chinese army. He took refuge in Yadong, near the Indian border. A share of the Treasury in gold dust and ingots, which he took with him along with his retinue, was buried in a cache in Sikkim.

Many exiled Tibetans bitterly criticize the negligence of the authorities in 1950, when urgent decisions should have been taken to defend the country against the invaders by any means available. Phuntsok Wangyal, Director of the Tibet Foundation in London, is among the critics. When we met in autumn 1989, I asked him to tell me about that time, knowing he had fought against the Chinese although only a teenager. 'Obviously the Tibetan government made mistakes. First and foremost, they didn't oppose the Chinese when they entered Tibet.' How was an army of 8,000 men to resist the onslaught of a force ten times its size? 'It doesn't matter. I'm convinced that even though the Tibetans were not trained militarily, they were prepared to fight. Unlike Westerners, almost all Tibetans had weapons, the majority at any rate. Very primitive weapons, to be sure, but weapons nonetheless and they were used to fighting, sometimes fiercely and often in a naive way. Once their mind had been made up to fight, they would lay down their life if need be. So if the Tibetan government had said: "The country is in danger. Everybody has to fight. There is no choice" the entire country would have taken up arms.'

When he talks about those tragic days in Lhasa, Phuntsok Wangyal can't help getting excited. With rising anger, he spits out his words. Yes, he says, the Tibetan aristocracy handed Tibet over to the Chinese. Although a monk, he joined the resistance in his native Kham. Now forty-five, he has never stopped fighting for Tibet's independence. In 1950, he points out, the Chinese could not be sure of an easy victory in Tibet because there were no roads to bring in military supplies. Chinese commanders had only vague notions about the terrain. Their troops were in no position to secure regular supplies and the Tibetan population was generally hostile to the incoming Chinese. 'This being the case, it was the Tibetan government that made it easy for the Chinese: it let them in. We were lulled and fooled by their promises. And the Chinese turned it all to their advantage.'

Tenzin Geyche Tethong, the Dalai Lama's private secretary, agrees. He explains: 'We Tibetans were really stupid before 1950. Instead of opening out to the world and establishing diplomatic relations with foreign countries, we deliberately remained in isolation, clinging tightly to a system comparable to what existed in your Western countries two or three hundred years ago! Tibet had done nothing to prepare for the arrival of the Chinese. Today we realize that if the Tibetan government had used the time available to establish diplomatic ties with some countries, even if only with India, it would have been much more difficult for the Chinese to claim sovereignty over Tibet in 1950.'

When I met the Dalai Lama in his Dharamsala home in northern India, in September 1989, I questioned him at length about the shortcomings of the Tibetan administration of the 1950s. While putting my questions, I wondered about annoying him. As I had come from China, would he think I was being impudent enough to call for a self-criticism? But he replied cheerfully and frankly, without a trace of anger:

'Oh yes, Tibet had totally neglected to make any preparations! Before his death in 1933, the Thirteenth Dalai Lama had placed a number of recommendations to that effect in his testament. But during the regency, all these things were thoroughly neglected. I cannot lay the blame on individuals. The whole society, the religious and official circles and the regent himself were far too ignorant. They had no idea about the outside world. They still believed Tibet was the Land of the Gods and that it lay beyond the realm of human strife and contention. It was blind faith.

'Most particularly, I very much regret that when India became independent at the end of the forties, the Tibetan government failed to seize the opportunity to send a very large delegation, led if possible by the old Regent, who was then over seventy. If at all feasible, I should have joined the delegation myself. Although I was very small, I could have toured a little and gone to the Zoo, for instance! That is what we should have done.'

Comparison.
ex. Mongolia

State
nation,
(
recognition by
Int. Comunity ?

farce k
1 April
ation re
g had b
ies, in his utterly courteous, amiable manner,
Foreign Minister Chou En-lai spoke honeyed words of welcome to the
delegation, as befitted a first-class diplomat whose negotiating skills were
renowned around the world. Thereupon, the Chinese government produced a seventeen-point document that formally enshrined the end of
Tibet's independence. While extending its sovereignty over Tibet, the
'central' government in Peking agreed in return to grant the Tibetans
a great deal of autonomy.

First and foremost, the point was made that neither Tibet's social
system nor its religion were to be changed. But the document explicitly
stated, starting in article one, that 'The Tibetan people shall return to
the big family of the motherland, the People's Republic of China,' In
the eyes of the Chinese authors of the document, was this an implicit
admission of Tibet's independence until 1951, since they acknowledged
that it was not currently a member of the 'great Chinese family'? The
Tibetan authorities, renamed 'local government', were to undertake to
'actively assist the People's Liberation Army to enter Tibet and consolidate the national defences'. Gradually, the remains of the Tibetan army
were to be merged into the People's Liberation Army.

In turn, the Chinese government promised 'not to alter the existing
political system in Tibet'. 'The Central Authorities also will not alter
the established status, functions and powers of the Dalai Lama', said
Peking. The Chinese side also vowed to respect religious freedom. A
further promise was made 'not to effect any change in the income of the
monasteries',[4] which were very big landowners at the time. While Tibet
was to immediately forfeit virtually every possibility of asserting its independence within the international community, China's promises were
no more substantial than bits of paper. Indeed, only a few years later,
they were unceremoniously consigned to the dustbins of history.

The Tibetan delegation, led by Ngapo Ngawang Jigme, signed the
agreement on 23 May 1951. Seals were affixed to the document. The
Dalai Lama maintains that the Chinese government went so far as to
supply the Tibetans with forged Tibetan government seals that it had
made itself, and which are still kept in storage as proof of the document's authenticity. Back in Lhasa, the Tibetan delegation declared that
it had been compelled to yield to the Chinese demands under duress.
While in Peking, 'They were insulted and abused and threatened with
personal violence and with further military action against the people of
Tibet, and they were not allowed to refer to me or to my government
for further instructions', says the Dalai Lama.[5]

[handwritten margin note: Tibet. Part of the Qing Dynasty not 'PRC' (→ 1949 –) how should they be son justified ?]

Conversely, Chinese Communist pu[...]
of the agreement brought epoch-maki[...]
in the history of the relations betwee[...]
motherland. It enabled the bitterly dist[...]
free of imperialist aggression and shac[...]
of the motherland composed of all its[...]

The Chinese government treasures in its archives a telegram sent to Mao Tse-tung on 24 October 1951, in which the Dalai Lama purportedly declared that: 'The Tibetan local government, the monks and the people have given their unanimous assent. Under Chairman Mao Tse-tung's and the central government's guidance, they are actively assisting units of the PLA to enter Tibet and strengthen national defence, expel imperialist forces and safeguard the unification of the sovereign territory of the motherland.'[7]

Apparently, this is all that China needed to justify an all-out armed attack on Tibet. The Tibetans did not have long to wait. 'On October 26, the People's Liberation Army marched into Tibet and the Tibetan people were liberated from imperialist aggression and returned to the big family of the People's Republic of China.'[8]

Today, the Dalai Lama maintains that the telegram – which was presumably dictated (he was only sixteen at the time) by China's representatives and by his own advisors – was in keeping with a policy of restraint to avoid making things worse. The Tibetan Cabinet wished to persuade the Chinese government that in the future, it preferred peaceful coexistence to armed resistance. Knowing that the Chinese would exact a high price, Lhasa was anxious to avoid confrontation and the inevitable bloodbath that would follow.

According to Chinese press reports, after the Seventeen-Point Agreement was signed, the Tibetans joyously set about preparing a welcome for the 'liberating' army. Other than a few pockets of resistance – Tibetan Khampas hostile to any compromise with China negotiated in Lhasa – the road to Lhasa was basically wide open. From all the provinces bordering on Tibet, from Gansu and Qinghai in the north and the north-east and from Sichuan and Yunnan in the east and south-east, Chinese units launched a simultaneous assault on the Roof of the World, long sheltered from the territorial ambitions of its neighbours.

Marching through the uplands of Tibet, columns of Chinese soldiers advanced through unknown wild and arid plains. For days on end they would not meet a soul, as its vast reaches are mainly uninhabited. On they marched through forests, valleys and mountains, and the occasional tiny hamlets, villages and towns of Tibet, but their progress was slow and bringing up the artillery, tanks and trucks was an extraordinarily difficult task. It took the People's Liberation Army an entire year to deploy its forces in the Land of Snow, from its initial attack on 7 October 1950 to the declaration of victory on 26 October 1951.

Official Chinese propaganda boasts that that Mao's army provided assistance to the Tibetan people with such exemplary enthusiasm and selflessness that 'its good deeds won the hearts of the Tibetans'. They praised the PLA men as 'Son and Brother Soldiers of the People' or 'New-Type Hans'.[9] The Han, who account for 94 per cent of China's total population, are the original Chinese race. Controlling the main positions of responsibility in the Party and the government, they are depicted living in perfect harmony side by side with the Mongolians, Manchus, Uzbeks, Uighurs, Miao, Yi and other ethnic minorities, now known as 'national minorities'.

The Dalai Lama returned to Lhasa in August, closely followed by the first columns of the Chinese army. The People's Liberation Army entered the capital on 26 October 1951, consolidating China's triumphant military adventure in Tibet. The first detachment marched into the city to the strident tune of Chinese trumpets and drums, waving the five-starred red flag of the People's Republic of China and huge portraits of Mao Tse-tung, emblems of the personality cult he was working to develop throughout China. Henceforth, out the five stars, one was to symbolize Tibet.

The annals of the Chinese Communist Party contain numerous descriptions of this historic moment. Here is a sample: 'On the memorable day, October 26, 1951, the vanguard forces of the PLA arrived in Lhasa after a long march replete with hardships and privations. Their arrival set the whole city astir. More than 20,000 laymen and monks lined the streets in welcome.'[10] The Tibetan 'masses' are said to have thunderously acclaimed the fraternal Chinese troops.

The testimony of exiled Tibetans provides a strikingly different perspective. According to them, Tibetan children pelted the Chinese soldiers with stones while the monks cursed the 'enemies of religion'. Among the crowd of ordinary Tibetans who gathered along the road to stare in amazement at this novel spectacle, only a few were able to fully assess the implications.

The representatives of the Chinese government explained the reasons for the arrival of the Chinese army to the Dalai Lama. It had come to help Tibet develop and to protect it against imperialist machinations that were being plotted abroad. Of course, he was assured, as soon as these tasks were completed, the Chinese army would withdraw, even if the Dalai Lama begged it to stay! While waiting for the better days that never seemed to dawn, the inhabitants of Lhasa watched with unease as the Chinese military presence grew in a matter of months to 20,000 soldiers – about equal to half the civilian population. According to the Seventeen-Point Agreement, Tibetan religious affairs were to be left intact. The Chinese commanders offered sumptuous presents to the Tibetan nobility, many of whom were happy to accept. Something was said about modernizing the city and the country.

It is true that as late as 1951, in many respects Lhasa was still living in the Middle Ages. Towering above the city, the Potala palace of the Dalai Lama – the 'Precious Protector' – was a magnificent sight, and so were Lhasa's three great monasteries, Sera, Ganden and Drepung. But in the 'lamaist Rome' there was no electricity, no running water and no sewers. Latrines were mainly open-air affairs in the empty lots surrounding the city. In the street, ragged beggars with pock-marked faces roamed around with mangy dogs. The homes of the poorer inhabitants could be unbelievably filthy inside.

Be that as it may, Lhasa was certainly not the hell on earth so lovingly depicted by Chinese propaganda. The testimony of contemporary foreign visitors invariably describes the City of the Gods as an animated, pleasant and peaceful town. The meanest parts of Lhasa never looked as grim as the sombre tenements in our Western cities and it seems that even the most destitute beggars never died of hunger. The altitude, nearly 12,000 feet, meant that fatal contagious diseases were rare, despite the lack of hygiene.

Still, the Chinese promised to provide better services: hospitals, roads and schools were planned. Soon after their arrival, their propaganda services devised a shooting schedule to record the popular festivities that would necessarily follow the Tibetan people's 'liberation'. It was probably not too difficult to provoke ecstatic smiles for such a good cause among the poor and the beggars given princely gifts by the 'New-Type Hans'. After a thousand years of serfhood, happiness had finally dawned in Lhasa, said the Chinese.

In the meantime, following the strategy planned by the Military Command in Peking, the army marched into the other important cities in Tibet, such as Shigatse and Gyantse west of Lhasa. Military camps were set up throughout eastern and western Tibet in the provinces of Amdo and Kham. In the space of a few months, almost all of Tibet fell under the control of the Chinese army. China had staked out the area well as a prelude to full domination.

Starting in 1951, in order to facilitate troop movements, ground was broken for two major highways that were completed in 1954. The one from Lhasa to Chengdu in Sichuan was 1,500 miles long, while the other one ran for 1,225 miles to Xining in Qinghai in the north-east. These two roads, with passes at 15,000 feet, the first scars of modernity on a particularly difficult natural environment, were of prime importance to Chinese strategists. In 1957, a third artery 730 miles long was carved out in the direction of the Muslim 'Autonomous region' of Sinkiang in the North.

The new roads facilitated the optimum deployment of the armed forces and brought within reach the rapid conquest of these remote areas. They were a breach in the walls of the Tibetan fortress, which had sheltered for so long behind the highest mountains in the world. Chinese propaganda played up the importance of the roads for the economic development of Tibet, where there had never been any network of highways. But it is quite clear that the economic aspect came a poor second in the minds of Chinese decision-makers, well after the narrowly military imperative.

China enrolled the Tibetan peasants in the construction of the roads. Mostly illiterate and uneducated, these young people were docile workers. To make them work faster, the Chinese introduced the concept of competition among individuals and groups. Quotas were set for the day's work – to be exceeded, of course. At the end of the day, the Chinese cadres organized 'mass meetings' during which rewards were handed out. Mao badges were given to the best workers and banners to the most deserving groups.[11]

Religion is poison, long live Chairman Mao!

Having presented themselves as 'liberators', the Chinese government cadres embarked upon a long-term campaign to gradually erode the immense political power and the pervasive spiritual influence of the Dalai Lama over Tibetan society. In order to consolidate their position in hostile territory as much as possible, to pave the way for Tibet's complete integration within the 'great Chinese family', they first had to neutralize the Ocean of Wisdom before attempting to destabilize his position. To promote the Maoist image of the New Man liberated from his chains, the Chinese leadership planned to capitalize on the past excesses of a partially feudal system and a fragile society that had been closed to the world for centuries.

To achieve their purpose, they first had to convince the lower strata of the Tibetan population that they must arise and unseat their oppressors – the handful of nobles and high lamas whose wealth dazzled the little people, harnessed to poverty by the twin yokes of religion and superstition. An entirely new order, they explained, now reigned in the valley. There would be no more prostrations, no bowing and kowtowing to the Buddhas and the gods; no more 'pujas', the prayers and litanies endlessly recited by the Tibetan faithful as they spun their prayer-wheels. Following the advice of the Great Helmsman, the Chinese masses had rid themselves of religion, the opium of the people.

The Chinese people had stood up and put an end to corvée labour and crushing taxes for the benefit of a bloodsucking aristocracy. There would be no more serfs nor slaves and no more beggars – instead, all men were to be rigorously equal. The phenomenal impetus of Mao Tse-tung's ideology had given birth to a burgeoning hope that surged in the hearts of 700 million Chinese to the tune of 'The East is Red'. After war, humiliation and poverty, an entire people had raised its head under the red banner of communism and the thought of Mao Tse-tung.

Israel Epstein, born in Poland in 1915, is one of the most illustrious apologists of the Chinese Communist regime. He is so well trusted that he has been appointed Editor-in-Chief of the official monthly publication *China Reconstructs*, an unprecedented honour for a foreigner in the People's Republic. I met him in spring 1988, an old man who has lived in China since the 1920s, rubbing shoulders with the prominent leaders of the Chinese Revolution. I questioned him about Tibet. Knowing I was a journalist, he was manifestly reluctant to respond to my questions concerning the causes of the anti-Chinese protests that had just occurred.

Here is his description of the liberation of Tibet, from *Tibet Transformed*, a 566-page book published in China in 1983. 'In the democratic revolution, with the help of the People's Liberation Army, which entered the region in 1951 and smashed the imperialist-backed revolt of the secessionist serf-owners in 1959, Tibet's million serfs and slaves rose to their feet. Step by step, they took the land and herds away from the feudal-theocratic rulers who for many centuries had held sway over their bodies and, even more crucially, over their minds. And they built up, from the village to the regional level, local organs of state power that could represent their own class interests and will. An irrevocable change had come to the "roof of the world".'

As the army set up camp in Lhasa after its triumphant arrival, problems of food supply soon became acute, since the Chinese army demanded the lion's share of the available grain to feed its men. This was really a loan, it claimed, to be repaid with Chinese assistance for the industrialization of Tibet. 'For the first time that could be remembered', says the Dalai Lama, 'the people of Lhasa were reduced to the edge of famine.'[12] The people protested about the forcible requisitions that quickly drove prices sky-high. Anti-Chinese posters sprang up around the city and the children aimed stones at all the funny men wearing identical green hats decorated with a red star.

Peking's representatives, under general Zhang Jinwu, accused senior ministers Losang Tashi and Lukhangwa of the Tibetan Cabinet of collusion with foreign 'imperialists', and the Dalai Lama was compelled to accept their resignation. In late 1953, Mao Tse-tung invited the Dalai Lama to Peking. Did he really think, as he claims today, that he would be able to extract concessions from Chairman Mao and Premier Chou En-lai? Despite the qualms felt by part of his entourage, he accepted the invitation. It was his first visit to the great 'Northern capital', an expedition decried by a good many of Lhasa's inhabitants who wept over his departure on 11 July 1954. Their God-King had promised to return soon, but many feared that Peking would keep him as a hostage.

In the company of several dozen nobles and church dignitaries, the Dalai Lama rode towards Chengdu, where for the first time in his life he boarded an aeroplane to Xian – ancient Chang'An, the old capital of the Chinese Empire – where he was met by the Panchen Lama with his entourage of 200 people. Another initiation into the marvels of civilization awaited them: the Tibetan delegation took the train – 'the fire wheel' – to Peking, where they were welcomed at the station with deafening applause by a throng of students and schoolchildren sent by the Communist Youth League, in keeping with protocol. In Communist China, where meticulous organization is an article of faith, official ceremonies are prepared with the utmost care, for no false note or impromptu gesture is tolerated. The Dalai Lama and the Panchen Lama were received by Zhu De and Chou En-lai. Several meetings were scheduled for the Dalai Lama and Mao Tse-tung. Some say the Chinese dictator was genuinely taken by the gentle charm of this adolescent who had become the King of the Tibetans through no effort of his own.

The Chairman uttered bland pleasantries about Tibet and the Dalai Lama and spent hours discussing the benefits of Buddhism with the shy, gawky youth. The Dalai Lama was left thinking that a *modus vivendi* could be reached with the master of Communist China. With his habit of chain-smoking and his careless attire, the emperor of Red China did not appear to be in good health.

The Dalai Lama recounted his meetings with Mao to me. 'He was consistently kind to me. Therefore I felt some sort of respect, an authentic respect for Chairman Mao. His manner of speaking, his way of explaining things made everything he said sound really convincing. Chou En-lai was not the same type of person. Straightaway, I felt he was a cunning man and when he spoke, his eyes always roving about, there was an unyielding look about him. He was nice, but it seemed artificial. Whereas Chairman Mao was not like that, you could open up to him in a discussion. Sometimes our talks went on for hours.'

Was Mao sincere when he spoke of autonomy for Tibet? 'Once, we gathered around a long table for an official meeting. I was sitting on one side of the table and Chairman Mao on the other, so that we were facing each other. The Panchen Lama sat beside me as well as some Tibetan officials. On one side of the table sat the two Chinese generals who commanded the troops stationed in Tibet. At one point, Mao pointed to the generals and said to me: "I've sent these generals to help you. If they don't behave the way you want, let me know and I'll have them withdrawn".'

The Dalai Lama recalls seeing Mao again at a meeting of the top Chinese leadership. They were seated next to each other. 'As the discussions dragged on, Mao turned to me and said: "You Tibetans are very backwards nowadays. We will help you. Over the next twenty years, you will develop, and then it will be your turn to help us. Your history is the history of a great nation." His choice of words revealed that he recognized our status as a nation. Another time, he suddenly asked whether we Tibetans did or did not have a flag. I replied that we did and he said: "You must keep that flag." On yet another occasion, he said to me that, "For the moment, we are sending you Chinese to enable you to develop. Once you have developed, all the Chinese will be withdrawn."'

The Dalai Lama remembers well his last meeting with Mao. It occurred suddenly and unexpectedly, while the Tibetan leader was attending a meeting of the Standing Committee of the National People's Congress, the governing body of the Chinese parliament. A messenger came to call the Dalai Lama away, saying that Mao wished to speak to him. Tenzin Gyatso asked Liu Shaoqi, who was chairing the meeting, to excuse him, and hurried to where Mao was waiting. 'We were sitting on a couch. As we spoke, he suddenly moved closer to me. He leaned towards me and calmly said, "you know, religion is poison. It is very harmful to the development of a nation. First of all it acts as a hindrance to material progress (this is not entirely false) and secondly, it weakens the race. Your mind is somewhat like a scientist's; so you can understand what I mean. Religion is poison." I was stunned! I immediately felt very ill at ease. I grasped at once that what he had said was very important and noted down his comments word for word.'

Before leaving, Mao Tse-tung advised the Dalai Lama to train some young Tibetans in radio communications, so that the two leaders could remain in touch. 'I returned to Tibet during the summer of 1955. A few months later, I think it was in early 1956, we first heard people were rebelling in eastern Tibet. Soon the rumours increased, then came very sad stories about what was happening there. I sent two or three letters to Mao, through official as well as non-official channels, to explain what was happening. There was no response. It was then that doubt entered my mind.'

On the way back to Lhasa, the Dalai Lama passed through the Tibetan parts of Amdo and through the village of his birth. He noted the inroads of Chinese influence with distress. Like well-oiled machines, the Tibetans brought to meet him said how happy they had become, thanks to Chairman Mao and the Chinese Communist Party. The Dalai Lama realized with dismay that Peking had decided to impose 'drastic' reforms in areas as distant from Lhasa as this one, in order rapidly to lay the foundations of the Communism that had already taken root in China.

The next step towards integrating Tibet was taken on 22 April 1956, with the creation of the Preparatory Committee for the Autonomous Region of Tibet, a body whose avowed purpose was to assimilate Tibet and cast it in the Chinese administrative mould. Photographs of the inauguration show Chinese Marshall Chen Yi at the rostrum in front of a gigantic portrait of Mao Tse-tung. On either side of the Living God of Communism hung smaller portraits of the Dalai and Panchen Lamas, as if to show the Great Helmsman's superiority. The background

(Autonomous) Tibet. - not after 'a nation' but as a name for just 'region' like Manchuria.

was made up by a gigantic Chinese flag. In the pit, a PLA band played the Chinese national anthem. As never before, the Dalai Lama and his assistants looked ridiculously out of place.

The Dalai Lama presided over the Committee, with the Panchen Lama and General Zhang Guohua, commander of the Chinese troops in Tibet, as Vice-Presidents. Ngapo Ngawang Jigme was named Secretary-General. With three Tibetans and a single Chinese member, the Committee could pass muster as a representative autonomous entity. In fact, its composition had been cleverly devised by the Chinese Communist Party: the Dalai Lama's supporters and the collaborators massed around Ngapo Ngawang Jigme could hardly fail to disagree. By then, the latter had quite openly espoused Peking's interests, and the Panchen Lama was easy to manipulate. It soon emerged that the Committee was no more than a device to ensure the smooth integration of Tibet with China. No longer any threat to Peking, the Dalai Lama had become an asset – however much against his will – providing crucial legitimacy to the Chinese, which they skilfully exploited.

As puppets in the hands of China, '[w]e were allowed to discuss the minor points, but we could never make any major changes', says the Dalai Lama today.[13] Henceforth, the real seat of power in Lhasa and the place where decisions were taken was to be the Committee of the Chinese Communist Party, led exclusively by ethnic Chinese. Tibet's political structures were so fragile that Peking had every reason to believe it would be easy to absorb its prey. Controlling the Dalai Lama was the key to success; then the Tibetans would be powerless. A cunning mixture of guile, threats and smiles soon managed to neutralize him. Thirty years later, the God-King explains that in the midst of all these intrigues, his prime concern was to avoid a bloodbath in Tibet. The Chinese, he says, had clearly indicated that in case of insubordination, Tibet would be taken by force of arms, and if it came to that, the balance of power was such that his people had no chance of survival. As for the aristocrats, a good number let themselves be bought and used.

From Peking's perspective, the story is quite different: 'The Preparatory Committee for the Tibet Autonomous Region was set up in April 1956 to systematically establish regional autonomy. Construction work, such as the building of highways, factories, farms and hospitals and developing trade, was carried out after full consultation with representatives of the upper social strata. The reactionary clique of the upper strata in Tibet headed by the Dalai Lama feigned compliance with the agreement while persistently obstructing and disrupting its implementation. They fomented trouble in Lhasa when the Tibetan Military Area Command was established. They persecuted those peasants and herdsmen who took part in construction work, accepted state loans or were treated by Han doctors who had entered Tibet.'[14]

The Khampas rebel

By this time, the experience of coexistence with the Chinese had already caused the Dalai Lama to lose any hope he ever had of reaching a substantial and lasting arrangement. In the areas under Chinese control, the Buddhist temples he had seen were no more than empty shells harbouring only a few aged monks, shunned like lepers by the people, who feared persecution if they were caught in such disreputable company. If religion was destined to die out in Tibet, as it had in China, what could be in store for the Tibetan civilization?

In the countryside, he had gauged the intensity of the growing hatred between Tibetans and Chinese. 'Among the Tibetans, I saw mounting bitterness and hatred of the Chinese; and among the Chinese, I saw the mounting ruthlessness and resolution which is born of fear and lack of understanding.'[15] At this stage, the government in Peking could still have salvaged the situation, avoided a confrontation and quite possibly achieved the smooth Sinocization of this peaceful race in the space of a dozen years at most. It seemed to hold every trump in its hand: a strong army, a powerful administration and an ideology to which the overwhelming majority of the Chinese people subscribed. One quality, however, was lacking – patience. Maoism had no time for that. All over Tibet, the Chinese cadres were in a hurry to complete their ideological work. The first revolt broke out in the Chamdo area in the winter of 1955–56. The guerrilla units organized by the Khampas attacked the Chinese positions with extreme savagery. The Chinese army was at a disadvantage in the impenetrable Himalayan foothills, where only the Khampa horsemen knew their way.

The revolt was sparked by a remarkably heavy-handed Chinese initiative: in 1955, PLA units were ordered to disarm the Khampas and confiscate the monasteries' stocks of weapons. For the very keenest Communist cadres, anxious to cover themselves with glory during the construction of communism in Tibet, this also implied the eradication of religion in Kham. They told the people that religion was poison. They organized *thamzing*, the notorious 'struggle sessions' during which the masses were invited to denounce the crimes of their oppressors. These tactical mistakes had grave consequences. A Khampa warrior's most cherished possession had always been his rifle. The response was instantaneous: the call to arms spread like wildfire.

The Chinese army had managed the feat of uniting against itself a whole spectrum of peoples and tribes throughout Kham and Amdo better known for their constant feuding. Tens of thousands of Khampa nomads joined forces with the common goal of attacking the Chinese army wherever it could be engaged. All over eastern Tibet, everywhere seething in turmoil, the Khampas inflicted deadly losses on the Chinese. Peking unsuccessfully called on the Dalai Lama to send his own troops to quell the revolt of the Khampas, the 'running dogs of imperialism' who were obstructing the implementation of democratic reform.

Phuntsok Wangyal was one of the Tibetans who took up arms in Kham against the Chinese. A novice monk in Derge monastery in the vicinity of Kanze town, he was not quite fifteen at the time. 'In the past, Derge Gompa had twice been destroyed in combat against the Chinese, burned and demolished. I was a young monk in this monastery that had yet to be subjected to "reform". But many "class struggle sessions" were being held in the area. In early 1958, some of us decided to leave the monastery and fight. At that time we had no guns, it was not allowed. When we left the monastery, there were eighty-one of us on horseback, and one monk on foot. We had seven carbines and two pistols between us!

'I was fourteen and a half. When we fought, we did well: by the time we reached the Yangtze river, the border of the "autonomous region", every one of us had his own weapon. Some even had machine-guns, taken from the Chinese. We lost many men. When we arrived in Lhasa, forty were left of the original eighty-two. Only seven made it to India, and I was one of the lucky ones. I was so young, that the weight of the machine-gun would drag me to the ground. It was guerrilla warfare: our first priority was raiding Chinese convoys. The small ones. We made thirty-six sorties against the Chinese. Every time, we joined battle not in the villages but wherever the Chinese would halt on the road to take on petrol or to eat. The road linking Sichuan and Lhasa was already open and occasionally we would ambush convoys of a hundred men. In the beginning, our skirmishes were indescribable. None of us had any training. But we had no choice, what else could we do?

'We never stayed down by the road. We lived in the hills and mountains, looking down on the enemy from above. Sometimes we would send local farmers scouting to find out how many Chinese there were. Sometimes we dressed up in local people's clothes to go and see for ourselves. The villagers gave us food. They were terrorized by the Chinese and helped us willingly. In those days, the food rationing system was not yet in place. They were able to feed us without attracting the attention of the Chinese. Later, through rationing, almost every grain of cereal could be traced. Every now and then, it was the Chinese who laid a trap for us, and we had to split into two groups. We were forced to hide and live off *shomay*, a tuber that looks like a small sweet potato. Occasionally, we would have nothing to eat for a fortnight.'

The Khampa rebellion spread so widely that it sparked the curiosity of the American government, openly hostile to Red China. The Korean War – a singularly bloody conflict – had compounded the antagonism between the USA and China. By means of a cut-rate operation code-named 'Garden', which ranks among the most outlandish capers it ever attempted in Asia, the CIA planned to destabilize China by opening a front on its western flank. Hundreds of Tibetan loyalists were transported in great secrecy from India to America for intensive training. In Washington, the idea was to train a Tibetan elite that would spearhead the anti-Chinese guerrilla offensive. David Wise, in 1973, was among the first American journalists to disclose details of the covert operation. Under the aegis of the CIA and its then director, Allen Dulles, Tibetan insurgents were trained in a valley lying at 9,300 feet, at Camp Hale, fifteen miles north of Leadville, Colorado. During the Second World War, the military had used this old base to train US Army mountain troops; the climate and topography were as similar as possible to the Himalayas and its remoteness protected the secrecy of the operation.

The Tibetans had been selected from among the rebel groups that were carrying on the struggle against the Chinese from safe havens in the neighbouring Himalayan countries. The CIA's objective was to train them in guerrilla tactics, provide them with modern arms and infiltrate them into Tibet. 'Some of these people were parachuted into Tibet; others went in overland. A small number came back out and contacted the CIA', writes David Wise. 'But', he adds, 'while this enabled them to harass the Chinese forces, it did not provide them with the means to liberate their country.'[16] One of the actors in this controversial operation was Gyalo Thondup, the Dalai Lama's eldest brother, who was to surface later on as a mild-mannered Hong Kong businessman before rejoining the political circle in Dharamsala.

These men who had never seen an aeroplane in their life were taught parachute-jumping, the use of heavy weapons and radio communications. But whereas Tibet's cries for help had fallen on deaf ears in 1950, when it was arguably still possible to restrain China's greed, CIA support for the Khampas' struggle came too late to make any difference at all. On the other hand, the Chinese government did not hesitate to take advantage of this brief episode to denounce with renewed ardour – and for once with some reason – the collusion between Tibetan separatists and foreign imperialists. American support for the Tibetan resistance came to a full stop after Secretary of State Henry Kissinger's secret visit to Peking in July 1971, which served as a prelude to the Sino-American rapprochement sealed by President Richard Nixon's official visit to China in the following year.

The CIA and the 'Garden' operation

Chime Namgyal is in his fifties. He belonged to the secret Khampa resistance organisation known as 'Four Rivers and Six Mountains', and his group was the last one to go for training in the secret American base in Colorado. He agreed to tell me his story, the first exclusive interview ever given to a foreigner.

'Our training took place from March 1962 to November 1964[17] in a secret place in Colorado that does not appear on any maps. There were 135 Tibetans in our group. We flew from India in a four-engined plane belonging to the US Air Force, flying over the east of Pakistan. It stopped in Thailand and Japan before landing in the USA. The portholes were covered and we were not told where we were going. But when the plane landed the first time, we were given soft drinks with straws that said 'Bangkok'. Some of us knew a few words of English and this enabled us to know where we had landed. Later the plane landed in Japan, somewhere out in the countryside, but we could see signs in Japanese.

'I was very happy to participate in this operation and I was impatient, because for me, this was a way of serving my country. The objective was to give us advanced military training with a course on guerrilla techniques to make us operational inside Tibet. The operation with the CIA dates back to 1957. I think about one thousand Tibetans must have been trained in the USA.

'We were taught how to use various types of equipment and intelligence techniques. This was to help us create and direct an organization in Tibet. We were also taught about Chinese intelligence, for observing Chinese military manoeuvres in Tibet. Life was not too difficult. We had time to sleep. But the training went on from eight in the morning until five in the evening. All the instructors were Americans who spoke to us through Nepalese interpreters. Of course we were not allowed to leave the camp.

'When our training was over, some of us were parachuted into Tibetan territory. Others, I among them, were to penetrate into Tibet overland. When the time came to enter Tibet, we were given just one pistol – no other weapons. We felt terribly let down. After having undergone such intensive training to end up armed with a single pistol! In fact, the first thing we were supposed to do was enter Tibet and set up groups. Once the preliminaries were completed, we would be receiving shipments of weapons. Five guerrillas made up each group, which had a transceiver that each of us knew how to use. We carried no identifying material, of course, in case we were caught. Later on, some shipments did arrive. I was in Pemakod at the time, in southern Tibet, north of India near the border with Burma. I stayed there for about one year.

'The essence of our job was to make contacts among the population in order to create resistance networks. On several occasions, we could have attacked Chinese positions, but that was not allowed. Our commanders had forbidden us to do so, on orders from India. Only the men who had been parachuted into Tibet were allowed to fight against the Chinese. I was furious, because I felt my skills were not being put to good use. This is why I dropped out after a year or so. All the obstacles originated on the Indian side. All it cared about was gathering military intelligence about Chinese armed forces in Tibet and avoiding any confrontation between Chinese and Tibetans that might provoke a border conflict.

'This state of affairs was accepted by the Americans – the overall operation had been designed by representatives of three countries: Tibet, USA and India. Those who were parachuted in fought valiantly, causing heavy losses among the Chinese.'

Before joining the 'Garden' operation, Chime Namgyal had been among the first Khampas in his home district of Tridu to take up arms against the Chinese, when he was only seventeen. He owns up to having killed a number of Chinese between 1958 and 1962. 'The Khampas in my district joined forces with another district against the Chinese, and together they obliterated 40 Chinese convoys in 1958 alone, killing some 700 Chinese. Sometimes, there would be non-stop shooting from nine in the morning until three in the afternoon. When we ran out of ammunition, we would charge them with our sabres. The Chinese were not very brave, because as soon as they saw us coming they would flee, leaving their weapons behind.

'My desire to fight for my country's freedom is as strong as ever, and if an opportunity arises, I am prepared to take up arms again', said this proud Khampa, who has now been elected Vice-Chairman of the People's Assembly of the Government-in-exile in Dharamsala.

As of January 1956, the Chinese government decided to stamp out the rebellion by any means whatsoever. Peking rushed fourteen divisions to Kham – more than 150,000 men. After a number of harrowing battles, this tidal wave of humanity drowned out the Khampas' desperate resistance. Equipped with Ilyushin Il-28s from the Soviet Union, the Chinese bombarded the resistance with devastating results, throwing them into total disarray. Protected from the 'balls of fire' that rained down from the sky only by the charm-boxes they wore over their hearts, the Khampas were soon decimated.

Terror and silence

After crushing the revolt in blood, the Chinese army terrorized the monasteries and villages. There is a great deal of testimony concerning the barbarous deeds committed between 1956 and 1958. The Chinese tortured the Tibetan clergy. Monks were burned alive. Tibetan refugees recall scenes of monks and nuns being forced to copulate in public in front of the Chinese soldiers. Many monks were deported to the labour camps in Qinghai, known to be the harshest in China. Children were forced to shoot their parents. The Chinese army employed an entire arsenal of methods to intimidate the local population: Tibetans were crucified, buried alive, decapitated and dismembered. Entire villages were razed and wiped off the map.[18] But the guerrillas did not lay down their arms. The atrocities caused the Khampas to close ranks against the

Chinese. PLA positions were raided by Tibetan guerrillas until the early 1970s, well after the beginning of the cultural revolution.

What was the level of response provoked abroad by this brutality? Almost nil. In 1956, the Dalai Lama was invited to attend the celebrations in India for the 2,500th anniversary of the Buddha's birth. Before his departure, he was tutored by the anxious Chinese representatives in Lhasa. He was requested not to make any statements on Tibet's internal situation that might embarrass the 'central' government. His Chinese protectors briefed him on the proper response to inconvenient questions from journalists. The Dalai Lama, who had been made a Vice-Chairman of the National People's Congress in the meantime (a purely ceremonial position), was warned to bear in mind that India was a country infested with reactionaries of every type and colour. He would have to be extremely cautious and, as a good Chinese patriot, it was his duty to convince every foreigner, journalist or diplomat that the Chinese Communist Party was very tolerant of religions all over China.

Could Tibet count on India's help? A further disappointment was in store for the Dalai Lama when he met Nehru in New Delhi. The head of the Indian government recommended that he pursue his efforts to arrive at a peaceful arrangement with China. India, the Prime Minister explained, did not have the means to help Tibet shake off the Chinese yoke. So, if they could not learn to live with the Chinese presence, the Tibetans would have to rely on their own resources. In Lhasa, according to persistent rumours, all of Tibet was about to rise up and expel the Chinese army. Having come to New Delhi for the same occasion, Chou En-lai advised Tenzin Gyatso to hasten home and defuse any such initiatives, adding unambiguously that they would immediately be met with merciless repression. At this very moment, Mao produced another display of his tactical genius. Realizing that Tibet was on its way to becoming a real powder-keg, he took a step back, in keeping with the techniques set out in Sun Tsu's ancient and renowned manual of strategy, the *Art of War*. In the 1930s, during China's 'liberation struggle', Mao himself had written: 'It is a well-known fact that just as in a boxing match, the smart fighter sometimes takes a step back, whereas his stupid antagonist charges forward and dissipates his strength, so that in the end, the one who yields often wins.'

Faced with the possibility of a general conflagration in Tibet, buying time was essential. Anyway, two steps forward and one step back still leaves you one step ahead. Since the Tibetan people were not yet ready for Communist reforms, the central government in Peking would wait for the time to be ripe, declared Mao in February 1957. China formally undertook to defer the introduction of reforms in central Tibet for six years. But was there anyone left in Tibet who didn't grasp his long-term intentions? Mao was merely offering a reprieve.

While battles raged and blood flowed freely in eastern Tibet, the tension in Lhasa and Central Tibet rose unrelentingly throughout 1958. Lhasa was swamped by the continuous influx of refugees. The Tibetan resistance, basically Khampas, numbered in the tens of thousands in central Tibet. Some put the figure as high as 80,000, stationed within 50 km. of Lhasa and united under the leadership of an organization called 'National Defence Volunteers Army'. The final meetings between the Dalai Lama and the representatives of the Chinese government were fruitless. The crisis loomed large; an explosive outcome could no longer be averted.

The Dalai Lama's departure

In Peking, after a thorough analysis of the increasingly critical situation in Lhasa, it was probably felt that the time had come for some serious decision making. The hardline faction in the Chinese government considered that the Tibetan people would never yield without the use of force. In Lhasa, their representatives set out to prove them right. On 1 March 1959, General Tan Guansan invited the Dalai Lama to attend the performance of a play inside the People's Liberation Army encampment, an area surrounded by a red-brick wall and christened Silingpu. The strange invitation was accepted by the Dalai Lama, who selected 10 March as the date. On 9 March, he recalls, a Chinese messenger bluntly came to inform the Chief Bodyguard that the Dalai Lama should come alone and unarmed, a peculiar request since he was always escorted by twenty-five armed bodyguards. 'Now I want to make this clear to you: there will be none of the ceremony you usually have. None of your armed men are to come with him, as they do when he goes to the Preparatory Committee. No Tibetan is to come beyond the Stone Bridge. If you insist, you may have two or three Tibetan bodyguards, but it is definitely decided that they must not be armed.'[19]

The Dalai Lama had not yet visited the military camp, lying less than two miles from the Norbulingka, his summer residence. What is more, the Chinese were insisting that the arrangements be kept secret. How could anyone fail to suspect a trap? Wasn't there a chance of the God-King being taken hostage? The rumour spread through Lhasa in a few hours, leaving desperation in its wake. There had been many cases of great Tibetan lamas being invited to Chinese receptions and disappearing. The people rushed immediately to the Norbulingka. Quite soon, a crowd of 30,000 Tibetans had gathered in front of the gates. The people of Lhasa would not let their Dalai Lama fall into such a crude trap. He could hear them shouting: 'The Chinese must go; leave Tibet to the Tibetans' – every slogan demanded an end to the Chinese occupation.[20]

The Chinese government now rejects this account of events. According to Ngapo Ngawang Jigme, 'the 1959 armed rebellion in Tibet was

fomented by baseless rumours and lies spread by the Tibetan aristocracy'[21] The Dalai Lama having expressed a desire to watch a spectacle
featuring the PLA's dance troupe, the Chinese Army had offered to
organize a 'cultural soirée' in the Norbulingka gardens. But it seems the
Dalai Lama had declined the offer, insisting on visiting the military camp
himself. 'When the day came, some people spread a rumour that the
Dalai and his principal assistants would be arrested and sent by air to
a destination outside Tibet.' In a separate statement, Ngapo Ngawang
Jigme maintains that the 1959 rebellion was not caused by the policies
of Chinese Government, for it had scrupulously abided by the seventeen points of the 1951 agreement: 'On the contrary, it was the outcome
of a plot hatched by a small number of reactionaries belonging to Tibet's upper classes.'[22]

In his memoirs, Tenzin Gyatso recounts that he informed General
Tan Guansan that it had become impossible for him to honour the
invitation. The Chinese commander lost control and flew into a violent
rage. The Dalai Lama's messengers were told that the patience of the
Chinese government was exhausted: measures would be taken to 'crush
all those reactionaries'. The Dalai Lama and the Kashag were alarmed.
Fearing that the army would unleash another bloodbath, they proposed
another date. A correspondence ensued between the Dalai Lama and
General Tan Guansan, in which the Dalai Lama wrote that he was being
held against his will in the Norbulingka residence, by elements who were
trying to 'sabotage the friendship between Tibet and China'.

All of this was designed to buy time, as the decision about the Dalai
Lama's flight into exile was hanging in the air. The Dalai Lama learned
from Ngapo Ngawang Jigme of a Chinese plan to attack Norbulingka
in order to 'liberate' him. Chinese batteries – heavy cannons and machine-guns – were already in place on the higher terrain surrounding
the park. Sizeable military convoys were heading towards the Norbulingka. There was no time to lose. On 16 March, the first two bombs
fell on the compound, without causing any casualties. It was no longer
possible to entertain doubts, and any lingering hesitations were dispelled.
The interpretations of these events by Western historians depend on the
differing accounts of contemporary eyewitnesses. On the whole, most of
them agree that the Dalai Lama left willingly and in fact on his own
initiative. He himself says so. Others, however, maintain that his conciliatory attitude towards the Chinese had reached such a degree of diffi-
dence that the Khampas were afraid he was about to irrevocably 'sell
out' Tibet, without putting up any resistance. They snatched the young
man from the Chinese claws that were closing around him and escorted
him willy-nilly to a cushioned life in exile in India.

The flight of the Dalai Lama took place in strictest secrecy on the
night of 16–17 March. The Chinese knew nothing about his departure
for a number of days. 'A soldier's clothes and a fur cap had been left for

me, and at about half past nine I took off my monk's robes and put them on. And then, in that unfamiliar dress, I went to my prayer room for the last time, I sat down on my usual throne and opened the book of the Lord Buddha's teachings which lay before it and I read to myself till I came to a passage in which Lord Buddha told a disciple to be of good courage. Then I closed the book and blessed the room, and turned out the lights. As I went out, my mind was drained of all emotion. I was aware of my own sharp footfalls on the floor of beaten earth, and the ticking of the clock in the silence.'[23] As he prepared to depart into exile, the Dalai Lama was embarking on one of the most unusual odysseys of our time.

Accompanied by a few parliamentarians and Cabinet members, his mother, his elder sister, his younger brother, his two tutors and some 400 Tibetan soldiers and loyalists, it took two weeks for the Dalai Lama to reach India, travelling on horseback, on foot, on mules and in yak-hide coracles. The caravan moved at an average speed of 20 miles a day over the snowy highlands of Tibet, crossing passes at 18,000 feet and narrowly missing Chinese patrols on more than one occasion. If Tenzin Gyatso had delayed his departure by a few days, he would probably have been killed by a bomb or captured by the army. On 20 March, at about 2 a.m., bombs started raining down on the fragile buildings of the Norbulingka.

'They started firing on the Norbulingka with mortars and cannons, from all four directions at the same time. Boom! Boom! Five or six thousand people died that night.' Eighty-year-old Tashi Gyaltsen, a humble monk living in exile in a monastery in Dharamsala, relives the horror of those days, with battles raging in the streets. 'Around four in the morning, they started firing cannons on the Potala', the Dalai Lama's imposing residence built on a hill near Lhasa. 'The bombardment went on all day. From morning till night they fired on the Potala, Ramoche temple and many other parts of Lhasa.'

There is no sorrow nor hatred in the eyes of this Lama, as he speaks in a strong and resolute voice, sitting on a brocade cushion and smiling broadly. As he describes the golden roof of the monasteries shattered by the Chinese bombardment, people's homes burned to the ground and countless lifeless bodies littering the streets on that evening of 20 March 1959, a bell tinkles softly somewhere in the inner courtyard of Tse Chok Ling, a peaceful little monastery built in the 1960s by a handful of Tibetan monks. Perched on a hillside in the Indian state of Himachal Pradesh, it lies over 600 miles away from Tibet. Thirty years have passed, but the memory of that insolent brutality is vividly etched in the mind of the old man with the peaceful Buddha's face.

'The Chinese had disguised themselves as Tibetans and we couldn't always tell them apart. They were all over. A cannon boomed and a few seconds later we could see the dust rising up into the sky where a bomb had landed. They also fired at Drepung monastery; five cannons were trained on the monastery from behind. Sera monastery was almost entirely destroyed. All the monks fled. You know, as a result of the teachings of our Buddhist religion, we monks have never wanted to fight. Ours is a peace-loving religion. To fight had never entered my mind. We believe in the Buddha, in the Dalai Lama, we had never given a thought to fighting and killing. Why? Nothing in our religion says that we should fight and kill. This is how the Chinese were able to enter Tibet so easily. The Dalai Lama was too young to organize a resistance. They came little by little, initially wearing civilian clothes. They settled in all over Tibet, saying: "We are going to help you. We will do everything for you". But in actual fact, what have they done?'

In 1959, the old Lama goes on, 'the Chinese became more vicious. There seemed to be no end to their appetite for destruction. The ranks of the army swelled without end and more and more weapons poured into Tibet. Ordinary Tibetans talked of nothing besides this unfamiliar situation. Over the past two years we had realized that it was beyond repair. The Chinese had arrived saying they wanted to liberate Tibet. But they meant the opposite. They said Tibet had become free, free from religion. They said civil rights had been restored in Tibet.' Many people who lived through this period gave us a similar account of events. In 1959, the Chinese opened a wound that is difficult to heal, even thirty years later.

The uprising of 1959

When the Chinese army cannons started spitting fire, the entire city was immediately thrown into a ferment. Locked for three full days and nights in mortal combat, twenty thousand civilian Tibetans rose up against a compact mass of some forty thousand Chinese soldiers armed to the teeth. Despite the insurgents' determination and their courage born of desperation, the match was too uneven. On 22 March, Chinese tanks entered the Barkhor square right in the heart of Lhasa and positioned themselves facing the Jokhang temple. Hundreds of Tibetan fighters fell before the onslaught. Shortly afterwards, the voice of Ngapo Ngawang Jigme was heard over the loudspeakers that the Chinese propaganda service had strung up all over the city. He called upon the remaining rebels to surrender. The Chinese government, he said, had reached an agreement with the Tibetans. So there was no point in going on fighting and it was time to lay down one's arms.

On that same day, the Chinese artillery targeted Ramoche, one of Lhasa's most important sanctuaries and the last target for the Chinese bombs. Lama Tashi Palden, also a refugee in Dharamsala, was in Ramoche that day. He shared his memories with me. 'They fired two salvoes at daybreak. Then nothing for a few minutes. They were adjusting their sights. The Chinese had been preparing their artillery for some time, making the required calculations well in advance so as to hit their targets when the time came. After those first shots, bombs hailed down on Ramoche with a deafening noise. At the end of the day, I saw fifty to sixty bodies strewn among the ruins of the sanctuary. But it was not yet over. When the firing ceased, the Chinese troops came to have a look.

'Right near Ramoche, there were three Tibetan policemen with a machine-gun. A bomb had severed both of one man's legs. The Chinese were coming nearer. A monk urged one of the policemen to shoot. "Not now, let's wait a little", the policeman said. There must have been fifty Chinese. They walked around the ruins and came into range. Then the policeman opened fire: rat-tat-tat-tat. I saw a good thirty Chinese die. We were very happy! All the more as we discovered the body of a high-ranking Chinese officer among the dead.

'In the evening, the Chinese returned. They set the ruins on fire. The buildings burned for two whole days. We fled towards the centre of Lhasa: that was when I saw the tanks in the street. I hid in the house of a friend. Outside, the Chinese were arresting thousands of people. An incalculable number of Tibetans were arrested and taken to an unknown destination, their hands tied behind their backs. There were corpses all over the streets. You couldn't count them all. Every step of the way you came across lifeless bodies; even women, children.

'One day my turn came to be made prisoner and I was taken to the Norbulingka garden where there were hundreds of others like me. There I saw the Chinese stacking up bodies and dousing them with kerosene before setting them alight. The smell was horrendous. The pyre burned for three days.'

When the cannons finally fell silent, the Chinese counted 4,000 Tibetan prisoners. They confiscated 8,000 handguns and a hundred machine-guns and mortars as well as 10 million rounds of ammunition. A Chinese estimate refers to 2,000 fatalities among the Tibetans but others speak of 10,000 and even 20,000 people killed during the three-day carnage. In the streets, the wounded were left to perish in agony, untended. At last, the Chinese flag flew over the breached walls of the Potala. Mao's troops had routed the separatists.

The time for reprisals had come. The army systematically searched the homes of all the families suspected of being 'reactionary'. Their belongings were confiscated. Summary executions were organized to serve as an example to the public, while many monks were deported to the sinister 'reform through labour' camps that remain the mainstay of the enormous Chinese gulag. Many others were forced to labour on large-scale construction schemes such as hydropower projects.

Teams of Chinese propaganda specialists filmed simulated exchanges of gunfire, using Tibetans as models. Their intention was to create 'proof' of the monks' participation in the rebellion in order to force confessions out of those who had remained silent. The Chinese government published photographs of monks laying down their weapons. Tashi Palden maintains that these photos are forgeries: they were taken at gunpoint during the simulation exercises.

In the meantime, an inventory of the most precious objects taken from the monasteries and from the homes of 'reactionary' families was drawn up with the greatest care. Gold and silver ornaments and utensils were packed in sacks, sealed with wax and sent to Peking. For several years more, convoy after convoy of trucks was to carry off to China the most cherished treasures of Tibet's cultural and religious patrimony.

The leaden yoke of Chinese authority was rammed down on Tibet with the utmost violence. Over the next few years, tens of thousands of Tibetans died, according to the most conservative estimates based on testimony provided by fleeing Tibetans and on the rare accounts published in the official Chinese press. 'They have not only been shot, but also beaten to death, crucified, burned alive, drowned, vivisected, starved, strangled, hanged, scalded, buried alive, disembowelled, and beheaded', in the words of the Dalai Lama.[24] After examining a considerable amount of congruent testimony, the International Commission of Jurists concluded in an official report that China was guilty of engaging in genocide in Tibet. While this catastrophe ravaged the Land of Snow, Tenzin Gyatso arrived safely in India, a new place of refuge. Between eighty and one hundred thousand Tibetans followed him into exile.

As soon as the Dalai Lama's flight came to their notice, the Chinese cancelled the promised six-year respite: all the measures required to bring Tibet as a whole into the Communist fold – euphemistically referred to as 'democratic reform' – would immediately be applied. The 1959 uprising 'accelerat[ed] the destruction of Tibet's reactionary forces. Tibet went on the shining democratic, socialist road sooner than expected', boasts an official Chinese publication.[25] A prophet in his own lifetime after all, Mao predicted on 6 April 1952 that 'if Tibet's reactionaries dare to unleash a general rebellion, the labouring masses will become liberated all the sooner. There is no doubt in that respect.'

Democratic reform was based on an accelerated and extreme collectivization of Tibet's rural dwellers and the neutralization of monasteries that were still active. 'The Million Serfs Stand Up', announces a publication controlled by the Chinese Communist Party.[26] 'The inhuman political oppression and economic exploitation of serfs forced them to live like animals. Agriculture and animal husbandry in Tibet were stagnant and backward', while the people lived in sickness, persecution and death. 'The savage rule of the Tibetan serf-owners served only to fan the flames of hatred among the serfs who would rise up at any time with violent force.'

Was this not the time for them to finally throw off their chains and

rise against the class of their oppressors? 'While the rebellion was being
quelled, the serfs were demanding that the democratic reform be carried out', the booklet goes on. The Chinese government proceeded to
expropriate the holdings of the wealthy peasants and the monasteries.
The land was distributed among the labouring masses. Old debts were
cancelled and the 'slaves' were officially given their freedom. The process of democratic reform was officially concluded in 1961. 'The democratic reform shattered the yoke of feudal serfdom and liberated the
productive forces, promoting the development of agriculture, animal
husbandry and handicraft industries. Later, the emancipated serfs organized themselves and embarked on the road to socialism.'[27]

According to Israel Epstein, this was not the single-handed accom-
plishment of the Chinese. They were helped by Tibet's serfs and slaves,
who were ready to overthrow the old system. 'Only the oppressed and
exploited themselves can really uproot old tyrannies, and change, in that
fight, into free men and women – masters of the land and of their own
fate.'[28] Mao's words are famous: 'Revolution is not a dinner-party.' Epstein
does concede that 'demolishing the old in order to build the new' did
not come about without violence. 'Between 1959 and 1965, a whole series
of mass struggles were waged by them', a euphemistic reference to the
public humiliations inflicted on the 'enemies of the people'. This compulsory element of the theory of class struggle far too often culminated
in torture and death, in practice. The victim was invariably beaten; many
were executed or driven to commit suicide as an alternative to the pain
or to avoid denouncing their companions. Chinese cadres specializing
in 'political work' were so effective that by 1960, Ngapo Ngawang Jigme
was in a position to report to the National People's Congress that: 'The
class consciousness of the peasants and nomads has greatly improved.
Now they warmly sing praises such as: President Mao is the father of
the different nationalities of our Motherland. He is closer to us than our
own parents.' The Panchen Lama chimed in, saying that the situation
had never been better in Tibet.

The techniques for class struggle and self-criticism meetings were quite
sophisticated, having been honed and polished throughout the Chinese
countryside since the fifties with the unfolding of the different stages of
the agrarian reform. The reform had produced a massive redistribution
of land to the poorer peasants. It had necessitated the denunciation and
elimination – often physical – of the big landowners. In the cities, the
'people's dictatorship' had been slammed down upon the head of any
citizen who opposed the relentless progress of socialism; the reactionaries, spies and running dogs of imperialism and capitalism had been
exposed to the people's righteous indignation. In this field as well, Mao
Tse-tung's faithful subjects had acquired a fair amount of experience. In
Tibet as in China, the script was very much the same and the drama
was played out in front of an 'invited' audience.

Along with the bread in the egalitarian 'big pot' of Communism, the regime offered games as a bonus. A 'People's Court' made up of political commissars would officiate on the rostrum, and extract a complete confession from the accused by whatever means were required. When appropriate, 'fraternal assistance' would be volunteered by representatives of the masses, including not a few professional agitators. In most cases, the combination of insults, threats and brutality would take care of the victim in a matter of hours. At other times, it would take a few days to break the will of the stronger spirits. Enough torturers were available to work in shifts, vying in cruelty to secure advancement. The strategy of the Chinese Communist cadres, in Tibet and elsewhere, was simply to destroy the bonds of traditional society: family ties and religion. In this climate of political terror, except for the more resolute who preferred suicide, who would hesitate to sell out a friend, a sister or a father?

By 1965, Tibet's administrative incorporation into China was felt to be complete with the creation on 1 September of the 'Tibet Autonomous Region'. The Chinese press loudly hailed the birth of a socialist paradise in Tibet. So much for the propaganda. Leaving aside the myth of the heroic march of socialism liberating Tibet, what was in fact the situation in the cities, towns and villages perched high on the Himalayan plateau before the arrival of the liberators? Was Tibet, as China claims, a land oppressed by the darkness of slavery? Was it an independent country in those days?

Notes

1. Wang Furen and Suo Wenqing, *Highlights of Tibetan History*, New World Press, Beijing, 1984, p. 171.
2. Wang Furen and Suo Wenqing, op. cit., p. 172.
3. Ibid., p. 175.
4. Michael C. van Walt van Praag, *The Status of Tibet*, Westview Press, Colorado, 1987, p. 339.
5. Tenzin Gyatso, *My Land and my People*, Potala, New York, 1983, p. 87.
6. Wang Furen and Suo Wenqing, op. cit., p. 177.
7. Xinhua News Agency, 22 May 1988.
8. Ibid.
9. Wang Furen and Suo Wenqing, op. cit., p. 178.
10. Ibid.
11. Dawa Norbu, *Red Star Over Tibet*, Sterling Publishers Ltd, Delhi, 1987 (Second Edition), p. 113.
12. Op. cit., p. 91.
13. Ibid., p. 133.
14. *Tibet: Myth Vs. Reality*, Beijing Review Publications, Beijing, 1988, p. 44.
15. Tenzin Gyatso, op. cit., p. 128.
16. David Wise, *The Politics of Lying*, Random House, New York, p. 174.

17. To be compared with David Wise, who dates the operation from 1958 to December 1961.

18. Michel Peissel, *Les cavaliers du Kham*, Robert Laffont, Paris, 1972, p. 114.

19. Tenzin Gyatso, op. cit., p. 166.

20. Ibid., p. 172.

21. *China Daily*, March 1988.

22. *Xinhua*, 2 March 1988.

23. Tenzin Gyatso, op. cit., p. 198.

24. Ibid., p. 222.

25. *Tibet: Today & Yesterday*, Beijing Information, Beijing, 1984, p. 88.

26. *Tibet: Myth Vs. Reality*, p. 43.

27. Ibid., p. 52.

28. Israel Epstein, *Tibet Transformed*, New World Press, Beijing, 1983, p. 45.

2

Heaven or Hell?

Chinese propaganda has been so effective that when most Westerners attempt to conjure up an image of old Tibet, what often comes to mind is the worst type of feudal society. We must be careful not to pass judgment hastily, for it is not always easy to draw the line between fact and fantasy. The difficulty is further compounded by the shortage of serious and objective studies on the religious, social and political structures in Tibet before the Chinese invasion. As far as Chinese propaganda material is concerned, the matter is settled: before their 'liberation', the Tibetans groaned under the yoke of a slave-owning tyranny more cruel than any of Europe's medieval societies. Just as many other colonial powers have done in the past, Peking has based much of the rationale for its presence in Tibet on the fraternal assistance its army and Communist cadres are said to have provided in order to rescue the Tibetan people from serfdom and slavery. The jargon of the Communist Party hints broadly at what cannot be said outright: it is the responsibility of the Chinese Hans to civilize ignorant barbarians. China, unsolicited, illuminated its neighbour with the torch of the new civilization, held to be the guiding light for all humanity under Mao's leadership.

Since the flight into exile of the Dalai Lama, Chinese criticism of the old regime in Tibet has lost little of its acrimony. Whenever he has offered to initiate a dialogue with the Chinese authorities about the future of Tibet, he has immediately been accused of seeking to restore the feudal system. Following in their leader's footsteps, Tibetans in exile no longer seek to conceal the shortcomings of the old society. They freely admit that drastic changes were long overdue in a society that had become ossified and set in its ways.

It was imperative for Tibet to break out of the near-total isolation into which it had receded by 1950. Today, those same Tibetans are trying with some success to break with tradition and build a working democracy. But they challenge and reject Peking's version of their history. They point out that until the Chinese arrived, Tibet was a country that had never experienced large-scale famine or war. We shall try to hear both sides, starting with China's arguments and those of its friends.

Feudal Tibet: myths and realities

We know where Ngapo Ngawang Jigme's loyalties lie; here is his account of life in Tibet before it embarked upon the shining path to socialism. 'In the old Tibet, the working people groaned under the rule of an oppressive, feudal serf system. Feudal officials, aristocrats and monastic autocrats – 5 per cent of the total population – owned almost all the land and most of the livestock. The serfs and herdsmen owned no land or livestock and had to toil the year round to eke out a bare subsistence. Freedom of the individual was denied them. The ruthless suppression and exploitation by the local government, the aristocracy and the monasteries severely hampered productivity. Tibetan society was stagnant for a long time. The old Tibet was a hell for the labouring people. It was a paradise only for the serf-owners, the tiny minority. Under the leadership of the Chinese Communist Party, the Tibetan people have instituted democratic reform, thrown off the shackles of feudal serfdom and taken the socialist road.'[1]

Concerning respect for human rights prior to 1959, this is the position of the Chinese government: 'Before democratic reform, Tibet was a feudal country of serfdom. All the instruments of production were concentrated in the hands of less than 5 per cent of the population, that is the government, the nobles and the monasteries, who were the three landowners. Most Tibetans were slaves or serfs. Considered to be chattels by their owners, the were reduced to working day and night, being sold, exchanged or mortgaged. If they disobeyed or did something wrong, they could be cruelly tortured or even killed. In such conditions, most Tibetans could not even think of personal freedom, let alone human rights.'[2]

Identical or comparable atrocities are described in another official Chinese publication which claims that serfs were indeed given 30 per cent of the land (the less fertile, of course) but they had to pay their masters back in kind. Additionally, they were subject to corvée labour, for the benefit of masters and government alike. As a result, most serfs were deeply in debt and could seldom provide for their family. Indebtedness was another way for the rich to perpetuate their dominion over the poor. 'All serf-owners in Tibet, including the Dalai Lama, were usurers. Manorial estates, monasteries and governments at all levels had special institutions for handling loans',[3] says this publication.

Torture was a common practice in Tibet, if one is to believe the Chinese booklets and magazines. Whereas the lords enjoyed the most extravagant pleasures in their luxurious homes, the vilest methods were used to punish wayward serfs. Noses were slit, eyes plucked out and limbs lopped off the hapless victims. There were families of professional torturers. In Lhasa, from time to time, a bugle would herald the public execution of a serf. The 'celebration' was about to begin: 'Some were first disembowelled and paraded through the streets of Parkor (in the heart of Lhasa) before they were executed. Others were tied naked to a red-hot copper horse mounted on wheels and paraded around Parkor three times before they were killed.'[4] Victims condemned to the most atrocious suffering were thrown into two dungeons infested with scorpions, one being sited in the Potala.

Tibetan society was divided into three classes and nine grades, say the 'historians' of the Chinese Communist Party. The aristocracy, the grand lamas and the leadership belonged to what was called the superior class. Monks and ordinary lamas among the Buddhist clergy, lower-ranking government servants and the agents of the landowners constituted a middle class. The rest made up the lower classes. Unlike the two higher strata, the last suffered the most severe punishments. 'The lives of the "inferiors" were as cheap and worthless as a straw rope. They had no right to claim "innocence" when persecuted. If a member of the "inferior class" witnessed the rape of his wife or daughter by a lord, his eyes would be gouged out.'[5]

Soon after gaining control of Tibet, the Chinese government built a Museum of the Tibetan Revolution in record time. This ungainly icon of the new regime, a concrete block of defiance, was erected right opposite the Potala by a brigade of 'model workers'. The 'Tibetan masses' who had never gained admittance to the splendours of the Dalai Lama's palace could wander freely in the halls of the Museum and contemplate the glorious episodes of the popular uprising against the tyrants of the old system. Also on display were the treasures of successive Dalai Lamas, said to be comparable only to the hoard of the late Tsar, accumulated from the sweat and toil of the Russian people. For a time, a whole range of instruments of torture allegedly used under the old system were displayed along with musical instruments manufactured from human bones – taken from people who had not died a natural death, it was carefully explained, but from the corpses of serfs assassinated by their masters.

During the cultural revolution, this gruesome exhibit was a mandatory stop for foreign visitors, particularly if they were from the Third World. In those difficult years, Chinese propaganda shrilled to a peak of hysterical denunciation. The depiction of the old system was based on an exhibit with an audiovisual presentation showing a serf carrying his master – eyes gleaming with hatred – on a mountain track in a snowstorm, a monk forcing into a box a terrified child promised as a religious sacrifice, and the skins of children fallen victim to these barbaric rites. The display concluded with the revolt of the serfs against their oppressors. A young Tibetan girl was shown drawing a red star on a rock with her own blood, to express the Tibetan serfs' yearning for liberation and their love for Chairman Mao and the Chinese Communist Party. With the passing of time and the appearance of a measure of restraint, the Chinese authorities seem to have closed down this type of 'shame' exhibit intended for the edification of the masses.[6]

Nevertheless, declarations from Peking are still replete with absurdities; if the situation were not so serious, they would be merely comical. Take Israel Epstein: for his servile praise of China's Tibet, he deserves the title of poet laureate. In a typically laboured attempt at trenchant irony, while showering undisguised contempt on Tibetan Tantric practices, he demurs, artfully conceding that the modern buildings that the architects of socialism have thrown up in Lhasa are not sufficient proof of progress in Tibet. 'If imperialism and not the Chinese revolution had triumphed in Tibet, it too might have added some towering edifices to Lhasa's skyline – a multi-storey Shangri-La Hotel run by some great international chain, perhaps, with oxygenated Potala-view luxury suites for those able to foot the bill. It would not be too far-fetched to imagine, among its features, a Reincarnation Dance Lounge with statues of many-armed Passion Buddhas engaged in ritual coitus unveiled each midnight to titillate the guests.'[7]

Communist China has another fervent admirer in the author Han Suyin. Over the years, she has managed to espouse the many twists and turns of the Chinese Communist Party's policies with extraordinary celerity and flexibility. While Mao lived, she praised him unreservedly. After Deng Xiaoping was rehabilitated, she became his most ardent supporter. Her testimony about Tibet should be taken with a grain of salt. In her opinion, in order to understand the atmosphere of terror in which Tibetan serfs and slaves lived in the old society, 'you have to turn to the darkest pages of the history of Europe in the Middle Ages'. The 626 highest-ranking Tibetan clerics owned 90 per cent of Tibet, she claims. Thanks to the reforms introduced in 1959, 'Tibet has put an end to centuries of darkness and terror. But this liberation was accomplished by the Tibetans themselves, the serfs and slaves who wish to make their contribution to the revolution.'[8]

When she describes socialist Tibet, however, Han Suyin is lavish with her praise. After a visit in October 1975 she reports that: 'In the streets, the few and rare policemen who direct the traffic carry no weapons, nor are there any patrols or barbed wire, or enclosures except around the young trees.' When she stops to photograph three Tibetan farmers in their fields, she notes that 'the almost palpable joy, the happy trust are more visible in Tibet than elsewhere, because these people have been so oppressed and exploited and the cruel memories are not far away'. Thanks to Chairman Mao's clairvoyance, 'a new class, the worker class, unknown in Tibet before, would be born!' 'Every young boy and girl now wants to become a worker, to drive a machine!' 'I see how suddenly the old myths were exploded, the old world of belief crumbled, and a new logic, a new understanding of the world took its place.' 'These are the new miracles, exorcizing the abject terrors of the past.' From her point of view, the achievements have been considerable, for that past was 'a monster devouring their lives ... a world of sumptuous terror'. By association, even the Potala becomes 'an evil, parasitic monster'. Fortunately, 'the apparatus of magic and terror, where all was explained by demons and supplication and incantation, is now gone'. Han Suyin is not impressed. She feels that 'the vast accumulation of treasure is slightly nauseating. It is all exacted service, corvée, squeezing grain and tribute from terrorized people.' Whereas now, 'There is no fear, no cowering servility, but an atmosphere of mutual trust and respect which is very impressive.' 'I can scarcely believe that here, in Tibet, that most backward and hermetic of regions, the leap from the seventh to the twentieth century has been made in one generation. ... [that] a new generation is taking the future in its own hands, and that it is Tibetan.'[9]

Foreign testimony about the old Tibetan society is rare, but there are more and more Tibetans writing about the period before 1950. Slowly but surely, the parts of the puzzle are falling into place. No truthful person in a position to evaluate the facts can deny that in the middle of the twentieth century, Tibetan society was still feudal in many respects. The same could be said for China. Would it not apply equally to a number of Asian and other nations at that time? Furthermore, it will be difficult to understand Tibet unless we look at it from a Buddhist perspective.

Buddhism is basically a philosophy of peace. A disciple of the Buddha strives for release from desire, which is held to be the source of suffering (samsara). His goal is Nirvana or Enlightenment, the sublime liberation of body and mind. According to Arya Deva, an eminent Buddhist philosopher:

Mental suffering torments the upper realms,
Physical suffering the lower,
This world is eternally consumed by mental and physical suffering.

For those who attain Nirvana, all suffering is extinguished. Buddhahood is a state of supreme enlightenment, leading to omniscience. Only a small minority can hope to attain this state. For disciples of the Small Vehicle (Hinayana), the search for enlightenment is an individual quest: the believer seeks to set himself free from suffering. For disciples of the Great Vehicle (Mahayana), seeking Nirvana is a collective enterprise for the benefit of all beings. To become a bodhisattva or a Buddha of Compassion is to serve the entire community, because a being with such a level of realization assists all suffering beings in their own search for deliverance. The third school is the Tantric Buddhist school (Tantrayana). It demands rigorous mental discipline in order to achieve the liberation of the mind. Its methods, similar to those used by Indian Yogis, are concentration, contemplation and meditation – difficult mental exercises requiring a strong will and great determination.

Tibetans have drawn on both Mahayana and Tantrayana in developing their own religion and disseminating the Dharma, the teachings of the Buddha. Over the centuries, several schools of Buddhism have vied for prominence in Tibet. The main ones are the Yellow Hats (*Gelugpa*) to which the main tutors of the Dalai Lama belonged, and the Red Hats (*Kagyu*). With the spread of Buddhism, starting in the thirteenth century, thousands of monasteries were founded and grew into Dharma Universities. Combining a number of administrative functions with the purely religious, these fortified citadels owned vast areas of land and lived off the work of the peasants who farmed it. Tradition strictly dictated the place in the hierarchy of the *getruk* (novice), *trapa* (monk), *Lama* (accomplished master) and *Tulku* (the reincarnation of an important figure in the Tibetan religious pantheon). The most highly revered reincarnations and teachers were addressed as *Rinpoche* (literally 'precious one'). At the height of the golden age of Tibetan Buddhism, several hundred thousand monks lived in *gompas* (monasteries) erected outside the larger towns or scattered widely in the vast solitudes of Tibet. Thousands of monks were not affiliated to any particular monastery, but lived as beggars, wandering along the roads. Last but not least, hermits who had chosen the ascetic path lived a secluded existence in remote caves tucked away in the mountains, far from the world below.

Alexandra David-Neel was one of the very few Westerners to travel all over Tibet in the early twentieth century and her accounts are extremely valuable. She says that a 'benign' (her own term) form of slavery still existed at the turn of the century. The 'slaves' generally became servants in wealthy families. As for Tibet's all-powerful religion, its grip on the people manifestly verged on obscurantism.

Tibetan peasants lived in a world of fanciful beliefs and superstitions that created irrational fears in their minds. They often relied on the services of magicians directly descended from the Bön shamans whose religion flourished in Tibet before the advent of Buddhism in the eighth century. The distinction between Tantric Buddhism and Shamanism was often blurred, producing a convenient syncretism. Evil spirits preyed on humans. Group trance was commonplace. For Tibetans, not all diseases had natural causes; some were caused by invisible spirits from other worlds who roamed about trying to steal 'life force' from earthly beings.

Sacred objects were sometimes made out of human bone. Some monks had *thug-treng* – ritual rosaries in which each of the 108 beads had been fashioned from a different human skull. The famous Parisian traveller recounts how she and her adopted son, Lama Yongden, once met a solitary pilgrim who asked to share their tea and whipped out from under his robe an unusual bowl that turned out to be half a human skull!

To make matters worse, peasant families often owed long-standing debts, with scant likelihood of relief, to the monasteries and *gyalpos*, the local lords and kinglets who never stepped outside the door without a servant to hold an umbrella over their head. Corvée and other taxes were the main source of misery and despair in other cases. Pervasive corruption undermined every level of the Tibetan hierarchy. When a Tibetan official – a *Pönpo* – travelled around the country, it was customary for the local people to feed him and his retinue, his servants and his animals. At each staging-post, a procession of men and women would 'offer' him, out of their scant possessions, a specified number of gifts in cash and in kind.

Alexandra David-Neel maintains, however, that Tibet was first and foremost a country where laughter rang out and people partied, feasted and rejoiced, a land where the inhabitants revelled in the pleasures of life and no one died of hunger, except in the most remote places where the climate was exceptionally harsh and inhospitable. The Land of Snow was a realm steeped in tradition and radiant spirituality.

From other accounts of daily life in Tibet, it emerges that Tibetan women played a prominent part in society. They related freely with men before marriage. Arranged marriages were common, but if the candidate was not to her liking, the young woman was free to demur. If necessary, she could ask for a divorce. Very often, a wife managed the accounts and ran the household entirely on her own. In Tibet, there was never any custom of binding women's feet, a common aberration among well-to-do Chinese. Unlike their Chinese sisters, who languished all day long in the women's quarters of the house and could only hobble outdoors and see the world on a handful of occasions every year, Tibetan women moved freely in and out of the home. Nor was there any question of veiling the women's faces as the Muslims do. For centuries, a Hindu tradition commanded that a woman unlucky enough to survive her husband be burned alive on his funeral pyre. There was nothing of the sort in Tibet. In fact, Tibetan women's status was so elevated that even today many Tibetans joke that in old Tibet, the men were the brawn and the women the brains, and when the two merged, they produced excellent results.

The belief in the Buddhist law of *karma* (the overwhelming majority never questioned the principle of reincarnation) led rich and poor alike to accept that in this life, each human being was enjoying – or otherwise – the harvest of the seeds sown in a previous life. Everyone understood the implications: in the next life, a person would be held to account for the good and the evil committed in this one. Respect for the working of *karma* also produced in the believer a feeling of satisfaction with however much or little he possessed – and perhaps also a feeling of resignation. This tended to neutralize envy, most of the time.

For the logical Western mind, it seems obvious that Tibetan Buddhism instituted a society based on privilege. The first to benefit were the high Lamas. They jealously guarded their prerogatives and their influence in society. A case in point: the lay schools that had been opened in the twenties in Lhasa, Shigatse and Gyantse were forced to close at the express request of the monasteries. Thinking that an English type of education would help his people, the Thirteenth Dalai Lama had personally called for these schools to be set up. But a great majority of the clergy was uncompromisingly hostile to outside influences and adamantly opposed to any changes in Tibetan daily life. 'The great monasteries had such power that they sometimes objected successfully even to His Holiness' plans', says Rinchen Dolma Taring, the daughter of an aristocratic Tibetan family that settled in India after 1959.[10]

The Dalai Lama: between the old and the new

What about other Tibetans in a position to speak freely? What do they have to say? I asked the Dalai Lama for his opinion about the shortcomings of the old society in Tibet. He made no bones about giving a forthright reply. He started by telling me how as a small child wearing the Dalai Lama's crown, he himself had been deprived of freedom and kept inside the Potala palace, cut off from the outside world, while all the other children his age played outdoors or looked after the family herds in grassy pastures. 'When I was small, sometimes I felt that if I had been an ordinary person, I would have been happier. Especially in winter. For almost five months every winter, I spent all day and all night in a room in the Potala. In keeping with tradition, I was expected to go into "retreat" and pass the time reciting mantras (Buddhist incantations). The room was gloomy, very cold and full of rats! There was an awful musty smell' – the Dalai Lama laughs at the memory. 'At the end of the day, when the sun was setting, I would go to the little window. As I watched the shadows engulf Sera monastery next door, I felt as if I was drowning in a well of sadness. To make things worse, my tutor, who had been appointed Regent, had a severe expression. He would stand beside me with that severe look on his face. Opposite the Potala, I could see the villagers driving their cows into the fields every morning. In the evening, the cowherds would come home, looking happy and carefree. I could hear the melodies they were singing so clearly! Maybe they envied me, sitting high up in the Potala. Little did they know how much the Dalai Lama would have liked to be with them!'

Was Tibet feudal? 'If you look at the social system and the different strata in the society, Tibet belonged to a feudal system. It sounds very bad. But in reality, generally speaking, the Tibetan community was very peaceful in those days. Very happy. The Chinese talk about serfs and landowners. Actually, the relationship between the landowners and their staff was rather good. In many cases, the simple people developed a feeling of belonging to the landowners, and displayed a type of loyalty. When it comes to the landowners, not only the lay people but also the monasteries, some had an acute sense of responsibility for their servants' well-being.

'As for the politics, the system of government – of course the social system was old-fashioned. It had to change. But since the general atmosphere was pacific and harmonious, I think the changes should have been introduced progressively. The political system was also part of a feudal system. Since the time of the Fifth Dalai Lama, the Tibetan government has been headed by a Dalai Lama. In this respect as well, there was no pressing need to change things abruptly. The necessary changes would have emerged gradually, on their own. The most vital requirement at the time, I feel, was the establishment of a modern educational system. To study and learn in an up-to-date educational environment and to develop some means of communication with the outside world: those were the real needs. We needed technology. Had these things been available, changes would have taken place quite naturally as we developed.

'The public, the community as a whole was very ignorant for want of education. One of the most striking examples of the prevailing ignorance is the fact that Tibetans were convinced that Tibet was the largest nation in the world! The Chinese entertained the same belief, but not without justification. In our case, it was unwarranted, don't you think?' Looking at me, the Dalai Lama goes off into peals of contagious laughter that ricochet around the walls of his residence for the next few minutes. Tenzin Geyche Tethong, his secretary, joins good-naturedly in the laughter.

Tenzin Gyatso is willing to discuss the corruption in the old Tibetan society. I tell him that from what Tibetans have told me, corruption had come to pervade every level of Tibetan society, including the monasteries. In some cases, it was a direct outcome of feudal-type customs. For instance, Tibetans believed that when a high Lama died, his reincarnation had to be found. The child, born within a year or two of the death of his predecessor, would inherit all his titles once he was recognized as the reincarnation. Finding the child involved a complicated procedure relying on divination and the occasional help of an oracle. I am not attempting to question something that is exclusively a matter of religious belief. But in Tibet, an important Lama wielded considerable religious – and sometimes also temporal – power. In theory, a reincarnation could appear in any family, even the lowliest. But it was not uncommon for the candidate to be found among the great aristocratic families: for the price of a few bribes, they could protect their prerogatives and their fortunes.

'Of course there was corruption,' replies the Dalai Lama, 'just as there is in any human society, isn't there? But in Tibet, there were also ways and means for the people to inform those in charge of fighting corruption.' In the monasteries, the corruption was of two types, he adds. Some monks, instead of devoting themselves to the spiritual well-being of their charges, sought material gain, prosperity and influence. The other type of corruption in the monastic universities was more easy to condone: out of a concern for maintaining the desired level of spiritual practice and avoiding an extended power vacuum, the search for a reincarnation might be carried out expeditiously, with little concern for the authenticity of the candidate. The Dalai Lama clearly states that in the period before 1950, the monasteries had degenerated to some extent. Buddhist precepts were no longer observed with the required rigour, to such an extent that vacant posts were occasionally filled with plainly incompetent monks. Lastly, influential Lamas might neglect their monastic studies in order to manage their family's affairs, in breach of the vows they had taken. Once a *trapa* or a Lama puts on the robes of a monk, he should cut the ties that bind him to his family and friends.

'In some monasteries, some important Lamas had acquired functions similar to those of a landowner, to the detriment of those of a spiritual centre. That was unfortunate', sighs the God-King of the Tibetans. The situation had deteriorated to such an extent that in the 1920s, a few years before passing away, the Thirteenth Dalai Lama had subjected all the high Lamas to a general examination to test their level of knowledge. The Lamas who had failed the test had been promptly relieved of their responsibilities.

What about the situation today? Inevitably, things have changed tremendously. In exile, Tibetan society has constantly been in contact with foreign civilizations and it has been compelled to open up and adapt. For the people who were left behind in Tibet, the basic situation is not so different. The Chinese intrusion and the ensuing political persecution thoroughly convulsed the pre-existing social order.

How has Tibet's unique religion adapted to the modern world? Many Western intellectuals who have inquired into the matter consider that Tibetan Buddhism is a philosophy of life that has a modern outlook and a scientific approach to what being human means. No longer archaic, it poses no obstacle to an individual's liberation or to finding one's place in society.

As for myself, I've come to know a number of Tibetans who have settled in the West. A few, a small minority, are obdurate when it comes to religious practice. Some superstitions are durable. But the younger generations don't take them seriously, and affectionately poke fun at those who do. I was told the story about a Tibetan lady living in Paris nick-named 'the Tigress', for she had fought the Chinese in Kham with ferocious strength in the 1950s and 1960s. At a reception after the wedding of a Tibetan and a Frenchwoman, she kept avoiding the centre of the dining hall, making complicated detours to get to and from the kitchen while casting anxious glances at the floor. Her strange behaviour attracted the notice of the other guests, who inquired about it. 'Well!' she replied, 'see that shadow on the ground. It belongs to a guest who has brought a pheasant that he has killed himself. He has drawn blood. Look at his

shadow, it is inauspicious. It will bring bad luck: it is evil karma!' The
Tigress was afraid of a shadow!

But when it comes to the Dalai Lama, as the twentieth century draws
to an end, he is still being treated like a church dignitary in the Middle
Ages. He is referred to and addressed as 'His Holiness'. It may be ar-
gued that the same applies to the Pope and other religious leaders around
the world, but for his followers, he is the manifestation of Chenrezig, the
Buddha of Compassion appearing in the guise of a human being. When
speaking about him, the epithets most commonly used by Tibetans and
Himalayan Buddhists are: 'The Wish-Fulfilling Gem' (*Yidzhin Norbu*), 'The
Presence' (*Kundun*), 'The Precious Victorious One' (*Gyalwa Rinpoche*), 'The
Highest' (*Gongsa Chog*). His official title is 'the Venerable Holder of the
Sacred Word, Heart of Wisdom, Ocean of Faith, Ruler over the Three
Worlds, the Unequalled' (*Jetsun Ngawang Losang Yeshe Tenzin Gyatso Sisum
Wangyur Tsungpa Nepai Dhe Palsangpo*). Some look upon him as the 'Guard-
ian of the Pure Lotus' and the 'Jewel of Fulfilment'. I wondered, didn't
he find this type of devotion excessive? What was he doing to bring his
people into the modern world? Here is what he replied:

'Oh yes! Sometimes they express unshakeable devotion. They think
I can do anything. When they ask for an audience, some come because
they are ill. They arrive with great expectations. But I always tell them:
you should see a doctor. Occasionally they ask me to blow on them,
thinking it will cure them. Sometimes it works!', he laughs. 'But sometimes it doesn't. Quite often, they really expect too much from me.' He
nods in assent: yes, it is a mistake to think he has supernatural powers.
But the Dalai Lama believes in reincarnation, quite naturally, and he
explains that his knowledge is rather broader than most humans and
that he has some special abilities as a result of experience gained in past
lives. 'That is why sometimes I can indeed relieve someone's suffering.
Sometimes my breath does have some effect. Occasionally they bring
me little bottles of water and ask me to blow on it. Later they drink the
water and sometimes it helps. But I am not a very extraordinary person.
Just a little bit extraordinary!' The Dalai Lama roars with laughter. 'This
is how there are a lot of things I know, although I was rather lazy as a
child. When I discuss with scientists or with experts, they seem to think
my awareness is on a par with theirs. So they congratulate me. I think
it is because of my past lives.'

Are Buddhism and science compatible? Yes, definitely. The key to
the survival of the Tibetan nation is probably to be found in the harmonious merger of the two. 'My own experience and the discussions
I've had with scientists lead me to believe that in some fields there is no
contradiction at all between Buddhism and the sciences. In other areas,
we are getting beyond the realm of science and that is another matter.
But, generally speaking, there is no contradiction. After all, Buddhism
is only an exercise for the mind. Researchers are presently experiment-

ing with Buddhist practices to try to explain how they work. On the other hand, if contradictions appear, they have to be resolved. According to some Buddhist scriptures, the world is flat. In areas like that, we must accept the rational explanations of science and reject the scriptural. Buddha himself was very clear in this respect: "You should accept my teaching only after practising it, on the basis of your own experience. When you yourself are convinced it is true, only then should you adopt it." In this way, the Buddha himself has given us the right to question his word and carry out investigations. So if we find science can produce proof that contradicts some scriptures, those scriptures must be abandoned. I explain to my followers that if researchers can experimentally prove that reincarnation does not exist, theoretically we will also have to abandon that concept!'

How does his audience respond when he makes such revolutionary statements? Again his laughter rings out. 'Every time I visit a monastery, I tell the Lamas and the Abbot: we must introduce courses on science and Western philosophy and psychology. These things are very important for us. In India, we don't yet have all the facilities we need. But we will some day. I explain to them that instead of explaining dead philosophies such as India's ancient religions, we should be studying the living traditions: Christianity, Judaism, Islam, the modern sciences. Particularly the modern sciences. We must study the scientific explanations for the world around us. But some of our older religious experts are sometimes very obstinate. I remember the day a man stepped on the moon for the first time. They weren't at all convinced, they were quite sceptical!' The Dalai Lama and his secretary laugh. 'So I made fun of them gently and said: maybe some of you should have gone up with the astronauts. From up there, you could have seen that the earth is round with your own eyes!'

After a good laugh, Tenzin Gyatso reminds me with a mischievous look that even the Dalai Lama is a man-made creation. The day the people no longer need him, he will cease to exist, and that will be the end of the Dalai Lama lineage. In the meantime, today's Dalai Lama wants to ignite a revolution of a different order in the lofty halls of the monasteries: it is high time, he says, to change the way the Dalai Lamas are selected. Since the time of the First Dalai Lama, born in 1391, the rules have remained unchanged. After one dies, the Tibetans start looking for the reincarnation. The search, more involved than for an ordinary Lama, can take months or even years until the right child is found. The high Lamas meditate and consult oracles. The right candidate is expected to immediately recognize objects that were among the personal belongings of the previous Dalai Lama. And this is how it went for Tenzin Gyatso, born in 1935 to a peasant family from Takster village in Amdo province in north-eastern Tibet. As it happens, Tenzin Gyatso was a fortunate choice for his people: he is nobody's fool and he dreams

of reforming his society to ensure its survival. But what if the next Dalai
Lama turned out to be a little bit dim? It would be a tragedy for the
entire Tibetan people.

'I have been saying since 1969 that the Dalai Lama institution can
either go on or disappear, depending on the wishes of the Tibetan people.
If it goes on, the next question is whether we should stick to tradition
or devise new methods. There are several possibilities. One would be to
select as a successor a Lama who has already proved his worth. Why
not? To do the same as for the Pope would be another possibility. When
he dies, the most eminent, the most highly qualified spiritual masters
gather and choose the next Pope. If the first method is adopted, I'll choose
my own successor before I die. That would be a good thing. It would
prevent quarrelling.' The Dalai Lama laughs again. 'I'm told that in a
Zen Buddhist sect in Japan, the abbot appoints his successor in his
testament, which he leaves behind when he dies. During his lifetime, all
the hopeful candidates serve him to the best of their ability! But when
I discuss this with the other Lamas, sometimes they are shocked and tell
me, "You shouldn't say such things. Succession within the Dalai Lama
lineage must continue in the same way as in the past." But as far as I'm
concerned, they can protest as much as they like, I won't let them change
my mind.'

Sino-Tibetan history, independence and interdependence

China's designs on Tibet did not originate in 1949. Well before the
founding of the Republic of China in 1911, the Qing dynasty (1644-1911)
had been clamouring with greater or lesser insistence that Tibet was
an integral part of its territory. But until 1949, Peking had neither the
time nor the means required to exercise the sovereignty it claimed over
the Land of Snow. It is also worth noting that the Chinese Communist
Party has not always displayed the same intransigence as it has since
1950. At the time of its birth in 1921, the first Congress declared that
it would be necessary to grant autonomy to Mongolia, Tibet and
Turkestan (Xinjiang) and to transform them into 'democratic federa-
tions'. According to that script, China would have become a 'Federal
Republic of China'. In 1928, the fourth CCP Congress decreed that
the unification of China could not proceed without a recognition of
the right of peoples to self-determination and secession. The wording
in 1931 was even more explicit, when the first Congress of Chinese
Soviets and the Constitution of the 'Soviet Republic of China' proclaimed the fundamental right of peoples to self-determination and the
right of small nations to split off and declare themselves independent
States.[11] Alas, when the Chinese Republic became the People's Republic following the Communist victory in 1949, might became right, and

the language of the CCP underwent radical changes. From 1962 onwards, the draft Constitution prepared by Liu Shaoqi proclaimed the
People's Republic of China to be a unitary and multinational state of
which the component regions and autonomous nationalities were all
declared to be inseparable parts.

Ever since, the Chinese government has compulsively sought to establish historical legitimacy for its presence on the Roof of the World.
Peking's thesis is stunningly simple: Tibet formally became part of the
Chinese Motherland in the thirteenth century and it has never looked
back. Tibetan independence is a pipe-dream invented by foreign imperialists who seek to weaken China and by a handful of reactionary Tibetans who want to restore the feudal regime. Always ready with an
answer, Peking is prepared to deal with any misgivings about its inter-
pretation of history. In December 1989, a Xinhua dispatch revealed to
the world that researchers working in a laboratory had found genetic
parallels that provided 'scientific proof' that the Tibetans belonged to
the Chinese Han race.

The Chinese position is contradicted by a large number of exiled
Tibetans in a position to speak freely, and by Tibetans brave enough to
risk their lives by speaking up inside Tibet; they consider their country
was independent and will be an independent nation again in the future.
They are convinced that truth will ultimately triumph over injustice: the
Chinese will all have to leave and the Tibetans will again live in peace
in Tibet. This conflict started on a tragic note with the arrival of the
Chinese army in Tibet; it will not end until a lasting agreement can be
found between Chinese and Tibetans. It is so sensitive an issue that both
parties to the fray are helplessly ensnared in a web of intolerance and
violence. This is not a topic one can discuss calmly with either a Chinese or a Tibetan. Those of us who are trying to understand will have
to turn to the pages of history.

One of the first obstacles encountered by researchers is of a semantic
nature. In past centuries, whether in China or Tibet, what could have
been the real significance of terms such as 'independence', 'sovereignty'
or 'suzerainty'? Unknown in Asia, these concepts were all imported by
British settlers in the nineteenth century. Let us delve further.

If you casually ask a Chinese to explain in what way Tibet can be
said to be Chinese, there are usually two possibilities. If he is an ordinary person without much education, you can safely bet that he will be
extremely hard-pressed to reply to your question. It will be abundantly
clear that Tibet is the last thing on his mind and that he probably knows
next to nothing about it. 'Yes of course Tibet is part of China. The
Tibetans are one of our national minorities', is what he may reply if you
are rude enough to flout the most basic rule of Chinese etiquette and
press for an answer on such a sensitive matter. You may also be told that
'Tibet has been part of China for many centuries. All our history books

say so.' Unless you are very fortunate, you are unlikely to get any further, let alone satisfy your curiosity.

The second possibility is comparable to finding a light in the dark: you meet someone who has already thought about the issue and who has realized that the official accounts of events in Tibet to be found in the history books are full of lies. It may happen – quite rarely, to be sure, but not quite as seldom as before – that you will hear a Chinese intellectual publicly question his government's dominion over Tibet. A sizable number of Chinese students will volunteer that the Tibetan people, along with all other peoples of the world, are entitled to be free and to enjoy the right to self-determination. Chinese dissidents are no longer the only ones who dare to hint that Tibet has the right to be independent if it so wishes. Among the overseas Chinese, while many remain adamantly opposed to the idea of an independent Tibet, many others accept the idea of self-determination for the Tibetan population.

In the autumn of 1989, I was invited to dinner by a family of Chinese intellectuals and artists who had settled in Paris. I seized the opportunity to talk about Tibet and found myself discussing the situation with the father, a historian in his sixties. I will not say more about him, except that his work is considered authoritative in China despite the fact that he never joined the Party. The old gentleman, his face creased by a thousand wrinkles, had arrived in France shortly after the Tiananmen square massacre of 4 June 1989. Having reached a certain point in the discussion, I screwed up my courage and asked him point-blank: 'When all is said and done, can one say that Tibet is part of China or not?' He thought for a minute. 'You know, the answer is clear: no. Tibet is not a part of China's historical territory. The official history for schoolchildren and students and official accounts in the media assert that Tibet is an inalienable part of China. By dint of repetition, the Chinese have heard it said so often that they believe it. But it is enough to look at the facts. Now I'm in France. My mind is free from any kind of political pressure. In China, I would never have given you the same answer – even if we had been alone.'

When some Chinese vociferously maintain that Tibet has been part of their territory for seven centuries, I am tempted to remind them that in the history of their glorious country, there was a period when Emperors had the peculiar habit of referring to any state that sent an ambassador or a representative to the Chinese court as a vassal state. This is how England, the Vatican, the Netherlands, Portugal, Russia and several Asian countries all became vassals of China!

Publishers in Peking continue to print quantities of 'works of reference' for the edification of the Chinese masses or for the foreign tourists who don't know anything about Tibet. Other than to vie among themselves for the liveliest portrayal of Communist miracles in Tibet, what do these righteous servants of Chinese Communist Party orthodoxy write about the history of China's Tibet? And what proof have their opponents, both foreign and Tibetan, produced in support of the thesis of Tibetan independence?

According to the Peking government, 'friendly' relations between Hans and Tibetans originated in the Sui dynasty (581–618) and expanded tremendously in the next few centuries. The alliance between China and Tibet was symbolized by the marriage in 641 of King Songtsen Gampo of Tibet to a Chinese princess, Wengcheng, offered by Emperor Taizong of the Tang dynasty. The bride arrived in Lhasa with a quantity of Chinese books and a retinue that included many experts in the fields of science, medicine and mathematics. The princess is seen as an early benefactor, bringing 'civilization' to Tibet. Out of this union were born, in the infelicitous words of a generally rather staid Chinese publication, 'very lengthy intimate relations between the Han and Tibetan nationalities'.[12]

Is there any special significance to this marriage? Strangely enough, most historical accounts published in the People's Republic of China neglect to mention another wedding, when the same Tibetan king married a Nepalese princess. In fact, Songtsen Gampo, who unified Tibet, had no less than five wives! The historians of the Chinese imperial court describe Tibet at that time as one of the great Asian powers and as China's main rival. If anything, that Sino-Tibetan alliance reflects favourably on the prestige of the Tibetan king: when he decided he wanted to marry a Chinese imperial princess, the Son of Heaven had to oblige him.

Tibet's influence was felt far and wide in Asia in the eighth century, to such an extent that in 763 Tibetan troops were able to take the capital of the Chinese empire, Chang'An, now called Xian. This is another episode that Chinese history books prefer to forget. The best effort to be found in a Chinese official account is a vague concession that 'Frequent exchanges (between China and Tibet) ... were sometimes interrupted by conflicts and wars, which were destructive to both sides. This kindled a strong desire on both sides for close friendship and peace.'[13]

While the Tang dynasty (618–907) ushered in a cultural and artistic golden age in China, the Tibetan empire of Trisong Detsen (755–797) and Tritsug Detsen Ralpachen reached the zenith of its military power, making its might felt through the Pamirs to the threshold of Arab and Turkish zones of influence to the west, to Turkestan in the north and Nepal in the south. A peace treaty was signed with China in 821, after part of its territory in present-day Gansu and Sichuan had fallen under Tibetan domination. Then came the triumph of the Mongol conquerors who founded one of the greatest empires known to man, starting in the twelfth century.

The Mongol emperors, and particularly Genghis Khan (1167–1227), gradually extended their sway over the Tangut Empire to the north of

Tibet, Korea and Song China. In 1279, China lost its independence. The Mongol influence spread to Siberia, Annam and the north of Burma; Tibet placated the invaders by pledging allegiance at the beginning of the thirteenth century. In mid-century, two Tibetan Lamas of the Sakya lineage paid a visit to the Mongol Khans and the Buddhism of Tibet spread to the Mongol court. This was the beginning of the special relationship between the two powers, known as *chö-yon*, which translates roughly as 'priest-patron relationship'. Under the terms of this association, the Lama was appointed *Ti-shi* or vice-regent of Tibet, and acted as the guru or spiritual guide of the Mongol emperor of China, in exchange for temporal protection.

For the Tibetans, this special relationship was to become the basis for ties between Tibet and China that lasted into the twentieth century. Unrelated to territorial sovereignty or military conquest, it was essentially a spiritual bond. Tibet did fall under the control of the Mongol court in the reign of Kublai Khan (1259–1294). But it regained its independence in 1350, well before China, which spent another eighteen years under Mongol rule. A deep spiritual affinity remained between the Tibetans and Mongolians, shared to some extent by the Yuan dynasty in China (1280–1367), but much less if at all by the Ming (1368–1643).

It is essential to study this period, because Chinese Communist Party historians hark back to the Mongol invasion of China in order to situate Tibet's integration into the Chinese 'motherland'. 'In 1271, Kublai Khan unified China and founded the Yuan dynasty. The central government adopted a series of important measures by which it shored up its administration of Tibet.' From Peking's perspective, this is how Tibet was forever after attached to China.

By means of an interesting sleight of hand producing instant assimilation, the Mongols are said to be Chinese. Just recently, the Chinese Communist Party promoted Kublai Khan to the rank of 'national hero'. In this connection, it is worth noting that in spite of having extended official recognition to the People's Republic of Mongolia in 1960, the Peking government finds it difficult to give up the idea that all of Mongolia belongs to China.[14]

The official version of history goes on to explain that the Chinese court set up a system of courier stations and military posts in Tibet; the Celestial administration was positioning its mandarins. It is claimed that armies and 'pacification commissioners' were dispatched to 're-establish order in Tibetan society' and that 'local officers were examined at regular intervals'. Not only did these ties remain intact under the Ming, according to this account; they are said to have expanded. Particular emphasis is placed on the following: 'According to the records of Ming Dynasty's Board of Rites, every year 300 to 400 Tibetans arrived at the capital city to offer tributes to the emperor and pay homage to him. By the 1460s, the figure was ten times larger.'

There is not a word about this in the Tibetan annals, says the Dalai Lama. For Tibetans, this version of China's and Tibet's history is fraught with lies and fabrications. Quite on the contrary, they consider that Sino-Tibetan ties loosened markedly throughout the time of the Ming, as the Chinese court showed little interest in Tibet. After the fall of the Ming, who yielded to the Manchu dynasty of the Qing (1644–1911), close spiritual links did develop. It was the Manchu emperor Shunzhi (1644–1661) who first invited a Dalai Lama to visit China. While Han China and Tibet had mutually ignored each other for centuries, the Tibetans and the Manchus displayed reciprocal curiosity and respect.

The visit took place in 1653. This was not – as asserted by the official history of the PRC – an episode in which the Tibetan leader came to pledge allegiance to the emperor of China, going down on bended knee like a vassal in the hall of his lord. The Son of Heaven had no intention of asking his guest to kowtow, a traditional gesture of respect that compelled all visitors, even foreigners, to kneel thrice in front of the emperor and touch their head to the ground nine times. On the contrary, out of deference to the rank of his guest, the Emperor rode out more than a dozen miles with his retinue to welcome the Dalai Lama and accompany him on the last stretch of the journey to Peking. When the Dalai Lama appeared in court, the Emperor stepped down from his throne to greet him. The two sovereigns sat together to talk and have tea, treating each other as equals, in a vivid demonstration of the *chö-yon* relationship between a religious master and his disciple – the former providing peace of mind and the latter protection in temporal affairs.

In 1720, Manchu troops entered Lhasa. According to exiled Tibetans, the soldiers came both to expel the Mongol occupants and to protect the Seventh Dalai Lama. However, they brought along a team of cadres from the imperial administration, whose task was to reorganize the Tibetan administration. The ensuing period was a difficult one. Peking considers that it constitutes irrefutable proof of Chinese sovereignty over Tibet. The new Tibetan government, led by the Kashag and the Kalons (ministers), was indeed placed under the control of two 'Ambans', or representatives of the imperial power in Peking. The Manchu court stationed a permanent garrison in Lhasa, of variable size, exceeding one thousand men on several occasions.

The Ambans' main job, retorts Tenzin Gyatso, was to keep the emperor informed about events in Tibet. For the court in Peking, he adds, it was a matter of 'supervising' Tibet's defence and, in particular, keeping the Mongols at arm's length. Towards the end of the eighteenth century, the Ambans became the 'advisers' of the Kashag, occasionally reminding their Tibetan counterparts about the 'protector' on his Peking throne and his commitment to the 'protected', the Dalai Lama and his people. But they were never directly involved in the deliberations or in the decision-making process of the Kashag.

For the present Chinese government, the opposite is true: they consider that starting in 1793, the representatives of the Imperial court enjoyed extensive decision-making powers. Ranking with the Dalai Lama and the Panchen Lama, they had absolute precedence over the Kalons, who had to carry out their orders. They allegedly had control over Tibet's foreign affairs. The Kalons apparently did not have the right to correspond privately with foreign powers, and mail from abroad was censored by the Ambans. Finally, when it came to selecting the reincarnation of the Dalai Lamas, the Panchen Lamas and other important Lamas, it was mandatory for the candidate to be approved by the emperor in Peking.

It is not easy for a foreign observer, happening along two centuries later, to draw a clear-cut line between independence and interdependence. When Emperor Qianlong (1736–1796) sent troops to Tibet in 1792 to repel the Nepalese invasion, it is generally accepted that Tibetan foreign policy fell into the hands of Peking for a short time. The Manchu emperor was able to impose a series of far-reaching administrative reforms in Tibet. Tibet's relations with the outside world came under his control: for a hundred years, the Land of Snow had to close its doors to Western visitors. It was during the final years of the Qianlong era that Tibet came closest to becoming a Chinese satellite. China's imperial court struck silver coins, both sides of which explicitly mentioned the fifty-seventh year of Qianlong's reign in Tibetan and in Chinese. By a curious coincidence, those coins are almost impossible to find in Tibetan circles in exile.

Michael C. van Walt van Praag is a legal adviser to the Dalai Lama and the Kashag on international affairs. Although he is certainly not a person likely to be accused of entertaining a pro-Chinese bias, he freely recognizes Manchu China's ascendancy over Tibet during that period. However, he is quick to point out that Tibet never lost the attributes of independence. 'On the one hand, the Qing Emperor exercised a vague supremacy, which the Tibetan authorities acknowledged. In addition, some Ambans derived considerable influence in Lhasa from the emperor's prestige. On the other hand, the Tibetans certainly did not consider themselves truly dependent on the emperor, nor did they submit directly to his authority. They guarded jealously against any interference in Tibet by the governance of the Ambans.'[15]

Another interesting and valuable perspective on this difficult yet decisive period for Sino-Tibetan relations is provided by Melvyn C. Goldstein. The American ethnologist and historian, a specialist on Tibetan affairs, is sharply critical of the Dalai Lama and his followers in India, and cannot be suspected of harbouring an anti-Chinese bias. He points out, nevertheless, that in the early eighteenth century, at the height of the Qing dynasty's power, 'China's overlordship was never formalized, the mutual rights and obligations of the two sides were not delimited in treaties or agreements.' During that period, he explains, 'Tibet became a loosely-linked protectorate of China, but Tibetan officials governed their country with their own officials and laws.' Later on, 'as Manchu power eroded during the nineteenth century and China became preoccupied with the onslaught of Western imperialism, its hegemony over Tibet became increasingly symbolic', concludes the historian.[16]

Qianlong's death heralded a steep decline in Peking's fates. It also closed the chapter on the Qing court's role as 'protector of Tibet', a part it no longer had the means nor the desire to play. From that moment onwards, not once did China's imperial army come to the assistance of the Dalai Lama when his country was attacked by a neighbour such as Nepal. The Ambans' duties became entirely symbolic, while the number of Chinese troops stationed in Lhasa dwindled to about a hundred men, a majority of whom were half-breeds born in Tibet. Of Peking's authority in Tibet, nothing was left but an empty shell, as all the power in Lhasa gravitated back into the hands of the Tibetans.

By the end of the nineteenth and the beginning of the twentieth century, Tibet had become the focus of the rivalry between China, Great Britain and Russia. The Thirteenth Dalai Lama, Thubten Gyatso (1876–1933), sealed the break with China by assuming full temporal and spiritual powers in 1894. With the pretext of sending a trade mission, Great Britain provoked a brief conflict in 1904 in southern Tibet. An 'escort' of three thousand soldiers reached Lhasa on 3 August. Peking turned a deaf ear to the Tibetans' appeals for help. Chinese Communist historians recognize this fact and consider it a serious breach of the Chinese government's obligation to defend 'its territory'. 'A feeling of estrangement arose between the central government and the Tibet local government which consequently caused the relations to deteriorate further' between Peking and Lhasa, concede Peking's official historians.[17]

The Tibetan forces were pushed out of the way without much difficulty and the British forced Tibet to sign a treaty on 7 September. Significantly, the 'Lhasa Convention' was exclusively bilateral, for London recognized Tibet's *de facto* independent status. Tibet undertook to seek British assent before signing an agreement with any other foreign power. When asked to countersign the agreement, which failed to recognize Chinese suzerainty, the Manchu court refused. Peking protested, declaring that '[t]he British should not conclude an agreement with Tibet directly because such an agreement robs China of its suzerainty'.

After lengthy negotiations, an Anglo-Chinese compromise text was finally signed in Peking on 27 April 1906. Neither one of the disputed terms – whether sovereignty or even suzerainty – appears with reference to China. China was exempted, however, from the list of foreign countries with which Tibet was not to sign an agreement without London's permission. The Middle Kingdom's right to protect Tibet's territorial integrity was also recognized. An Anglo-Russian treaty signed on 31 August 1907 recognized a measure of Chinese suzerainty over Tibet. London and Moscow undertook to refrain from violating Tibet's territorial integrity and from interfering in its internal affairs. Both parties were precluded from entering into negotiations with Tibet except through the good offices of the Chinese government.

In June 1909, after a stormy visit to Peking by the Dalai Lama, the Qing Court decided to send an army to Tibet. Two thousand soldiers from Sichuan invaded Lhasa in February 1910. Amban Wen Zongyao promised that the Chinese troops would act with the utmost restraint. But Chinese historians note that '[a]fter entering Lhasa, they looted and threw the whole city into chaos'.[18] The Dalai Lama was forced to flee and seek refuge in India. Never before had Peking intervened against the will of the Tibetan authorities; the show of force in 1910 was the first military act of aggression by the Manchus. They were not to have time to settle in Lhasa, for the Qing dynasty fell in 1911, swept away by the Chinese Revolution. For Tibet, the time had come to make a clean break with Peking and to proclaim its complete independence, which it did at the first opportunity.

As a first step, the Tibetan government announced the expulsion of all Chinese residents, including the Ambans, in the summer of 1912. The last group of Chinese left the Tibetan capital on 6 January 1913. On 13 February, having returned to Lhasa, the Dalai Lama officially declared Tibet an independent country and called for the proclamation to be disseminated throughout the land. 'We are a small, religious and independent nation. To keep up with the rest of the world we must defend our country. In view of past invasions by foreigners, our people may have to face certain difficulties, which they must disregard. To safeguard and maintain the independence of our country, one and all should voluntarily work hard.'[19]

Letters requesting foreign support were dispatched to India, Great Britain and Russia. On 11 January 1913, Tibet signed a 'Treaty of Friendship and Alliance' with Mongolia, which had proclaimed its own independence in December 1911. The Dalai Lama gave orders for distinctively Tibetan currency and postage stamps to be introduced. From 1911 onwards, the government struck coins bearing its own name and seal in Tibetan script, with no reference to China. The first Tibetan banknotes were printed soon after, and were initially numbered by hand; they remained in circulation until 1959. Although Tibet printed its own stamps from 1912 onwards, it did not belong to the international postal organization, and its stamps were valid only within its own boundaries. A letter addressed to a foreign country had to be stamped with Indian stamps at the border. Tibet also had its own flag.

Tibet was to gain another token of its independence as of 13 October 1913, thanks to the tripartite negotiations with China and Great Britain held in Simla, in northern India, to put an end to hostilities along the Sino-Tibetan border. The three delegations were led by plenipotentiary representatives of their respective governments. The British plenipotentiary, Sir Henry McMahon, proposed to mediate in order to allow the two contenders to save face. While maintaining 'suzerainty' over Tibet, China undertook to respect its full 'autonomy'. There was no longer any reference to sovereignty. On 27 April 1914, the text was finally initialled.

The Simla conference divided Tibet into two areas: 'inner' Tibet to the north and 'outer' Tibet to the south and centre of the Himalayan Plateau. China could continue to wield a certain influence in inner Tibet but had to refrain from interfering in any way in the administration of outer Tibet. Only one Chinese representative was allowed to reside in Lhasa, with a maximum escort of three hundred men. Great Britain would be allowed to deal directly with the Tibetan authorities on matters such as borders and trade. The Peking envoy signed the document, but his government rejected the agreement on the very next day and to this day continues to declare it null and void.

Here are a few lines from the official Chinese version of this episode: 'In 1911, after the bourgeois democratic revolution overthrew the decadent feudal Qing dynasty, the [Tibetan] hirelings in British pay took advantage of the central government's inability to deal with its affairs from afar to betray the central government and sabotage the unity of the country. The high commissioners resident in Tibet were expelled. Many noted Tibetan personages who adhered to the unification of the motherland were killed.'

The Dalai Lama drew my attention to a further consideration that provides, in his eyes, conclusive proof of Tibet's status as an independent nation prior to 1950. At no time in its history did U-Tsang pay one penny in taxes to the government in Peking, unlike the Chinese provinces and the areas under China's suzerainty. 'Some parts of Tibet that had come under China's administrative control did pay taxes. But central Tibet, which constitutes the larger part of Tibet, never did. For almost two thousand years, it paid no tax at all. I think this is a clear indication', he concludes.

Over the centuries, adds the Dalai Lama, many internal squabbles were played out in the vast expanse of Tibet, all to the benefit of China. 'At times, there would be a number of Tibetan chiefs, there not being any central authority, and lamas from this or that region would rush headlong into China's embrace hoping to enhance their status and maybe get a few presents in addition to support!' The Dalai Lama goes on: 'but when it comes to the Tibetan people, the entire population considered itself a Tibetan entity, not Chinese. A separate nation.'

Today, the People's Republic can claim with some justification that the Kuomintang government never relinquished the principle of

China's sovereignty over Tibet, although it had been considerably weakened by years of warfare against the Japanese and later the Communists. Equally steadfast, the Thirteenth Dalai Lama (and after his death in 1933, the Regent and the Lhasa government) unremittingly proclaimed Tibet's independence. The Tibetan government announced the creation of a Foreign Affairs Bureau in 1942. Why so late? This protraction in developing an active diplomacy reveals the administration's lack of experience at a time when it had the best chance – in fact the only chance before the arrival of the Chinese troops – of gaining recognition for Tibet's independent status abroad. In 1947, a Trade Mission left for India and the United States. Its members carried Tibetan passports. Washington announced that in accepting the delegation, the American government was not calling into question China's sovereignty over Tibet. In the following year, the Mission visited Great Britain, where it was warmly welcomed by the British government.

This was the Tibetan government's last major attempt to engage in active diplomacy. In the West, the inexperienced Tibetan administration revealed a disconcerting lack of political awareness. It was already too late for Tibet to try to break out of its isolation. A formidable enemy was massing at the gate. Less than a year later, Mao Tse-tung was to lead his Communist fighters to victory down the avenue of Eternal Peace (Chang-An) in the heart of Peking. Almost immediately, Radio Peking announced that 'Tibet is part of China's territory and no foreign aggression will be tolerated; the Tibetan people are an inseparable part of the Chinese people. Aggressors who do not recognize this fact will shatter their skulls against the fist of the People's Liberation Army.'

It is not for us to take sides in the debate about the aspiration to independence of many Tibetans. The reader must be the sole judge and form an opinion on the basis of the historical facts described. It must be added, however, that although no country has officially recognized an independent Tibet, it clearly enjoyed the principal attributes of independence in 1911. A CIA report from the late 1970s, declassified in early 1992, openly recognizes the historical reality of Tibet's independence – in sharp contrast to the official position of the US government. 'Historically, Tibet has been independent, a fact recognized by the 1959 investigation of Tibet's legal status by the International Commission of Jurists. This legacy of independence and strong feelings of a Tibetan national identity have contributed to the Tibetan resistance potential.'

Fosco Maraini, the noted Italian ethnologist, states that the Chinese and Tibetan peoples, 'undoubtedly have distant common roots in prehistorical times' but he adds that 'during the fifteen centuries or so of Tibetan history that are known to us, except for a few specific moments, the distance [between these peoples] grew more and more, from the cultural and religious point of view even more than from the political'. In the opinion of this expert, '[t]his is how the present situation emerged, where two peoples who seem to have quite a similar appearance and language, have nothing at all in common when it comes to their way of thinking, their approach to life and to the world, in short, everything that constitutes the priceless spiritual heritage of a group of human beings, of a race or of a nation'.[20] Another great expert on Tibetan affairs, Hugh Richardson from the United Kingdom, is also very precise on this point: 'It is clear that when the Chinese Communist army attacked Tibet in 1950 and subsequently occupied the whole country, it was committing an act of unprovoked aggression against a country that was enjoying actual independence.'[21]

Notes

1. *Tibet: Today & Yesterday*, Beijing Review, Peking, 1983, p. 8.
2. *100 questions about Tibet*, Beijing Information, Peking, 1989, p. 38.
3. *Tibet: Myth Vs. Reality*, Beijing Review, Peking, 1988, pp. 38–9.
4. Ibid, p. 40.
5. Ibid, p. 41.
6. John F. Avedon, *In Exile from the Land of Snows*, Wisdom Publications, London, 1985.
7. Israel Epstein, *Tibet Transformed*, New World Press, Peking, 1983, p. 35.
8. Interview in *Femina*, a Swiss magazine, 18 May 1977.
9. Han Suyin, *Lhasa, the Open City*, Putnam, 1977, pp. 30, 35, 54, 107, 113, 116, 127, 153.
10. Rinchen Dolma Taring, *Daughter of Tibet*, 1970, London, p. 71.
11. Pierre Gentelle, 'Le Parti communiste chinois et la question nationale', in *l'Etat de la Chine*, La Découverte, 1989, p. 287.
12. *Beijing Information*, June 1983.
13. *Tibet: Today & Yesterday*, p. 73.
14. According to a circular dated 24 March 1992, issued by the secret police of Inner Mongolia, the very concept of Mongolian nationalism is flawed, since the entire territory of Mongolia, both Inner and Outer and including Buriatia (in Russia) are part of the 'Mongolia region of our country'. Excerpts from the circular were published by Reuters on 30 April 1992.
15. Michael C. van Walt van Praag, *The Status of Tibet*, Westview Press, Colorado, 1987, p. 19.
16. 'The Dragon and the Snow Lion: The Tibet Question in the 20th Century', Melvyn C. Goldstein, in *China Briefing, 1990*, Westview, Colorado, 1990.
17. *100 Questions About Tibet*, op. cit., p. 17.
18. Wang Furen and Suo Wenqing, *Highlights of Tibetan History*, New World Press, Peking, 1984, p. 147.
19. Michael C. van Walt van Praag, op. cit., p. 49.
20. Fosco Maraini, *Tibet Secret*, Arthaud, p. 324.
21. *Tibet un autre monde*, La Maison du Tibet-Olizane, Genève, October 1993.

3

The Maoist Fury

The repression that followed the 1959 uprising devastated the country. But the worst was yet to come. Tibet lived through its darkest hours during the 'Great Proletarian Cultural Revolution' launched in 1966 by Mao Tse-tung. Threatened by the opposition he felt growing within the Party's Central Committee, he turned to China's young generation to recapture the power that was slipping from his grasp. The story of the ten years of chaos that ensued is a tale of destructive fury that ravaged China and caused excruciating suffering – in Tibet far more than elsewhere – until well after the death of the Great Helmsman in 1976. The cultural revolution tore through China like a raging typhoon, but in Tibet it escalated into full-scale war on a people and a civilization. The violence was so traumatic that Tibet and its people may never recover from the horrors they had to endure. More than fifteen years after Mao Tse-tung's demise, the scars left by the Maoist terror are still in evidence. His Red Guards, often children in their teens, sallied forth in their thousands to attack Tibetan religion and traditions; they came close to immolating Tibet to an ideology based on homicidal insanity.

Ask any of your Chinese or Tibetan friends and acquaintances about the cultural revolution: they will unfailingly respond with deep-seated disgust. Most will have undergone some uniquely ghastly trial and will feel compelled, or perhaps relieved, to tell you about it down to the smallest detail, so long as no inconvenient witness is present. There is probably not a single Chinese citizen over the age of forty who has not been adversely affected in some way or another by the cultural revolution. Time and time again I was taken aside by a person anxious to recount in minute detail the atrocities suffered by his or her family during that period. When the speaker is Chinese, descriptions of the most painful experiences will constantly be interrupted by loud peals of laughter, a very Chinese way of expressing unease or embarrassment . . .

The same openness does not grace the declarations of the Chinese Communist Party or the government leaders, nor the pages of the official media. As sole repositories of the right to define China's political orientation, the Party's Central Committee and the Political Bureau that crowns it have been cautiously re-evaluating Mao's legacy since 1978. Nowadays, he may be criticized to some extent for having committed 'serious mistakes' towards the end of his life. The Peking government acknowledges that the cultural revolution was a 'great national catastrophe' that plunged the country into chaos and squandered precious time on the difficult and tortuous path towards economic development. The Party is remarkably circumspect, however, when it comes to explicitly recognizing the magnitude of the disaster. This is particularly noticeable with reference to Tibet and other areas inhabited by non-Chinese 'ethnic minorities'. In China, the official media has published only the sketchiest accounts of the atrocities committed during the cultural revolution. Other than a handful of speeches in the most abstruse Party jargon, very few specific statements have been made about the persecution and destruction in China and Tibet. Mao and his cultural revolution have yet to be called to account. An open debate would lay to rest the demons that continue to haunt the corridors of power in Peking and in the provinces, not to speak of Tibet.

The Deng Xiaoping regime condemned Mao's widow Jiang Qing to death. The sentence was soon commuted to life imprisonment, for in China, with very rare exceptions, disgraced leaders do not suffer the fate of the common people, not even for the worst mistakes. The regime, with infinite forbearance, provides gilded prisons for them. Deng Xiaoping and his allies never tried to eliminate Maoism. Although they had been its victims, they were keenly aware that any such attempt would very likely put paid to what little was left in China of the Party's influence and authority, thus sealing the end of their own power. Their determination to keep hidden the darkest pages of the cultural revolution led them to muzzle anyone in the country who tried to establish the truth. Many tried, among the intellectuals and historians, but every single one was defeated by the censors. In 1987, the famous theorist Yan Jiaqi was obliged to restrict to the upper echelon of the Party the circulation of his very detailed book on the events of 1966–1976, despite the fact that he enjoyed the support of Party Secretary Zhao Ziyang. Following the massacre of 4 June 1989, Yan Jiaqi sought refuge in France.

After the cultural revolution, when the entire population was calling for the country's honour to be cleansed of ignominy, the government affected a diffident attitude. The leadership has never entirely repudiated Mao Tse-tung, nor his ideology, nor even his works. 'We will never do to Mao Tse-tung what Khrushchev did to Stalin', declared Deng Xiaoping to Italian journalist Oriana Fallacci in 1980. The portrait of Chairman Mao, he added, will forever adorn the portals of the Forbidden City that towers over Tiananmen square, the political heart of the People's Republic at the centre of Peking. Mao's thought, insisted the aged dictator, will remain as one of the four pillars of China's official ideology, along with Marxism-Leninism and the 'people's democratic dictatorship', the leadership of the Communist Party and the socialist path. After 4 June 1989, entire chapters of Mao Tse-tung's thought were again given prominence in the economic, social, political, artistic and literary fields. On another plane, for over a decade, the Chinese Communist Party has been maintaining come hell or high water that every province and region in China suffered equally during the cultural revolution, including Tibet. This claim is contradicted by every available report.

Before 1966: the forced march
towards integration

Mao did not wait until the cultural revolution to unleash violence and destruction in Tibet. While China was still basking in the afterglow of the ten years' honeymoon that followed independence, and the famines produced by the catastrophic 'Great Leap Forward' still lay in the future, while hundreds of millions of Chinese were rediscovering their pride and dignity, and were still moved, in the main, by the ideal of genuine egalitarianism that Mao had managed to instil in them, in Tibet, the crushing of the 1959 uprising signalled the beginning of large-scale and systematic brutality. Now that the Dalai Lama had taken refuge in India and the policy of peaceful coexistence was left in tatters, it was no longer necessary to seduce the Tibetan people. For Mao Tse-tung, the time had come to apply naked force to rapidly and thoroughly integrate Tibet with China. Starting in 1959, energetic, massive purges were organized to decapitate the religious hierarchy and the Tibetan aristocracy, to crush any hint of dissent and to isolate the Tibetan 'masses', the better to control their fate. The old society had to be eliminated to make way for the new one; the dreaded *thamzings*, or struggle sessions, were held throughout Central Tibet, Amdo and Kham.

The two latter provinces were simply detached from Tibet and merged with China 'proper'. About half of the territory inhabited by Tibetans was divided up among the Chinese provinces of Yunnan, Sichuan, Gansu and Qinghai. Parts of Tibetan Amdo had already been incorporated into the newly-formed province of Qinghai by the Nationalist authorities of the Republic of China in 1928. This time, a stroke of the pen over a map of China abruptly halved the demographic, economic and political importance of Tibet: suddenly, it had only two million inhabitants. The other three or four million just disappeared, absorbed into the Chinese masses of the neighbouring provinces. Nowadays, you can pore over as many official maps of the People's Republic of China as you like, but you will never again find the names of Amdo or Kham. In the towns and villages of Amdo and Kham, any person with power or authority became the target of the incoming Communist Chinese. The People's

Liberation Army carried out sweeping raids in the monasteries and continuously 'visited' the homes of people who were blacklisted. As the political purges picked up steam, the 'reform through labour' camps in the Chinese borderlands were filled with countless 'counter-revolutionaries', 'reactionaries', 'spies', 'class enemies' and 'bad elements', among which the Tibetans were particularly well represented.

The harshest camps were located in Qinghai and Gansu, whose arid and desolate wastes saw the birth of a gigantic gulag. The Chinese penal universe is still an enigma today. No Western journalist has ever been able to visit these camps where millions of prisoners lived – and died – as unpaid slave labourers in the service of the government. According to a Tibetan survivor's personal account, in 1959 to 1961 alone some 70,000 Tibetans were held in camps north of Lanzhou, the capital of Gansu. Thirty-five thousand died of hunger, he says. In these death camps, despite their rugged constitution, the Tibetans were soon reduced to skin and bones. They even ate their clothes and items made of leather, bit by bit, eking out the nourishment they provided, trying to make them last. Lucky prisoners found worms, insects or the leaves of trees.[1]

In the meantime, the first monasteries were being closed down. Others were simply destroyed. The Chinese authorities now acknowledge that the destruction began well before the cultural revolution, contradicting their staunchly-defended earlier position. At press conference in Lhasa on 18 July 1987, a Vice-Chairman of the Tibet Autonomous Region, Mr Buchung Tsering, revealed that in 1966, at the eve of the cultural revolution, only 550 monasteries were still active in the Autonomous Region as compared to 2,700 in 1959. Mr Buchung went on to say that in 1959, the monasteries in the Autonomous Region were inhabited by 114,000 monks, but by 1966 there were only 6,900 left.[2] Kham and Amdo were not spared the destruction.

Labrang, one of the six holiest monasteries of the Yellow school, was founded in 1709. Situated in Amdo, over 600 miles from Lhasa, Labrang housed 3,000 or more monks in the fifties. It was responsible for the administration of four dozen smaller monasteries dotted over a vast area that included Peking. It was closed in 1956 on Chinese government orders. All the monks were arrested or sent back to their village of origin.

In November 1960, the land reform was declared to have been completed in Tibet. The land taken from the 'lords', 'agents of the lords' and 'rich peasants and nomads' had been distributed among the poor peasants and beggars. Two hundred thousand titles to land, bearing Mao's portrait flanked by red flags, were presented to the new socialist landowners.

Addressing the National People's Congress in December 1960, the Panchen Lama reported that the Tibetans were ardently and courageously marching on Mao Tse-tung's great shining path. 'In short, a wonderful situation prevails in Tibet today. Prosperous scenes of labour and production are found in every corner of the vast countryside and the towns. This is the main trend of our work in Tibet', were his words.[3] In reality, a devastating famine was raging throughout China; millions died between 1959 and 1961. The 'three black years', the result of the dramatic failure of the Great Leap Forward, had made tens of thousands of victims in Tibet as well. Compared with the disastrous dearth of food in China, the situation in the Land of Snow suddenly took on the appearance of an unexpected treasure trove of grain for the Chinese masses 'inside' China. Among Tibetans in exile, the most harrowing accounts of this famine, lasting until 1963 in Tibet, are commonplace. When mothers were reduced to mixing some of their own blood with water to feed their children, the fate of the Tibetan prisoners in the labour camps defies the imagination. Jean Pasqualini, a survivor of the Chinese gulag, provided some of the earliest testimony about China's labour camps. In his book, *Prisonnier de Mao*, he tells how he narrowly missed dying of hunger more than a hundred times, and how in December 1960, since there was no longer enough food to go around, the prisoners were introduced to their new staple: cellulose pulp![4]

The ironies of history – at the very moment that the Panchen Lama was in Peking presenting his optimistic report on Tibet, the Chinese army was raiding Tashilhumpo, his monastery in Shigatse. Tashilhumpo was one of the few that had so far escaped the iron fist of democratic reform, for the Chinese leadership had been making some effort to appease the Panchen Lama. After all, unlike the Dalai Lama, he had kowtowed to the Communists in the clearest possible terms. Additionally, he would be a valuable ally when it came to ensuring the success of the projected assimilation that was underway in Tibet. The truce was broken on the day the People's Liberation Army ransacked Tashilhumpo and seized its 4,000 monks. They were accused of plotting against the Chinese government. After a few had been executed, the rest were deported to join the many other monks in the labour camps. Tashilhumpo was extensively damaged by the army.

This is probably the reason why the Panchen Lama reneged on the policy of collaboration that he had been following so far. He committed his first 'crime' towards the end of 1961: he criticized – however subtly – the policies of Mao Tse-tung. Horrified by the starvation and the widespread destruction of Tibet's temples and monasteries, he wrote a 70,000-character memorandum addressed to the Great Helmsman himself. Naively, he appealed to him to correct the abuses being perpetrated in Tibet's towns and rural areas. He implored the Chinese dictator to genuinely implement the autonomy that Tibet had been promised. Mao was not amused. During a 1988 press conference in Peking, the Panchen Lama revealed that the memorandum signalled the beginning of his disgrace.

In 1964 he indulged in a far more serious 'mistake': he openly defied his Chinese handlers. The annual Monlam Chenmo or Great Prayer Festival is the Tibetans' most important religious holiday. Although it traditionally lasted for two weeks, a special one-day Monlam Chenmo had been authorized for the Panchen Lama to publicly denounce the Dalai Lama. Instead, speaking to the crowd of 10,000 Tibetans expressly assembled in front of the Jokhang, he proclaimed his support and faith in the Tibetan God-King and in Tibet's independence, in a loud and sonorous voice.

'Today while we are gathered here I must pronounce my firm belief that Tibet will soon regain her independence and that His Holiness the Dalai Lama will return to the Golden Throne. Long Live His Holiness the Dalai Lama!'[5] The Chinese government immediately had him placed under house arrest. He was tried in August 1964 in front of an assembly of baleful Communist cadres. During the trial, which lasted almost three weeks, he was manhandled and insulted, and accused of having fomented an armed revolt. Then he simply disappeared, along with his family and the closer members of his retinue. From December onwards, he was branded a 'reactionary' by the Peking government. Chou En-lai himself was heard to use this epithet to describe him. Until the end of the cultural revolution, the Panchen Lama was never seen again in public. For fifteen years, he was held in prison and under house arrest in Peking.

The last phase of Tibet's administrative integration with China was the official creation in September 1965 of the 'Tibet Autonomous Region'. Its Chairman was Ngapo Ngawang Jigme, the only remaining pro-Chinese collaborator of any importance from the original Tibetan government. The Tibet Work Committee of the Communist Party was renamed 'Chinese Communist Party Tibet Autonomous Regional Committee'. General Zhang Guohua was appointed First Secretary of this all-Chinese body, the only one with any real power in Tibet. At the inauguration of the Tibet Autonomous Region, General Zhang declared that '[t]his represents another great victory of the Party's policy of national regional autonomy. The national regional autonomy is part of the people's democratic dictatorship. As far as Tibet is concerned, this means that the working class, the peasantry and herdsmen, other working people, patriotic elements, and all those in support of socialism, are all rallied under the leadership of the Party, to establish a people's democratic national regional autonomy. It imposes dictatorship on the serf-owner class, reactionary serf-owners and their agents, counter-revolutionaries who resist the socialist revolution and sabotage the socialist construction, elements who took part in the rebellion and other bad elements. The formal establishment of the Tibet Autonomous Region signifies the consolidation of the people's power.'[6]

The clarion call of the cultural revolution

The 'clarion call of the Great Proletarian Cultural Revolution' started reverberating throughout China on 8 May 1966, when the *Liberation Army Daily* launched a call to arms against the 'black anti-Party anti-socialist line'. The new radical ideologues aligned with Mao Tse-tung, who had taken control of Red China's fate, wanted to make way for an immense tidal wave of revolution, by completely eradicating the culture, the thinking, the customs and the traditions of the past. On 1 June 1966, the editorial in the *People's Daily* set the tone: 'In a few months, responding to the call to arms issued by the Central Party Committee and Chairman Mao Tse-tung, millions and millions of workers, peasants and soldiers, as well as the great masses of revolutionary cadres and intellectuals armed with his thought, have swept away a large number of evil spirits who had taken up residence in ideological and cultural positions. With the speed and power of a storm or a hurricane, they have shattered the fetters imposed for so many years by the exploitive classes and have comprehensively routed and deflated the arrogance of bourgeois 'specialists', 'scholars', 'authorities' and 'mentors'.[7]

The cultural revolution was set in motion by the 11th Plenary Session of the Eighth Party Central Committee. Meeting from 1 to 12 August, its members called for a struggle against 'capitalist-roaders' who had infiltrated the higher echelons of the Party. They were to be crushed without pity. In parallel, the customs inherited from the old society were to be eliminated at any cost. From the Party's perspective, it was essential to strengthen the 'left' and isolate the 'right' so as to unite the 95 per cent of cadres and activists who were 'good' or who were ready to correct their mistakes. On 18 August, a million Red Guards with *Little Red Book* in hand paraded with military precision through Tiananmen square in front of their idol Mao Tse-tung. The spectacle provoked a frenzied feeling of quasi-religious exaltation. A million fanatical Chinese screamed with joy, wept with happiness and sang a hymn to their god.

> The East is Red
> The sun is rising
> In China Mao Tse-tung has appeared
> Chairman Mao
> Loves the people
> He is our guide.

The violence started two days later in Peking. Fired up to the point of incandescence by the atmosphere of hysteria that reigned in the city, the Red Guards attacked anyone suspected of opposing the Party, or who might be a remnant of the bourgeoisie. Teams of Red Guards sprang up unbidden and roamed through the streets of the Chinese capital, proudly brandishing Mao's portrait as they tracked their quarry to their homes. They committed abominable murders. Elderly citizens were dragged out of their house to be publicly judged in the street by impromptu 'People's Tribunals'. Many old people died from the beatings administered by deranged adolescents. Others committed suicide. Bloated with pride, the Red Guards marched through the city, flaunting crimson hands stained with the blood of their victims and shouting: 'I have just re-educated an opponent of the cultural revolution!'

The smaller children were taken to watch the atrocities by the older ones. Under the banner of the campaign against the 'four olds' (old thinking, old culture, old habits and old customs) and the need to set China free from five thousand years of feudal traditions, thousands of homes were sacked. With righteous anger, the Red Guards frenziedly demolished anything that reminded them of the banished past. All books, photographs and personal belongings were confiscated and works of art were vandalized. Pets were brutally put to death in front of terrified children whose terrified gaze betrayed total incomprehension.

They broke pianos, antique furniture, invaluable cultural relics. Any churches that were still open in Peking were closed, along with the Buddhist temples and Taoist places of worship; these were soon to be devastated. Chinese traditions were declared to have been abolished. This applied particularly to wedding feasts, New Year greetings and funerals. Students with long hair had it shaved whether they liked it or not. Cemeteries harbouring the remains of foreigners were desecrated. The carnage and persecutions dragged on for over a week in the capital.

As Mao gradually draped himself in an extravagant cult of his personality, elsewhere in China a crescendo of apocalyptic encounters produced ever-growing abominations. In Shanghai, the stronghold of the Maoist factions' most radical leaders, the red terror spread by Mao's new soldiers outrivalled the horrors Peking had endured. In 1967, all over China, extremely violent clashes pitched 'Revolutionary Committees' against the army or the workers. In some cases, more than a thousand people were killed or wounded during a confrontation in a single factory. Rival factions accused each other of reactionary thinking, claimed the mantle of real revolutionaries for themselves, and set to killing each other with gusto. Wherever they went in China, the youthful Red Guards struck at the local authorities, quickly dispatching people who gave any indication of being unfaithful to Chairman Mao or of obstructing the revolution.

As the months passed by, China slowly sank into anarchy. By 1968, the Communist Party felt threatened with disintegration by the onslaught of the Revolutionary Committees and Mao called in the army to cool down the now superfluous and even dangerous ardour of the Red Guards. His naive foot-soldiers were no longer needed. Once they had enabled Mao to recover his power, they were abruptly betrayed by their master.

The army made a clean sweep in dozens of Chinese cities; there were thousands of casualties. For weeks, bodies floated down the Pearl River in Guangdong province and piled up on the beaches of Hong Kong. Mao's China sent daily reminders of the butchery that was taking place on the other side of the Bamboo Curtain.

In terms of human lives, a conservative estimate of the toll of the cultural revolution – a gigantic piece of humbug that duped countless admirers in the West – runs to well over 500,000 hapless victims, killed as a result of physical and mental torture, summarily executed, or reduced to taking their own lives. Not to mention the hundreds of thousands of intellectuals, painters, poets, musicians and young people whose lives would never be the same again. The cultural heritage of five thousand years of civilization was smashed, desecrated, scattered and lost. At the time of Mao's death, China was an enormous, ravaged country just emerging from a devastating civil war, full of tormented people desperate to forget the iniquities they had suffered.

When Mao Tse-tung was compared to Emperor Qin Shihuang, who united China in the second century BC but then ordered the killing of hundreds of intellectuals and the burning of all the classic texts, he retorted: 'What was so special about Qin Shihuang? He only executed 460 scholars. We have executed 46,000! This is what I have replied to some democrats: you think you are insulting us by calling us Qin Shihuang, but you are mistaken, we have outdone Qin Shihuang a hundred times! You call us Qin Shihuang, you say we are despotic. These are qualities of which we are proud. Our only regret is that you understate the situation and compel us to join in and add substance to your allegations!'[8] Experts who have studied the situation in China between 1949 and 1976 estimate that Maoism was responsible for the deaths of more than 20 million Chinese, including those executed in prisons and labour camps or by the 'People's Tribunals', those who died of hunger during the successive famines and those who decided to put an end to their suffering themselves.

Harry Wu Hongda spent nineteen years in the Chinese gulag. He estimates that 'a minimum of 50 million' people have been sent to Chinese reform-through-labour camps over the past forty years. He thinks that today, the camps still hold between twelve and sixteen million prisoners.[9] In *Chine, l'archipel oublié*, a scholarly tome dedicated to the Chinese penal world, the sinologist Jean-Luc Domenach draws attention to the fact that 'since 1949, tens of millions of Chinese have been locked up in the archipelago, often in terrible conditions, and millions are still there'. He suggests a range of 4 to 5.7 million prisoners for the years 1985 to 1988, as compared to 9.6 million around 1955. Referring to the Land of Snow, the French expert adds that: 'There were probably several tens of thousands of prisoners in Tibet in the late 1980s. Overall, since the end of the 1950s, over 300,000 people have been jailed in Tibet.'[10] He goes on: 'the testimony is conclusive. A witness estimates that from 1956 to 1959, 65,000 Tibetans were killed and 200,000 were incarcerated.'

Peking's story

The cultural revolution was the 'most monstrous display of obscurantism ever achieved by any tyrant on earth' according to Etiemble.[11] What was the impact of this murderous ideology as it swept over Tibet, almost causing the Land of Snow to vanish in its wake? According to the Chinese government's most faithful Tibetan ally, Ngapo Ngawang Jigme, 'the cultural revolution dragged all of China into an abyss of suffering and pain. Tibet was caught up in a groundswell that suddenly placed all its promising achievements in jeopardy. "Taking Tibet's actual conditions into consideration", a principle advocated by China's moderates, was denounced for betraying a defeatist attitude, while the "gradual development of Tibet" was held to signify preparing the ground for the restoration of capitalism. The "United Front" approach based on respect for Tibet's national identity and religious beliefs, designed to win over the population to socialism, was stupidly forsaken. Religious leaders and patriotic members of the well-to-do classes were branded monsters and demons. The monasteries, seen as the vestiges of obsolete superstitions, were often razed. Particularly after 1969, "People's Communes" were set up all over Tibet with no thought for productivity. These measures seriously dampened the enthusiasm of the Tibetan peasants and nomads, and production dropped, leading to a marked deterioration in the population's standard of living.'[12]

This is as far as Ngapo has ventured in his denunciation of those nightmare years. He does concede that Tibetan people were often heard to murmur: 'We detest both ends', a reference to the two extremes of the old society on the one hand and the cultural revolution and the people's communes on the other. These words mark the outer limit of China's repudiation of the cultural revolution.

Concerning the cultural revolution in Tibet, here are a few excerpts from a number of official publications, all placed under the direct control of the Propaganda Department of the Chinese Communist Party: 'During the ten years of the "cultural revolution" (1966–76), however, normal religious activities were proscribed and temples and monasteries shut down or laid to ruin by wilful destruction. The scars of this widespread disaster were especially evident in Tibet.'[13] 'During the 1966–76 "cultural revolution", due to "leftist" errors, the religious policies of the Chinese Communist Party were disrupted. Many temples and monasteries in Tibet suffered serious destruction. But this problem was not exclusive to Tibet. Temples and monasteries in other parts of China also suffered. Now the catastrophe has passed, and the Party's policy of religious freedom is being fully implemented.'[14]

The *New World Press* booklet is even more succinct: 'After liberation, and especially after democratic reform, Tibet advanced by leaps and bounds. Though it suffered along with all of China from the disastrous ten years of the "cultural revolution", it still developed much faster than old Tibet. Brilliant achievements have been made in the last twenty years, and particularly since 1980.'[15] Nothing further is said in the three official publications from which we have quoted, although each one is supposed to provide the reader with a comprehensive picture of contemporary Tibet. The cataclysmic cultural revolution is dismissed in a few lines, eclipsed by the glowing descriptions of the colossal progress achieved since 1950.

Without exception, all of China's official publications certify that Tibet and other areas inhabited by ethnic minorities did not suffer any more than the rest of China during the cultural revolution. For example, a study of all China's ethnic minorities states that: 'The ten-year period of chaos, generally known as the "cultural revolution", was a disaster for all the nationalities of China, the minority peoples and the Han majority included. Like the minority peoples, religious believers among the Hans were forbidden to engage in religious activities and were subjected to severe dress restrictions. Han men were confined to wearing the Chinese drab tunic suits of grey, blue and grass green and Han women were browbeaten if they wore skirts. So, the minority peoples and the Han shared the same fate during the "cultural revolution". The turmoil of this period was not the result of one nationality pitting itself against another, but the two counter-revolutionary cliques headed by Lin Biao and Jiang Qing directed their spearhead against the people of all nationalities.'[16]

There remains the task of arriving at a more accurate vision, for it has been established that these statements misrepresent historical events. In one of Israel Epstein's very rare references to the cultural revolution the falsification is so gross as to be offensive. He claims that: 'On the "roof of the world", as elsewhere in China, the distortions of the decade in which the "gang of four" ran riot, and the effects of the ultra-Leftism they fed and fostered, had their negative effects. Some, as in the sphere of education, were part of the country-wide picture. Others, concerning national and religious matters, had to do with local problems. But in Tibet, due to direct attention by Mao Zedong and Zhou Enlai, the relative steadiness and continuity of the region's leading bodies, and the great distance which put it out of the range of much of the disruption, these effects were in general less than in other national autonomous regions.'[17] Epstein's loyalty to Maoism cannot be questioned: in the 566 pages of his book on Tibet the cultural revolution is never criticized again. Page after page, the Chinese regime is praised and Tibet's religion and traditions are decried, while photographs show smiling young Tibetans, red communist flags and model workers striving for a radiant future.

Despite its best efforts, the Chinese regime has managed to generate a number of critics and detractors. It is safe to assume that they would have been legion if freedom of expression were granted. Most of the discordant voices within the chorus of acclamation have been rapidly muzzled. Nevertheless, a handful did manage to make themselves heard before they too were silenced: as we will see later on, shortly before his death the Panchen Lama painted an uncompromising portrait of Communism's darkest hours in Tibet. Hu Yaobang, the former General Secretary of China's Communist Party, displayed genuine courage before his death in disgrace in April 1989. Several times, as he waited for important foreign guests, I was able to meet and exchange a few words with the short, highly-strung Party leader; alone among the entire crew of China's political leadership, he was brave enough to formulate a self-criticism of the mistakes made in Tibet in the name of the Party and of the government. Many of his peers in Peking never forgave him. When he was purged in January 1987, in the wake of the first great wave of student protests, his criticism of Chinese policy in Tibet was held up as an example of his 'ideological laxity'.

The crimes of the Red Guards

The regions inhabited by ethnic minorities were potentially the most vulnerable to the devastating storm that was brewing in China. Unlike the areas where most of the population was Han – the original Chinese – these regions had preserved their own customs and cultural identity, and this was considered reactionary from Peking's point of view. Inhabited by people speaking a language other than Chinese, sometimes openly hostile to incoming Chinese settlers, these regions were often suspected of harbouring separatist impulses. In Xinjiang – originally East Turkestan and inhabited in the main by Muslims – the Red Guards quickly tore down the mosques. To further discredit religion, they forced believers to raise and eat pigs. Among the strongholds of the 'four olds' according to Mao's New China, Tibet quite naturally topped the list. In the eyes of Mao's ideologues, it was in Tibet that the most archaic beliefs and customs still remained. In other words: Tibet still had far to go before it was completely 'liberated'. The first teams of Red Guards reached Lhasa in July 1966; the cultural revolution started in August in Tibet. It was officially launched in Lhasa at a 'rally in support' of the 11th Plenary Session of the Eighth Party Central Committee that had just met in Peking, signalling the official opening of a China-wide hunt for 'capitalist-roaders'.

The Jokhang and Ramoche temples in the centre of Lhasa were the first targets of the Red Guards. Ribhur Tulku, a Lama who found refuge in Dharamsala a few years ago, witnessed the sacking of the Jokhang. 'It was the twentieth day of the sixth Tibetan month (6 August) in 1966.

Several hundreds of Chinese and Tibetan Red Guards in their late teens or early twenties suddenly burst into the Jokhang, in the company of some Chinese cadres. There were several hundred chapels in the temple. Only two were spared. All the others were thoroughly looted and soiled. Every single statue, holy scripture and ritual object was smashed or taken away. Several hundred of us monks and Geshes (doctors of religion) stood watching this spectacle, with tears running down our cheeks. The Red Guards shouted slogans under the watchful eyes of the Chinese cadres. Only the statue of Sakyamuni Buddha at the entrance of the Jokhang escaped their fury. Brought by Chinese princess Weng Cheng when she married Songtsen Gampo, it was a symbol of the links between China and Tibet. The rampage went on for almost a week. Then the Jokhang was turned into barracks for Chinese soldiers. They used a corner of the temple as a toilet, and we saw them urinating on the floor. Another part of the Jokhang was used as a slaughterhouse.'

For five days, the crowd of Red Guards kept a bonfire burning, in which they threw all the relics they found. Since 1959, the Jokhang had been used as a warehouse for Tibetan treasures brought from neighbouring monasteries that had been looted by the Chinese. Unique pieces of Tibet's cultural heritage were burnt to ashes. Chenrezig, the protector of Tibet, the Buddha of Infinite Compassion represented in the form of a large statue with eleven heads and a thousand arms, was smashed to bits by the Red Guards. When they were finished with the Jokhang and Ramoche, they moved on to Norbulingka, the Jewel Park, and methodically destroyed every treasure in each one of its pavilions. Fragments of statues, decapitated Buddhas, pulverized figurines were piled in every corner. Then the struggle against the 'four olds' spread throughout the Tibetan capital. Only the Potala and thirteen other places of worship in Tibet were placed off limits and protected by army detachments on orders from Prime Minister Chou En-lai. At any rate, this is what is claimed by the Chinese government and by a number of Western scholars who attribute to Chou En-lai a concern with the fate of the most important cultural sites in China such as the Forbidden City in Peking.

In Lhasa, street-signs were torn down and replaced with new ones bearing revolutionary names. In every home, the Guards tore down the images of the Buddha and ransacked the shrines. To compensate, tens of thousands of photographs of Mao Tse-tung were zealously handed out. Every home and office in Lhasa was adorned with his portrait and gigantic banners to the glory of the cultural revolution were raised over the Potala and other key locations. All over China, the Red Guards were challenging Party leaders and stigmatizing any whom they suspected of opposing Chairman Mao and the Revolution. The entire country seethed with relentless power struggles.

Until the fall, the leadership of Tibet's Communist Party Committee was able to keep under control the initiatives taken by the Red Guards. By December 1966, however, the Red Guards had multiplied substantially. One fine day, a coalition of fifty or so groups of Guards felt powerful enough to announce on Radio Lhasa that they intended to seize power shortly, as General Zhang Guohua and his allies had betrayed the revolution. The Chinese general hurriedly left Tibet and did not return until the following October. In March 1967, the 'Rebel' faction of the Red Guards managed to gain control of the *Tibet Daily*. In April, their ranks swelled with the arrival of 8,000 additional Red Guards from inside China. This increase brought their numbers up to at least 20,000 – all young people grimly intent on dislodging the 'traitors' who held power in Lhasa. In the Tibetan capital, street fights soon broke out between rival factions. By the autumn, these had spread to other large towns like Shigatse, Gyantse and Nagchuka. In Lhasa, the most violent engagements occurred in January 1968, when hundreds of people were killed.

The mounting chaos permeated every corner of Tibet, cutting off communications throughout the region by late January. In the army, entire units defected to join one or the other of the Red Guard factions, taking their weapons with them. After having receded for a few years, hunger reappeared in parts of Tibet.

Among China's twenty-nine provinces, regions and municipalities, Tibet and Xinjiang were the last to form cultural revolution committees. The central government had brokered a fragile truce between the two opposing tendencies. It goes without saying that the Chinese in Tibet suffered as a result of this strife. Several thousand died in combat. Countless others were detained and tortured. But how does this compare with what the Tibetans had to experience? Not to speak of the fact that the entire ideological controversy was completely alien to them.

Ribhur Tulku was subjected to thirty-five struggle sessions, staged in front of crowds of thirty to four hundred people. Now well over seventy years old, he recounts his memories in a calm voice, always smiling. 'During *thamzing* I was made to wear a tall, pointed hat. And my monk's robes, to make the point clearly that my class background was bad. All manner of badges and ritual instruments would be pinned to my robes to make me look ridiculous. I was paraded twice through the Lhasa marketplace to the music of trumpets and gongs and the insults of the Red Guards. The *thamzings* were usually held in the evening after work, from eight to eleven. During the day I had to work, doing construction work and breaking rocks. My accuser was naturally a Chinese. His name is Guo Xianzhi. I remember him perfectly well. He was in charge of the Lhasa district in which I lived. He accused me of having secret links with the Dalai Lama, of contacting "foreign reactionaries" and of trying to foment a Tibetan independence movement. I had to bend over with my hands on the floor and hang my head in front of the crowd. Then they would start beating me and criticizing me. Once they hit my right ear so hard with a rifle butt that I haven't been able to hear very well ever since. While the beatings went on, I could only see my attackers' legs. In fact, in Lhasa, I was one of the Lamas who suffered the least. The proof is that I am still alive today to tell you about it. Luckily I never lost my faith. It carried me through all the humiliation and suffering. And anyway, we all felt the situation could not last forever. From his position in exile, the Dalai Lama would do something to make Tibet free again.'

Ribhur Tulku is a *Rinpoche* – 'Precious One' – an honorific title used for reincarnations and the most learned and deserving monks. How does he feel about the Chinese? Does he hate them or does he feel compassion for them, in keeping with the Buddha's teachings? 'Of course I hate them. After living through such a harrowing time, how could I fail to hate them? Compassion is not at issue here. They destroyed our culture and our civilization. There is nowhere they can hide from our hatred. Compassion for them is out of the question. After 1979, China devised a policy of liberalisation and the Chinese tried to fool us with sweet-sounding words and higher salaries. But they are wasting their time. The Tibetans will not let themselves be duped twice. As a matter of fact, I decided to leave Tibet because the hatred in my heart was getting to be more than I could bear.'

In 1966, every type of religious practice was strictly forbidden, with no exceptions. This prohibition extended to Tibet's folk fairs and festivals. Even traditional Tibetan songs were banned. People caught praying were given exemplary punishments. The Red Guards removed the Tibetan prayer-flags that hung in every village, along the roads and on the mountain passes and replaced them with red banners. Tens of thousands of copies of Chairman Mao's *Little Red Book* were distributed – according to *Xinhua*, 740 million copies had been printed in China by late 1968. Portraits of Mao were hung all over the cities, at major crossroads, and in the villages, offices and factories. Families had to display at least one portrait in the house, if they didn't want serious problems. Big Brother had arrived in every home.

The braids worn by men and women in Tibet were labelled the 'dirty black tails of serfdom' and lopped off in passing. Just as in the rest of China, house pets were soon sacrificed. It became mandatory to wear Chinese clothes, which meant a pair of cotton pants and a jacket, and the only permitted colours were blue, grey or military green. The shortage of cloth was so severe that many Tibetans continued to wear their traditional costume. Tens of thousands of Tibetans were arrested, sometimes repeatedly, by each of the rival factions in turn. Sometimes, when a victim was released by one faction, he would be detained by the other, who vied to outdo its rival in subjecting him to the most inhuman treatment. A considerable number of these unlucky people were never seen again. Tibetans who had a 'bad class background', the sons and daughters of landowners or noble families, were unrelentingly persecuted by the Guards.

As the fighting escalated between the two factions of Chinese Red Guards, the punishments inflicted on the Tibetans became more and more ferocious. According to the testimony of exiled Tibetans, gang rapes became common, with victims including children. Women were undressed and forced to stand on frozen lakes. Brutality and torture in public became a common sight all over the Tibetan plateau. A victim's hand, ear, nose or tongue would be chopped off. People about to be executed were forced to dig their own graves. Whereas elsewhere in China the Chinese army intervened to pacify the situation, in Tibet it often participated in the Red Guards' felonies.

This frenzied period has left deep imprints in the minds of Tibetans who were small children at the time. A student from the Tibetan Children's Village school in Dharamsala once told me about an incident from his childhood in Lhasa, at the beginning of the cultural revolution. Although he was no more than five or six at the time, he has not been able to forget. 'That day I had been playing with other children. I had found a photo in the street and taken it home. It was a portrait of Mao with a red cross on it. I didn't know what the red cross meant and I wanted to ask my parents. So I showed it to my grandmother. As soon as she set eyes on it, she looked terrified! She told me to put it right back where I had found it, immediately. So I put it where I had first spotted it, in a little hole in a wall. Sometime later, a little girl found it. She was punished. Someone had seen her holding the photo and she was accused of drawing the red cross. She was severely punished. In fact, I remember they arranged a meeting, a struggle session. They called in the parents of the girl. She was older than my friends and I. She was punished to teach the others a lesson. They beat her in front of everybody. I was still too small to really understand, but I remember distinctly!'

A murdered civilization

In addition to these iniquities, which the Chinese government has never admitted, the Red Guards committed yet another heinous crime in Tibet, and it has proved far more difficult for China to deny it and to try to conceal it from the outside world since the death of Chairman Mao. From 1966 onwards, the dictator's followers engaged in the systematic, methodical, calculated, planned and comprehensive destruction of the Tibetan civilization. Quite naturally, one of the priorities for this enterprise was to eradicate the monasteries, which were held to be spawning-grounds for counter-revolutionary notions. There were some six thousand temples, holy sites and monasteries before 1959. A fair number had already been razed, badly damaged or closed by 1966. The few surviving ones were virtually all destroyed. The operation got under way in September 1967, a year after the launching of the cultural revolution. To facilitate their task, the Red Guards had access to an inventory of the Tibetan treasures that the Chinese had not yet managed to carry off to Peking.

Works of art containing gold, silver or precious stones, along with the better antique tangkas, were sometimes spared and thrown into sacks that were sealed and dispatched to the Chinese capital. In 1983, riding on the current of liberalization, a team of Tibetans visited Peking to search for some of the looted treasure. They found over 26 tons of Tibetan devotional objects in a warehouse in the Forbidden City in the heart of Peking! The statues and ritual instruments were packed into 136 crates and returned to their places of origin in Tibet. A further 6 tons of Tibetan relics were found in the Temple of Confucius (Kongzi Miao) in Peking. These were also crated and sent back to Tibet. By the time they returned, the team had located 13,537 statues and repatriated them packed in 600 crates.[18]

All of this, however, accounted for only a tiny percentage of all that had been wrecked or stolen. Ribhur Tulku, who headed the Tibetan mission, says that most of the Tibetan treasures were destroyed. Statues and objects made of pure gold or silver simply disappeared. Items made of brass, tin and other metals were sold to foundries in Shanghai, Sichuan, Taiyuan, Peking and elsewhere. To give just one example, the Shiyou Qingru (Precious Metal) Foundry, three miles east of Peking, bought 600 tons of looted metal objects from Tibet's temples and monasteries.[19] The smelting of Tibet's treasures only ceased in 1973, when it came to the attention of top cadres Li Xiannian and Ulanfu, himself a Mongolian.

Countless other ritual objects and sacred scriptures were thrown into huge bonfires in the grounds of the monasteries. The Red Guards would invite the Tibetan masses to attend these 'celebrations'. Material taken from sanctuaries and monasteries was used in building stables and public toilets and for surfacing pavements. The intention was not only to desecrate, but also to humiliate; to identify religion with the lowly and the vile. Predictably, holy Dharma texts were converted into toilet paper. When the temples and monasteries had been gutted, Tibetans were forced at gunpoint to level the walls by hand. The task was arduous, for the monasteries had been built to last. To deal with the thickest walls, the Red Guards brought in dynamite and artillery. Testimony abounds: in extreme cases, the holy sites were bombed from the air. In a matter of months, there was nothing left but collapsed roofs, shattered walls, crumbled metal, crushed stones and shapeless, unrecognizable ruins. The remains of the temples and monasteries are curiously reminiscent of Western cities that were bombed and razed during the Second World War: inanimate ghost towns.

Ganden, 25 miles from Lhasa, one of the largest monasteries, where several thousand *trapas* and *lamas* had studied and prayed, was soon reduced to smoking heap of rubble. Ribhur Tulku remembers: 'Before, there were thousands of monasteries in Tibet. Most were destroyed in the period before and after 1959. The Chinese thought that they were the centre of Tibetan cultural activity, that they harboured members of the Tibetan resistance and that they interfered with the forward march of socialism. Before the cultural revolution, some were left standing as proof that religious freedom prevailed in Tibet. But during the cultural revolution, even those that had remained untouched suffered the same fate as the others. Ganden is one of the most striking examples. According to our calendar, the demolition began on the third day of the seventh month of 1966 (19 August 1966). First they tackled the large hall where the monks met. Then they knocked down every single room where the monks had lived. To speed up the process they had recourse to dynamite. They just inserted sticks of dynamite in the walls and blew them up. Then teams were brought with hoes to put the finishing touches. The villagers managed to hide the statue of the founder, Tsongkhapa. That is the only thing that was not crushed to bits. Everything else was reduced to rubble. Anything valuable had been removed earlier and taken by truck to Lhasa and then to China. The destruction of Ganden resumed in 1969, when its stones were used as construction material and distributed all around. At that point, you could have said there was nothing left of Ganden at all.'

Generally speaking, the other monasteries and hermitages in Tibet suffered the same fate. When they disappeared, centuries of Tibetan architecture were lost. Needless to say, for the Tibetan people, the shock was unbearable. For humanity as a whole, the damage is more difficult to quantify, but it is an inestimable loss to our common patrimony. The Tibetan plateau offered an eerie vision of ruin and desolation. Much against its will, the home of Shangri-La had been engulfed in the convulsions of a ruthless ideological battle that was entirely alien to its own people. The land of the gods had become a hall of mirrors, where fear and death alone were reflected in infinite succession.

And yet, despite the political terror, the military and police presence and the teachings of Tibetan Buddhism (which forbid acts of violence) many Tibetans continued to fight the '*Gya Mi*' – 'Chinese' in Tibetan – the little men from the lowlands who had come to Tibet uninvited. Lost among the dark deeds of the cultural revolution, many acts of heroism or desperation went unrecorded. Fewer yet attracted any attention beyond China's borders. The country had closed in on itself like an oyster. Periodically, in the late 1960s and early 1970s, *Xinhua* would print a few lines about 'Tibetan rebels' guilty of 'sabotage', 'criminal acts' and 'separatist activities' in the boundless expanse of Tibet – and even in the heart of Lhasa. Occasionally, the Tibetan capital would bloom with posters calling for Tibetan independence and the death of Mao. The awesome military and police apparatus seemed powerless to stop them.

Among the accounts that filtered to the West, one relates an encounter on 7 June 1968 in Lhasa between Chinese troops and young Tibetans that left a dozen dead and about fifty injured in the Jokhang temple. Called in as reinforcements, the soldiers had fired point-blank on the unarmed 'rebels'. From their vantage-point in the Himalayan heights, bands of Tibetan warriors, mostly Khampas, grouped and regrouped to carry out guerilla operations against an enemy that was thousands of times stronger in number and infinitely better equipped. In 1972, guerrillas were active in sixty of the seventy-one districts of the 'Tibet Autonomous Region'.

Interestingly, Ngapo Ngawang Jigme's son Jigme Ngapo has openly repudiated the Chinese policies for Tibet that his father has been faithfully serving since 1950. Now residing in the USA, he and his co-workers have been shedding light on hitherto little-known episodes of the cultural revolution in Tibet. His testimony has provided much additional information about the Tibetan resistance in the late sixties, at a time when all of China was still in the grip of terror, when any act of resistance was a great act of courage. He revealed that in 1969 a revolt was staged by 1,000 Tibetans in Nyimu district, in the western outskirts of Lhasa. Led by a nun, the rebels took a police station. Sent in to put down the revolt, the army was unable to defeat the rebels, who fled to the mountains. When they were finally captured, they were dragged to Lhasa to be 'tried' and executed.

The rebellion was followed by a considerable number of arrests. Many Tibetans were thrown in jail or sent to the already overcrowded labour camps. 'All the prisons and labour camps were full. Little is known about the 1969 rebellion, even in China. After 1959 and 1969, a great majority of the families (including those living in Qinghai, Gansu, Yunnan and Sichuan), whether nobles or serfs, monks or laymen, had lost one or two members. Or else they had a relative in jail, under surveillance or in exile abroad. If you count all the people who suffered during the cultural revolution, you can say this includes several members of each family', in the words of Jigme Ngapo.[20]

From 1970 onwards, the Chinese authorities launched a new campaign to uproot resurgent hotbeds of rebellion. Peking's propaganda machine targeted the Dalai Lama and branded him a 'bandit and a traitor' and 'a butcher with bloody hands who lived off the flesh of the people'. The police and the army in Tibet took issue with 'traitors, conspirators, saboteurs, criminals' and other 'bad elements'. Executions were repeatedly held in public to serve as an example for the masses. Lhasa's prisons became increasingly crowded.

As if these trials were not enough for the long-suffering Tibetan people, a further calamity was waiting in the wings. It was a drama that had already played to full capacity in China, the creation of Mao's famous 'people's communes' in the rural areas, the cornerstone of his programme for full collectivization of agriculture and animal husbandry. The land, livestock and tools were taken away from the peasants and became the collective property of the people's commune, the Maoist's new administrative unit. Each commune was subdivided into production brigades. Family holdings and privately-owned fields were banned. Formalized by 1958 and vaunted by Communist cadres as the 'golden bridge to the paradise of socialism', some people's communes had already been set up here and there in Kham and Amdo, with the advance of Chinese colonization. News of those experiments had reached the ears of Lhasa's inhabitants. Individualistic and protective of their personal freedom by nature, the Tibetans – and particularly the nomads – immediately developed a deep-seated feeling of aversion to the concept. The people's communes were seen as just another type of prison or labour camp.

In theory, the people's communes were multi-dimensional entities with economic, administrative, social and educational functions. As in China, the communes were a formidable method of population control for the Maoist cadres. The family unit was destroyed, along with the power structures in the villages. The Communist Party and its cadres were left in absolute control of the situation. In Tibet, the peasants concurrently lost all freedom of movement. To venture beyond their living and working quarters, special permission was now required. In China, a single commune might regroup as many as five thousand villages and hamlets. The communes were smaller in Tibet, generally consisting of one to two hundred families. By the summer of 1970, over one thousand were already in place. In parts of the country where resistance to communal ownership was strongest, the army was called in to help. By December 1975, the collectivization of Tibet's countryside was virtually complete, and there were almost 2,000 communes scattered throughout almost every district of central Tibet (U-Tsang).

The workers' day began as in China with the piercing wail of 'The East is Red' blaring over the commune's loudspeakers. For political reasons, Tibet was forced to live on Peking time from 1959 onwards. When the sun rose in Peking, it was still pitch dark in the Land of Snow. In the evening, after long hours of intentionally exhausting field-work, the workers had to attend the daily political indoctrination classes. Attendance was compulsory. It became increasingly difficult to find any privacy or time to oneself because the commune's Party Committee controlled every waking hour of the workers' time. Lunch was eaten in the fields or in the communal canteens. The rare moments free from political control or brainwashing came while eating the family supper at home, before bedtime.

Soon after the people's communes were established, the Chinese cadres forced the Tibetan farmers to plant wheat. From time immemorial, Tibetans had grown barley, better suited to the fragile soil and short growing season of the Himalayan plateau. The Chinese leadership also ordered the farmers to bring in one crop every year. In Tibet, farmers customarily let the land lie fallow every other year, so as to regenerate its capacity. The Chinese methods soon depleted the soil, the harvests were bad and grain production went through the floor. Tibet, traditionally considered a granary until 1950, became totally impoverished in the space of a few years. These mistakes triggered off yet another wave of famine in some parts of Tibet. The situation was further aggravated by China's war preparation campaign, begun at the end of the sixties. In those days, Mao and his government believed that a third world war was inevitable. The countries surrounding China were almost exclusively hostile, starting with the powerful Soviet Union and all its allies. Mao concluded that there was no time to lose and started making active preparations. The Chinese army was given priority in the distribution of grain, including in Tibet, where the government had stationed hundreds of thousands of troops along the border with India.

However detailed or succinct, any description of the cultural revolution would remain incomplete if it did not contain a reference to one more element, which is very revealing of China's intentions in Tibet: the arrival of tens of thousands of Chinese settlers, sent by order of the central government in Peking. By the sixties, there were already a great many Chinese in Kham and Amdo, but in central Tibet, not counting the Chinese army, there were still relatively few Chinese cadres. The massive transfer of settlers started in earnest in 1975. From then on, their numbers rapidly swelled. A China-wide census carried out in 1982 put the number of Chinese in Tibet at 96,000, which reflects only the number of Chinese officially registered on the government's lists, and fails to take into account their wives, children and other relatives who joined them on the Roof of the World. In Lhasa, for a population of 50,000 Tibetans, there were soon over 100,000 Chinese. New quarters were built specially for them, and the grey, box-like buildings soon surrounded and dwarfed the old Tibetan city.

According to the Tibetan government-in-exile, no less than 600,000 Chinese were sent to central Tibet between 1975 and 1980. This means that whereas in 1912 not a single Chinese was left in Tibet after the government had expelled the last Ambans, by 1980 there was at least one Chinese for every three Tibetans in the heartland of Tibet. In Kham and Amdo, the number was much higher. Nowadays, in some areas, it is the Tibetans who are visibly very much in the minority. The number of People's Liberation Army troops is a closely-guarded secret and they are not included in population figures. Following the Sino-Indian conflict in 1962, China considerably upgraded its military presence in Tibet. Current estimates of Chinese military strength in Tibet by Western specialists vary considerably, ranging from the 1962 high of 500,000 to as few as 200,000 men stationed in central Tibet, Kham and Amdo.

After ten years of the cultural revolution, how could anyone in Tibet have any doubts about the real nature of the socialist paradise promised by the Chinese Communist Party? And yet, with no apparent qualms about sardonic laughter from his fellow Tibetans, this is how Ngapo Ngawang Jigme described the years of hatred and cruelty in 1976: 'I am over sixty now and I have never seen the Tibetan people so happy, so well-disposed and so firmly determined ... Even our enemies are compelled to recognize it. In the world it is rare thing for a people to go from an extremely backward, feudal serf system to an advanced socialist society in only a quarter of a century, as it has been the case for Tibet.'[21] At a time when the communist world has fallen apart and its ideology is well and truly defunct, this rhetoric can sound amusing. Unfortunately, this is how China's aged leadership still states its case today.

A million dead?

In 1980, four years after the end of the cultural revolution, the Dalai Lama's eldest brother returned to Tibet. Thubten Jigme Norbu was part of a fact-finding delegation sent by Tenzin Gyatso at the invitation of the Chinese government. He was horrified by what he saw when he first caught sight of the extent of the destruction: 'When I left, there were many Buddhist monasteries, nunneries and temples. Ganden Monastery, once the third largest in the nation with nearly three thousand monks, was completely obliterated. Drepung Monastery, which was the largest in Tibet with a population of ten thousand, is now a ghost town. The Chinese said there were two hundred monks, but I only saw six or seven in monk robes. Sera Monastery as well was practically destroyed. Only a few monks live there now. All the Tibetan monasteries are in ruins and semi-ruins.' At the end of the cultural revolution, the Potala was intact, but many objects had disappeared and been replaced with copies.

When he visited his birthplace, a village near Kumbum in Amdo, now re-named Taersi by the Chinese, Thubten Jigme Norbu heard nothing but heartbreaking stories about the devastation visited upon his relatives during the cultural revolution. 'When I asked them about their life now, they would just cry; they had no words. Others told me how their families and friends were killed, imprisoned, sent to labour camps, maimed and crippled. Some were beaten so severely over and over again with clubs and boards, that they had lost their hearing or sight. Others had bodies that were bent and twisted from being forced to pull heavy carts, like animals. Many were compelled to stand in public places while people were forced to pull out their hair in 'struggle' (*thamzing*) sessions.

Thousands died from exposure and starvation, unable to survive on the worms, garbage, dead dog bones, pig food, etc., which hunger drove them to eat. They told me that in 1959–60 all men were rounded up, put in trucks and sent away to labour camps; that the only people you saw then were women, children and the aged.'

Travelling through the countryside, he noticed that Tibet, once a paradise for wild goats, antelopes, deer, bears, wild yaks and horses, had lost most of its wildlife – not to speak of the destruction of the environment. Entire forests had been cut down. The fragile soil was exhausted. As for the level of education of its people, leaving aside a few privileged children, none of the Tibetans had been to school for thirty years. The small minority that could read and write only knew Chinese. Many of the fellow Tibetans he met whispered in his ear: 'Never, never trust the Chinese!' or 'Tell the Dalai Lama not to come back!' He goes on, '[t]he Chinese have the audacity to say that they liberated Tibet from a feudal society, and that the Tibetans have always been Chinese. Tibetans are not and have never been Chinese. Tibet is dominated today more than ever.' But, he concludes, '[t]hough the country is wounded socially and economically, these Tibetan people are not defeated in their hearts, nor have they become the "Chinese" that the Chinese officials say with their lips that they are'.[22]

Even in the absence of precise figures, it is obvious to an outside observer that hundreds of thousands of Tibetans died from unnatural causes during the cultural revolution. The Dalai Lama and the Tibetans in exile have compiled a tally of more than a million of their compatriots who died between 1950 and 1976 as a result of Chinese policies in Tibet. According to the recently-published statistics prepared by the Department of Information of the Dalai Lama's government-in-exile in Dharamsala, 173,221 Tibetans died in prison or in labour camps between 1950 and 1983, 92,731 were tortured to death, 156,758 were executed, 432,705 died fighting the Chinese, 342,970 died of hunger and 9,002 took their own lives. The total comes to 1,207,387 victims of China's first thirty-three years in central Tibet (U-Tsang), Kham and Amdo. On the basis of these figures, the Dalai Lama and his followers accuse China of committing genocide in Tibet. The Chinese government denies these figures and holds them up to ridicule, alleging that only one million Tibetans lived in central Tibet in 1950, as compared to nearly 2 million today. Peking, however, never includes the Tibetans from Kham and Amdo. Nor has it ever published figures of its own for Tibetan victims of the cultural revolution.

In the light of these events, it is understandable that Mao may have assumed that he had struck a fatal blow against Tibet. In this way, the Tibetan question would have been settled once and for all. Yet it is quite clear, seventeen years after his death, that his calculations were inaccurate. While it was child's play for Mao's battle-seasoned troops to sweep the Tibetan army out of its way and invade Tibet in 1950, neither the 'democratic reforms' begun in 1959, nor the Great Leap Forward from 1959 to 1962, nor even the cultural revolution lasting until 1976 were able to overcome the Land of Snows. For a time, Mao could crow about having annexed Tibet to the general indifference of the international community. But he has not been able to conquer, nor tame – even less to subjugate – the Tibetan people.

On the day the Great Helmsman breathed his last, the spirit of the Tibetan people was not only still alive, it was stronger than ever. The murderous savagery and the destruction wreaked by the Red Guards bound the Tibetans closer together, irrespective of their origins in Lhasa, Kham or Amdo. Whereas pre-1949 Tibet was constantly rent by domestic quarrels between clans, religious sects and small local lords, at the end of the seventies the Tibetans were more united than they had ever been in recent history. Having set out to extinguish Tibetan Buddhism and Tibet's cultural identity, Mao Tse-tung had achieved the exact opposite. Whereas a Chinese policy of peaceful cooperation with a genuinely autonomous Tibet would have had a good chance of overcoming its deeply-rooted traditions, bringing about the desired assimilation of the Tibetan people within the 'great Chinese family', the cultural revolution's wanton violence laid the foundation for a wide-ranging and enduring reawakening of Tibetan nationalism.

Notes

1. John Avedon, *In Exile from the Land of Snow*, Wisdom Publications, London, 1985.
2. Tibet Information Network Update, 30 April 1990, p. 21.
3. Ibid., p. 291.
4. Jean Pasqualini, *Prisonnier de Mao*, Gallimard, 1974.
5. John Avedon, op. cit., p. 338.
6. Michael C. van Walt van Praag, op. cit., p. 172.
7. Jacques Guillermaz, *Le Parti communiste chinois au pouvoir*, Payot, 1972, p. 365.
8. *Mao Zidong Sixiang Wansui*, Peking, 1969.
9. Testimony presented to the 48th Session of the United Nations Commission on Human Rights, Geneva, Spring 1992.
10. *Chine, l'archipel oublié*, Fayard, pp. 29 and 498.
11. Etiemble, *Quarante ans de mon Maoïsme*, Gallimard, 1976.
12. *Tibetans about Tibet*, China Reconstructs, Peking, 1988, pp. 187–8.
13. *Tibet: Today & Yesterday*, op. cit., p. 33.
14. *100 Questions About Tibet*, op. cit., p. 59.
15. *A General Survey of Tibet*, New World Press, Peking, 1988, p. 50.
16. *Questions and answers about China's national minorities*, New World Press, Peking, 1985, p. 73.
17. Israel Epstein, op. cit., p. 37.
18. Ribhur Tulku, *The Search for Jowo Mikyoe Dorjee*, The Office of Information and International Relations, Central Tibetan Secretariat, Dharamsala, 1988.

19. Ibid.

20. *Emancipation Monthly*, Hong Kong, December 1987.

21. *China Reconstructs.*

22. Thubten Jigme Norbu, *Tibet is my Country*, Wisdom Publications, London, 1986, pp. 273–5.

TWO

Clouds over the Roof of the World

4

The Revival of Nationalism

As soon as Mao Tse-tung was dead and his embalmed body safely tucked away in a glass coffin in the Monument to the People's Heroes in the centre of Tiananmen square, China's ideology sharply changed course. With the dictator gone and the Gang of Four behind bars, the new Communist leadership had no choice but to draw the lessons from the failure of Maoism: China was an enormous, impoverished country, cut off from the international community. The largest nation in the Third World, having aspired to enlighten humanity with a doctrine based on megalomania, was left toiling under a bankrupt, moribund system. Not only could the People's Republic no longer make its presence felt beyond its borders, it was being mocked and derided by many of its erstwhile admirers – not entirely without reason.

Thirty years after its foundation, one Chinese out of three could neither read nor write and 800 million peasants were still living in dire poverty. In parts of Anhui or Gansu, two of the country's most backward provinces, the people were still dying of hunger, plagued by recurring famines. The mighty Red China of Mao's dreams – he who had so often scoffed at the American paper tiger – had turned out be nothing more than a paper dragon.

At the same time, the first accounts to reach the West about life in China's concentration camps had finally opened people's eyes to the atrocities committed in the Chinese gulag – a worthy disciple of its Soviet model. The 'distinguished foreign guests' and other gullible tools of China's Friendship Associations became a little less amenable to Chinese propaganda's heavy-handed bluff. Western observers, even when they favoured Peking, spoke in critical terms and denounced the massacres of the Mao Tse-tung era. As for the Maoists and fellow-travellers of the Great Helmsman in the West, their cheeks burned crimson as they hurriedly packed pens and slogans away, picking feverishly through the revolutionary cant that now rang quite irretrievably hollow.

Confronted with such an utter rout, a radical review of the Party line was obviously required. For Peking, abandoning Marxism was definitely

93

out of the question. Since 1979, senior economist Chen Yun had sensed the danger inherent in too much liberalization: 'The masses want to raise the lid of the pot. Once the lid is off, we run the risk of losing power.' The men who were still in power faced the challenge of reforming Communism just enough to survive, in a fiercely competitive world dedicated to achieving 'progress'. At its December 1978 Third Plenary Session in Peking, the 11th Party Central Committee celebrated the victory of the Party's reform-minded wing led by Deng Xiaoping, freshly rehabilitated after a period of political disgrace.

China changes course

One fine morning, all of China woke up to read in the pages of the *People's Daily* that the East was no longer the blood-red hue Mao had favoured. The editorial went on to explain that the class struggle and the witch-hunt for counter-revolutionaries were no longer the priorities. From now on, overriding importance was to be attached to the 'Four Modernizations' programme, which focused on agriculture, industry, science and technology and military defence, in decreasing order of importance. For the rank and file of well-disciplined Party cadres, the new political credo was contained in two slogans: 'economic reform' and 'open-door policy'.

Mao's model workers, the icons of an entire generation, were allowed to sink into oblivion. With unnerving abruptness, the propaganda machine latched onto the theme of 10,000 yuan households' – China's new heroes; the rising stars of 'socialism with Chinese characteristics' were showered with praise. In the villages, the peasants were better off. The reason was simple: when they had been mobilized for communal work during the campaigns to collectivize the country, the peasants had worked as little as possible. As soon as their small plots were returned to them, they worked harder than ever. The people's communes receded into the nightmare of the past as the government extolled 'family responsibility'. Newspaper and radio programmes urged the smashing of the iron rice-bowl of the Maoist era, when workers were guaranteed the same income irrespective of their abilities and the quality of their work. Maoist egalitarianism had had its day. Long live Dengist inequality! The results were not long in coming: grain production increased spectacularly, rising from 300 million tons per annum in the 1970s to a record 407 million tons in 1984. The Chinese were again able to eat their fill.

In the cities, October 1984 brought similar improvements with the launching of an ambitious programme of urban reforms. Its originator, Chen Yizi, was to seek refuge in France after the massacre of 4 June 1989. The 'one big pot' for all the workers in each factory yielded to a system of bonuses for those who performed better than the rest. Communist China legalized the private sector, that ultimate symbol of the

exploitation of man by man, unrelentingly pilloried in Mao's time. Starting from about 300,000 in 1976, the year of Mao's death, the number
of 'private entrepreneurs' or self-employed traders and craftsmen soared
to over twenty million by 1988! In some parts of the country, 'contrac-
tors' were managing private factories that boasted a thousand or more
employees. All of China had caught the new fever: to get rich. Child
workers, or more specifically the exploitation of children's labour, made
a comeback in New China's industrial cities. Corruption had become
rare, carrying the death penalty during the cultural revolution; now it
poked its tentacles into every sector of society. A new class of *gaogan zidi*
(children of high cadres) took over the controls in China. Under the
envious stare of the man in the street, China's new Golden Boys revved
their top-of-the-line motorcycles.

Having lionized Mao, the West wasted no time in acclaiming 'tiny'
Deng Xiaoping. Gratified at being chosen Man of the Year by several
Western publications, he often aired his magic recipe: 'It doesn't matter
if a cat is black or white, so long as it catches mice.' The capitalist press
solemnly announced a new economic revolution in China. Some inno-
cents assumed that China had become a democratic country. Others
predicted a revival of capitalism. But the question remains, what was
there to be proud of? And how much courage does it take for a leader
finally to discard the policies that have proved to be irredeemably nox-
ious a hundred times over? China was fated to change its course; it was
left with no choice at all.

For intellectual and artistic circles in China, the open-door policy let
a welcome ray of sunshine shine through otherwise leaden skies, despite
successive campaigns against 'spiritual pollution' and 'bourgeois liberalization' that the regime was prompted to launch, fearing on more than
one occasion that the situation was getting out of control. On university
campuses and in the official media, the discussions and debates had not
been so bold and so 'free' for twenty years. This did not discourage the
regime from throwing in jail any political dissidents who looked threat-
ening. Wei Jingsheng, the best known among them, was one of the first
to pay the price for having questioned Deng's legitimacy during the short-
lived Peking Spring. For venturing to call for a 'fifth modernization' –
democracy – he was kept incommunicado in a tiny cell from 1979 to
late 1993. He used to have a Tibetan girlfriend, Phuntsok Dekyi, the
daughter of a Tibetan high cadre, who later emigrated and now lives
in Germany. Many other dissidents were jailed after expeditious political trials.

Turning its attention to religion, the government proclaimed that the
freedom of worship enshrined in the Constitution would be granted.
Proselytism was closely monitored. But in the cities, many Buddhist
temples, numerous mosques and different churches were reopened. The
Chinese Constitution of 1982 explicitly provides for freedom of belief.

Article 36 is entirely devoted to this principle and states that: '[c]itizens of the People's Republic of China enjoy freedom of religious belief. No state organ, public organization or individual may compel citizens to believe in, or not to believe in, any religion; nor may they discriminate against citizens who believe in, or do not believe in, any religion. The state protects normal religious activities. No one may make use of religion to engage in activities that disrupt public order, impair the health of citizens or interfere with the educational system of the state. Religious bodies and religious affairs are not subject to any foreign domination.'

'Chinese Communists are atheists, but they are not opposed to others having religious beliefs. They do not stand for the abolition of religion by force', says Peking.[1] The tactics have changed since Mao's time, but the objective presumably remains the same, for it would be naive to think that the Chinese Communist Party has abandoned its commitment to eliminate all religions. It continues to look upon them all as the manifestation of harmful superstitions that retard the liberation of the individual and his integration within a socialist, materialist society. Since naked force conspicuously failed to achieve their elimination, the new Chinese ideologues hope religions will disappear on their own, without a struggle, with the growth of social and economic progress. The experience of the industrialized countries would tend to prove them right.

Generally speaking, the period from 1979 to 1989 can be said to have provided a welcome respite and a time of renewal for a severely traumatized people. The decade of reform and open-door policies gave a billion men and women time to lick their wounds and rediscover a taste for life, while they became aware of their country's poverty and discovered a world beyond their borders, the very existence of which had escaped the great majority. By coming to grips with the magnitude of its economic backwardness, China took a giant step forward. There was again reason to hope.

Hu Yaobang weeps for shame

How did the decade of reform affect Tibet? The opening act consisted of a formal self-criticism and an acknowledgement of China's dramatic mistakes in the Land of Snow proffered by Hu Yaobang, then General Secretary of the Chinese Communist Party, during a memorable fact-finding tour in 1980. No Chinese leader had ever spoken so frankly about the tragedy of Tibet. This highly-strung, intelligent and conceivably honest man displayed real courage in saying out loud what everyone else in Peking preferred to keep quiet. A privileged spectator of the internal debates in the corridors of power in Peking, Jigme Ngapo remembers the reaction of Hu Yaobang and his deputy, Vice-Prime Minister Wan Li, when they took stock of the misery in Tibet. 'When Hu Yaobang and Wan Li went to Tibet, what shocked them most terribly was the poverty. It hit you in the face. China had put in a lot of effort for thirty years and invested several billions, but the Tibetan people and Tibet were still in a condition of grinding poverty. At that time in Lhasa there was not a single modern building. Hu Yaobang wept. "The Central Government has spent several billions in Tibet, how did you spend it? Did you throw it in the Tsangpo river?" He saw that the Tibetan economy, far from being self-sufficient and autarkic as before, had swung to the opposite extreme: it was completely dependent on mainland China.'[2]

Professor Wang Yao, Head of the Tibet Department of the Central Institute for Minorities in China and advisor to Hu Yaobang during the visit, remembers his words to a gathering of five thousand cadres in Lhasa: 'We feel that our Party has let the Tibetan people down. We feel very bad! The sole purpose of our Communist Party is to work for the happiness of people, to do good things for them. We have worked nearly thirty years, but the life of the Tibetan people has not been notably improved. Are we not to blame?'[3] These words, spoken by the head of the Chinese Communist Party and quoted by an unimpeachable source, can be taken as an outright condemnation of every facet of the Chinese government's policies in Tibet since 1950.

'All consumer goods had to be imported, even food', adds Jigme Ngapo. 'Tibet exported some minerals, medicinal plants and timber. If supplies from the mainland had been interrupted, the Tibetan economy would have been paralysed and collapsed. Hu Yaobang said one thing no one in China had dared to say: "this is plain colonialism". He realized that Tibet had suffered a lot of damage: monk or layman, every Tibetan was nursing deep wounds and the relations between the Han and the Tibetans were very tense. Everywhere he went, Hu Yaobang criticized the Han cadres and praised the Tibetans for their long history, rich culture and highly developed civilization and lauded the people's diligence, intelligence and courage.'[4]

The first result of the visit was that Secretary Ren Rong of the Regional Communist Party Committee was replaced by Yin Fatang, a military commander stationed in Tibet since 1950. A series of drastic measures were dictated by Hu Yaobang in hopes of revitalizing a Tibet that was tottering on its last legs. No more taxes would be levied on the peasants or the nomads for a period of three years; 85 per cent of Chinese cadres were to leave Tibet; Tibet's autonomy was to be enhanced. 'If the policy of the Central Government is not in keeping with the reality of Tibet, then Tibet has the right to refuse to implement it or to revise it' declared Hu Yaobang. Many Chinese cadres who had settled in Tibet promptly criticized his decisions and wrote to Peking to complain about the initiatives taken by a Party Secretary who was misguided, as far as they were concerned. 'Hu Yaobang was a liberal, frank and sincere. He recognized his mistakes. His new policy reduced the tension and probably avoided another large-scale ethnic confrontation. If one looks at China's long-term interests, Hu Yaobang's political decisions were wise ones', in the opinion of Jigme Ngapo.

Immigration: China's secret weapon

Although some members of the leadership in Peking were now more favourably inclined towards Tibet and had better information about the conditions, China certainly had no intention of relinquishing its claim to sovereignty over that territory. What is more, efforts to carry out Hu Yaobang's orders met with dogged resistance from the legion of Chinese cadres known as 'big Han chauvinists'. At least one of Hu Yaobang's decisions not only failed to yield positive results, it produced the exact opposite of what he sought to achieve. His decision to withdraw 85 per cent of the Chinese cadres met with violent opposition. The matter was very soon dropped in Peking and no more was said about it. In Tibet, the number of Chinese immigrants increased even more rapidly, primarily in response to the wage increments or bonuses given to Chinese willing to go there.

Incentives are required to overcome the cadres' reluctance. As a result, the salary of a cadre in Tibet is often three times higher than a comparable salary 'inside' China. To be precise, in a 1987 statement to the Tibet Standing Committee of the National People's Congress, the Panchen Lama complained that 'the expense of keeping one Chinese in Tibet is equal to that of four in China. Why should Tibet spend its money to feed them?' Plainly speaking, there is probably not a single Chinese who is pleased at the idea of going to Tibet and no place within China's borders where he will feel more cut off from his *guxiang* or birthplace, for which Chinese harbour intense feelings their whole life long. But the lure of easy money has attracted Chinese from many walks of life to Tibet's inhospitable highlands. In the towns, a whole series of occupations has changed hands: numerous workshops and stores owned by Tibetans have been forced to close by the unexpected competition.

The most recent figures in a report published by the Department of Information of the Dalai Lama's government-in-exile indicate that 7.5 million Chinese have settled in central Tibet and in the traditional Tibetan areas that were merged into Qinghai, Gansu, Sichuan and Yunnan. This would imply the presence of up to two million Chinese in central Tibet (U-Tsang), at least 2.5 million in Amdo and three million in Kham, versus 1.9 million, 0.8 million and 3.3 million Tibetans in the respective provinces. The report concludes that '[t]he transfer of Chinese to Tibet has attained alarming proportions. The real fear is that if the present Chinese policy is successful – and indications are that it will be – Tibetans will be reduced to a small and insignificant minority in their own country in the same way as the Manchus (35 Chinese to one Manchu), the Turkic people (3 to 1) and the Mongolians (5 to 1) have been. The object of this policy is to forcibly "resolve" China's territorial claims over Tibet by means of a massive and irreversible population transfer.'[5]

This is all baseless nonsense, replies the Chinese government. 'How things actually stand is that groups of educated and technically trained Han people go to work in Tibet to help develop the local economy and culture. But because of the highland climate and adverse reactions due to the high altitude, most of those people take turns to [*sic*] working there. Usually they return to the hinterland provinces after a few years of employment in Tibet.'[6] Peking's figures are based on the fourth national census carried out in June and July 1990. It established that the Han population accounted for 91.96 per cent of the 1,133,682,501 Chinese and the 'national minorities', basically the Muslims and the Tibetans, for only 8.04 per cent. For central Tibet (the Tibet Autonomous Region) the 1990 total is 2,196,000 inhabitants of which only 81,217 are stated to be Han – 3.7 per cent of the total population.[7]

These figures reveal a significant increase of the Tibetan population and also of the Han presence, since the previous official figures were 73,000 for the Hans and a total of 2,024,000 inhabitants for central Tibet in late 1986. At the time, the breakdown for the Tibetan population was given as 1,786,544 Tibetans in the Autonomous Region, 922,024 in Sichuan, 754,254 in Qinghai, 304,540 in Gansu and 95,915 in Yunnan. According to Peking's figures, the total Tibetan population scattered over several Chinese provinces has grown continuously, from 2,501,174 in 1964 to 3,847,875 in 1982 and from 3,863,277 in 1986 to 4,593,330 in the 1990 census. No explanation is given for the much higher increase (fifty times!) of the Tibetan population in the second four-year period, from 1986 to 1990, as compared to 1982–86.

When it comes to the figures for Chinese settlers, an attentive observer will note that they only pertain to central Tibet and fail to include the old Tibetan provinces of Kham and Amdo, where the Chinese overwhelmingly outnumber the Tibetans in certain areas nowadays. Nor do the Chinese statistics incorporate the troops stationed in Tibet, currently estimated to number at least 300,000. My esteemed colleague Jasper Becker quotes a 'secret' Chinese Government report dated July 1990 that puts total troop strength in Tibet, including the paramilitary People's Armed Police, at 'slightly over 40,000' – versus 240,000 Indian Army troops stationed right across the border. Whereas the Indian Army has deployed three army corps, nine divisions, 24 brigades, 11 airborne units, 400 aircraft and 90 tanks along the common border, this would be to say that China can only marshall two brigades of mountain infantry, 13 public works regiments and 65 units of People's Armed Police to protect its territory against the Indian menace. This scenario puts only one regiment of mechanized infantry in Lhasa.[8] Personally, I have reason to believe that the document – while probably authentic – broadly underestimates the actual Chinese military presence. First of all, it seems to apply only to the Tibet Autonomous Region, which means that it fails to include the troops stationed in the large Tibetan areas in the neighbouring provinces. Secondly, my feeling is that a report prepared for Chinese Communist Party General Secretary Jiang Zemin and People's Liberation Army Commander-in-Chief Chi Haotian's visit to Tibet, even if labelled 'secret', is unlikely to contain the actual figures, which are likely to be known only to an extremely restricted number of Chinese leaders.

Another omission relates to the already considerable and steadily growing number of traders, craftsmen, restaurant owners and other Chinese businessmen who emigrate to Tibet on their own initiative and for their own purposes. It can safely be assumed that the figure for Chinese cadres detached by the government is broadly underestimated and does not include family members. Last but not least, whereas the government-in-exile of the Dalai Lama always refers to six million Tibetans, China only records 4,593,330. Where are the 1,406,670 missing Tibetans? Peking and Dharamsala each have their own compelling reasons for publishing vastly underestimated, or conversely, generously inflated figures.

As Jigme Ngapo points out, the Tibetan autonomy advocated by Hu Yaobang remained a dead letter. 'Tibetan cadres have been promoted – but they do the daily housekeeping while the Han cadres are the masters. This situation cannot and will not change, as the autonomy has no substance. There is no substantial difference between this "Autonomous Region" and a mainland province. ... As for the right to "veto" central government policy, I wonder whether this isn't something that Hu Yaobang said on the spur of the moment. Who would ever dare to veto?' The tax exemption was probably the most successful measure. It was extended for a further two years after the first three. Alas, over and above this modest financial incentive, far more extensive measures would have been necessary to revive Tibet's economy, and the gap between its standard of living and that of the Chinese mainland has done nothing but widen since 1979. There is good reason to worry that one by one, the areas inhabited by ethnic minorities will come to be seen as no more than convenient parking-places for the overspill of the rapidly expanding Chinese population. Concerning Xinjiang, the *China Daily* announced on 5 December 1992 that the Peking authorities had chosen the Kashgar region as the new home for almost 500,000 Chinese who will be displaced by the immense Three Gorges Dam project. Once the massive dam on the Yangtze river is operative, a great deal of farmland in central China's Hubei province will be permanently under water. When the final go-ahead is obtained for the project, says the official Chinese daily, 100,000 Chinese farmers will immediately be relocated in Kashgar prefecture, which is expected to absorb 480,000 in the long run. It goes without saying that a population transfer on this scale runs a real risk of further destabilizing an area where, as we have already seen, considerable Chinese Han immigration has taken place since the 1950s.

Early negotiations with the Dalai Lama

As applied in Tibet, the open-door policy ushered in a dialogue between the Chinese authorities and the Dalai Lama's entourage. In 1978 the Dalai Lama's older brother Gyalo Thondup met in Hong Kong with an emissary from Deng Xiaoping. The envoy explained that Deng Xiaoping wished to close the chapter on twenty years of hostility and wanted to resume the cooperation that had been interrupted by the uprising of 1959. Gyalo Thondup was invited to Peking to meet the aged patriarch, who availed himself of the opportunity to admit that 'mistakes' had been made in Tibet. He invited the Dalai Lama to return to the motherland and contribute to the development of Tibet and of the People's Republic as a whole. This implied from the outset that he would have to abandon any notion of an independent Tibet.

When he was consulted about the desirability of engaging in a dialogue with China, the Dalai Lama agreed; in his reply to the Chinese, he offered to send a few preparatory Tibetan missions. Headed by Lobsang Samten, another one of his brothers, the first delegation toured Tibet in January 1979. The proposal called for a total of four delegations to take stock of the situation in Tibet. The first one met with an emotional welcome everywhere it went. Prodigious crowds of Tibetans lined its path and thronged to meet the delegates in the towns and villages. Scenes of hysteria were a daily occurrence, to the utter dismay of the Chinese in attendance. Sobbing Tibetans begged to be told when the Dalai Lama would return. Others, on the contrary, warned that he should not be allowed to fall into the clutches of the Chinese.

The second delegation visited Tibet in May 1980. Its passage through Lhasa created so much excitement, and the overwrought people were so haunted by memories of 1959 that the Chinese authorities panicked and decided to cut the visit short. The third delegation, also present in Tibet at the time, had to pack its bags as well. A fourth delegation visited Peking in 1982. It was composed of three important members of the Dalai Lama's cabinet and its mission was to clear the way for genuine negotiations with its Chinese counterparts. It was a total failure from the start, and so was a fifth delegation that spent some time in Peking in 1984.

Were the Chinese genuinely sincere? Were they merely playing for time? Were they prepared to make any real concessions? Or were they hoping to get the Dalai Lama back in China where they could neutralize him again as they had in 1959? A former Chairman of the Assembly of Tibetan People's Deputies (the parliament in exile) Lodi Gyaltsen Gyari, who served briefly as 'minister of foreign affairs' in the Dalai Lama's cabinet in the late 1980s, was a member of the last two delegations. During an interview at his home in Dharamsala in October 1988, he recalled the circumstances surrounding his two visits to Peking.

'This is my impression after making the two trips: whether the Chinese actually had some specific ideas to put forward or whether they were just in a tight spot for reasons of domestic policy, they were basically in no position to make any proposals. Was it never their intention at all? They just played a sort of game designed to captivate our attention for awhile, while they pursued their policy of demographic aggression in Tibet. I'm afraid that seems to be China's final solution to the Tibetan problem, unfortunately.'

During the meetings held with the last two delegations, the Chinese team was led by Xi Zhongxun from the Chinese Communist Party's Politburo, Yang Jingren and Wu Jinghua. Soon afterwards, Wu Jinghua was appointed Party Secretary in Tibet. The Tibetan delegation felt cheated and used by the Chinese, who had cleverly manipulated the media to create a false impression about the meaning of the visits for the edification of the Tibetan and Chinese public. One day during the second visit, without any consultations about inviting the press to the talks, the Tibetan delegation was suddenly ushered into a room packed with Chinese journalists. The trap had been sprung, and the Tibetan delegation was filmed side by side with the Chinese delegation. The Chinese explained to the journalists that the government in Peking, in a spirit of reconciliation, was going to allow the Dalai Lama to return: in fact, if the Dalai Lama behaved himself in the future, the government would go so far as to reward him with the post of Vice-Chairman of the National People's Congress.

That, Lodi Gyaltsen Gyari recalls, 'quite naturally led observers to believe that there had been nothing on our agenda during the discussions other than the return of the Dalai Lama and furthermore, it showed the Chinese treating us like little children: If you behave now, if you don't act naughtily like you did before, we'll let you come back.'

Opening Tibet to tourism

At the very same time as it sounded out the possibility of finding common ground with the Dalai Lama, the Chinese government decided on another major measure: Tibet's doors were thrown open to Western tourists. This was to have tremendous consequences that the Chinese Government had undoubtedly not anticipated and for which it had definitely not provided. Since 1950, with only extremely rare exceptions, no one besides a handful of Soviet advisers and harmless 'friends of China' had been allowed to travel to China's Tibet. Starting in 1981,

Lhasa was declared an open area accessible to tourists. Only a 'routing certificate' (*luxingzheng*) was required to purchase an air ticket to Lhasa. Several hundred lucky travellers rushed to Tibet, paying premium prices for organized tours with the inescapable official guides.

Their numbers grew rapidly. In 1987, China earned 130 million yuan (35 million dollars) from the 43,000 tourists who visited Tibet. In the Lhasa offices of *Luxingshe*, the Chinese tourist company, shiny new graphs displayed the unlimited growth potential of State income derived from tourism in Tibet. In 1985, the person responsible for Tibet's tourist industry, a Han, told me that official forecasts predicted that the number of foreign tourists would reach the fabulous total of 500,000 in 1990! In Lhasa and Shigatse and a few other towns, hotels were feverishly built in record time, to a standard of luxury unheard of in Tibet. Teams of workers were imported from China to build the prestigious Lhasa Hotel, right opposite the Workers' Cultural Palace. It hardly needs to be said that its design owes nothing to Tibetan architecture. What is more, and this can hardly be a fortuitous occurrence, the Chinese designers managed to orient the building so that none of the rooms have a view of the Potala! To compensate, perhaps, they provided a tea lounge called The Rambo Room and decorated with a poster of Sylvester Stallone.

In order to feed the exotic fantasies of the 'foreign friends', greater efforts were made to promote the restoration of some monasteries and temples. A quick coat of paint was splashed on the facades and pillared porches of a number of haphazardly renovated structures. The achingly empty halls of the formerly holy buildings were decorated with brand-new plaster Buddhas. Inevitably, the new tourist attractions had an ersatz look. The Chinese government claims that it has spent over 43 million yuan from State coffers for the reconstruction and restoration of more than 1,400 monasteries and temples. Starting in 1989, it decided to earmark 40 million yuan payable in several stages for repairs to the Potala.[9] In reality, the Tibetans were only too happy to participate in the rehabilitation of their patrimony and contributed a great deal of money themselves. Tibetan artists volunteered their time and skills – to retouch the frescos, to regild a roof.

Most Chinese, try as they will, simply fail to understand why Tibet is so fascinating to Westerners, why they find it so moving. But rather than wonder, Peking decided to turn Tibet into a Mecca for wealthy tourists around the world. Why not let those loud, overweight Americans come, so long as they leave their precious foreign currency in Tibet!

Other, unavowed, hopes may have also motivated Chinese strategists; many are keenly aware that a tourist invasion in Tibet will sooner or later put paid to Tibetan traditions. Where the violence of the cultural revolution failed utterly, mass tourism will succeed. Has any country in the world survived intact the onslaught of hundreds and thousands of tourists? They often lack the most elementary respect for local traditions and customs. The power of money and the seductions of western materialism will soon corrode even the most rebellious society, thought the Chinese decision-makers. China – who will blame it – charges premium prices to travel agents who advertise the 'marvels of eternal Tibet' and the 'treasures of the Roof of the World'. A package tour to China that includes a few days in Tibet is seldom to be had for less than £1,700.

In the USA and Europe, Tibet has become a fashionable destination. But for a few tourists, the price of a stay in Shangri-La is more than they can afford. The long voyage by air, the sudden exposure to the altitude and other rigours of the Tibetan plateau can overtax the capacity of an elderly person used to the comfort of an apartment in Paris or New York. Every summer, the Chinese airline flies back to Peking with the coffins of those whose heart was not strong enough.

Starting in 1985, Lhasa was opened to individual tourists. Gradually, other Tibetan towns were added to the list of open cities in the People's Republic. Tibet became the destination of choice for the horde of young travellers who wander around the world with backpacks, looking for new thrills. The road to Katmandu now continued on to Lhasa. Often travelling solo, intrepid young men and women with or without permits probed the farthest reaches of Tibet, sometimes spending months on end quite happily and illegally roaming from village to village, in places where no white faces had ever been seen before. After the first moment of amazement on both sides, they were given a remarkably warm welcome by the Tibetans. In a very easy and natural way, a feeling of closeness developed between these welcome strangers and the local people. Having seen the massive destruction in Tibet, how could anyone help feeling sympathy for the Tibetans?

Just as an organized tour can only yield the most fleeting impressions of Tibet, travelling alone encourages the development of a genuine interaction with the Tibetans. For the first time, Westerners and Tibetans, two peoples who had not met before, looked deep into each others' eyes. Protected from eavesdroppers in the dark gloom of the temples and monasteries halls, the monks delighted in describing to the visitors what the situation was like in Tibet. Their version, of course, had nothing in common with the inevitable paeans in the brochures from Chinese tourist offices. In order to develop these precious contacts, hundreds of young monks stayed up late to study English.

In private homes as well, over steaming bowls of butter tea, tales were told about the hated omnipresence of the Chinese. A Western traveller would have had to be deaf not to hear at least once the whispered phrase 'Chinese no good!' The more curious visitors compiled quantities of invaluable first-hand testimony about the history of the thirty stormy years gone by. Having found an interested and mostly sympathetic audience for the first time since 1950, the Tibetans poured out their hopes and fears in a flood of words whenever the Chinese were out of earshot. Messages detailing human rights violations were slipped to visiting Western journalists notwithstanding the eagle eyes of their ubiquitous Chinese minders. After shaking hands with a Tibetan a tiny ball of paper would be left in your hand, right in front of the Chinese officials.

After decades of total isolation, the Tibetan people had found witnesses and a forum. The visitors revived their hopes. For the first time as well, the Tibetan tragedy awakened powerful echoes in the Western press. As for China, it realized, but too late, that the opening of Tibet had been a mistake.

Religion rises from its ashes

The new policy of greater religious tolerance adopted in 1979 was also extended to Tibet. It would be rash – not to say completely wrong – to talk about 'religious freedom', which is an expression that Peking affects and deploys in order to beguile international public opinion. The leadership of the Chinese Communist Party has certainly not relinquished the hope of eliminating all religions, the opium of the people. A close look at the Chinese official press is very edifying: 'according to Marxism, religion comes under the ideological system of idealism. It is categorically opposed to dialectical materialism and historical materialism.' '... it cannot be abolished by fiat. It takes patient, meticulous and repeated education over a long period of time to weaken its influence. Religion cannot be completely abolished until the future, upon the attainment of certain stage in the development of communist society.'[10] The rules of the game could not be more clearly stated.

Thanks to a programme for the reconstruction and restoration of the principal monasteries in Tibet, the Land of Snow is experiencing something that resembles religious activity. The Chinese media make believe that things are almost like they were: '[e]verywhere you can see clouds of incense spiralling up from the monasteries. The butter lamps burn night and day in front of the Buddhist statues. Crowds of the faithful walk around the monasteries and prostrate in the streets to pray. Most Tibetan families have shrines for Buddha statues and the rolls (sic) of sutras are openly displayed.' 'China implements a policy of religious freedom. The Tibetan Lamaists can freely carry out their religious activities. They can install shrines in their homes or build sutra-chanting halls for daily prayers. They can also go to any monastery to pray and make offerings. The celebration of the different religious activities is also permitted.' According to Peking, there are some 34,000 monks in Tibet's monasteries,[11] the youngest aged barely sixteen.

There is no gainsaying that starting in 1979, the Chinese authorities considerably loosened the ideological straitjacket and decreased police surveillance. By loosening their grip on the reins ever so slightly, they hoped to stay in overall control of the process of relative liberalization. But they had neglected to take into account the Tibetans' attachment to their religion and their deep spiritual yearning. The religion had the effect of a cultural leaven and twenty years of Chinese presence had hardly made a dent in their faith. As soon as the new policy came into force, hundreds of thousands of Tibetans, young and old, rural and urban, workers and intellectuals, nomads and farmers, all went back to their practices, which can appear to us to hark back to the beginning of time.

In front of the Jokhang temple in Lhasa, many questions jostled each other in my mind as I watched the extraordinary spectacle of the crowds of pilgrims who prostrate over and over with seemingly boundless energy and inexpressible devotion. In a swift movement, the faithful raise their hands folded in prayer first to the crown of their head, then lower them in front of their face, then to the level of the heart; dropping to their knees, they stretch full-length on the floor with outstretched arms and press their forehead to the ground. Other pilgrims remain standing, their prayer-wheels spinning uninterruptedly, endlessly murmuring mantras such as *Om Mani Padme Hum* or praises to the Buddha. All day long, pilgrims measure their length in prostrations on the circuit known as the Little Barkhor that surrounds the Jokhang temple and along the Big Barkhor around Lhasa. For mile after mile they prostrate lying full-length in the dust, rise up and walk a few steps and prostrate again, tirelessly, with their prayer beads firmly clutched in one hand, elbows and knees scratched and bleeding. Peasants arrive on foot from distant regions, wearing on their chests the charm-boxes, amulets and other relics that are supposed to protect them from adversity. Blind faith? Fanaticism? Remnants of a feudal past? I leave the answers to others; as far as I can see, this shows that in Tibet, the transplanted ideology definitely did not take.

Just as they used to do before 1950, many Tibetans scrimp and save in order to make generous offerings of money and yak butter to the monasteries. Some families will borrow money to buy butter for the thousands of lamps that flicker and glow in the holy places of Tibet. Before the turmoil in 1987 and 1988, the monasteries had to some extent resumed their pre-1959 function as religious universities, but on an infinitely smaller scale, if only because of the small number of monks. The Chinese have never permitted novices to enrol freely. The number of Lamas and trapas is not one-tenth of what is was before 1959. Nevertheless, despite constant Chinese surveillance, the monks were getting back to the study of the Dharma. Once again, one might come across an open-air debate session, where hundreds of monks arrayed in pairs or in small groups mutually test and sharpen their theological knowledge by firing long strings of questions at each other in an atmosphere of friendly emulation.

When the Panchen Lama was allowed to return to Tibet in 1982, for the first time since 1964, his appearances in public provoked scenes of surreal devotion. When he visited Lhasa for the second time in August 1985, I saw Tibetans suddenly start shaking, going into a sort of trance at the mere sight of the religious leader wrapped in his brown gown trimmed with gold brocade. The news of his arrival travelled all over the city. When the people heard that he would bless the faithful in the Jokhang the next day, an impressive queue formed during the night. By early morning, it had grown several miles long, under the nervous gaze of the Chinese police armed with electric cattle-prods. The Panchen Lama may have consented to collaborate with the Chinese, but it had not affected his religious charisma in Tibet.

It was open season on Dalai Lama photographs. Any foreigner arriving in a village would quickly be surrounded by a crowd of children chanting 'Dalai Lama picture, Dalai Lama picture'. If you gave one to a monk, he would raise it to the crown of his head then hold it to his lips, his face suddenly transfigured with ecstatic joy. The photograph of Tenzin Gyatso decorates every altar of every monastery and every sanctuary. Photos of the Panchen Lama and other important Lamas of the Tibetan religious pantheon are systematically placed in the background. If Chinese leaders still cherished any doubts, they were compelled to acknowledge that the Dalai Lama's prestige had not suffered one iota from twenty years of Communism. Quite the contrary: if anything, his absence had magnified his aura for his people. The Communist Party's insults and verbal attacks had not even scratched the surface. He always had been, and he remained, the God-King of all Tibetans. Many of his subjects decry the wisdom of his recent overtures to China; yet I doubt that any Tibetan would fail to show him respect, highlighting ever more sharply the glaring ineffectiveness of the ideological lobotomy that the Chinese government has tried to perform in Tibet. The renaissance of religion was the manifestation of another phenomenon that Peking did not fully grasp in time; it reflected a profound revival of Tibetan nationalism. Apparently, the Communist leadership has never been able to comprehend the power of the nationalistic feelings that burn in the hearts of the Tibetans. The arrogance and contempt displayed by so many Chinese cadres and their inability to fathom the soul of the Tibetans were paving the way for another disaster.

Within the moderate faction of the Communist Party, in power since 1978, some of the more enlightened Chinese leaders must have aspired to restore the trust between the Chinese and the Tibetan people. Others hoped a historic compromise would emerge. But in Tibet itself, the wilfully impervious Chinese bureaucracy rendered any such mission impossible. On more than one occasion, the Peking government has criticized 'the survival of leftist influences' in Tibet, a piece of Communist jargon that refers to cadres who were promoted during the cultural revolution, and who, far from Peking, obstinately cling to their jobs in the Party and local government of Tibet. The post-1979 purges in China that cleared away the cadres afflicted with Maoist nostalgia hardly had any effect in Tibet. In his 1987 statement the Panchen Lama criticizes the cadres in Tibet, saying that 'many among them ... still have not got over their leftist hangover, and are guilty of atrocities during the cultural revolution'. The outward calm in Tibet indicated a storm was brewing, but China had no inkling.

The anti-Chinese explosion of 1987

Act One: on 21 September 1987, the Dalai Lama's ten-day visit to the USA took on a very special character when the local Tibetan lobby's efforts produced a warm welcome from the House Committee on Foreign Affairs of the American Congress. Addressing this august body for the first time, the Dalai Lama made a landmark statement advocating dialogue and moderation. It contained a Peace Plan based on five points:

1. All of Tibet would be transformed into a zone of peace. Buddhist Tibet would draw on its peaceable traditions to resume its role as a buffer-state between the great regional powers.
2. China would relinquish all policies designed to transfer the Chinese population to Tibet.
3. Respect for human rights and fundamental freedoms in Tibet: the Chinese government would release the thousands of political and religious prisoners it holds; the Tibetan people would be left free to determine their own future in a spirit of openness and reconciliation.
4. Tibet's natural environment would be restored and protected. China would renounce programmes to deploy nuclear weapons and store nuclear wastes in Tibet.
5. The opening of frank negotiations on Tibet's future status and on the relations between the Chinese and the Tibetan people.

Eight members of the American Congress publicly voiced their support for the Dalai Lama's initiative and wrote to the Chinese Prime Minister, who was Zhao Ziyang at that time. The anger of the Chinese government knew no bounds at the unprecedented success of the Dalai Lama's visit to the USA. It accused the American Congress of flagrant interference in China's internal affairs. The Chinese Minister of Foreign Affairs produced an extremely lengthy statement in which he expressed his regrets and strong dissatisfaction with the US government's failure to prevent the Dalai Lama from indulging in political activities in the United States.

Act Two: on 24 September 1987, the Chinese government organized a huge public trial in Lhasa. Fifteen thousand Tibetans were herded into the Triyue Trang stadium to watch eight Tibetans being sentenced to terms in jail. Two others were condemned to death. One of them, Kelsang Tashi, was executed on the spot with a bullet in the back of his neck; the other, Sonam Gyaltsen, was dealt with in the same fashion two days later. Peking claims that the two victims were murderers. Exiled Tibetans maintain that the two men paid for their commitment to Tibetan independence with their lives. The Chinese Communist regime has a tradition of holding public trials in stadiums, which it considers to be a very effective way of educating the people. Some Tibetans feel the trial was the Chinese government's response to the Dalai Lama's visit to the USA; many see it as the signal that triggered off the impending revolt.

Act Three: in late September 1987, posters appeared on the walls of Lhasan homes and office buildings. Credible testimony indicates that they were pasted up by foreigners. The posters set out the text of a resolution adopted on 16 June 1987 by the Human Rights Sub-Commission of the US House of Representatives. China stood accused of violating human rights in Tibet, and in particular, it was held responsible for the death of a million Tibetans since 1950.

Final Act: only six days after the Dalai Lama's statement in Washington and three days after the trial, something happened in Lhasa that caught the Chinese authorities completely by surprise. On a sunny Sunday morning, dozens of foreign tourists were wandering peacefully around the city. A number of them were contemplating the treasures of the Jokhang, in the heart of the old town. Hundreds of pilgrims from all over Tibet had gathered as usual on the square in front of the Jokhang, after a long journey by bus or by truck, on foot or on horseback. It was 10 a.m. Suddenly, twenty-six monks clad in their long maroon robes started running around the temple, holding up the blue, red, white and yellow flag of free Tibet. Two roaring lions face each other in front of three snow mountains (symbolizing U-Tsang, Amdo and Kham) and the Tibetan Buddhist Wheel of the Law. In front of the gaping bystanders, they shouted 'Tibet wants independence!' and 'Chinese leave Tibet!'. Running along the Barkhor, the group circled the Jokhang five times, then veered towards the seat of the People's Government of the Tibet Autonomous Region. The entire performance had taken less than an hour.

Once they had recovered from their surprise, the police arrested the demonstrators. Although *Xinhua* usually doesn't mention inter-ethnic incidents in China, it did issue an account two days later. Since the cultural revolution, nothing of the sort had taken place in Lhasa. On the next day, Ngapo Ngawang Jigme, as Vice-Chairman of the National People's Congress, explained that 'the troublemakers were an isolated group that did not enjoy the support of the people'. A certain dose of courage was required for those few Tibetans to dare to defy China's power openly and to voice their desire for independence. That small group of protesters must have known the type of exemplary punishment that awaited them for having done something that Peking considers tantamount to treason. But this first alert merely pointed to a much more dangerous outbreak of violence.

Less than a week later, still reeling from the first affront, the Peking leadership was dealt an even more powerful blow. On 1 October 1987, all of China was celebrating the thirty-eighth anniversary of the People's Republic. In Peking the atmosphere was relaxed, for the National Day is also a public holiday. Since 1949, 1 October has been a traditional opportunity for cadres to feast at State expense and to congratulate each other on the giant steps taken on the road to socialism. But this particular 1 October was about to become a nightmare for Peking. In Lhasa, conversely, it was a day of great joy. Starting early in the morning, the hotline that permanently connects the centres of power throughout China didn't stop ringing.

By about nine o'clock in the morning, several hundred Tibetans had gathered as usual on the square in front of the Jokhang. Following their daily routine, pilgrims walked around the temple reciting the mantra *Om Mani Padme Hum.* There were a few monks in purple robes. Beggars too, an overpowering smell rising from their dirty clothes and pock-marked skin. There were also a great many Westerners. Their eyewitness testimony concurs: all of a sudden, forty or so monks flew out of the Jokhang, each one holding a small Tibetan national flag and shouting slogans against the Chinese presence in Tibet. They started marching around the temple, shouting: 'Tibet is a free and independent nation!' This time the police response was almost immediate. A few minutes later, most of the demonstrators were being dragged into the nearby police station, a three-storey building that dominates the square, the better to keep a permanent eye on the situation.

A great clamour rose from the crowd. Soon several thousand Tibetans were crowding around the entrance of the police station. A hail of stones rained down on the building. A hundred more police arrived as reinforcements, of which perhaps fifty were carrying AK-47 machine-guns, a Chinese copy of the Soviet model, made in China and exported around the world. In Tibet, public order is not the province of the police but of the People's Armed Police, special paramilitary units deployed to protect official buildings, embassies and foreign residences. The confrontation went on for several hours. The atmosphere grew increasingly tense, but for the armed forces there was no question of releasing the demonstrators.

Outside, the Armed Police faced the crowd in front of the gate, only a few feet separating the hostile camps. The Chinese police were facing thousands of men, women and children who were screaming their hatred of all things Chinese. A hatred further inflamed by the recent arrests. A hatred that could no longer be contained. Children threw stones at the helmeted men. At one point, a twelve year-old boy found a rifle that a policeman had dropped in flight. Grabbing it by the barrel, he struck it on the ground until the butt shattered into pieces. The police did not move a muscle, petrified by the unimaginable scene. But their distorted features revealed their fear of the riot yet to come. To protect themselves, they moved a dozen vehicles into position around the building.

The Tibetans set them on fire. In a moment, thick black clouds of smoke rose up to the sky. Then the police station itself caught fire. Long flames darted from the windows. The police raised their weapons and the sound of automatic gunfire rang around the square. The first shots were presumably warnings, fired over the heads of the crowd. It was a policeman standing on the roof of the building who first fired directly into the crowd. He was deliberately aiming at living targets. Then the machine-gun fire was directed straight at the Tibetans. Several people fell to the ground and blood ran brightly in the street.

Some of the monks and laymen who were being held in the burning police station managed to escape through the windows. Several were shot dead on the spot. 'I saw three dead in front of the temple. One was a young boy shot in the back, another was a man shot in the heart and a third died from head injuries', declares Dr William Kerr, from Buffalo, New York. 'I saw one man lying on the ground with a piece of his skull blown off and blood pouring out of his head', states Lars Petersson, a Swedish traveller from Kristinehamm. Leon Schadeberg from London reports that another Tibetan who looked about fifteen years old was hit in the head and died on the way to the hospital. 'He died as I was watching him. Blood was spewing from his mouth.' Another eyewitness recalls: 'a woman came up to me and led me into a small alley nearby. She told me in Chinese that a person had been wounded and was dying, and she wanted me to take a photograph. The man was lying on a cart. He was twenty-five and had been wounded in the chest. Quantities of blood were pouring out of his mouth and nose. The crowd parted to let me take a picture of the dying man. I took several. It was enough for me.'

When the blood bath started, the confusion became an uproar in the vicinity of the Jokhang. The clatter of the Chinese weapons sowed panic in the ranks of the Tibetan protesters. Many fled. Others stood their ground despite the danger. Tibetans beat and pummelled policemen in plain clothes who had been posted on a nearby roof and were recording the scene with video cameras. Their equipment was smashed to bits. The crowd placed the body of a dead Tibetan on a board and lifted it above their heads. They charged at the police, who yielded and let them through. Many Tibetans turned to the foreigners who were present and asked them to bear witness to the events, to photograph them and inform the world. 'We are fighting the Chinese', a Tibetan told a German tourist. 'Many Tibetans told us they were very happy this was happening', another tourist reported. In the neighbourhood shops, Tibetans harassed Chinese civilians. The whole Tibetan quarter was caught up in the rioting. Stones flew back and forth for several hours, keeping the fire-fighters away from the burning police station. Around one o'clock in the afternoon, the roof collapsed with a tremendous crash, to the applause of the crowd. It continued to burn right through the night.

The young Tibetan who died on Jokhang square had a brother called Sonam Tseten. He is a refugee now, living at the Tibetan Children's Village in Dharamsala. The day I went to meet him at the school, I found myself talking to a child who stood before me with lowered eyes, shy in the presence of a stranger. He was still wearing his worn Chinese trousers and jacket. It was particularly difficult to interview him for he was still in a state of shock, as the Director told me.

— What's your name?
— My name is Sonam Tseten.
— How old are you?
— Eleven.
— When did you arrive here?
— In 1987. I can't remember which month.
— Can you describe to me what happened the day your brother was killed?
— I saw all the monks of Sera monastery arriving. Many came. Maybe 200.

Sonam Tseten breaks off. Outside, his schoolmates are playing in the yard in between classes. We can hear them distinctly.

— Do you know that your brother was hit by a bullet and killed?
— Yes, I know.
— How did it happen?
— It all happened during the demonstration. My brother was also pro-testing. A friend of my brother's was fighting with the Chinese. They were fighting, hitting each other. My brother tried to keep his friend from fighting with the Chinese. That was when he was hit in the head. He died almost straight away.
— How old was he?
— My brother Khasel was about eighteen.
— Did you also throw stones?
— I was with my own group. We were also protesting. I spotted a mo-torcycle and we set it on fire. Some of us took petrol from the bike's tank and set it alight. There were six or seven of us. The Chinese were busy trying to stop the demonstration. The motorcycle had been left behind.
— Why did you do that?
— The older boys had said that everything that belonged to the Chi-nese had to be burned. So we set fire to the motorcycle.

—Do you think that was the right thing to do?

Sonam doesn't know what to say.

—What happened to your brother when he was hit?
—He died almost straight away. He was hit in the head. We put him on a stretcher and we took his body to be incinerated. The Chinese didn't object to that.
—What do you feel when you think about those events?
—I feel sad.
—Where are your parents?
—In Tibet.
—Was an apology offered to them?
—No, there was none.
—Are you happy here?

Sonam says nothing but nods his head in assent.

—What do you want to do when you grow up?
—I want to be a monk.
—What does your father do in Lhasa? Do you get letters from him?
—He is a farmer. I don't get mail from him.
—Do you have brothers and sisters?
—Yes, I have a brother at Bir (near Dharamsala). He is older than twenty. He arrived a few years ago. Sometimes he comes here to see me. I'm very fond of him.
—What are you learning here?
—I'm learning Tibetan, English, maths and science.
—Who brought you here?
—My father took me to Khassa (on the border with Nepal). We met Nepalese who dressed me in clothes like theirs and then took me to Nepal. I have an uncle in Nepal. He brought me here. At the end of last year.
—Do you hate the Chinese?
—Yes. I hate them.
—Do you want revenge?
—Yes.

On the day of the protest, the Chinese authorities shut down almost every telephone and telex line from Lhasa to Peking. It became that much more complicated for correspondents in Peking to get information about the situation in Lhasa, which of course was the whole point. Several journalists did manage to reach Lhasa by the next day. Oblivious to the growing amount of testimony, the Chinese Government started out by denying energetically that the police had fired into the crowd. Two days after the protests, *Xinhua* announced that Tibetan demonstrators had 'seized the policemen's weapons' and fired on them. A little bit later, a Chinese spokesman for the local government, reached by telephone, admitted that 'several policemen who did not know how to use their weapons might have let a few shots go off' in the direction of the protesters. But, he added, their instructions had been to fire in the air. On Friday night, the walls of Lhasa were covered with posters that said: 'Twenty people have died, there will have to be many more!' and 'Let us seize this opportunity, Chinese go back to China!' In a new official version of the events, *Xinhua* explained that 'some shots were heard in the confusion'. It went on to say that the protests had been 'fomented and prepared' by the Dalai Lama's followers. 'The riot is considered to be the direct result of the Dalai Lama's actions to split the motherland.' It added that, at the beginning of the demonstration, 'some rioters ran through the streets, knocking on the doors of the houses and shouting: "The Dalai Lama is giving back its independence to Tibet and we should all follow him. Those who refuse to join the demonstration will find their houses destroyed."'

The hero of the day was Venerable Jampa Tenzin. The daring and valour of the forty-nine-year-old monk have made him famous: braving the raging flames, he raced inside the police station to rescue his detained compatriots. Later on, with serious burns on several parts of his body, he was raised up on the shoulders of the crowd and paraded in triumph through Lhasa. A photograph that shows him raising his fist in a sign of victory, long strips of burned flesh dangling from his arm, has travelled around the world. He was initially arrested, then set free a few months later at the express request of the Panchen Lama. On the night of 22 February 1992, he died in peculiar circumstances. According to the local police, he was found dead in his bed at the Jokhang temple, with a thin rope tied around his neck and wound around one of the feet of the bed. The police decided it was a suicide. Other sources argue that suicide can be ruled out. Jampa Tenzin had never renounced his beliefs and he continued to approach foreign tourists whenever possible in order to tell them about the situation in Tibet. They are convinced that he was cold-bloodedly assassinated by the local police.[12]

The Chinese government announced that six persons had been killed, all of them policemen. When correlated, the reports by foreign witnesses indicated thirteen deaths – six Chinese policemen and seven Tibetans – as well as dozens of injured people. Most of the injured Tibetans refused to go to hospitals for treatment, out of fear of immediate arrest. The Western journalists who did manage to reach Lhasa on Friday and Saturday, after the rioting, saw dozens of Tibetans engaged in destroying and sacking the burned-out police station. On Monday, despite an overnight curfew imposed by the authorities and severe police surveillance, the main Lhasa monasteries such as Sera, Drepung and Ganden managed to smuggle an appeal to the United Nations to the foreign journalists. 'The Chinese rule our country through violence and we want them to leave Tibet. We call upon the United Nations and all the countries of the world to support our just cause. We are suffering. We Tibetans always recognize the Dalai Lama as our leader. We hope that people who defend respect for human rights will come to Tibet to see for themselves.' Other posters encouraged the people to 'carry on the struggle'. On Monday, the official English-language *China Daily*, published in Peking, printed more broadsides against the Dalai Lama and affirmed that the blood bath in Lhasa had provoked the 'disgust of the Tibetan people and the condemnation of the local Chinese authorities'. 'Despite the forgiveness and the well-meaning advice conveyed to him by the Chinese government, the Dalai Lama has appointed himself as the advocate of Tibetan independence. His undertaking is doomed to failure', the newspaper added. On the same day, Chinese Communist Party spokesman Wu Xingtang accused foreigners of helping the partisans of Tibetan independence.

Once again, the Chinese government was caught napping. On the day after the turmoil, in Chengdu, I interviewed the Director of the local office of Tibetan affairs, Gesan Namjie. He informed me that neither the Chinese Communist Party Secretary nor the Governor of Tibet were in Lhasa on the day of the disaster. Wu Jinghua, the Party Secretary, the real strongman in Tibet, had been in Peking since September, helping to prepare a forthcoming Party congress. As for Doje Cering, governor and representative of the government on the high Himalayan plateau, he had been undergoing treatment for two months at the Military Hospital in Peking. Many other important cadres from Lhasa had also returned 'inside' for the celebrations pertaining to the thirty-eighth anniversary of the founding of the People's Republic. The ensuing paralysis of the power structure in Lhasa produced a catastrophe when the cadres left behind inherited the crisis.

Gesam Namjie was Tibetan, but he soon let me know that the protesters were all 'counter-revolutionaries' against whom the Chinese Communist had the duty to perform 'class struggle'. This type of political vocabulary had almost lapsed into oblivion, but it was now being revived, eleven years after the death of Mao Tse-tung. 'Class struggle still exists in China in certain situations. In a case like this, we have to apply it against a minority of separatists in Tibet who are trying to split the country. They are counter-revolutionaries!'

Five days after the protests, I saw two important cadres from the Department of Propaganda of the Chinese Ministry of Foreign Affairs on the flight from Peking to Lhasa via Chengdu. One of them was Liu Rucai, a high-level official in charge of political work. They told me they were flying to Lhasa 'to understand the situation'. The Chinese airline, CAAC, was ordered on Monday not to sell any more tickets to Lhasa to foreigners. 'This is to stop you from spreading information about Tibet' a CAAC employee informed me. Westerners who had remained in Lhasa heard police sirens wailing in the streets of the Tibetan part of town, while the shops in the Chinese areas closed earlier than usual. The terrified Chinese were locking themselves in before dark. In the Tibetan quarter, the raids took place between midnight and two in the morning. Small, unmarked vans would stop in front of Tibetan homes and take the inhabitants to an unknown destination. It was said that the police had lists of names and photographs of wanted Tibetans and others who were suspected of having had something to do with the demonstrations.

Two flights, each ferrying a hundred officers and policemen, landed in Lhasa on Sunday. Another one landed on Monday. On that same day, a Canadian television team saw a convoy of twelve trucks loaded with People's Armed Police on the road to the Lhasa airport. Starting from the day after the protests, about thirty plain clothes police were posted on the roof of the Jokhang while entire columns of the People's Armed Police took up positions in the vicinity of the larger monasteries. Armed and helmeted policemen were visible on the roof of the buildings surrounding the square, ready to intervene at a moment's notice. Several dozen policemen erected barricades to impede access to Drepung, Sera and Ganden. Simultaneously, 'work teams' composed of Chinese cadres and policemen in civilian garb took up residence inside the monasteries, embarking on a long effort to 're-educate' the monks. The hunt for the leaders went on. From the beginning of the next week, vans equipped with loudspeakers criss-crossed Lhasa all day long. Appeals were broadcast calling upon the people to 'uphold the unity of the motherland' and 'denounce the separatists'. At Gonggar airport, the highly visible People's Armed Police kept a close watch on foreigners leaving Tibet. On the outskirts of Lhasa, they guarded the main highways, which were all closed except for the road to the airport.

Notwithstanding the awesome apparatus of repression, another demonstration occurred on 6 October 1987. Sixty or so monks from Drepung, wearing lay clothes to slip past the watchful police, headed towards the town centre in mid-afternoon, hoping to reach the seat of the local government and call for the release of their detained brethren. About thirty were arrested at the edge of the town, in front of the Workers' Cultural Palace. Westerners witnessed the brutality with which they were treated. The police beat them with clubs and with the butts of their rifles. They were all thrown into trucks and driven away. The remainder reached the government building, where a dozen army trucks and police armed with machine-guns had been stationed. They were all beaten and arrested. On 8 October, the fourteen foreign press correspondents who were in Lhasa were given forty-eight hours to leave Tibet. Mr Yu Wuzhen, Director of the Tibet Autonomous Region's Department of Foreign Affairs, accused the press of having contravened article 16 of a set of regulations governing the work of foreign correspondents in China.

The article requires every foreign journalist to inform the local authorities in China, at least ten days ahead of time, of any movement outside
Peking. I can vouch for the fact that those rules had not been invoked
by the Chinese government for quite a few years. It became increasingly
obvious that they were trying to get rid of inconvenient witnesses. After
all, it is traditional in China to 'beat the dog behind closed doors' (*guanmen
dagou*).

The police gave Tibetans who had participated in the demonstrations until 15 October to turn themselves in. They were promised leniency. Those who did not would feel the weight of the full force of the
law. On 8 October Nepal announced that China had closed the border.
On the same day, Thailand announced that it had refused to grant a
visa to the Dalai Lama, who had been invited to attend a Buddhist
symposium. The Thais swore this had nothing to do with Chinese
pressure.

On 12 October, *Zhongguo Xinwen* (China News), a Chinese press agency
that is *Xinhua*'s (New China) competitor, published its own 'official' version
of the events. Here is an extract: 'During the unrest on 1 October, eleven
still cameras and three video cameras were smashed and destroyed, eleven
vehicles and four motorcycles were set on fire and destroyed and twenty-
seven vehicles were smashed and damaged. Direct losses are estimated
at over two million yuan. During the unrest, some 350 police were injured
by thrown rocks. Nine were severely wounded and six were killed. An
official of the Autonomous Region has explained that "a handful of people
incited the masses, ignorant of the truth, to split the motherland, in
coordination with the Dalai Lama who was directing them from afar.
Their criminal plotting will never succeed."'

What a strange account this is, that lists material losses ahead of
human lives! Should this be taken as a measure of the value that the
Chinese Communist regime assigns to human beings? This report does
not even mention any Tibetan victims.

On 16 October 1987, Deng Xiaoping publicly mentioned the events
in Tibet for the first time: 'The Dalai Lama and a few members of the
American Congress have created a few small problems for us, but this
will not affect our overall situation, which is good. On the contrary, this
has exposed their ignorance and their arrogance and has shed light on
their real nature.' A few days earlier, the Dalai Lama had voiced his
profound grief. He added, however: 'I am glad that the Chinese government have found in me a scapegoat for the Tibetan people's demonstration in Tibet just as they blamed the "Gang of Four" for the
madness and chaos during the Cultural Revolution. I appeal to all human
rights groups to prevail upon the Chinese government to stop the executions and to release those imprisoned.'

Three weeks later, the 13th Congress of the Chinese Communist Party
was held in Peking. A congress is one of the most important events in

the life of a communist party. The 13th Congress was of paramount importance to the reformist wing of the regime, under the leadership of Zhao Ziyang. In the ferocious power struggle that has rent the Chinese Communist Party since its inception, this was an opportunity the reformists planned to use to triumph, once and for all, over the camp of the orthodox conservatives opposed to reform. In January 1987, the balance had swung towards the orthodox camp with the humiliating disgrace of Hu Yaobang, the Party leader ousted as a result of conservative pressure. He had been blamed and made to pay for the sweeping wave of dissent that had agitated the universities in December 1986. The disturbances in Tibet served to further consolidate the positions of the last living fossils of the revolution. They were able to maintain that the reform and open-door policies should be blamed for the chaos in Tibet. In addition to the negative impact of these events on China's image abroad, what effect would this deplorable example have on China's other minorities?

What little information transpired from the corridors of power in Peking indicates that the crisis in Lhasa did generate a lively debate within the Central Committee and the Politburo of the CCP. On the surface, the reformers triumphed during the Congress. In late October, a number of hardline Maoist purists were finally retired. China's open-door policy was forcefully restated and so was the commitment to reform. But there was no going back on what had happened in Lhasa. The police firing machine-guns into a crowd will live on in history as a painful symbol of the lack of understanding between two peoples.

1988, Lhasa: fire in the sky, blood in the streets

Faithful to its Celestial ancestry, China's Communist bureaucracy has a distinct fondness for *kaihui* – meetings. They are manifold, interminable and with honourable exceptions, useless. They account for the lion's share of the work of the average Chinese cadre. Cut him off from his *kaihui* and he will be lost in space. The events in Lhasa precipitated innumerable meetings in Peking. After much hesitation, in early 1988 the government decided to allow the Monlam Chenmo to be held in Lhasa. The Great Prayer Festival usually lasts eleven days, starting after the New Year celebrations according to the Tibetan lunar calendar. It is the most important religious festival in Tibet. Founded in 1409, the Monlam Chenmo was forbidden in the 1960s and it was only in 1987 that the authorities granted permission to revive the tradition. In 1988, Peking hoped a successful festival would make it easier to forget the other recent events. China wanted to refurbish its image by displaying to the world a pacified and 'stabilized' Tibet.

Every effort had been made to avoid an upsurge of nationalistic feeling. On 15 February, the Chinese Buddhist association, a body controlled by the authorities in Peking, warned the Tibetan population: 'During this period, insults and quarrelling must cease and people must treat each other with respect so that the lamp of Buddhism will shine on the summit of the world.' In mid-February, thousands of pilgrims started pouring into Lhasa. There were 20,000 by the 15th. The veneer of calm was deceptive; many of the faithful had been turned back at the outskirts of the city, particularly the Khampas who always top the list of undesirables.

No vehicle was allowed to circulate in Lhasa without a special permit. Special anti-riot units had been deployed several weeks before; several were stationed in the buildings surrounding the Jokhang. According to certain sources, 6,000 policemen were on active duty. The centre was swarming with plainclothes police and informers. On the roof of a building that dominates the Jokhang square, an early-warning system with video cameras and sophisticated radio broadcasting equipment was kept operating around the clock with look-outs permanently on the alert. In the monasteries, the 'work teams' had held countless meetings to educate the monks about the history of Tibet, patriotic feelings and the dangers of separatism. Many monks in the larger monasteries declined to attend the public gathering, saying they had no stomach for a celebration while their fellow-monks remained in jail, including the well-known Lama and academic Yulu Dawa Tsering, jailed since December 1987 for talking openly about Tibet's past history of freedom and the Chinese oppression with a visiting Italian tourist. The authorities bullied and bribed and promised to release some prisoners if the monks attended the public gathering and behaved appropriately.

From October 1987, access to Tibet was made much more difficult for western tourists and virtually impossible for journalists accredited in Peking. Towards the end of February, the Chinese government obviously felt it had done enough to ensure that the Monlam Chenmo would be a success, for it nonchalantly invited five foreign journalists to admire the smooth unfolding of the celebration that had begun some days before. Among the happy few were a correspondent from *Agence France-Presse*, two from Reuters and one from the *Los Angeles Times*. I went to Chengdu, hoping to benefit from the unexpected goodwill and travel to Lhasa on behalf of my agency. Alas, after hours of negotiations with the local authorities, I found out that I was not welcome in Tibet.

Everything went well at the Monlam Chenmo until the penultimate day. The government was already patting itself on the back. Things were were going so smoothly that four of the five journalists had already packed and left. Their editors thought nothing was going to happen. On 5 March, there was only the AFP correspondent, Patrick Lescot; the man from the *Los Angeles Times* had left in the early hours of the morning. A few hours later, Lhasa was on fire and blood ran in the streets.

On Saturday 5 March 1988, by five past nine, several hundred monks led by a few Lamas had congregated in the court of the Jokhang, transformed into an ocean of purple and gold. Twenty-five thousand worshippers sat in the square in front of the sanctuary. On this final day of the Monlam Chenmo, the only ceremony scheduled was called 'welcoming the Buddha Jampa', the Buddha of the Future, whose statue carved in wood would be carried around the Jokhang by a procession of Lamas and monks. Afterwards, the crowd was expected to disperse and the day would finish with a horse-race and dancing. But the monks had other plans. Instead of following the prescribed itinerary, some monks went boldly up to the dais where the authorities were sitting and challenged a Tibetan hardline collaborator, Deputy Party Secretary Ragti, to show the released prisoners, since the monks had kept their part of the bargain. The authorities, fear outweighing the ignominy, scrambled to their feet and fled. Amidst the clamour of the chanting, dozens of raised fists stabbed the air. Surging forward, the younger monks grabbed the microphones and the whole square rang with their shouts of 'Free Tibet! Free Tibet! Free Tibet! We want freedom for Tibet! Independence for Tibet! Independence for Tibet! Independence for Tibet! Independence for Tibet! Down with Chinese oppression! Down with Chinese oppression! Long live the Dalai Lama! Long live the Dalai Lama! Long live the Dalai Lama!'

The monks knew they were being filmed and videotaped by the Chinese security forces. They knew they had no chance of escaping their wrath. They knew the combat was desperately unequal. They knew Lhasa was hemmed in by six military camps and a trained army that could easily crush any revolt, however heroic.

Soon the stones were raining down on the police, so much in evidence around the temple. A few minutes later, several hundred monks started circling the temple. Thousands of Tibetans joined them, chanting nationalistic songs. From the roof of the Jokhang, monks dropped stones on the vehicles of the armed police and on the mobile unit belonging to the Lhasa television station that had been filming and broadcasting the Monlam Chenmo ceremonies. By then, no force on earth could have stopped the demonstration. Twenty minutes later, a dozen police vehicles arrived. It was another ten minutes before 2,000 armed police, helmeted and armed with bludgeons and shields, ringed the square and cleared the open area using tear gas grenades. A hundred monks were taken away in trucks. Shortly after noon, the security forces located the AFP correspondent and ordered him back to his hotel, where he was forced to stay for a few hours. Lhasa had already been cut off from the rest of the world. All the telephone and telex lines had been cut.

Soon afterwards, the air was filled with the distinctive rat-tat-tat of automatic weapons. The authorities had tried to avoid this extremity, for in the morning the police had not been armed. Six thousand Tibetans confronted the police for the rest of the afternoon. Numerous shops owned by Chinese were looted and burned. The demonstrators were particularly hard on the headquarters of the Tibetan Office of the Chinese Buddhist Association and on a police station. Many policemen were lynched and beaten.

The *Xinhua* agency's description is quite candid. 'These hysterical trouble-makers screamed: "Let's destroy everything that belongs to the Communists!" The extremely ferocious lamas and crowd ran to take control of the strategic points around the Jokhang in the hope of attacking the unarmed police with stones.

'In the evening of 5 March, a certain number of hooligans attacked the "Juleyuan" (Palace of Happiness) restaurant on the East Peking street and put all the tables and chairs outside and set them on fire. These hooligans destroyed all the equipment in the restaurant.' Many other restaurants owned by Chinese suffered the same fate. When the Tibetans started turning cars over and setting them on fire, they shouted 'Let's break everything that belongs to the Communist Party and the Hans', explained the *People's Daily*.

The official press, usually so full of praise for the unshakeable brotherly love between China's 'national minorities', was trying to discredit the protesters. But had the Chinese Communist Party given a thought to the fact that by describing these feelings they were enabling the Han population to gauge for the first time how very much they were detested by a large number of Tibetans?

At nightfall, Lhasa still echoed with AK-47 gunfire. The whole of the Tibetan quarter had risen up against the Chinese. In the middle of the crowd, a twenty-year-old monk fired a stone with all his strength at a plain clothes policeman in full flight. Further on, an even younger monk lobbed a stone at the security forces before crumpling to the ground with a bullet right between his eyes. Three witnesses saw a policeman in plain clothes take aim and fire at the teenager. Young and old, every Tibetan in the street was caught up in the revolt, helped by women who piled up the stones. Far from being an isolated handful, as Peking maintained, the monks were actively supported by thousands of Tibetans. In the morning, when the police ordered the attack on the Jokhang to arrest the monks, the people put ladders against the back of the building to help them escape.

At two in the morning on Sunday, the wail of the sirens was still audible several miles from the centre. A few hours later, the AFP correspondent was escorted to the airport at Gonggar and sent back to Peking. Lhasa had lived through sixteen hours of bloody confrontation.

The Tibetans counted eight dead, some say more. The final tally of the Chinese government was one police fatality and 309 'casualties', twenty-nine of whom were seriously injured. Once again, not a word was said about the Tibetan victims. On 4 April 1988, during a press conference, the Panchen Lama was more frank: he announced there had been five deaths, including one policeman, and that 330 men had been wounded among the troops. The riot, he said, was 'first staged by a hundred or so lamas who were later joined by several thousand civilians. If onlookers were included, the number came close to ten thousand.'

On Sunday 6 March 1988, Radio Lhasa announced that 'a few separatists engineered a terrible spectacle ... This small minority of separatists has committed new crimes against the people and the region as a whole. Their spectacle, organized in full daylight, has further exposed their black purposes and their criminal aims, vainly trying to split the motherland and sabotage national unity ... Once again, the facts have demonstrated that the forces of evil cannot succeed.'

On Monday, the *People's Daily* described the way in which the policeman had been killed by being thrown from the upper storey of a building. A colleague of the unfortunate victim recounted the scene. That story, avidly read by millions of Chinese readers, speaks volumes about the violent resentment felt by the Tibetan population against the Chinese. 'First they just threw stones at us. I was hit in the face several times', says Yang Yuchen from his hospital bed. He hid in a toilet, but 'they broke the door and started attacking us with sticks and stones. They took away our helmets. A young man cut me with a knife several times, on my face and my back. The others didn't stop throwing stones at us and hitting us with sticks. They tried to throw me out of the window of the building but I gripped the frame with all my strength. My chief Yuan, the squad leader, had been injured on both hands. He couldn't hang on and he was pushed out the window by four or five people.' He was rushed to the hospital's intensive care unit, but died shortly afterwards, adds the *People's Daily*.

Also on Monday, the *Xinhua* news agency issued an appeal for exemplary severity against the protesters, which indicated that the Party leadership was jittery. The leaders were reported to 'consider that the People's Government has acted with too much restraint and has shown too much patience and tolerance to those people'.

On 10 March, the Panchen Lama broadcast a message on Radio Lhasa: 'If Tibet becomes independent, this will unfailingly bring great calamities down on the Tibetan people as a result of the discord and unrest that will certainly ensue in Tibet. For this reason, to call for "Tibetan independence" is an act of treason against the great motherland, it sabotages the unity among the fraternal nationalities and is prejudicial to the fundamental interests of the Tibetan people.' He added that he would never abandon his 'four loves': his love for the Chinese Communist Party, his love for the motherland, his love for the Tibetan nationality and finally, his love for his religion.

On the day after the rioting, the police embarked on a new series of midnight round-ups. Several hundred Tibetans were taken to Lhasa's prisons for 'interrogation' – and torture according to many of them. In the space of a few days, between 300 and several thousand Tibetans were thrown in jail, Western sources report. On 4 April the Panchen Lama spoke of 200 arrests. On the same day Ngapo Ngawang Jigme announced that the murderers of the policeman would be 'sentenced to capital punishment in accordance with the law'. By 1 May, the Tibetan government-in-exile claimed that 2,500 arrests had taken place. Nevertheless, despite the fearful atmosphere in Lhasa, something extraordinary occurred. About fifteen Tibetan nuns demonstrated again on 17 April, in front of the Jokhang, shouting 'Long live the Dalai Lama!' and 'Brotherhood'. Knowing full well what to expect, they had brought along some warm clothes. They were immediately arrested.

Generally speaking, Chinese justice is known for quickly judging and executing delinquents. But for several months, the Lhasa authorities did not dare to stage the trial of the policeman's murderers. In such a charged atmosphere, they were afraid it would trigger an explosion. Finally, on 19 January 1989, the Lhasa People's Court staged a sentencing rally, attended by 5,000 people. The sentences were remarkably lenient. Lobsang Tenzin, a Lhasa University student, was found guilty of pushing policeman Yuan Shisheng out of the window and condemned to death, with a two-year reprieve. Sonam Wangdu, a businessman in his early thirties, was found guilty as an accomplice and given a life sentence.

Twenty-five other Tibetans were given sentences ranging from three to fifteen years in detention. Three who were found guilty of 'misdemeanour crimes' were simply released. The authorities were trying to mollify the Tibetan people and the Dalai Lama. The moderate wing of the Party had again managed to gain the upper hand. In another gesture of appeasement, Hu Jintao, one of the youngest members of the Peking leadership and said to be open to a dialogue, replaced Wu Jinghua as Party Secretary of the Tibet Committee in late autumn. Unfortunately, the Tibetans had come to like Wu Jinhua, a member of the Yi minority who had shown respect for the Tibetan culture and sensitivity, and they did not appreciate his replacement. In Lhasa, it was too late for accommodation and the mood had swung to icy determination.

In 1991, Lobsang Tenzin's suspended death sentence was changed to life in detention. He was initially held in Drapchi prison, where he was reportedly kept incommunicado for eighteen months chained hand and foot in a tiny, damp cell. His health is said to have deteriorated greatly from ill-treatment. Shortly after being put back with other prisoners, he and another detainee handed a petition to US Ambassador James Lilley, who was being given a tour of Drapchi on 31 March or 1 April 1991.

The piece of paper was quickly retrieved by a guard, and Lobsang Tenzin and his friend were severely beaten. The two of them, as well as a number of prisoners who protested in sympathy and were also given severe beatings, were all transferred to a distant prison in Powo Nyingtri.

As for Sonam Wangdu, numerous reports stated that he could no longer stand upright and that he had serious kidney problems, to the point of incontinence, from being kicked and tortured in jail. Despite petitions and appeals to Peking not only by his family and friends but even by US Congressmen and the United Nations, a recent photograph shows a prematurely aged, broken figure slouched in a wheelchair. A plastic pipe leads out from the blanket over his knees. He is said to be near death.[13]

China loses face

In early December 1988, Peking had been actively making preparations to commemorate the fortieth anniversary of the signing of the United Nations' Universal Declaration on Human Rights. Never before had Peking taken any notice of this date, which falls on 10 December. This time, however, they were going about it with maximum visibility. For a week, the newspapers had been replete with articles about China's commitment to respect for human rights. Once again, Peking was trying to refurbish its image abroad. Let us give them the benefit of the doubt: for a few Chinese cadres among the moderates, it could also have been linked to a desire for progress in an area of endeavour where everything had yet to be done. The Tibetan nationalists, for their part, had already decided to ruin these plans and give the Chinese government a black eye.

Almost every morning for the previous few weeks, Tibetan flags and posters in favour of Tibetan independence had been appearing on city walls, pasted up as high as possible to delay their removal. The walls of Tibet University had been covered several days in a row in early December with chalk drawings that caricatured the Chinese cadres who come to Tibet to get rich. One depicted an obese Chinese official whose belongings were so heavy they had to be lifted by a crane. The caption said: 'Thin on arrival, fat on departure!'

On Saturday 10 December 1988, shortly before eleven, in full view of the crowd of pilgrims in the area, a few Tibetan monks suddenly pulled Tibetan national flags out from the folds of their robes. They knew they were signing their own death warrants. Only a few minutes separated the signal for the beginning of the demonstration and the arrival of several hundred anti-riot police, who squared off 20 yards from the protesters. The first line of helmeted soldiers, armed with AK-47s and pistols, broke into a run towards the protesters. When they were a few yards away, they raised their weapons, took careful aim at their human targets and fired point-blank without any warning. The weapons crackled for a few minutes. Several Tibetans dropped to the ground. Christa Meindersma, a twenty-six-year-old Dutch woman who had been working as an interpreter for a Swiss Red Cross team, was hit in the shoulder from about thirty yards away. At first, the frightened people scattered and ran in every direction. But the security forces were soon compelled to fall back, because despite the chaos and the panic, everybody on the square was throwing stones at them. Two hours later, tear gas grenades were still being fired in the streets leading into the square to try and break up the crowd.

The police shooting claimed up to twelve fatalities that day, and dozens of people were injured. The *Xinhua* news agency reported that the Lhasa police had been 'compelled to fire warning shots when the troublemakers, refusing to heed appeals for calm, threw stones and bottles'. This is a lie, say all the foreign and Tibetan witnesses. The police fired on an unarmed and peaceful crowd.

On 17 December 1988, at the Hong Kong Press Club, Ron Schwartz, a professor of sociology at a Canadian university, accompanied by Christa Meindersma and a freelance British journalist, told us about his own experience. 'On 10 December, the three of us along with many other foreigners in Lhasa saw a group of unarmed, peaceful protesters carrying a flag, marching towards the Barkhor. We watched them as they were struck down without any provocation on their part and as far as we can tell, without any reason. The look in the eyes of those young men as they marched with their flag was a combination of indescribable fear and tremendous determination. They knew what they were doing and they knew what was going to happen to them. They knew something we didn't know. Not a single one of us Westerners present in Lhasa at that moment could have imagined what we were about to see.'

Christa Meindersma had been in Tibet for fourteen months at the time of the tragedy. What she has to say is important: 'Those young monks are mostly between twenty and twenty-four years old. They are fighting against what they have experienced up to now. They never knew the old pre-1959 regime. They are not trying to restore anything. They are trying to put an end to the violations of their basic rights, of their fundamental freedoms. They live in constant fear about something they might say or do. They can be thrown into jail, they can be tortured. And I think now things have come to a point where not only the monks but the Tibetan people as well have realized that there has been no genuine improvement in the situation and that the things that the Chinese government puts on paper are nothing but lies. So there is a tremendous solidarity and an incredible feeling of urgency. I think the Tibetans now feel they are on the verge of being completely exterminated by the Chinese and they have to do something to show the world that they are prepared to die to defend themselves.'

Although many were still in shock, for several days the Tibetans came to the scene of the tragedy with candles, prayer flags and white silk scarves – the traditional Tibetan *khatas*. The bloodstains were still visible on the pavement. Weeping Tibetans recited prayers to the 'protector of Tibet' (the Dalai Lama), begging him to throw the 'barbarians from the East' out of the Land of Snow. Foreigners were confined to their rooms, awaiting expulsion.

The list goes on: on 19 December 1988 in Peking, seventy students from the Central Institute for Minorities demonstrated in the vicinity of Tiananmen square, shouting 'Our comrades have been killed!' The people were still not cowed in spite of the wave of terror in Lhasa. On 30 December more than 500 Tibetan students, ignoring a new decree that banned all demonstrations, marched to the headquarters of the regional government calling for a 'peaceful solution to the Tibetan problem'. Their banners condemned the 'cold-blooded killing' on 10 December. The police stayed at home that day. The Tibetan resistance showed it was still active: on 7 February 1989, for several hours, the Tibetan national flag flew over the roof of the Jokhang for the first time in thirty years. The police did not make an appearance. By the end of the day, the foot of the flagpole had disappeared under a pile of white scarves. On 20 February, the national flag and some tracts turned up at sixteen different places in the Jokhang area. There was no Monlam Chenmo that year, but there were other protests . . .

Martial law in Lhasa

This recent chapter in the Tibetan rebellion has been by far the bloodiest since the end of the cultural revolution. It has also had the weightiest consequences, for it led China to decree martial law in Lhasa. For a long time after, Tibet was forced to retreat behind a wall of silence. The rioting started on 5 March 1989 and developed along the now familiar pattern for a people no longer capable of enduring what it experiences as colonial domination. Once again, in their hundreds, the monks and the inhabitants of Lhasa dared to defy China's rule with cries of 'Independence for Tibet!' in front of their Jokhang temple. By the thousands, they attacked Communist Party and local government buildings, police vehicles and the shops owned by Chinese. This further outbreak of despair was drowned in blood. The Chinese government had managed to keep almost all foreign journalists at a distance. But the tragic violence found witnesses. Some two hundred foreign visitors were in Lhasa and several dozen witnessed the scenes described below. Their testimony is fully consistent: once again, the Chinese police had no qualms about opening fire with no warning and directing it at unarmed people. Again, men, women and children were gunned down in cold blood in the streets of Lhasa. This time, the Peking authorities did not even try to play down the massacre: 'The police were obliged to shoot, because there was no other means of stopping the rioters', *Xinhua* announced. What statement could be more revealing of a people's determination to fight to the bitter end, and of a government's equally icy resolve to crush them by any means?

On Sunday 5 March, ten Tibetans and a policeman were killed and over a hundred people were wounded according to Peking's tally. Far more, said the witnesses. In the evening, the streets were still full of dead bodies. On Monday, the terror continued. During the day, Radio Lhasa broadcast a warning: 'The rioters are certainly not preparing a happy ending for themselves. This has been proved by history and by reality. How did the rebellion led by the Tibetan reactionaries end in 1959? And what about different revolts in the past? Was their outcome not sufficiently clear? If the separatists dare to continue to act against the will of the people, cause trouble, start riots and engage in beating, fighting, smashing, looting and burning, the iron fist of the people's democratic dictatorship will certainly deal them a crushing blow!'

For the second consecutive day, the Chinese police fired on the demonstrators and claimed new victims, dead and injured. The fighting went on in the evening in the Tibetan quarter. Throughout the day, Tibetans carrying national flags demonstrated in groups of several hundreds all over the city, in the centre of which they erected barricades. *Xinhua* claimed that rioters had been seen carrying guns. No independent source has ever confirmed this claim. The Bank of China building was raided and partly destroyed, along with four police stations and other official buildings. Jasper Becker, a correspondent for the British *Guardian*, tells of a Tibetan holding a stone, standing up to a truck full of armed troops. Chinese residents of Lhasa, including some Muslims, were stoned and shops and restaurants were burned, but never looted. 'Many foreigners saw Chinese bleeding that day. I saw one Chinese guy in an alleyway with a huge gash in the back of his head' says Chris Helm, a twenty-nine-year-old American. A Chinese tourist who had just arrived from Hong Kong, unaware of the rioting in Lhasa, had the fright of his life walking on Dekyi Sharlam, renamed Peking Street by the Chinese – but held by the Tibetans that day. 'He was just walking, looking for the Yak Hotel, and he looked so Chinese that he had to carry a Dalai Lama picture in his hand', remembers Zumi Picarelli, a thirty-nine-year-old American. At midnight on Monday night, the Chinese police embarked on a gigantic manhunt. Westerners staying in small Tibetan inns heard police banging on doors with their rifle-butts, then the sound of blows and screaming. Tibetans certify that in several cases the police opened fire indiscriminately with their automatic weapons as they entered a house, randomly killing parents and children.

Tuesday 7 March 1989 was the third day of quasi-anarchy in Lhasa. Many Chinese were seen gathering their belongings to leave the city in a disorderly, mad panic as the thirtieth anniversary of the anti-Chinese uprising of 1959 drew near. At midnight on Tuesday, the Chinese government took an unprecedented step, unthinkable even at the time of greatest tension in 1959 or during the cultural revolution: it declared martial law in Lhasa. Drawn up and signed by Prime Minister Li Peng for an unspecified period of time, the martial law decree was announced by Doje Cering, governor of Tibet, along with an official curfew and the following measures:

— All 'assemblies, demonstrations, strikes ... petitions and other get-togethers' were forbidden;
— Any person or vehicle entering the area under martial law required special passes and would be searched;
— Any firearms or ammunition possessed illegally would be confiscated immediately;
— The security forces were given 'the right to search the riot-creating suspects and places where criminals are possibly hidden';
— the security forces were authorized to arrest any 'trouble-makers' on the spot and to take 'any appropriate measures' against anyone resisting arrest.

On the same day in Peking, the *People's Daily* emphasized that the advocates of Tibetan independence were 'preparing another large demonstration in the next few days' with a view to 'settling accounts once and for all with the supporters of the communist government'. By Wednesday, Lhasa was in a state of siege. At midnight the night before, thousands of soldiers in combat dress (2,000 according to Peking) fanned out through the city and took up positions at strategic locations such as the major crossroads and government buildings. Loudspeakers attached to military vehicles broadcast the martial law regulations at full blast while sirens wailed throughout the city.

Calling from Lhasa, Jacques Launey, a twenty-seven-year-old French traveller, described the following early morning scene in the capital: 'There are soldiers everywhere. I can see at least one hundred from here. There are only a few children playing in the street and the odd cyclist riding past the smoking debris of the Chinese shops and restaurants ransacked by the Tibetans.' Here is the picture provided by *Xinhua* in an urgent dispatch dated 8 March 1989: 'At present, soldiers and armed police are stationed throughout the city. The soldiers are armed with pistols, tommy-guns, machine-guns, rocket launchers and wireless equipment. They are on duty day and night, guarding this city which is the highest place in the world and where the temperature can shift from one extreme to the other in twenty-four hours. The Army has orders to stay in Lhasa until martial law is lifted.'

Everywhere, arrests were being carried out in full view. In despair, screaming women hurled insults at the soldiers. The terrorized Tibetan population locked itself indoors. Dozens of military jeeps and lorries, some mounted with heavy machine-guns, scoured the streets. On Thursday, an AFP correspondent who had been trying to reach Lhasa, unsuccessfully, witnessed the following scene at a roadblock less than five miles from the city: a man with curly black hair, wearing indigo blue work clothes, was held by young soldiers from the People's Liberation Army. Twisting his arms behind his back, they tied his hands. An officer struck him in the face with the butt of his rifle. Other soldiers kicked his ankles to make him fall to the ground and bound his feet. Others kicked and prodded him as he lay on the ground. The man looked more shocked than afraid. He was hurled 'like a slab of meat' into the back of a jeep. No one could explain why he was stopped at the checkpoint, manned by some twenty soldiers armed with AK-47 automatics. Looking fit, tanned and well-fed, they seemed unaffected by the altitude.

The three-day rebellion had caused fifty to sixty deaths and hundreds of injuries. In Lhasa, hundreds of Tibetans were being dragged off to Gutsa prison and other places of detention.

On 8 March, at around three in the morning, the Chinese police burst into the hotels where the Westerners were staying. They were given forty-eight hours to leave Lhasa. A new decree dictated the conditions for visitors: they would have to obtain a 'special authorization' and be accompanied at all times by an official guide, even if they were the guests of the Chinese government.

Starting on Thursday 9 March, Chinese propaganda rounded on the Dalai Lama: 'The Dalai clique will never succeed in dividing China and destroying national unity', declared Li Zhaoxing, speaking for the Ministry of Foreign Affairs. In the words of a typically meticulous official communique, the rebels had attacked, damaged or destroyed twenty-four government units (offices of the administration), ninety-nine private shops and restaurants, more than twenty vehicles and dozens of bicycles. On the day before, India had voiced its 'concern' while quickly reaffirming that it considered Tibet to be an integral part of China's territory. London expressed 'great anxiety' while Washington 'deplored' the violence and use of force by the Chinese police.

As for the Dalai Lama, he declared from Dharamsala: 'No amount of repression, however brutal and violent, can stifle the voice of freedom and justice.' Confronted by violence on both sides, Tenzin Gyatso continued to preach moderation: 'For the Tibetans, to engage in armed struggle would be suicidal. It will be very easy for the Chinese to respond with brutality. The demonstrators must never take up arms, even when fired upon with machine-guns. Such an attitude will be much more difficult for Peking to control.' But now that the foreigners – witnesses – had been expelled, he was afraid that 'Lhasa may become like a house of slaughter'. His words had little impact on events, for Peking had already decided to slam shut the doors of Tibet. On 10 March 1989, the *People's*

Daily commented that a 'necessary shock' had been dealt in Tibet, while admitting that 'some residents still misunderstand this necessary shock, a few even oppose it'.

The Hong Kong press condemned the Tibetan rebels. 'The Tibetans are Chinese, not foreigners' was the headline of *Xin Wanbao* on 8 March: '[n]o one will allow Scotland to separate from the United Kingdom any more than California will be given independence. It is a matter of principle. The government of every sovereign State is allowed to take any measures it deems necessary to suppress splittist activities. Therefore, it is unnecessary for London and Washington to deplore anything. The regrets they have expressed are very deplorable regrets!'

As for the media in the People's Republic, they reverted to the sinister tone so familiar to anyone who experienced the cultural revolution. From Radio Lhasa on 11 March: 'Since the liberation, separatist forces in China and abroad have not ceased their criminal activities designed to restore the old Tibet for a single day. Have they not always been smashed to bits? In the future, the Chinese Communist Party will unswervingly maintain its leadership role over the people of every nationality in Tibet and thus help them to progress on the socialist path of unity, civilization and prosperity. The Chinese Communist Party will lead the people of every nationality in Tibet to inflict devastating blows on anyone who dares to hinder the advance of the Tibetan people and engages in separatism or in attempts to restore the old regime. ... We have the conquering, invincible and heroic People's Liberation Army as well as the People's Armed Police, which are loyal to the motherland and to the people. They sow terror in the ranks of the separatists. With the People's Liberation Army, the people have everything they need.' On 10 March 1989, the anniversary of the 1959 uprising, *Xinhua* announced that 'Over the past few days, one after the other, people telephoned the Communist Party Committee and the government of the Tibet Autonomous Region to express the satisfaction of the population with the troops on duty. Letters conveying heartfelt gratitude have been forwarded by various channels to the officers and men on duty.'

In late March, Zhang Shaosong, Political Commissar of the Tibet Autonomous Region, noted that there had been '600 victims' in the course of twenty-one 'incidents' since 1987 in Lhasa in his report to the Chinese National People's Congress. This was in marked contrast to the official figure of twenty-eight deaths and an unspecified number of people injured. After a ten-year era of moderation, as the last foreign visitors left Lhasa, Tibet was cast again into the darkness. For a long time, little news filtered out of Tibet. In mid-September, the Chinese government announced that nine nuns who had called for independence had been arrested.

In October 1989, the Reuter's correspondent in Peking, Guy Dinmore, was given permission to travel to Lhasa. Although he had been expelled from Tibet three times in the past two years, the Chinese Ministry of Foreign Affairs chose him as the first journalist to be given the right to enter Tibet. His visit to the Tibetan capital made a chink in the wall of secrecy that surrounded the situation. Wang Naiwen, a spokesman for the regional Public Security Bureau (the police) informed him that more than 400 Tibetans had been arrested after the events of March 1989. Sixty-three Tibetans and two dozen nuns had been sent without trial to work in labour camps for periods of up to three years. Some 320 Tibetans had been released, he said, and four more were still in detention pending trial. He added that there was no likelihood that martial law would be lifted in the foreseeable future, and acknowledged that without the help of the army, the police 'probably would not' have been able to regain control of the situation in Lhasa.[14]

A Tibetan nationalist and a source in the Public Security Bureau, speaking confidentially, told Guy Dinmore that over 1,000 Tibetans were being held in the three main prisons in Lhasa. The Tibetan showed him the scars left by torture on his body and declared that 'he had been tortured with an electric prod to extract the names of the leaders of the demonstrations'. The Lhasa population did not seem intimidated enough to remain silent, for when he visited Sera monastery with his inseparable official guide, the monks did not hesitate to tell him how many of them had been imprisoned. Nor did they fail to express their delight at the fact that the Nobel Peace Prize had been awarded to the Dalai Lama, to the great mortification of the guide.

In Lhasa, the implementation of martial law was far more severe than in Peking after 4 June. A Western academic in China likened the situation in Peking to a 'Sunday picnic'. But severe or not, it was not enough to stifle the expression of Tibetan hostility to the Chinese presence, since quite a few more demonstrations occurred during 1989. On 25 September, an article in the *Tibet Daily* announced that five more nuns had been sentenced to re-education through labour. 'They shouted "Independence for Tibet" and other reactionary slogans in a hysterical and frenzied manner', it explained. It seems that there was also trouble in the Tibetan region called Aba in Sichuan, for a number of political commissars from the army were dispatched to the monasteries and nunneries to strengthen 'patriotic attitudes' through military discipline.[15]

Tiananmen Square, 4 June 1989

Having seen with what savagery the Chinese army crushed the student movement in full view of world public opinion, it is easy to imagine the methods used in Tibet to decapitate the resistance behind closed doors. Millions of Westerners, lulled by the creations of Chinese propaganda, were in no position to recognize the real nature of the Chinese regime until roused from their slumber by tragedy. Abroad, the blood bath had the salutary effect of exposing the true face of a gerontocracy willing to commit heinous crimes to maintain its grip on power. Similarly, after witnessing the monumental Chinese government campaign to cover up its tracks after the 4 June massacre, beguiling credulous governments abroad while discrediting the students' and workers' demands for more democracy in the eyes of the rural and urban 'masses' at home, it is not unreasonable to feel sceptical about the information published by Peking about Tibet.

Just as it claims that the armed police did not fire directly at the Tibetan demonstrators in Lhasa, the Chinese government affirms that no one died on Tiananmen square on 4 June 1989, and that only 300 citizens and policemen lost their lives during the 'unrest'. But the many witnesses unanimously agree that somewhere between 1,000 and 3,000 Chinese died in Peking in the night of 3 to 4 June, mowed down by the machine-guns and automatic fire or crushed under the tanks of the People's Liberation Army. Tanks that had just reduced students or soldiers who refused to open fire to a pulp, backed up again over any bodies that were still squirming. In addition to the many exemplary public executions, other Chinese workers and dissidents were secretly put to death during the summer of 1989 near the Marco Polo (*Lugouqiao*) Bridge, a notorious site in the suburbs of Peking. Thousands of Chinese were arrested. Many have never been seen again. The intellectuals who were not detained were muzzled, or pressed into service during the campaign against 'bourgeois liberalization'. The repression that followed 4 June 1989 placed a heavy damper for several years on the open-door policies that Deng Xiaoping had been actively promoting since 1979. It was experienced as a profound humiliation by the Chinese, who are aware that most of their neighbours enjoy healthy rates of development.

The similarity in the terms used by the scribes of the regime to describe the bloody events in Lhasa and Peking, then under martial law, does not do credit to Chinese propaganda. In the media, the thousands of Tibetan demonstrators were described as 'a tiny handful of splittists trying to sabotage the unity of the motherland'. The hundreds of thousands of Chinese dissidents were dismissed as a 'small minority of criminals trying to overthrow the Chinese Communist Party'. In the same way, the Tibetans protesting in Lhasa and the Chinese in Tiananmen Square were all lumped together and branded 'counter-revolutionaries'. In the language of the Chinese government, peaceful demonstrations in Lhasa and Peking became 'acts of sabotage that perturbed the society' and 'threatened the stability of the country'. In Lhasa as well as in Peking, the demonstrators were accused by the regime of being 'hooligans' and 'bandits' engaging in 'looting, theft and attacks against innocent citizens'. If one is to believe the official media, 'the great majority of Tibetans resolutely oppose' the Tibetan protest movement, just as in Peking, 'the great majority of the people are energetically opposed' to the youth movement for more democracy. Both in Lhasa and in Peking, the police and the army 'gloriously put an end' to the rebel agitation, in March and June 1989 respectively. In both cases, the army was said to have displayed both discipline and restraint. Yet the Chinese government felt compelled to add, when speaking of both Peking and Lhasa, that the 'struggle' was not yet over,

There was, however, a crucial difference: in Peking many foreigners and journalists had remained behind in a position to follow events, but not in Lhasa. Whatever happened in the Tibetan capital after the imposition of martial law?

Despite the increasingly sophisticated equipment and methods of surveillance and repression that were installed in Tibet and particularly in the monasteries, Tibetans continued to protest throughout the period of martial law. In fact, more than fifty demonstrations took place between late 1987 and spring 1993. In the single month of May 1992, Lhasa was shaken by at least four pro-independence demonstrations. Several dissident monks and nuns were immediately arrested.[16] Twelve nuns were arrested on 15 June 1992 during another demonstration in Lhasa.[17] The protest movement has now spread to many other parts of Tibet. It has found an echo in the 'Tibetan Autonomous Prefecture' of Aba (Ngapa) in Sichuan and in a Tibetan area in Tongren, in Qinghai, where several demonstrators were already jailed in 1989.[18] Gyaltsen Norbu, then governor of Tibet, recognized the existence of a rural protest movement when, in a speech delivered in January 1992, he accused independence activists of 'vainly trying to find support for their separatist activities in the rural and pastoral areas'. He appealed to the Communist Party to 'launch the struggle against separatists in rural and pastoral areas'.[19] Since then, dozens of monk and lay Tibetans have been arrested outside Lhasa, and five farmers who were tried in Lhasa in November 1992 were sentenced to between thirteen and fifteen years for interrrupting an official political education meeting by shouting 'Tibet is independent'. The severity of the sentences – double the current average – is a throwback to the pre-1990 period and suggests increasing Chinese concern about growing political involvement in rural areas well beyond Lhasa.[20]

Clearly, the Tibetan resistance has not been reduced to silence. All we can do is hope that the few open-minded leaders in Peking who believe in dialogue will triumph over the fossil warlords who have lost touch with the realities of our modern world. In Tibet as in Peking and elsewhere in China, State-sponsored violence, torture behind prison walls and executions will provide no lasting solutions. On the contrary, these will only precipitate more extreme political changes after the fall of the present regime. As for Tibet, unless a stable and lasting political compromise with the Tibetan people is achieved, granting them a very broad autonomy, or they are rapidly and thoroughly extinguished as a nation – the genocidal final solution – China cannot hope to put effectively into practice the open-door policy it requires to grow beyond economic, social and political under-development.

In Xinjiang too

In the Xinjiang Autonomous Region, the area in the north-west of China previously known as Chinese Turkestan, there are occasional outbreaks of anger. The Muslim tribes have difficulty cohabiting with the atheistic Han. Xinjiang is peopled by a mosaic of ethnic groups who resent the inroads of Sinocization just as much as the Tibetans. The largest group are the Uighur, who account for some six million inhabitants or 46 per cent of the total population in an area that borders on Pakistan, India, Afghanistan, Kazakhstan, Tadjikistan, Kirgizstan and Mongolia. About a million Kazakhs, a nomadic people of Turkish ancestry, also live in Xinjiang, mainly in the north at the foot of the Tianshan range, in the Yili valleys and south of the Altai mountains. Near Kashgar, there are 120,000 Kirghiz people, 633,000 Huis (Chinese Muslims), 265,000 Tadjiks in the Pamir range, 12,000 Uzbeks in the Tarim basin and a few thousand Tatars in the north.

In 1949, the Han (Chinese) population of Xinjiang accounted for only 6 per cent of the total. By the end of the 1980s, it was 36 per cent! In some of Xinjiang's larger towns and cities, such as the capital, Urumchi, the Han are already a majority. For a number of years, the non-Chinese population was not subjected to the birth control policy applied in most of China since 1979: one couple, one child. Starting on 1 July 1988, new regulations dictated that urban dwellers could have two children at most per couple while rural dwellers were allowed three. Officially, the goal was 'to restrain excessive population growth in the region and improve the quality of new-born infants'.[21] A great deal of the available testimony indicates that the regulations provoked intense dissatisfaction among the population.

Since it was 'liberated' in 1949, displays of anti-Chinese feelings have often occurred in Xinjiang, a region long coveted by Russia and later by the USSR. The Kazakhs protested strongly in 1962, shortly after the break between China and the USSR, and 60,000 Kazakhs from the Yili area were compelled to seek refuge in the USSR. In the early 1980s, the local people rose up in armed rebellion against the Chinese presence in the regional centre of Payzawat. The Chinese army was called in to put down the uprising and the death toll was high. In 1981, Kashgar was paralysed by anti-Chinese rioting. This type of incident is hardly ever mentioned in the Chinese press. As a result, very little information about these events ever reaches the outside world unless some Western witnesses are present. The more recent protests suggest not only that the friction caused by Chinese immigration has not been resolved, but that nationalistic feelings remain very close to the surface.

In fact, part of the population is willing to fight for Xinjiang's independence.

On 2 January 1986, two to three thousand Muslim students demonstrated in the streets of Urumchi for an end to nuclear testing in Xinjiang. On 15 June 1988, again in Urumchi, 600 Uighur students protested against having to live in the same dormitories as Han students. In Yili, in the beginning of the summer of 1988, there were some far more serious incidents. The scant information available is not very detailed. According to well-placed sources in Peking, it seems that the Chinese police, on the basis of material provided by Soviet intelligence, arrested a number of Kazakh dissidents belonging to underground organizations that were active on both sides of the border between the then USSR and China. From July 1988, articles reflecting apprehension and anxiety appeared in the official Chinese media.

On 19 July, Radio Urumchi broadcast an alarmist speech by Wang Enmao, Chairman of the Xinjiang Chinese People's Political Consultative Committee, who was Peking's trusted strongman in the region for many years. 'Some people say that those who oppose the Han are heroes and that those who seek close union with the Han are traitors. This way of looking at things is not only absurd, it is very reactionary. Of course, there are a few, very few people who think this way ... Are there any people who are against the Han and would like them to return inside [China]? Yes there are, but not many. Just a small number, a very small number. The Hans are against those people and the Uighurs, along with the other national minorities, are against them too. These people sabotage national solidarity and act against the fundamental interests of people of every nationality ... It is really reactionary, very reactionary to say that the national minorities have been enslaved for thirty years and more.'

Radio Urumchi reported on 22 August 1988 that Deputy Secretary Janabil, of the Xinjiang Committee of the Communist Party, had successfully undertaken an 'inspection tour' of the Yili area that shares a 450-mile border with what was then the Soviet Republic of Kazakhstan. This is one of the points he emphasized: 'As we take stock of this good situation, we must also realize soberly that a small group of people inside China and abroad, with hidden aims, are deliberately sabotaging national solidarity in hopes of splitting the unity of the motherland and ruining the stability and unity of the political situation in the region. We must attach great importance to this.' On 1 September, 1988, the *Xinjiang Daily* commented on the economic situation and reforms in Xinjiang, claiming that they enjoyed the support 'of the entire country, including the people of the many different nationalities in Xinjiang'. 'However', the editorial went on, 'there is a very small group of people who are making a big noise about the exploitation of Xinjiang's resources, grumbling that Xinjiang's oil is flowing towards the East and that its cotton is sent away and that a lot of products leave Xinjiang while very few come in. They even suggest banning exports of Xinjiang's resources. Their ideas are extremely wrong.' The figures provided showed that 27,359 million yuan in subsidies had been allocated to Xinjiang from 1950 to 1987. On 25 October 1988, writing in the Shanghai daily *Baokan Wenzhai*, Wang Enmao revealed that secret organizations based abroad sought independence for Xinjiang and were sending spies to overthrow the Chinese by committing acts of sabotage and 'separatism'. He listed seven clandestine groups, including a National Committee for the Salvation of Turkestan, a Revolutionary Front of Eastern Turkestan and a World Muslim Alliance.

A further indication of the irritation felt by China's Muslims was the 12 May 1989 march in Peking, when several thousand young Muslims demonstrated, shouting 'Punish China's Rushdie', to protest against the publication of a book which they felt slandered the Koran. On 16 May, more than 30,000 Muslims demonstrated in Xian (north China). The offending volume, entitled *Sexual Customs*, described Islamic religious customs and practices in provocative terms: mosques were compared to erect penises, for instance. It was banned on 14 May 1989 and all copies of the 'blasphemous' book were seized and burned.

Western travellers report that far more serious incidents occurred in early April in Akto, a county lying north of Kashgar, the hub of the old Silk Road. The encounters between ethnic and security forces are said to have caused sixty civilian and eight police fatalities. The Chinese authorities conceded there was trouble when the regional television station in Xinjiang announced that fifteen civilians, six policemen and one Muslim official had been killed on 5 and 6 April during an 'armed counter-revolutionary rebellion' in Baren, a city lying 45 miles south of Kashgar.[22] Akto and Baren are both part of the Kizilsu Kirghiz Autonomous Prefecture bordering on what used to be the Soviet Republic of Kirghizia, now Kirghizstan.

In a further admission that all was not well, Xinjiang's governor Tomur Dawamat felt compelled to announce a crackdown 'on national separatists' at a 15 March 1992 meeting of the regional People's Congress. He added that 'international and domestic hostile forces' had stepped up their activities 'of infiltration, subversion and sabotage'.[23]

The veteran leader of the East Turkestan freedom movement is Yusuf Isa Alptekin, now aged over ninety. Once Secretary-General of the 'East Turkestan Republic', Isa Bey, as he is respectfully known, has been living in exile in Istanbul since 1954. Although he regularly issues statements condemning excesses arising out of the Chinese presence in Xinjiang, the leader of Turkestan's nationalists has a Turkish passport, and his prestige with China's Turkish and Muslim minorities does not compare with the Dalai Lama's influence over the Tibetans.

Notes

1. *100 Questions About Tibet*, op. cit., p. 59.
2. *Emancipation Monthly*, No. 115, Hong Kong, December 1987.
3. In *Tibet Information Network*, News Update, 30 April 1990.
4. *Emancipation Monthly*, op. cit.
5. *The Facts About Tibet*, Department of Information, Dharamsala, 1988.
6. *100 Questions About Tibet*, op. cit., pp. 54–5.
7. *Agence France-Presse*, 15 November 1990, quoting information broadcast on 8 November by Lhasa television. The figures were provided by China's State Statistics Bureau.
8. *South China Morning Post*, 8 June 1992.
9. *About Tibet (8)*, 'Freedom of Religious Belief', New Star Publishers, p. 7.
10. *Questions and Answers about China's National Minorities*, op. cit., pp. 174–5.
11. Ibid., p. 7.
12. *Tibetan Bulletin*, March-April 1992, p. 5; *Tibet Press Watch*, pp. 7–8.
13. *International Campaign for Tibet*, Urgent Action Appeal, December 1992; *Political Prisoners in Tibet*, Asia Watch & Tibet Information Network, February 1992.
14. Reuters, 22 October 1989.
15. *Jiefangjun Bao* (the People's Liberation Army daily), 12 October 1989.
16. *Tibet Information Network*, 21 May 1992.
17. *Tibet Information Network*, 2 and 3 July 1992.
18. *Agence France-Presse*, 23 April 1990.
19. *Tibet Information Network*, 18 June 1992.
20. *Tibet Information Network*, 21 January 1993.
21. *Xinhua*, 8 May 1988.
22. *Agence France-Presse*, 23 April 1990.
23. *Tibet Information Network*, 22 April 1992.

5

Pride and Fall

Barring the sudden outbreak of a singularly murderous conflict that would bring China to its knees, it is difficult to imagine the Chinese authorities spontaneously relinquishing their oft-proclaimed sovereignty over Tibet, if only for strategic reasons. The geopolitical balance being as it is, what Chinese government, whether Communist or not, would dream of giving up Tibet unless it were forced to do so? No country has ever parted willingly with any of its conquests, and it would be utopian to expect states to indulge in altruistic gestures out of generosity or exclusively humanitarian considerations. What is more, a Chinese government that took such a step would be exposing itself to accusations of high treason from rival factions. The Nationalist government in Taiwan – the island off South China where troops loyal to the Kuomintang sought refuge in 1949 – used to claim Tibet as an integral part of China's sacred territory with the same zeal and ardour as the Communist regime in Peking.

It must be said for the Taiwanese authorities that the political climate on the island has changed considerably in recent years, tending towards a genuine democracy. Taiwan is already perceived as a model of democracy for the Chinese world as a whole, including Singapore and Hong Kong. It is no longer preposterous to think that Kuomintang policies on Tibet could change in the near future. In June of 1992, government spokesman Jason Hu explained to me that when the time came to discuss a new formula concerning Tibet, 'obviously nothing could be forced on the Tibetans'. In April 1993, after long years of silence, the government of Taiwan formally extended an invitation to the Dalai Lama to visit the island. Speaking on behalf of the government, John Chang, President of the State Commission for Mongolian and Tibetan Affairs, stated that no conditions were attached to the invitation, specifically any obligation to renounce publicly the claim to Tibet's independence. The Taipei authorities expressed respect for the Tibetan leader's Five-Point Peace Plan. In fact, the Tibetans already enjoy the overt support of the Progressive Democratic Party in Taiwan, which has more than 30 per cent of the vote and openly advocates independence for Taiwan. The party's secretary-general in charge of international affairs, Mrs Yang Huang Maysing, told me frankly that her party 'is in favour of Tibetan self-determination' and 'supports the idea of an independent Tibet'. In early May 1993, the Dalai Lama's elder brother Gyalo Thondup spent some time in Taiwan, his first stop on the island since the fifties. Manifestly, the purpose of his visit was to reopen the dialogue with the authorities and plan the Dalai Lama's future stay on the island. This dialogue between Chinese and Tibetans is undoubtedly of great importance to the future of the Tibetan people.

Taiwan's example suggests that in time, if China becomes truly democratic and Tibet has not yet succumbed to the campaign to make it completely Chinese, new ways of thinking would allow for a reassessment of Tibet's status, within, for instance, an overall 'Federation of China' with mainland China, Hong Kong and Taiwan. Chinese dissidents who fled to France and to the USA after the massacre of 4 June have set up a kind of government-in-exile called the 'Federation for Democracy in China'. In late September 1989, then President Yan Jiaqi announced that once China was free of the Communist clique presently in power in Peking, Tibet could become part of a Federation, the articles of association of which remained to be defined. This proposal is not unlike that of the Dalai Lama, who speaks favourably of a 'Confederation' including both China and Tibet.

Why is Peking so obstinately unyielding? A cursory glance at a map is enough to show the strategic importance of Tibet, and its potential capacity to accommodate the expansion of China's economy, population and military ambitions. This is why, over the last few years, Peking has unrelentingly pursued a policy designed to secure Tibetan integration. More discreet and underhanded, it is no less formidable than the murderous frontal attack of Mao Tse-tung's time. If the inroads it has already made into Tibetan society are anything to go by, the 'soft' Sinocization policy could easily turn Tibet into a tawdry theme park in the space of a decade or two. Some see this as a classical example of strong-arm colonialism; others as a case of blatant expansionism. For many Tibetans, the Chinese policy in force since 1979 displays all the characteristics of genocide – a 'final solution' that offers no alternative to assimilation other than the complete extinction of the Tibetan people.

From the point of view of economic performance, after forty years of Chinese Marxism, Tibet's situation looks disastrous from any angle. Today's Tibet is still by far the most backward region in China, lagging well behind the inland Chinese provinces, not to speak of the prosperous coastal zones. Despite all the idyllic descriptions in official Chinese publications, it is not so sure that the Tibetan population is better off now than it was before the arrival of the Chinese army.

Paradise lost

The prize in the rivalry among the regional powers, Tibet lies in a mountain range that boasts every single one of the fourteen peaks that top 24,000 feet, including Mount Everest – Chomolangma in Tibetan – the highest of them all at 24,028 feet. The Kailas range runs along the west of the country and the Kunlun along the north where it borders on Pakistan. Mount Kailas is the supreme holy mountain for both Hindus and Buddhists. The former believe it is the throne of Shiva, and that it confers enlightenment; the latter think it is the centre of the universe and the protector of Tibet. For the faithful who circumnambulate it – a 32-mile pilgrimage – going around eight times atones for a life of sin and doing 108 rounds leads to Nirvana.

Although more than half of ethnic Tibet was amputated at the beginning of the 1960s and merged with the neighbouring Chinese provinces, the area of the 'Tibet Autonomous Region' is still 750,000 square miles (almost five times the United Kingdom), lying at an average altitude of 12,000 feet. Tibet borders on Burma, India, Nepal and Bhutan as well as on the the Chinese provinces and regions of Sichuan, Yunnan, Qinghai and Xinjiang. It borders on old kingdoms that have been taken over by the Indian administration, thus losing their sovereignty and sometimes also their identity, such as Sikkim, Ladakh and Zanskar.

Tibet and the Himalayas are a gigantic water reservoir for all of southern Asia and its teeming population. The Brahmaputra, known in Tibetan as the Yarlung Tsangpo, is born from the glaciers that grace Tibet's peaks. It runs for 1,285 miles through the Tibetan highlands before bestowing its welcome water – and less welcome floods – on the valleys and plains of China, Bangladesh and India. The source of the Indus is also in Tibet: it flows through Pakistan from north to south. The Ganges, India's holy river, springs up in the Himalayas. Burma's Irrawaddy, the Mekong, which irrigates Laos, Thailand and Cambodia and one of the mightiest rivers in the world, the Yangtze-kiang, all come forth in Tibet's province of Kham in the eastern Himalayas. The Yellow River (Huang He), China's other major waterway, originates in the north of the Tibetan plateau.

From the commanding heights of the natural fortress constituted by the Tibetan plateau, the Chinese army has carved out for itself a privileged position, towering over a vast expanse of territory. Sheltered behind a colossal barrier more than 1,500 miles long, China feels safe from the past, present or future ambitions of openly or potentially hostile neighbours such as India and Russia. In addition to the several hundred thousand soldiers stationed in Tibet, including Amdo and Kham, various sources report that China has gradually carved out a dense network of underground bases with gigantic depots for food and ammunition that communicate through long tunnels dug by the unpaid efforts of its captive population. Most of these installations are difficult for Western spy satellites to spot and identify.

Relying exclusively on the Chinese soldiers in its ranks, the People's Liberation Army is said to have built several maximum security nuclear missile bases. This effort took a heavy toll of the labourers, working like ants over many years and unaccustomed to such high altitudes. China exploded its first atomic bomb in 1964, making a triumphal entry into the still somewhat exclusive club of the nuclear powers, behind the USA, the USSR, the United Kingdom and France. As the pride and joy of the Chinese people with its rockets and satellites, the nuclear industry was protected by Mao Tse-tung and Chou En-lai from the long series of domestic political upheavals, even during the worst moments of the cultural revolution. In the hope that a proven first-strike capability would provide independence from the major superpowers, then the USA and the USSR, the military's nuclear activities were given absolute priority and were spared all the cutbacks that affected the army after 1979.

According to the Department of Information of the Tibetan government-in-exile, Indian intelligence and comparable sources in Taiwan, China has installed at least five nuclear missile bases in Tibet. They are located at Kongpo Nyitri, Powo Tramo, Rudok, Golmud and Nagchuka. Some informants report that Nagchuka, only 150 miles north of Lhasa, has become since 1976 the most important nuclear base in China; this is difficult to verify. Tibetan refugees insist that the Tibetan population has been evicted from the area around Nagchuka. It is strictly off limits to Tibetans and Chinese civilians alike. Reportedly, a minimum of eight ICBMs, 70 MRBMs (medium-range missiles) and twenty IRMBs (intermediate-range missiles) are said to be scattered among the various bases in Tibet. From the heights of this impregnable sanctuary, the missiles are aimed primarily at Indian and ex-Soviet territory, the main cities and industrial targets of which are well within range. Not counting several secondary landing strips, Tibet is also said to contain no less than seventeen radar stations and fourteen military airfields. Only Gonggar, 50 miles southeast of Lhasa, is open to non-military aircraft. It is probably for all these reasons that most of Tibet's airspace remains closed to international civil aviation.

In 1989, the *People's Liberation Army Daily* commented on a ten-day series of exercises held in August 1988 in Tibet to provide 'comprehensive chemical defence in high-altitude zones' by testing 'newly developed equipment'. These manoeuvres 'greatly strengthened coordinated chemical defence measures for PLA troops', specified the report.[1] At very much the same time, Peking announced that airborne units were receiving parachute training in Tibet. It was emphasized that 'the recent experimental parachute landing and survival training on the Qinghai-Tibet plateau indicates that the airborne units have basically mastered the technique of airdropping and parachuting on the plateau and are capable of conducting operations there'.[2]

Exiled Tibetans also accuse the Chinese of testing nuclear weapons and disposing of nuclear wastes in Tibet. In April 1993, the International Campaign for Tibet released a comprehensive account of China's nuclear activities in Tibet that reveals the existence of a top-secret nuclear city called 'the Ninth Academy'. It also reports radiation sickness among Tibetans, prison labour in nuclear facilities and the dumping of nuclear waste.[3] China, it goes without saying, issues wholesale denials. 'China has never deployed nuclear weapons nor dumped nuclear waste material in Tibet. The natural environment in Tibet has not suffered from nuclear pollution', declares the government in Peking.[4] Western experts point out that Peking's largest known nuclear testing ground is in Lop Nor, in the middle of the vast deserts of Xinjiang. That top-secret base is where a sizable number of China's nuclear tests have been held since 1964.

In the middle of the 1980s, the Federal Republic of Germany and China initiated negotiations relating to exclusively peaceful uses of nuclear power. The Chinese side proposed an original way of financing the purchase of new technology and equipment for its nuclear plants: West German nuclear waste would be buried in Chinese soil in the less-densely inhabited areas in the west of the country. The Bonn government and MBB, a West German company, examined but declined the offer, fearing a scandal and a violent reaction from the Green Party, whose political influence was on the rise. In November 1990, Japan and China did sign an agreement to undertake jointly the design of storage capacity for highly-radioactive nuclear wastes. The agreement, signed between the Nuclear Industry Forum of Japan and the Chinese government, stipulates that the two parties will jointly evaluate the safety of equipment used to process waste from nuclear plants.[5] Nothing is said, however, about potential storage sites. The threat is unfortunately not confined to nuclear wastes. There is a distinct risk that Tibet could become a dumping ground for industrialized countries. In March 1992, an environmental watch-dog agency reported that the city of Baltimore had signed an agreement with a California agency to ship 20,000 tons of city sludge to Tibet, for the price of 1.4 million dollars. This deal came on the heels of an agreement between the government of the Tibet Autonomous Region and a Chinese partner of the California agency, the Hainan Sunlitt Group, covering the storage in Tibet of up to 1.5 million tons of sewage sludge from US cities.[6]

Tibet and the Himalayas contain some of the last remaining virgin territory on our planet. They are home to an extraordinary variety of fauna and flora: more than 5,760 different types of plants have been identified. Among the wild animals, there is the golden entelle (Himalayan monkey); the argali sheep; the snow leopard; the Tibetan antelope; the pashmina goat, source of cashmere wool; the delicate black-necked cranes; the yak; the lammergeier, which is one of the largest birds of prey in the world and flies with ease at 18,000 or 20,000 feet; the Barbary falcon, capable of flight up to 27,000 feet; the kiang, a sort of cross between a horse and an ass; various types of bears; the musk deer; the bharal, which has features in common with both sheep and wild goats and the drong, a black-haired wild yak. The vegetation in Tibet and in the Himalayas ranges from the profusion seen in the well-watered valleys to the desolation at 15,000 feet, the lowest limit of the eternal snows. Some of the most extensive old growth forests in the world are found in Tibet, where they function as lungs for our old Earth. Taken together with what has been left standing in Mongolia and Manchuria, these are the largest forests in China. According to recent Chinese figures, in central Tibet (U-Tsang) alone, there are still 6,320,000 hectares of forest.

Tibet is dotted with lakes, over fifteen hundred lakes in all, with water that ranks among the clearest and purest in the world. The soil is rich in minerals such as copper, uranium, chromite, tungsten, bauxite, gold, silver, lead, lithium, borax, barite, sulphur, sulphides and several exceptionally pure forms of graphite. Known deposits of lithium constitute half of the world's entire reserves; the considerable deposits of uranium and borax are said to be the largest in the world. The Chinese press has reported on the activities of eight gold mines in Qinghai (Amdo), two of which are located in Madoi and Baima districts, in the land of the Golok. It was stated that the gold dust collected in the mines was bringing in 'fortunes' for the operators.[7] Official Chinese figures reveal that gold production in Qinghai (Amdo) rose to 177 kilograms in 1991, a 73 per cent increase over 1990.[8] Indeed, mining operations seem to be flourishing in Tibet and in the areas inhabited by Tibetans. According to a survey undertaken by the exile authorities in Dharamsala, 100,000 tons of different minerals were extracted in 1990 from the soil of the Tibet Autonomous Region alone, including 70,000 tons of chromite. A total of 500,000 tons was mined between 1979 and 1989, and the objective for the nineties is said to be 90,000 tons per annum.[9] When it comes to uranium, Chinese geologists have apparently located considerable reserves in the Tibet Autonomous Region, in the Tibetan Autonomous Prefecture of Aba (Ngapa) in Sichuan (Kham), in the Tibetan Autonomous District of Tianhu (Pari) in the province of Qinghai (Amdo) and in the Qaidam basin, also in Qinghai. Several mines are already said to be in operation.[10]

China uses unpaid workers (labour camp inmates) in many of its mining operations, but it still lacks the technical know-how to exploit the deposits fully. It definitely intends to make up for lost time, and whenever possible with the help of Western capital and technology. Tibet's hydropower, geothermal and solar energy assets are also considerable. The Chinese government estimates the Yarlung Zangpo's hydropower potential at 110 billion kw/h, only slightly below the estimated potential of the Yangtze, China's largest river. More than three hundred geysers have been located in Tibet.

The Himalayan landscapes and the Land of Snow rank among the most breathtaking vistas on Earth. This unique environment is one of nature's gifts, one of the crown jewels of the common heritage of mankind. It must not be allowed to degenerate into a dumping ground for the waste products of our civilization. Almost intact only twenty ago, the Tibetan environment has now been placed in jeopardy. In some places, the damage is beyond repair. Some of the unique species mentioned above are well on their way to extinction, not to speak of the larger species that were machine-gunned into oblivion by the People's Liberation Army in the 1960s and 1970s. Many others are vanishing as their natural environment deteriorates. Others fall prey to poachers. The forests are being razed, in Tibet as well as in Nepal. Whole mountainsides are being stripped for terraced cropping or simply for the sake of the timber, felled for sale in the valleys – or left behind to rot when proper arrangements for transport are wanting. Gone are the dense forests at the foot of Mt. Everest that so delighted Sir Edmund Hillary and his Sherpa, Tenzing Norgay, the first conquerors of the magic summit in 1953.

Is there really much deforestation in Tibet? The situation is too serious to be passed over in silence. The June 1992 Earth Summit in Rio provided an opportunity for the Tibetan authorities exiled in Dharamsala to prepare a substantive presentation on the condition of Tibet's ecosystem. The document, entitled 'Tibet: Environment and Development Issues 1992' is partly based on official Chinese statistics. According to this report, over 40 per cent of the old growth forest in Tibet and in the ethnic Tibetan areas of Kham and Amdo (now sited in Sichuan, Yunnan, Qinghai and Gansu) has been cut down since the fifties. The forest cover has shrunk from 25.2 million hectares in 1950 (about 9 per cent of the total area under consideration) to 13.57 million hectares in 1985, or about 5 per cent. Much of this coniferous forest, where the pines are often hundreds of years old, lies to the east of the Tibetan plateau, along the valleys of rivers such as the Yellow River, the Yangtze, the Mekong, the Salween and the Brahmaputra. Timber extraction is said to have totalled 2,990 million cubic metres, or 46 per cent of the available forest stock in 1950. The logs were transported to 'inner' China, and often exported abroad; the Chinese government's income from the timber has been valued at US$ 54 billion. Since 1985, felling has continued, hindered only by difficulties of access. New roads are being built, particularly in Kongpo and Powo Tramo, two areas that had been relatively overlooked within the Tibet Autonomous Region. Some 20,000 People's Liberation Army personnel and Tibetan prisoners are said to be working in this area, employed in intensive clear-felling operations.[11]

Seldom offset by new planting, the deforestation has provoked a severe depletion of Tibet's fauna, including some endangered species. It has accelerated soil erosion and caused landslides, and it contributes to the progressive build-up of silt in rivers such as the Yellow River, the Yangtze and the Brahmaputra, which further aggravates the murderous flooding in the area, extending to India and Bangladesh.[12] In the opinion of Bradley Rowe, a British expert on Tibet's environment and a member of the Royal Geographical Society, when the logging carried out since 1985 is included, fully 70 per cent of Tibet's forests in the neighbouring provinces of Sichuan and Yunnan have been destroyed.[13]

For decades, the Chinese authorities have not spared a thought for the pollution caused by industrialization and other environmental abuses. As a result, many a Chinese city looks just like Western industrial centres did in the fifties: a blighted megalopolis. The air is poisonous, the water is loaded with deadly germs and bacteria and the concrete housing blocks breed delinquency. The mortality rate due to cancer is so high and the urban landscape so squalid that China is gradually realizing what kind of dismal future is in store for the next few generations. China is poor. Industrial development will remain a priority, which bodes ill for to-morrow's children, but at least the press has started to sound the alarm. Anti-pollution regulations are reining in the worst offenders. Yet there is still much to be done, compared to the achievements in terms of environmental protection in Japan, South Korea or in the West. China, a huge country, continues to pollute on a such scale that in a few decades, according to many specialists, the entire world may have to pay the price for its mistakes.

When it comes to Tibet, with few exceptions, silence is very much the rule. In late 1988, the *People's Daily* published a short article that spoke volumes about the massive destruction of Tibet's forests. 'The primal forest in Tibet is among the best preserved of all in our country. But to our discredit, for ten years, this forest has suffered serious sabotage as a result of haphazard cutting and fires. Anyone who looks at a Tibetan forest will notice that large tracts have disappeared. Everyone who loves our country's patrimony will feel regret. I visited the township of Mi where wood was piled in every corner. All the farms, whether state-run or private, were felling trees. Even young trees were being cut for sale. The waste is enormous. A considerable number of large trees have been left lying on the ground, for lack of transport. The forest that used to lie south of the township has been completely razed. Several dozen fires break out in Tibet every year. Tens of thousands of hectares are lost in this way. We hope that the departments concerned will take energetic measures to protect Tibet's timber resources.'[14]

Tibet's lakes are likely to suffer the same fate as those of neighbouring Xinjiang and Qinghai. The English-language *China Daily* has reported on the catastrophic situation. Lake Kokonor, which lies in a Tibetan area, has been renamed Lake Qinghai and is held to be China's largest lake. However, the water-line has been going down by four inches or more every year. Since 1949, it has dropped almost ten feet. Some of Xinjiang's lakes have already turned into salt pans. Over the past forty years, following the fast-paced transfer of Chinese immigrants to that region, the area under cultivation has increased threefold. This new element, coupled with the population explosion and an exponential demand for irrigation, has sealed the fate of these lakes.[15] In central Tibet, Yamdrok Tso is the most seriously threatened. Lying about 75 miles south of Lhasa, it is known as the 'Turquoise Lake' and it ranks third in Tibet for size. Its area of 500 square miles and location at 14,000 feet set the stage for a controversial project to supply a hydropower plant on the Yarlung Tsangpo river in the next valley. Chinese engineers devised a plan to tunnel almost four miles through the mountains. On completion of the project, the lake water will rush down 3,000 feet through the tunnel to feed a 15,000 kw turbine; by the year 2000, six generators with a total installed capacity of 90 Mw are planned. According to the Chinese authorities, part of the water would be pumped back into the lake during periods of low demand, slowing the drop in the Yamdrok Tso waterline to 3 inches a year. Many Tibetans are alarmed at the prospect of muddy water from the river being pumped into the pure and limpid lake, and by the inevitable deterioration this will cause in the lake's ecosystem. Until his death, the Panchen Lama was among the most energetic opponents of this Herculean project. Peking admits that a special detachment of 1,500 troops is required to guard the construction site.[16]

Low-budget tourism has brought pollution to remote areas of the Himalayas. The amount of rubbish left behind has reached alarming proportions in some places. China's plans for Tibet, when it comes to tourism, border on megalomania. Fourteen months of martial law set back the schedule. Nepal had 10,000 tourists in 1960; it was welcoming 250,000 a year in the late 1980s. By the year 2000, the Nepali government hopes to quadruple the figure. Incoming tourists invariably transform the local economy and slowly but surely erode ancient but vulnerable traditions and customs. It is a safe bet that the survivors of 'modernization' will succumb to the impact of modernism.

A fourth world within the Third World

During an official visit to France in late 1987, former Chinese president Li Xiannian was asked several times about the situation in Tibet. French public opinion had been deeply moved by the turmoil in Lhasa and by the brutal repression that followed. In a quavering voice, the exasperated eighty-year-old replied without batting an eyelid that before the arrival of the Chinese army, Tibet had been inhabited by savages. After all, had the immense majority of the Tibetans not been serfs at the mercy of the clergy and the aristocracy? And had Tibet not been a medieval society at the time? Confronted with such a situation, what alternative was there for China, other than to intervene? Westerners, he insisted, should think twice before criticizing China. China's mission in Tibet had been to bring civilization, nothing more. Li Xiannian, one of the most conservative members of the Chinese Communist Party leadership, probably failed to notice how much he had embarrassed his audience. With every word, he had brought back vivid memories of what the French had said in colonial times about Algeria – or nearer to Tibet itself, Indochina.

Peking's arguments are despicable, as regards both style and content; yet they have been formulated in almost identical terms since 1950. Their absurdity would appear in even starker relief if out of curiosity, an open-minded observer were to take a closer look at Tibet's much-vaunted economic progress after forty years of untiring pursuit of 'socialist civilization'. If the Chinese appear to rank among the poorer inhabitants of the planet – on paper at least – the Tibetans are definitely the last of the least, a fourth world within the Third World.

For a start, a world of difference exists between the China of the People's Republic and most of its neighbours. In China, between 70 and 100 million rural dwellers still live below the poverty line on a yearly income of less than 200 yuan (£22), according to official Chinese statistics. Over 10 million people belonging to ethnic minorities fall into this category, according to Mr Ren Yinong, a high official from the Chinese National Commission for Minority Affairs. He adds that malnutrition is still a problem for this group.[17] Yan Mingfu, formerly responsible for ethnic minorities for the Central Committee of the Chinese Communist Party, states that 33 million people belonging to ethnic minority groups still live below the poverty line. They tend to be illiterate, their food intake is not adequate and they lack suitable clothing and housing within the Chinese definition of the threshold of poverty.[18] The Panchen Lama contributed another interesting fact – in Tibet as a whole, the average per capita income is only 300 yuan![19]

Is it necessary to spell out how unlikely it is that a Western tourist enjoying a package tour of China, staying in the best accommodation in the country, will ever come across any pockets of extreme poverty? Lying well off the beaten track, they are not something to be found on any carefully sanitized tourist itinerary. In terms of national economic development, China falls in the same category as India. In Japan, a country reduced to rubble by the Second World War, the per capita Gross National Product (GNP) easily tops $23,000. In Taiwan, an island governed by Kuomintang 'reactionaries', per capita GNP was $7,500 in 1989. In South Korea, it is over $5,000. In Hong Kong it borders on $11,000.[20] How to explain that China's GNP remains stagnant at $400 to $500 per capita, other than to blame the system for an utter failure to deliver results? Deng Xiaoping's cherished goal is to raise per capita GNP to $1,000 by the year 2000. Well and good! But even if his dream comes true, where will his neighbours be by then? The embarrassed Chinese leadership always comes up with the same explanation: China is an immense country, difficult to manage and subject to natural catastrophes. Be that as it may, when it comes to profitability, China's state enterprises return one of the lowest figures in the world. The only dynamic area in the national economy is the private sector. If we compare the standard of living in Tibet with the prevailing levels in the Asia–Pacific region's newly industrialized or industrializing countries, the gap widens into a gaping chasm. The disparity reflects badly on Peking's pretentious claims, despite the recent take-off of its economy.

The famines provoked by Mao's political campaigns may be a thing of the past in Tibet. But the disparity between China and Tibet continues to grow. The Chinese government says it injected more than 12 billion yuan in financial subsidies into Tibet between 1952 and 1986. In capital construction, its share of the financing accounted for 3.43 billion yuan between 1952 and 1987. To this should be added another 5.91 billion yuan of funding from the 'central' government for various aid programmes in Tibet between 1979 and 1986.[21] Yet the question put by Hu Yaobang in 1980 still remains: on what has the money been spent? Owing to the liberalization and de-collectivization of the rural sector since 1979, grain production rose to 467,000 tons in 1987, a per capita average of 233 pounds. In 1990, grain production was said to have reached 560,000 tons, 0.13 per cent of China's total production figure.[22] Providing only 253 kilos of grain per capita, it remains well below the all-China average of 335 kilos for the same year.

If we turn to the industrial sector, the contrast is humiliating. According to Chinese government statistics, industrial production in Tibet for the month of August 1988 was just 11 million yuan, or 1/10,000th of China's total industrial production. This was 130 times lower than the figure for Gansu province, one of the poorest in China! Furthermore, despite ten years of reforms, Tibet's economy is not exactly poised to take off. The same official statistics show that in Tibet, starting from a base that is practically nil, industrial growth was 22.2 per cent higher in August 1988 than in August 1987. For the same period, the all-China figure was 18.3 per cent. It was 36.1 per cent in Guangdong, bordering on Hong Kong, and 28.1 per cent in Shandong, directly opposite the Korean peninsula, two of the most highly developed provinces in the country. Hainan island, off southern China, lying opposite the Vietnamese peninsula, showed record growth with a comfortable 42.4 per cent.[23] The situation has not fundamentally improved since then. Official statistics put Tibet's industrial output at 235 million yuan in 1990, a 6.3 per cent increase over 1989. Its share of China's total industrial production remains unchanged at 1/10,000th of 2,385 billion yuan.[24]

Trade with the outside world accounted for 245 million yuan in 1990, less than 0.5 per cent of China's total.[25] If we leave out the expensive imported equipment required to upgrade tourist facilities, the result will probably be closer to zero.

In China's two-tiered system of economic reform, while the coastal provinces are set to act as locomotives for the rest of the country, Tibet is visibly destined to remain in the grip of poverty, despite the much-advertised decision in 1992 to proclaim the region a Special Economic Zone.

On the educational front, the situation is nothing to boast about. The Chinese produce a remarkable amount of propaganda material describing extraordinary advances achieved in Tibet where, except for a few lords, nobles and high lamas from the ruling classes, it is stated over and over, 95 per cent of the Tibetan population was illiterate up to 1950. But looking at other declarations of the same official media, it appears that things have not improved all that much. Thirty-eight years have passed and 1.4 million Tibetans – at least 70 per cent of the Tibet Autonomous Region's population – still cannot read or write![26] Educational facilities in Tibet are euphemistically described as very modest and the number of teachers is said to be inadequate. Earlier, Tibet's official daily had reported that the real percentage of Tibetans who were totally illiterate was as high as 80 per cent![27] The average for China as a whole was then 23 per cent. This leads us to wonder what exactly has China's civilizing mission contributed to Tibet? What could be said to be its achievements?

China claims to have spent 700 million yuan (about 500 million dollars at 1985 rates) on educational facilities in Tibet between 1980 and 1987 and 130 million yuan in 1987 alone. Nevertheless, a considerable number of Tibetan children have never seen the inside of a school. According to official Chinese statistics published in 1991, out of a total of 2,469 schools in Tibet, there are 4 institutes for higher learning, 15 secondary-level vocational training schools, 68 secondary schools and 2,300 primary schools. These cater to 177,000 students or 54.4 per cent of school-age Tibetans. There are also 17 scientific research institutes active in the fields of forestry, biology, environmental sciences, solar energy, astronomy, medicine and the Tibetan pharmacopoeia.[28] Some Tibetan students – 5,278 in 1987 – have been sent to study in secondary schools in the provinces and prefectures of 'inner' China. Reportedly, 1,500 Tibetans will have earned a university degree by the year 2000, and another 10,400 should have qualified in a technical specialization.[29] Last but not least, a university was inaugurated in Lhasa in July 1985. Tibet University offers 17 courses taught by 17 professors and assistants. Three of the eight departments concentrate on exclusively Tibetan topics, including Tibetan language and medical science. The first 246 students graduated in 1988. So much for the figures. The facts are less inspiring.

Peking admits that 50 per cent of school-age Tibetan children in the Tibet Autonomous Region do not actually go to school at all.[30] This low figure seems optimistic, compared to the statistics for some districts of Qinghai (formerly Amdo), where only 11.2 per cent of school-age Tibetan children attend classes. In other districts, attendance rises to 21.6 per cent; the highest attendance figure is put at 88 per cent. The vice-governor of the province, Bainma Dandzin, is quoted as saying that 'as a result of a scarcity of economic and natural resources, basic education is still under-developed in the province, and the development of education is very unevenly spread throughout the various parts of the province'.[31] The situation is far worse in central Tibet. The testimony compiled over the past few years, from the Tibetans themselves and from the foreign travellers who have been able to tour extensively, paints a bleak picture of the situation.

In the villages there are primary schools only. The buildings often consist of no more than a few planks and a corrugated iron roof; frequently, neither tables nor chairs are available. The teachers tell the time by looking at the sun's position. These establishments offer a four-year course, on completion of which the teenage graduates theoretically should enter a district school, often two to three days' walk away from home. A majority of young Tibetans never get there. Peasant families are loath to part for four more years with the young people's help in the fields, particularly when it is so difficult for anyone to fathom the purpose of what is taught when almost all the schools are mere outlets for Chinese propaganda.

For China, the schools are a powerful weapon in the campaign to Sinocize Tibet, reaching far into the most remote inhabited areas. In some cases, Chinese is even being taught at the primary level. The teaching of history and other subjects is carefully geared towards instilling the benefits of Tibet and China's 'reunification' into unsuspecting young minds. The old system is painted in lurid colours. For young Tibetans, this functions as a daily brainwashing. Tibet's culture and traditions are passed over in silence while much ado is made about China's. Leaving aside the total lack of interest in Tibetan civilization – sometimes verging on contempt – that this type of education can leave in the minds of the young generation, there is a distinct risk that the Tibetan language will be gradually forsaken. As for religion, the life-blood of Tibetan society, it is simply ignored in school – when it is not openly derided.

For the last forty years, the Chinese Communist Party has tried to develop a Tibetan elite that wholeheartedly supports its goals. Ever since the fifties, thousands of Tibetan students have been sent to schools and universities in Peking, Chengdu, Xining, Lanzhou, Shanghai and elsewhere in China. These young people have been uprooted and separated from their family and their community to prepare the ground for their

political indoctrination; these Sinocized Tibetans were being groomed
to be Tibet's future cadres. Had this enterprise succeeded, the Chinese
government would have been in a position to boast to the world that the
Land of Snow was governed by Tibetans. But the constant protests and
demonstrations and the fact that the latest Party Secretary sent in from
Peking has felt the need to purge Tibetan officials accused of loyalty to
the Dalai Lama seem to indicate that it has failed. Peking has still not
succeeded in winning over the Tibetans. When all is said and done, many
of these Tibetan intellectuals have remained quite nationalistic and their
undercover resistance is all the more effective, originating as it does within
the government apparatus itself.

The weapons of Sinocization

'A holocaust is taking place on the Roof of the World and the Free World
is still not paying attention. The situation in Tibet is intolerable: 500,000
troops and a quarter of China's nuclear arsenal are stationed there',
claimed the late Petra Kelly, formerly the leader of the German Green
Party.[32]

The Chinese authorities swear this is not true. An honest appraisal
of the situation in Tibet today will reveal nothing beyond the tenacious
but discreet campaign to transform every inch of Tibet into a piece of
China. Tibet is besieged from all sides and may soon find itself with no
choice but to surrender. There is little time left. The government continues to proclaim its innocence: 'Chinese government policy is based
on respect and protection for the traditional cultures of all the minorities. The traditional culture and the priceless historical heritage of the
Tibetan nationality are no exception.' The press now admits that the
destruction caused during the cultural revolution produced irreparable
losses, but it claims that the excesses were committed by some 'leftists'
and have now been corrected. There is a perceived need to specify that
'[p]eople often confuse the destruction of traditional culture by the "red
guards" during the "cultural revolution" and the correct policy carried
out by the people's government during the greater part of the post-lib-
eration period'. For the benefit of any reader that has managed to keep
a straight face, it is stated that '[t]raditional Tibetan literature and art
is an important component of China's traditional culture. The Chinese
government attaches great importance to traditional Tibetan literature
and art.'[33]

Official guidelines stipulate that 'Han cadres are expected to respect
the ways and customs of the Tibetan people and study their language,
while the Tibetan cadres, for their part, are expected to study the Han
language. The Han cadres should pay particular attention to overcoming any thinking of Han chauvinism, while the minority cadres should
guard against localist tendencies in their thoughts. All cadres should in

earnest study Marxist-Leninist theory on the national question and continuously raise their political awareness and ideological level.'[34]

In reality, forty years after the 'peaceful liberation' of Tibet, the goal of China's orthodox strategists has not changed. They remain intent on eliminating Tibet's traditions and customs. They are committed to breaking the resistance of a hostile society and forever extinguishing any yearning to be different. Success in restoring China's independence by evicting the foreign occupants was probably the main factor in the 1949 victory of the Chinese Communists. To this day it remains their sole unmitigated achievement. It goes without saying that it deserves admiration and respect; but if China's intellectuals were invited to voice their gratitude to the Chinese Revolution and to its veterans, their praise would focus exclusively on the struggle for China's independence. This is how Chinese theorist Yan Jiaqi explains the situation: '1949 was not an ideological (Marxist) but a victory for Chinese nationalism. The decisive factor was the struggle against the Japanese occupation. Had it not been for the Japanese invasion, the Chinese Communist Party might not have come to power. With the disintegration of the tissue of society, the communist victory came about quite naturally. But when the Chinese Communist Party gained control, it fell back into the traditional dynastic pattern. It produced a dictatorship.'[35] As in Vietnam and elsewhere on the planet, the Communists built solid popular support and a formidable war machine on the foundation of a national liberation struggle. Ever since it came to power, the leadership in Peking has been haunted by the spectre of partition. With the emergence of regional differences in development, along with the ongoing changes all over the world, the spectre has been rattling its chains. More than at any other time since 1949, China's leaders have good reason to shiver at the thought. With the daily erosion of the Chinese Communist Party's dominance and uneven economic growth, powerful currents are dragging China in different directions.

As a result, Peking attaches overriding importance to the integration of China's borderlands, which is precisely where the majority of the ethnic minorities live. These frontier areas are peopled by most of the fifty-five ethnic minorities identified by Chinese research in demography and ethnography. Taken together, the non-Chinese population adds up to 67 million people, less than 6 per cent of the total population: a drop of water in the ocean of Han Chinese. But their attachment to their own customs and their potential – or active – hostility to the communist system imposed from outside, transforms these groups into permanent hotbeds of rebellion and secession. The Sinocization of those areas is felt to be imperative, today more than ever. On another tack, it is enough to recall how enthusiastically the Chinese have been destroying their own traditions for the past forty years, and how blindly they have been embracing and losing themselves in every cultural current from abroad, to shudder at the fate that awaits Tibet if it opts to follow in China's footsteps. It is no exaggeration to imagine Tibet transformed into a pathetic theme-park, on the model of America's Indian reservations, where the Chinese state would generously distribute free liquor to contribute to the Tibetans' degradation.

In Tibet, the worm is already in the apple. Overt or covert, various methods are used by the Chinese government in its campaign to make Tibet Chinese. One of them, as we have seen, is to generalize the teaching and use of the Chinese language at the expense of Tibetan. Mastery of Chinese is a *sine qua non* for Tibetan cadres, for their Chinese counterparts rarely speak Tibetan. Knowledge of Chinese is gradually becoming indispensable in the shopping centres of the towns and larger villages. Some educated Tibetan children already speak in Chinese to each other and in adulterated Tibetan to their parents. If this trend continues unchecked, Tibetan will become a mere dialect spoken only by old people warming their bones in the sun.

In 1987 the Chinese government adopted legislation to establish Tibetan as the main official language in the Tibet Autonomous Region. Chinese officials were instructed to study the language. The intentions of the proponents may well have been honourable, but the new regulations were seen as a hilarious joke from the very outset and the Chinese in Tibet are still laughing about it. Another injunction decreed that from late 1990 onwards, government offices in Tibet could refuse to consider any official document that did not have a Tibetan translation attached to it. For many officials, this was all part of the same farce. The law decrees that all official documents as well as the signs outside government office buildings must be written in both languages, Chinese of course being given pride of place. Although it dates back several years, this order is often ignored. How many Tibetan prisoners have been shown documents written only in Chinese, of which they understood little if anything? A Tibetan version of the *China Daily* has been coming out for twenty years. Its main purpose seems to be to convey the political code of conduct of the Chinese government to the Tibetan working masses. More preoccupying is the fact that some members of the new Tibetan aristocracy whom the Chinese have managed to win to their side prefer to converse in Chinese, the better to flaunt the superior status conferred by that language.

From 1950 onwards, the new Chinese administration started changing the Tibetan names of a number of places; the same fate lay in store for the principal actors in Tibet's history. They were systematically given Chinese names based on a phonetic transliteration. Peking's official Pinyin system was pressed into service, and more often than not, the Tibetan names became unrecognizable. It is unsettling to see how easily a number of rather serious Western publications have fallen into the Chinese trap. The names of some monasteries and some heroes of Tibetan history have suffered this fate in the fourth and latest French edition of the *Nagel* guide to China; it must be said in passing that its version of Tibet's recent history is extraordinarily faithful to China's views on that score. We are told that a Tibetan king, one 'Song zan gan bu', married Princess Wengchen. The reference is to Songtsen Gampo, the founder of the first Tibetan empire. Further on, the reader is informed that the oldest piece of architecture in the Tibetan capital is the 'Da zhao si'. If you try out this word on a Tibetan, however many times you may repeat it and however hard he tries to catch it, he is not likely to understand. But if you ask him how to get to the Jokhang, he will be happy to show you the way. As for Ramoche, the other great temple in Lhasa (which never appears on Chinese maps, for it was destroyed in 1959), the *Nagel* calls it 'Xiao zhao si'. The names get better and better: Drepung monastery is rendered as 'Zhe bang si', the city of Shigatse 'Ri ga ze' and Tashilhumpo 'Za shen lun bu si'!

The promotion of mass tourism in Tibet is another component of the plan to remake Tibet into a Chinese zone. Peking's vision of Western tourism as a means of undermining Tibetan traditions is not even denied by the Chinese authorities. Certain official publications contain words to that effect. Ngapo Rinchen, one of the cadres responsible for tourism in Tibet, holds that 'tourism encourages open-mindedness. Tibet's lengthy state of isolation gave birth to, and preserved, a number of conservative and backward ideas. The arrival of numerous foreign visitors, their life-styles, their way of thinking and of enjoying themselves, cannot fail to have an effect on the spirit of this very ancient nation. Mental progress invariably produces social progress.'[36] This artful use of foreign influences has already affected the customs and lifestyles in Lhasa and in the other towns included on the map of destinations tourists may visit. According to Chinese official figures, only 1,362 foreign tourists visited Tibet between January and April 1990, and only a thousand in the same period in 1989.[37] The numbers have increased, but not yet to pre-1987 levels.

Martial law undoubtedly delayed the full implementation of the programme to develop tourism in Tibet. But if the published target of 500,000 foreign tourists a year is met, Lhasa will offer a pitiful sight as 500,000 gum-chewing and Coke-swigging Westerners armed with cameras go trudging through the streets of a city that only boasts 50,000 Tibetans. Ten tourists for each Tibetan! Hemmed in by a crushing majority of Chinese settlers, encircled by the numerous military camps dotted all over Lhasa, the unfortunate Tibetans may come to feel more and more like exotic animals in a zoo. In these circumstances, how will the City of the Gods manage to avoiding losing its soul?

The effort to transform Tibet into a Chinese outpost is abetted by the mountains of products from China that swamp Tibetan markets: the textiles, clothes, shoes, thermoses, household goods and appliances, preserves, soft drinks, alcoholic beverages – and tons of other items of every description that are carried and flown in from all over China. All this is sold in shops or market stalls by an army of Chinese traders, mostly from Sichuan or one of the other neighbouring Chinese provinces. A great deal of smuggling goes on under the benign – not to say corrupt – gaze of the customs authorities at the borders with Nepal and India. These activities have created new demands in Tibet. Traditional life-styles and centuries-old customs are being modified without a shot being fired. All over Tibet, the men have folded away their attractive traditional clothing; they wear the standard Chinese uniform, drab but cheap and available in abundance. In the towns and villages, Tibetan children have green Chinese army caps and blue or olive cotton Chinese jackets. Synthetic fibres and colours have replaced the natural cloth and hues of days gone by. The women are holding out, but many of them only wear a Tibetan *chuba* with its traditional embroidered apron and an elaborate hairstyle on special days.

Tibetans selling their jewellery, knives, prayer-wheels and charm-boxes to tourists for a few dozen yuan have become a common spectacle. Their paltry earnings will often be gone by nightfall, spent on drinks in a tavern owned by a well-fed Chinese newcomer. It is heartbreaking to see proud Khampa horsemen, with their bold eyes and striking faces, untie their braided hair and remove the traditional coral beads and turquoises to sell to a tourist for a couple of ten-yuan notes. In the alleys around the Jokhang, these very Khampas, who not so long ago were still resisting the Chinese encroachment on Tibet, have turned into black-market money-changers. They unaffectedly greet tourists with a ringing 'Change money?' Just as the small dealers and speculators do in Peking and Canton, they offer almost twice the official rate for the Foreign Exchange Certificates that the Bank of China gives foreigners in return for their convertible currency. FECs are very much in demand, for they buy better-quality Chinese goods or imports in special shops. Some of Tibet's precious works of art find their way to the West, where they command extremely high prices. After being looted by the cultural revolution, Tibet is slowly losing the authentic treasures that remain, which are rapidly being replaced by counterfeit relics.

'Fashion comes to Tibet', proclaims a *Xinhua* headline. 'Every popular item in China's large cities soon finds its way to Lhasa', the agency dispatch explains with ill-concealed glee in an interview with young Tibetans. 'I prefer to wear large sweaters when I go out, but to go dancing, I have to dress up', confides a young girl. 'Tibetans used to wear long-lasting garments, but now they prefer flashy clothes', claims a young man. The Tibetans are ready to pay large sums to buy Chinese textiles. To keep up appearances, a young Tibetan woman must have a number of Western-style outfits; Tibetan tailors are beginning to use synthetic material and colours, even for traditional Tibetan clothing.

Traditional hand-made footwear no longer finds any buyers. Over two hundred types of tennis shoes selling at 160 yuan a pair (a month's salary) were snapped up in four days in a Lhasa shop, according to the news agency.[38] The traders on Lhasa's Beijing Street clothing stalls buy their goods in Chinese cities like Hangzhou, Canton and Shanghai, China's fashion capital. About a third of Lhasa's inhabitants work in the garment trade, according to *Xinhua*.

The Chinese press is not exaggerating. Sceptics may be glad to hear that in Lhasa, both Chinese and Tibetan neighbourhoods swing to the latest Western pop hits. Two to three months after its release, Sting's latest hit will be playing all over Lhasa. In 1987 and 1988, Tibetan guys and dolls were rocking the night away in discos located within hailing distance of the Potala. The campaign against 'bourgeois liberalization' hardly made a dent in these antics, which seem quite droll against the background of the high Himalayas. In Lhasa, the new rites of Sinocization are staged at the 'Deluxe' discotheque, where Chinese and Tibetan musicians play rock 'n' roll with state-of-the-art amplifiers and synthesizers from Japan. In the soft darkness, the patrons bury their differences for a few hours every Saturday night. But they rarely dance with each other. Most couples are either Chinese or Tibetan.

Traditional ways are being abandoned even in the farthest reaches of Qinghai. Another official publication relates that 'except for a few nomads in pastoral areas, few Tibetans in Qinghai still wear traditional costumes. Zhuobao, a young Tibetan employed by the local administration of Qonghe, the district capital, wears a modern Western suit and speaks fluent Chinese. He says, "I prefer Western clothing to Tibetan dress. It is much more practical. But I still wear traditional costume for our celebrations".' The magazine goes on to explain that as a result of contact with Han, the Golog people, one of the most primitive tribes in Qinghai, have given up using stone instruments to cut wool and plough the earth. Since 'liberation', they have been introduced to progress, symbolized by running water and electricity.[39] Another Chinese magazine goes one step further with an 'investigation' entitled 'A Living Buddha turned Businessman'. The extravagant narrative describes a monk from Tashilhumpo monastery in Shigatse who is trying his luck in business. 'I'm known as the businessman in monk's robes or the Lama-trader. One might think there is a conflict between these two activities. But I feel both are connected and I remain a devout Buddhist', he says.[40] I remember reading somewhere that Tashilhumpo had set up an import-export agency. There's no stopping progress.

Almost all the food markets and restaurants in Tibetan towns are by now in the hands of Chinese families, who can rely on an abundance of cheap labour: so many Tibetans are unemployed! Their Tibetan customers are open-handed *bon vivants*. They enjoy eating and drinking and talking in loud voices over a plate of good food. Some are known to spend all their money in restaurants. Just as the foreign concessions in Shanghai were off limits to Chinese and dogs, some of the more upmarket restaurants in Lhasa adamantly refuse to serve Tibetan customers.

In Tibetan homes as well the decor is changing: the furniture is often Chinese nowadays, and so is the bedding. A television set often dominates the main room. This is a wonderful tool for Chinese Communist propaganda, unrelentingly instilling alien values based on materialism and consumerism in the minds of its Tibetan audience. To provide maximum exposure, China has invested heavily in ground facilities to secure optimum reception of Chinese television programmes relayed by satellite. China Central Television programmes have been available in Lhasa since 1978. After an experimental phase, the network expanded rapidly. By 1990, there were 2 radio broadcasting stations in Tibet, 14 short- and medium-wave stations, 74 cable radio stations at the district level, 2 television stations, 98 television relays and 163 ground stations to receive radio and television programmes relayed by satellite. Thanks to this growing network, 21.8 per cent of the Tibetan population can listen to medium-wave radio broadcasts and 34 per cent can watch television.[41] The political value attached to this propaganda weapon by the Chinese authorities was revealed by a high-ranking official in charge of the radio and television department of the Tibet Autonomous Region in a Lhasa television broadcast on 30 April 1991. 'Hostile forces abroad regard broadcasting as the only effective means to subvert the socialist system', he said. 'Therefore, we must have a sense of urgency, be fully aware of the impact and the importance of radio and television in the political struggle and in social and cultural construction, and develop the region's radio and television services as quickly as possible.'[42]

When a village is connected to the power lines, the local Party committee will often donate a television set to the community. At twilight, when work in the fields is done, the peasants congregate around the box to watch an incongruous combination of Peking Opera peppered with rather ham-handed advertising. Little programming is in Tibetan. The little that is can be hard to understand, for the speakers affect Chinese-inflected tones. Just as it put paid to the traditional customs and life-styles of the rural communities in Western Europe, television is killing off a culture in Tibet.

The West is not watching idly from the sidelines. On 31 March 1991, the Voice of America (VOA) started broadcasting a daily 15-minute programme in Tibetan. Often jammed, but very closely followed in Tibet, it keeps Tibetans up-to-date on the latest developments in the international arena relating to their cause.

Tibetan architecture is also undergoing irreversible changes. A Westerner arriving for the first time in Lhasa with no preparation will be disenchanted: most of it looks just like any other Chinese town. On the outskirts, the traveller's gaze will be riveted by the graceful golden roofs and massive red façade of the Potala, the Dalai Lama's residence and seat of the government, built in the seventeenth century. A powerful, majestic symbol of Tibet, it soars 375 feet from its base on a small hill and towers over the city. But once in Lhasa, the transformation of the city is overwhelming. The traditional houses are gone. Tall Chinese buildings are everywhere. The few old neighbourhoods left have been gutted in preparation for new edifices to be built, more often than not by workers brought in from China. The elegant rows of low, half-timbered dwellings with their white façades and black or blue-trimmed windows have been replaced by bleak Chinese cement cubes. Here again, the official media is ready with an answer: 'Tibetan religious devotees used to drag themselves in the mud while reciting their scriptures around the Jokhang in Lhasa. Now they can walk on a granite and asphalt path that runs 600 yards along Barkhor street.'43 Socialism coming to the rescue of religion?

The Chinese government claims it spent 40 million yuan from 1979 to 1989 to 'renovate old houses'. From the Barkhor, the historical nucleus of Lhasa, 1,300 families living in 'dangerous' houses were compelled to relocate to new housing – which does provide some running water and a toilet on each floor, seldom available in traditional buildings.44 Tibetans complain that the rooms are smaller, however, and the thin concrete walls offer no protection from the cold. These achievements seem modest in comparison with the sums spent since 1989 on the rest of the city. In the first quarter of 1991, a considerable amount of 'renovation' was carried out to prepare for the celebration of the fortieth anniversary of the signing of the Seventeen-Point Agreement, which consecrated China's intervention in Tibet and cemented its integration with Chinese soil. Many houses were demolished to widen the streets. To get an idea of how much Lhasa has changed, one must bear in mind that since 1959 the built-up area has been multiplied by a factor of 12, for a total of 3 million square metres. Needless to say, the new buildings are Chinese-style reinforced concrete, even those which have been given a slightly Tibetan look. The authentically Tibetan part of Lhasa that has not yet been attacked by Chinese bulldozers now covers only 2 per cent, if not less, of the total area of the city. On the 'modern' square that was built from scratch in front of the holy Jokhang temple, the Chinese flag is flown under the watchful eye of three members of the People's Armed Police on permanent duty. No description of today's Lhasa is complete without a mention of a new monument, a masterpiece of poor taste that was erected in May 1991 in the centre of a busy roundabout by the Chinese authorities – two gigantic golden yaks.

'With its 1,300-year history, Lhasa is the economic, cultural and religious centre of Tibet. It used to be a small town with no roads or factories. There were only a few workshops. The city covered only 2 square kilometres and the population did not exceed 30,000. Now, with 120,000 inhabitant and covering 34 square kilometres, Lhasa has developed and has become a modern town with new hotels, theatres, hospitals, a cultural centre for children and an art gallery', according to *Xinhua*. The same words apply to the other larger towns and cities in the rest of Tibet, including Amdo and Kham. In each case, a new city inhabited by Chinese cadres and their families has mushroomed, and continues to spread unchecked as it accommodates the flood of new arrivals from the Middle Kingdom. China's excess population is overflowing into the unpopulated vastness of Tibet.

The campaign to Sinocize and amalgamate is going strong even in the monasteries, the last redoubts of Tibet's identity. At the great Kumbum monastery near Xining in Qinghai – renamed 'Ta Er Si' by the Chinese – the authorities have sandwiched in among the Tibetan ritual objects a set of reproductions of the 6,000 clay warriors and horses discovered in the tomb of emperor Qin Shi Huang near Xian, the former imperial capital of Chang'an! These warriors are known as the paramount symbol of Han civilization. Also well in evidence in the monastery are some brightly coloured butter sculptures depicting the marriage of Songtsen Gampo and the Chinese princess, Wengchen. At Labrang monastery in Gansu, we saw another marriage of convenience of the sacred and profane, another blatant deception foisted on the Tibetan monks: one of the restored halls contained a massive butter sculpture of the entrance to the Forbidden City in Peking. On the façade, in the best Chinese socialist-realist style, the 'artists' had drawn a portrait of Mao Tse-tung and the two slogans that have graced the original structure since the fifties: 'Long live the Chinese Communist Party' and 'Proletarians of the World Unite'. Butter sculpture is a specifically Tibetan art-form going back to the thirteenth century. In that same hall, displayed in parallel with reliquaries and other Tibetan Buddhist ritual objects, I found a bust of Mao and some butter figures representing the present leadership of Communist China. Just in case anyone was tempted to think that in a monastery lying over 800 miles from Peking, the joke was in rather poor taste, the official guide will clarify that these works of art are a token of the 'patriotic spirit of the Tibetan people' and of their loyalty to New China.

Human rights violations

This is a sensitive, difficult and painful topic, but it is one we cannot elude or even less pass over in silence. People in a position to speak out, and the governments of the countries that are free, have an imperative duty to intervene and get involved. We feel obliged to provide assistance to a person in danger. What about an entire people? If 'human rights violations' are defined in the same terms in Lhasa and in London or in

Washington, then the truth of the matter is that violations in Tibet are numerous, frequent and extremely serious. Since they are covered up whenever possible, they often escape notice. In the opinion of Alexander Solzhenitsyn, the Chinese Communist regime in Tibet is 'more brutal and inhuman than any other Communist regime in the world'.[45]

China ratified the International Convention Against Torture and Other Cruel, Inhuman or Degrading Treatments or Punishment on 5 September 1988. In a statement on 14 November 1988 to the Third Committee of the United Nations General Assembly, announcing China's ratification, Mrs Gao Yanping of the Chinese delegation highlighted the fact that 'as a vast country with a large population, there is still a great deal to be done in China with respect to forbidding torture and other inhuman treatment or punishment'. This is commendable frankness.

China has a permanent seat on the Security Council, and it has endorsed the Universal Declaration on Human Rights of 10 December 1948. According to the *People's Daily*, the official mouthpiece of the Chinese Communist Party, 'inhuman acts such as segregation, genocide, trade in slaves, persecuting refugees and terrorism must be condemned at the international level and the acts of other countries against such crimes cannot be considered "interference".'[46] The rights and duties of citizens, the protection of minorities, women and children and legal sanctions against criminals were felt by the newspapers, however, to be matters that fall within the scope of the internal affairs of a State. China systematically rejects any allegations of human rights violations emanating from foreign organizations and, more rarely, foreign governments. It specifically rejects any that concern Tibet. Over and over, it has asserted that China will 'not tolerate, under any pretext whatsoever, the slightest further interference by any foreign government or organization in Tibetan affairs, which are exclusively the internal affairs of China'.

Here is a summary of Peking's position on the matter: 'Bourgeois and certain unscrupulous persons attack the socialist system on the basis of human rights. The imperialists and Western bourgeoisie have never stopped using human rights to attack and slander China, nor have they lessened their efforts to infiltrate China ideologically. The instruments of Western propaganda have continuously presented a distorted picture of Chinese activities in favour of human rights and social conditions. They maintain that the socialist democratic system violates what they call human rights. Some have even supported people engaged in illegal activities in China, with the pretext of promoting human rights ... Anyone who is unprejudiced can see that the rights of the Chinese citizen stipulated in the Constitution are superior to the individual human rights of the Western bourgeoisie. Of course, the rights enjoyed by the citizens of a country depend first of all on its social system and therefore on its economy, its culture and other objective conditions. This is how, in a developing socialist country such as ours, the full implementation of citizens' rights will take some time.'[47] In other words, dear citizens, kindly be patient, we'll have jam tomorrow . . .

As far as the Chinese authorities are concerned, there never have been and never will be any human rights violations in Tibet. Any allegations to that effect that have gained currency in the West are 'baseless rumours', 'gossip', 'lies' and 'fabrications' spread by foreign circles that 'harbour ulterior motives'. For a few years, from 1985 to 1988, the official Chinese press made a few timid but genuine attempts to bring about greater transparency. (In Chinese, *glasnost* is called '*toumingdu*'.) But the endeavour was relegated to the back burner after the disastrous repression of the student demonstrations on 4 June 1989. When it comes to the overall picture, independent observers agree that China's official spokesmen and the media that carry their statements have never hesitated to lie 'for reasons of State'. The sinister campaign that followed the events of 4 June serves as a constant reminder.

Starting in autumn 1990, after the July visit to Tibet of Jiang Zemin, the new Chinese Communist Party Secretary, the authorities modified their approach to reduce its negative impact on China's image abroad and to increase the effectiveness of their increasingly subtle methods of repression. The new tactics, which left the basis and the objectives of China's presence in Tibet unchanged, are clearly set out in Circular No. 20, a confidential document that emanated from a meeting in Lhasa on 17 October 1990 known as the 'Regional Conference on Basic Work on Public Security in Grassroots Units (Gongan zhian jiceng jichu gongzuo huihi).[48] Armed with these new guidelines, the Chinese government has struggled to improve the quality of its public relations with foreign countries. One of the new measures has been to grant access to Lhasa to a few foreign delegations essentially composed of diplomats or parliamentarians, despite their expressed intention to investigate the human rights situation. Some have even been taken on lightning tours of Drapchi, officially 'Lhasa's only prison', after it had been carefully prepared for the occasion. But Peking's hoped-for results have been elusive. Although the delegations were closely watched by a crowd of officials, the distressing conditions in which the Tibetans live were quite apparent to them. For example: a delegation of twelve parliamentarians and academics sent by the Australian government in July 1991 concluded that the lifting of martial law had not made much difference on the ground. 'Martial law continues to exist in every respect except in name', it emphasized in its report. During its visit, the delegation observed that 'Tibetans unconnected with the Government overwhelmingly opposed Chinese control of Tibet, sought independence and the return of the Dalai Lama'.[49] In December 1991, a delegation composed of four Swiss diplomats visited Drapchi; a political prisoner shouted a few words in support of the Dalai Lama and independence for Tibet. With the additional eight-year sentence he has been given as punishment, Tanak Jigme Zangpo will be spending a total of forty-two years in jail.[50] Also in 1991, the delegation of the US–China National Committee inconveniently asked to see the women's quarters, which had not been suitably prepared; so did the Austrian delegation in 1992. At the close of his 29 March to 2 April 1991 visit to Lhasa, US Ambassador James Lilley described the staging of his tour of Drapchi prison as being 'as phoney as a three-dollar bill'.[51] Two prisoners tried to hand him a petition; it was snatched away by a Chinese official, and the petitioners, as well as a dozen others who supported them, were severely beaten and placed incommunicado.

The tour of Drapchi as a feature of official visits to Lhasa was inaugurated in November 1990 by the ambassadors of Denmark, Sweden, Finland and Norway to Peking. It may be replaced by Trisam, a brand-new prison completed in late 1992 at the opposite end of Lhasa, well away from Drapchi and two other major unacknowledged prisons, Sangyip and Gutsa, which hold from several hundred to over a thousand people. Several smaller detention centres have sprung up in the vicinity of the monasteries.

Human rights violations in Tibet can be classified in three broad categories:

— ill-treatment by Army, police and paramilitary forces, show trials, summary public executions and torture in detention;
— excesses in the implementation of the birth-control policy, with forced abortions and sterilizations;
— segregation between Hans (Chinese) and Tibetans at school, in daily life, and in access to positions of power and responsibility.

Fortunately for Tibet, the main non-governmental organizations active in the field of human rights, such as Amnesty International, Asia Watch, the Minority Rights Group and the International League for Human Rights have been closely following developments in Tibet. There is so much credible testimony and so many reports concerning the brutality of the Chinese government and its officials in Tibet that it would be impossible to list them all here. Suffice it to say that in 1992, a UN body found it necessary to call for the compilation of material relating to violations. As we have seen in the past, summary executions without trial or following show trials and maltreatment of prisoners were common in Tibet in the 1960s and 1970s. Although the volume was turned down when the granting of greater religious and social tolerance became policy in 1979, the persecution has never really ceased; it remains as oppressive as ever. The cases of torture have multiplied as a result of the first demonstrations for Tibetan independence since the cultural revolution, in October 1987. Aside from the prisons mentioned above, the other detention centres in the vicinity of Lhasa and the notorious labour camps in Qinghai, there are said to be at least four big 'reform-through-labour' camps in central Tibet: Nachen Thang on the Kyichu river a few miles from Lhasa; Golmo to the north in the Tsaidam basin; Tsala Karpo also to the north and Powo Tramo in Kongpo, in the southern forests. The Chinese authorities have never allowed a Western journalist into these camps. They admit the existence of one prison (Drapchi) and two 'reform-through-labour' facilities in the Tibet Autonomous Region, holding fewer than 900 prisoners. This is a highly improbable figure; the true number is likely to be at least ten to twenty times higher. Peking claims that a total of 121 Tibetan rioters were sentenced between 1987 and early 1992 out of 1,025 who had been arrested. In 1991, a joint report by Asia Watch and the Tibet Information Network listed the names and details of 360 Tibetans arrested for political offences, of whom 240 were still being held in September 1991. More names arrive constantly. The two organisations emphasized that the list only accounted for 'a fraction of the total penitentiary population in Tibet'.[52]

Torture, rape, electric cattle prods

In early September 1988, Daniel Southerland, the *Washington Post* correspondent in Peking, compiled the testimony available on the treatment meted out to the people who had been arrested on 5 March that year. The results were edifying. One Lhasa resident who prefers to remain anonymous for obvious reasons had spent time in Gutsa prison. For over three months, he had shared a tiny cell with seven other Tibetans. 'Not a single one of those arrested on 5 March escaped the beatings ... They hit us with whatever came to hand' – fists, sticks, electric prods. A common technique used on detainees is called Chinese rope torture: 'I saw people hanging several feet off the floor, from ropes tied around their hands folded behind their backs. Two of the people I saw had dislocated shoulders from the pull of the ropes. Many became unconscious as a result of this treatment.' The worst treatment is reserved for the nuns. The most brutal wardens are not the Chinese but the Tibetans; one used to mock their slogans by punctuating his blows with: 'I'll give you independence'. Once a month, three or four Chinese and Tibetans in uniform would lecture the prisoners, explaining how Tibet is part of China.

Testimony gathered from Tibetans by Western residents reports torture with electric prods applied to the tongue, the toes, the chest and the genitals of the prisoners. Electric cattle prods have been inserted in the vaginas of some Tibetan nuns. Other nuns had cigarette burns on their faces. 'I was arrested on 1 October 1987, during the first riot', a fifty-year-old Tibetan woman told an AFP correspondent in March 1988. 'I had thrown stones at the police. In jail, I was beaten with the electric prod. The guards were Tibetans and Chinese. There were thirteen of us women, arrested in two batches. One was pregnant and had a miscarriage after she was kicked in the stomach. In prison, they kept telling us independence was nothing but a dream. They called us the Dalai Lama's separatists.' In November 1988, British television's Channel 4 showed a documentary by Vanya Kewley called 'Tibet: A Case to Answer'. Filmed covertly in Tibet, it revealed the plight of Tibetan men and women who had all undergone torture with the electric prod. One young nun out of a group of four who spoke openly into the camera wept as she said: 'They led me away in handcuffs to the police station and flung me on the ground. They stamped on my face, they beat me with the electric prod and kicked me in the chest. They undressed me completely. There were three or four of them, poking us with the electric prods.' One of the others chimed in: 'We were raped repeatedly by seven or eight people. We were completely naked. They told us that since we opposed the Communist system, we would be executed.' In the film, a Tibetan man tells how his wife was forcibly sterilized after the birth of their second child. Others spoke of being forced to have an abortion.

Valerio Pellizzari, from the Roman daily *Il Messaggero*, heard similar accounts in August 1988. One Tibetan recounted his ordeal: 'The police took me to Gutsa prison. They tied me hand and foot and started beating me with sticks and iron bars. Then they touched my genitals with the electric prods. I fainted. They threw cold water on me to revive me, tied me to a bed and continued.'

Another ex-prisoner, now twenty-nine and living in exile in Dharamsala, agreed to speak under the pseudonym of Jayang. He told the AFP correspondent in New Delhi how he was tortured after being arrested on 15 October 1987 at Dingri, 60 miles from the Nepalese border, as he tried to escape after the demonstrations of September and October 1987. 'I knew the police had my photo and had been looking for me since October 4th. I had left Lhasa on the 8th; I was caught and arrested five days later. They tied my feet with the heels digging into my thighs, and then bound my hands twisted behind my back. I spent days and nights like that, my legs numb from not moving and the cold.' At night, the hapless man slept on 'a cement bed with a blanket as a mattress'. One month and ten days later, he appeared in court, where he was asked to identify the leaders of the independence movement. In early December, he was sent to the hills to gather wood with the other prisoners. It was snowing and very cold. While his guards weren't looking, he managed to escape. This time he crossed the Nepalese border successfully, but he was relieved of his last personal belongings by Nepalese. His wife and four children stayed behind in Tibet.

Several Tibetans have told me that Geshe Lobsang Wangchuk, a high Lama and resistance hero from early times, died from the injuries caused by torture in prison. In spite of the treatment inflicted by his gaolers after his initial arrest in 1959, this Tibetan martyr never betrayed his convictions. Set free in 1979, he was arrested again a few years later. His Chinese torturers must have thought he was impossible, because they granted him 'full liberation' in 1987. He died a few days later. The Chinese government maintains that he 'died of illness' – unspecified – despite all the 'care' that was lavished on him.

John Ackerley and Blake Kerr, after visiting the country several times and interviewing many victims, have published a thorough report on torture in Tibet. It appears that in general, prisoners suspected of 'separatist' activities are systematically beaten when they are arrested. The use of the electric prod seems to be very extensive. Other forms of torture that are used in Tibet are even more degrading and dangerous, such as plunging a naked prisoner into icy water in winter, hanging someone upside-down, forcing a person to eat human excrement, setting dogs on prisoners and injecting substances which are claimed by several witnesses to have a very disturbing physical and also mentally deranging effect.[53] Testimony about such practices continued to accumulate throughout 1991 and 1992, brought by arriving Tibetan refugees.

If any more were necessary, here is an excerpt from the testimony of Adhi Tapey, a Tibetan who spent twenty-six years in Chinese prisons until she was let out in 1986. She fled to Nepal in the following year. 'I was chained, tortured, forced to watch my brother-in-law's execution, raped over and over again by Chinese gaolers until I was ready to admit anything', she testified in November 1989 in Copenhagen at a debate on Tibet organized by the local Support Group. 'We were hardly given anything to eat. We had to eat herbs, roots and worms to survive', she told the audience, mainly composed of Danish parliamentarians representing the entire political spectrum.

For anyone who feels sceptical about this testimony, it may be enough to recall that the Chinese press itself, as a result of the exemplary action of a few brave journalists, actually published investigations into some particularly odious cases of torture in police stations or 'detention centres'. To give a single example, in October 1988, the *Youth Daily* gave front-page treatment to the story of some Chinese policemen who had spent an entire night 'to the rhythm of disco music' beating a man hung from a rope with electric prods, iron bars and the handle of a hoe. When one torturer was tired he would yield to the next, stopping only for a snack. His entire body bruised and bloody, particularly the genital area, the victim obstinately refused to confess to a crime he had not committed. He died in the morning. A photograph of the man's daughter, her little face contorted with grief, appeared along with the article. Threatened time and again with reprisals, it took both courage and perseverance for the *Youth Daily* journalists to go through with their investigation and publish the results. The policemen went unpunished until the case was aired in public in Peking, at which point the Chinese leadership felt compelled to 'do something' to appease the 'anger of the masses'. A court finally sentenced the policemen to a few months in jail. It is safe to assume that they were released early. In China, particularly in rural areas, the local police still feels it is above the law and has every right, including the right to torture and kill.

It may also be worth recalling that the Chinese authorities are not too worried about international censure. They think nothing of offering labour-camp prisoners as cheap labour to Western companies that set up a plant in China. Volvo, the Swedish automobile manufacturers, received just such an offer. As soon as the deal was made public, Volvo blew the whistle on the offer of 'slave labour'. Other industrialists were approached with the same offer. They were told not to worry, for Chinese wardens would be assigned along with the prisoners to handle security. The Western partner could expect to pay these 'captive' workers only one-third of the rate for ordinary Chinese labourers. The Chinter company, with offices in Brussels and a Chinese–Belgian Chairman, has also had offers of this kind made to it.

China did release a number of Tibetan prisoners in 1988, less out of leniency than as a result of the pressure brought to bear by Western governments and humanitarian organizations. While living in China, I was approached several times by Chinese who begged me to intervene with the 'higher authorities' in order to obtain redress for a miscarriage of justice or for some hideous instance of police brutality. I was able to visit Prison Number One in Peking and a re-education-through-labour (*laojiao*) camp in the suburbs of Peking. These were 'model units' that are *duiwai kaifang*, meaning 'open to the outside'. In essence, they are special facilities designed to meet the needs of the regime's propaganda. No foreigner has ever been allowed to visit reform-through-labour (*laogai*) camps or the cells where known dissidents are held, not to speak of the punishment cells. The descriptions I heard from ex-inmates of the Chinese penitentiary world lifted the veil on a hell where mental and physical cruelty reign supreme. The gulag of Mao's time may have improved with the open-door policy in force since 1979. But with the wave of repression that followed the massacre of 4 June 1989, Chinese jails are again packed with political prisoners.

When it comes to Tibet, however, any media coverage of these topics is taboo. Very seldom does any information filter through. In early 1988, the *Tibet Daily* explicitly mentioned 'torture' as a practice the police should 'avoid'. Another remarkable admission – concerning the existence of political prisoners in Tibet – was made by an unidentified prison official.[54] And in June 1988, Radio Lhasa announced that a special police unit was being set up to contend with 'separatist' riots. 'Detachment Number Two' was placed directly under the orders of the People's Armed Police and told to be 'prepared to coordinate its activity at a moment's notice with the Public Security organs in case of any incident, in order to deal resolute blows to the separatists who sabotage the unity of the motherland and the solidarity among the nationalities' in China.[55]

Official depictions of life in Tibet's prisons would be funny if the topic were not so serious. On 1 March 1990, on the occasion of the Tibetan New Year, the official Chinese press agency lauded the relations between prisoners and wardens. They are so harmonious, it said, that some detainees are 'reluctant' to leave the prison once their sentence has been served. In the prison visited by *Xinhua*, the prisoners 'are light-hearted and as happy' as if they were free. The New Year celebrations organized by the authorities were 'as joyous for the inmates as for people outside' and the food was 'delicious'. 'Wardens never beat the prisoners', the agency maintains. Six to ten prisoners live in each cell, which are not locked until nightfall and 'resemble university dormitories'. In February 1991, *Xinhua* published further dispatches praising the prison administration. 'In the only prison' in Tibet, 'if the prison regulations were not posted on the wall, it would be hard to know it was a prison'. The detainees do manual labour five days a week. Those who attend the clinic are usually suffering from dysentery or a cold. As for the women, 10 per cent of the prison population, they are given 'special attention' and sometimes 'giggle when they wash their clothes or watch television'.[56]

Forced abortions and sterilizations

The 'stringent' implementation of the birth control policy in areas inhabited by Tibetans is another domain in which there are human rights violations. With almost 1.2 billion inhabitants and probably more than 1.5 billion mouths to feed by the year 2050, China is bowed under the weight of its immense population. Although figures published in 1993 seem to indicate unexpected improvement, the explosive growth is by no means under control, It was caused in part by Chairman Mao's poor judgment in the 1960s. Both Chinese and foreign experts agree that China's poverty cannot be overcome until it restrains the growth of its population. Recent projections show that by the year 2000, new Chinese births may more than make up for the industrial and agricultural surplus accruing from economic reforms. It is easy to understand why the government is keen to implement the birth control measure it has adopted. In the countryside, traditional attitudes are strong: a family with ten children is a prosperous one. When the first family planning measures were announced in 1979, Peking specified that the poorer rural areas and the areas inhabited by ethnic minorities would enjoy a measure of exemption. Underpopulated areas (like Tibet) inhabited by minorities were to be fully exempt. It now seems that whatever was left of this 'favour' to the minorities is being withdrawn, since the January 1992 announcement by the Chinese government specifying that birth control measures shall extend to Tibetan farmers and nomads. These have unofficially applied to urban Tibetans, particularly those employed by the State, for a number of years. Explaining the measure, Gying Puncog, Vice-President of the Lhasa government, said that the population of the Tibet Autonomous Region had risen to 2.2 million and would exceed 2.6 million by the year 2000. The authorities, he added, would 'gradually push the family planning work forward to include central Tibet and herdsmen', who had previously benefited from the exemption.[57]

It is difficult for Western journalists to wander unnoticed in the villages outside central Tibet, for most of these areas are off limits to foreigners, but there is too much testimony to doubt that alarming excesses do occur. In 1988, I drove from Lanzhou, the capital of Gansu province, to the 'Autonomous District of Gannan', a mountainous region in the south that used to be part of Tibet's Amdo province. I wanted to admire the now fading splendour of Labrang monastery. In the nearby village of Xiahe, whenever I managed to escape my driver's watchful eye, I asked local people and monks in the area how the birth control regulations were being enforced. I was told how worried the Tibetan people were about this problem. I learned that the Chinese State Commission for Family Planning has offices and delegations in each of the nineteen provinces, regions and townships in China, to make sure that the orders of the central government are applied. In Peking, the official position is that the 'one child policy' does not apply to the Tibetan minority. Only those Tibetans who are Party cadres or high officials are expected to 'provide an example'. The grass-roots reality is quite different.

The mission of the local authorities is to strictly control births in the areas inhabited by minorities, no matter how remote. Cadres who achieve results that improve on the quotas assigned to them will be given a reward and a promotion. Those who fail will be reprimanded or demoted. In this region of Gansu, inhabited by hundreds of thousands of Tibetans, specially-trained Chinese teams continuously make the rounds of the villages to find women pregnant with a third or fourth child – and sometimes even with a second child. When caught, they are forcibly taken to a clinic for an abortion. Many cases have been recorded of women being sterilized without their consent. No statistics are available, but I have listened to tale after tale of women being hunted down, dragged away screaming with fear and thrown into the back of a jeep with no more consideration than if they had been a sack of potatoes. The clinics' hygiene is such that the operations often lead to infections. Tibetan women have died or been scarred for life as a result. Several have testified that 'if a woman resists, she will be given no post-operative care – as a lesson'. Other Tibetan sources have informed me that identical scenarios are common in Qinghai, in Sichuan and even in parts of the Tibet Autonomous Region. In December 1987, several hundred students from the Middle School for National Minorities and the Teacher Training College in Tongren, along with monks from Rekong monas-

tery in eastern Qinghai, demonstrated for several days against these practices, shouting 'Down with family planning!' as they marched through
the streets.

For the Tibetan communities that have been reduced to the status of
a small minority in the areas outside central Tibet (in Qinghai the 810,000
Tibetans now constitute less than 20 per cent of the total population)
the struggle is far too unequal. There are grounds for wondering about
genocide being committed in Tibet.

I questioned three young Tibetan monks who had just fled into exile.
Lobsang Gyatso, twenty-one, Lobsang Shenpen, eighteen and Gyanpa
Gyatso, twenty-one, had come from Qinghai and from Sichuan. We spoke
in Chinese, with no one listening to us. All three confirmed that forcible
abortions and sterilizations had become commonplace in their home
regions.

Lobsang Gyatso comes from Qinghai: 'The birth control policy was
not extended to Tibetans in 1986, as some people claim. It was in force
by 1983. I don't know about the situation in China, but in areas where
there are Tibetans, all women who have borne one or two children are
expected to accept sterilization. The operation will be done by force if
necessary. Local medical personnel carry out these operations. From 1984
to 1985 onwards, they started forcing Tibetan women to go to hospitals
or clinics for the operation. At the time, the operation was free of charge.
Now, the price is going higher and higher. It varies from place to place.
If a woman does not submit willingly to the operation, there will be a
fine of 700 or 800 yuan. As further punishment, the authorities may
confiscate the ration tickets and residence permits to which the family
is entitled.'

What is the situation elsewhere?

Lobsang Shenpen is from Sichuan: 'Our region, now called the
"Autonomous District of Aba" is richer than Qinghai. The policy is two
children at most. But some wealthy Chinese and Tibetan cadres prefer
to pay for a chance to have more children. The Tibetans have to pay
more bribes to the Chinese so that they will accept this irregularity. We
also have sterilization by force.'

Do women ever die or fall ill after these operations?

Lobsang Shenpen: 'I know some have died. Many lose their health
after the operation, they become sickly.'

The Chinese authorities deny it all, particularly since the USA with-
drew support for the United Nations Fund for Population Activities
(UNFPA) in 1985 to protest against the use of these methods in China
as a whole. Two contemporary US Congress resolutions had declared
such practices 'crimes against humanity'. Shen Guoxiang, Deputy-Di-
rector of the State Commission for Family Planning, claims that the
Chinese government issues only general guidelines on this matter for the
areas inhabited by ethnic minorities: 'Our policy is to try to encourage

national minorities to practice family planning. Specific regulations setting the number of children allowed are drawn up by the local authorities.' She has of course never heard of any particular case of an abortion or a sterilization practised without the patient's consent: 'As far as I know, no family planning programme has ever been applied to the national minorities, and especially to the Tibetans. The central government confines itself to issuing instructions recommending that family planning be explained to populations that belong to national minorities. The specific regulations are formulated by the authorities at the local level.'[58]

China's national media is habitually close-mouthed when it comes to describing birth control practices in areas inhabited by ethnic Tibetans. One article in a local daily does however provide information on the situation in Amdo (Qinghai): in the Tibetan Autonomous Prefecture of Haibei, the natural growth rate of the population was substantially reduced between 1979 and 1984, dropping from 21.11 per cent to 10.07 per cent. 'Facts demonstrate that the masses among the minorities are willing to adopt birth control; this great event concerns all the families and every individual', adds Zhang Wei, the author.[59] Other Chinese sources announced that 18,000 women in the Tibet Autonomous Region had volunteered for sterilization in 1990, which works out at about 3 per cent of the women of childbearing age. Another 7,000 were said to be using contraceptives.[60] The transfer of Chinese settlers into Tibetan areas is accentuating the population imbalance. In this field as well, more and more testimony is becoming available, while official Chinese denials multiply apace. During a visit to Tibet in June and July 1991, John Ackerley, Director of the International Campaign for Tibet, and Susan Hatwick, a Sinologist, undertook an investigation of this phenomenon in the areas inhabited by ethnic Tibetans in Kanze (Ganze) and Ngapa (Aba) prefectures, at present amalgamated into Sichuan. According to their survey, 71 per cent of the Chinese settled in these areas said they had arrived since 1980. The majority of the new arrivals were shopkeepers or restaurant-owners. The remaining restaurants were owned by older Chinese who had been sent to Tibet with the People's Liberation Army or with the work crews employed in road-building during the 1950s and 1960s. Every town they visited now boasts a Chinese majority, whereas in the 1950s, each one was almost exclusively Tibetan. According to a Chinese census in 1982, Kanze and Ngapa prefectures were 56 per cent Tibetan. Today, the Tibetans are clearly a minority.[61]

Returning to Lhasa for the fourth time in 1992, a seasoned visitor commented: 'In June 1990, I was struck by the growing number of Chinese in Tibet as compared to 1987. Today no comparison is possible: Tibet is just becoming China. From Gongkar airport [50 miles away], new buildings can be seen everywhere. The outskirt of Lhasa have spread out dramatically. In Lhasa new shops are everywhere.' She added, '[s]ince

Deng Xiaoping announced his new [economic] policy in early 1992, I am told that thousands of Chinese have already arrived in Tibet to make money. All the construction spreading in every direction is undoubtedly destined to welcome thousands more.'

Segregation between Han and Tibetans

The third category of human rights violations in Tibet covers a set of practices that are both hard to pinpoint and acutely felt, difficult to quantify yet extremely common. The feelings that Han (Chinese) living in China proper harbour for Tibetans range from blank indifference to open contempt, quite rarely if occasionally tinged with curiosity. A sizeable number of Han are convinced that they embody civilization and progress whereas Tibetans are semi-barbarians enslaved by some medieval religious traditions. When it comes to Hans who live in Tibet, their feelings are even more sharply expressed and are often unmistakably racist. I am not about to forget a young Chinese, no more than eighteen years old, whom I asked about his life in Tibet. We were standing at an open-air market in the vicinity of the Jokhang in Lhasa. When I asked whether he was happy in Tibet, he gave me an incredulous look. 'Happy? Here? You must be joking! My parents brought me here. I don't want to stay long. I'm doing a little trading, but I don't want to stay. Just look at the Tibetans. They're worthless! They are as dumb as yaks!'

The simmering resentment between the Han and Tibetans is palpable wherever you go. When the hostility reaches a peak, fights break out in shops and restaurants. When a Chinese saunters into a temple, a cigarette dangling from his sneering lips and a green cloth cap firmly stuck to his head, quite impervious to the spiritual atmosphere of the place, he stands a good chance of being copiously insulted by the Tibetans. If alone, he may choose to quicken his pace and leave without a word. But if he has friends with him and they are feeling feisty, they will almost certainly reply in kind. In a restaurant, when the owner refuses to serve a Tibetan, plates and chairs will fly all around. When a Tibetan woman tries to peddle trinkets in a restaurant, she will be hustled out with insulting jokes. When Chinese try to visit the sites where the Tibetans carry out their 'sky burials', the traditional method for disposing of a corpse by cutting it up in small pieces for the vultures, the Tibetans chase them away.

In matters such as gaining admission to the better schools in Tibet and in the areas inhabited by Tibetans, it is the Han who have the priority, with few exceptions. The situation is the same in the hospitals. In the administration, the positions with decision-making power are virtually monopolized by Han cadres. Chinese statisticians claim that 37,000 of the 55,000 official positions in the Tibet Autonomous Region are held by Tibetans: 66.6 per cent of the total. But the figures are impossible to verify and nobody is fooled. Not once since 1950 has the position of first secretary of the Tibet Committee of the Chinese Communist Party been entrusted to a Tibetan. Why ever not?

The steady stream of testimony has become a torrent with the arrival of Tibetans fleeing the Chinese takeover of the temples and sanctuaries in Tibet. Starting in late 1987, entire families of Han cadres moved lock, stock and barrel into the monasteries, the better to monitor the monks' activities. Having initially taken up their posts as individual political cadres, they soon brought in their wives and children. In a few of the monasteries, so many have moved in that they now outnumber the monks! They bring constant pressure to bear on the senior monks in the monasteries and temples; their job is to sniff out in advance any planned protests or independence activities. The 'plotters' will immediately be separated from the rest and punished.

Lobsang Gyatso's testimony is explicit, and it tallies with other accounts:

— What is the situation like in Gansu?
— In 1981, 1982 and 1983, it was all right. Now it has become difficult. It is hard for us to express our faith. After the events in Lhasa, the response reached all the way here. It is difficult to bear for us monks. The police come to the monasteries every day to search and check up on us. They come every day. We don't know why they are coming. My monastery is called the Meiwujusi, it lies 55 miles from Labrang in eastern Gansu. The situation relaxed a little in 1980, and it lasted until 1987. The people felt living was easier. After the first incidents in Lhasa, a Chinese Work Team came to monitor our monastery. Ever since those incidents, a great number of police and local cadres regularly visit our compound and hold meetings. They inspect new arrivals and ask about our visitors, family and friends. We feel uneasy all the time. When we get up in the morning, we don't know what may happen by the evening. Since last year (1987), there is no real freedom of belief.
— Concretely, how does the pressure manifest?
— It had gone down after the end of the cultural revolution. What we are experiencing now is the constant monitoring of our monastery. There are so many Han among us now that the alleys are packed with them. If I want to go to fetch water, the street is full of Hans. There are more Chinese every day inside the monastery.
— Why do so many come?
— My impression is that the Chinese started populating our area in the 1950s. It is a settlement policy. As they arrive, they take control of the area. They take control of the local Tibetan population. In the monasteries, the settlers are basically cadres and their family. Bit by bit, they bring over their friends and acquaintances. The result is a huge number of Chinese. They open shops and stalls in the monasteries! By now, 65 to 70 per cent of the people living in a monastery will be Chinese and

the people they control. The other 30 to 35 per cent are the real inhabitants, the monks and Lamas.

— Don't the high Lamas protest about this to the Chinese?

— We never stop saying that the situation is intolerable and asking the Chinese to settle outside the perimeter of the monasteries. But our comments must first be approved by the 'competent authorities' among the leadership. Who are the 'competent authorities'? The Chinese. So this implies one set of Chinese protesting to other Chinese; a protest transmitted by the Chinese Communist Party to the Chinese Communist Party! In our monastery, we have already protested many times, but the results have been the very opposite of what we wanted. Look at this fountain. If we complain that we can't go to get water because there are too many Han around, a little sign will appear on the fountain saying it is not working!

Notes

1. *Jiefangjun Bao*, 16 September 1988.
2. *Zhongguo Xinwen She* (China News Service), 30 July 1988.
3. *Nuclear Tibet*, International Campaign for Tibet, Washington DC, 1993; *Far Eastern Economic Review*, 29 April 1993, p. 14.
4. *100 Questions About Tibet*, p. 90.
5. *Jiji Press*, a Japanese agency, 2 November 1990.
6. *Greenpeace Waste Trade Update*, 22 March 1992.
7. *China Daily*, 15 May 1989.
8. *Xinhua*, 4 February 1992.
9. *Tibet: Environment and Development Issues 1992*, Department of Information and International Relations, Central Tibetan Administration-in-exile, Dharamsala, 1992.
10. *Tibet, A Land of Snows Rich in Precious Stones and Mineral Resources*, Department of Security, Central Tibetan Administration-in-exile, Dharamsala, 1991.
11. *Tibet: Environment & Development Issues 1992*, p. 49.
12. *Tibetan Bulletin*, May–June 1992, pp. 11–19.
13. *Agence France-Presse*, 11 February 1991.
14. *Renmin Ribao* (People's Daily), 20 October 1988.
15. *China Daily*, 20 July 1988.
16. *Xinhua*, 5 August 1991.
17. Interview in the *South China Morning Post*, 26 October 1988.
18. Interview in the *China Daily*, 3 February 1989.
19. *Beijing Information*.
20. Statistics for 1989, *Japan, an International Comparison*, Keizai Koho Centre, Japan Institute for Social and Economic Affairs.
21. *100 Questions About Tibet*, p. 84.
22. *Xinhua*, 15 and 24 February 1991.
23. *Xinhua*, 8 September 1988.
24. *Xinhua*, 24 and 26 February 1991.
25. *Tibet, A General Survey*, The Tibetan People's Right to Autonomy, New Star Editions, Peking, 1991.

26. *Xinhua*, 3 August 1988.

27. *Xizang Ribao* (Tibet Daily), June 1988.

28. *About Tibet*, 'Big changes in 40 years', New Star Publishers, Peking, 1991 and *About Tibet*, 'New Developments in Tibetan Culture', New Star Publishers, Peking, 1991.

29. *Xinhua*, 30 November 1988.

30. *Xinhua*, 14 June 1988.

31. Radio Xining, 29 August 1988.

32. PTI Press Agency (India), 27 November 1988.

33. *100 Questions About Tibet*, pp. 75, 76.

34. *Questions and Answers About China's National Minorities*, p. 176.

35. From a September 1989 interview in the French daily *Libération*.

36. *Tibetans About Tibet*, p. 139.

37. *About Tibet*, 'Big changes in 40 years' and *About Tibet*, 'New developments in Tibetan Culture', New Star Publishers, Peking, 1991.

38. *Xinhua*, 10 October 1988.

39. *Beijing Information*, October 1988.

40. *Tibetans About Tibet*, p. 121.

41. *About Tibet*, 'New Developments in Tibetan Culture', New Star Publishers, Peking, 1991.

42. *Tibet Information Network*, News Update of 30 August 1991, p. 51.

43. *Xinhua*, 17 March 1988.

44. *Xinhua*, 6 December 1989, in *Tibet Information Network*, News Update of 30 April 1990.

45. Statement made in Tokyo, 10 October 1982.

46. *Renmin Ribao*, 3 December 1988.

47. *Beijing Information*, 2 August 1982.

48. For additional information about the main components of the new 'velvet glove' policy, see Corinne Vigniel's thesis: '*The shift from "Merciless Repression" to the "Comprehensive Management of Public Security" in the Tibet Autonomous Region*', School of Oriental and African Studies (SOAS) London University, 1991.

49. *Tibet Information Network*, News Update of 3 September 1991, p. 72.

50. *Tibet Information Network*, 9 January 1992.

51. *Tibetan Bulletin*, September–October 1991, p. 4.

52. These various figures were submitted to the United Nations Commission on Human Rights in February 1992.

53. *The Suppression of a People: Accounts of Torture and Imprisonment in Tibet*, by John Ackerley and Blake Kerr, Physicians for Human Rights, November 1989.

54. *China News Service*, 1 March 1988.

55. Radio Lhasa, 15 June 1988.

56. *Agence France-Presse*, 17 February 1991.

57. *Tibet Daily*, 3 January 1992.

58. Interview on 21 June 1988 by Daniel Southerland.

59. *Xibei Renkou*, North-West Population, April 1986.

60. *Tibetan Bulletin*, July-August 1991, page 25.

61. *The Long March, Chinese Settlers and Chinese Policies in Eastern Tibet*, International Campaign for Tibet, Washington DC, 1991.

6

A Happy Ending?

What chances are there for a peaceful resolution of the Tibetan conflict? More specifically – and this is a *sine qua non* – what chance is there of the Chinese and the Tibetans coming to an agreement? China has invited the Dalai Lama to return to China – 'his motherland' – to work for the well-being of his countrymen. There are two preconditions: he must relinquish for ever any claims relating to the independence of the Land of Snow, and he must publicly pledge allegiance to the Chinese authorities. The leader of the Tibetans has a different perspective. From where he stands, what is at issue is not his own future but the fate of his entire people. This is why, since the early 1980s, he has displayed commendable and growing moderation in hopes of arriving at a negotiated solution with Peking. He has invited China to open negotiations with a view to defining a durable compromise solution for Tibet's future.

The Dalai Lama has an unshakeable belief in non-violence. Whatever may be the motivations of Tibetans fighting to regain their independence, he continues to hold that violence against the Chinese would be suicidal. As a fervent admirer of Mahatma Gandhi, the Dalai Lama is convinced that violence is contrary to our human nature. What is more, it would provide ammunition for the factions in Peking that favour a harder line in Tibet and it would weaken the position of moderate Chinese. The Dalai Lama's position is bitterly rejected by the radical fringe among the Tibetans in exile, who consider that no solution is acceptable other than full independence. The Tibetan Youth Congress, an organization that has thousands of members, openly advocated terrorism against the Chinese inside Tibet until 1989. In Tibet as well, many members of the Tibetan resistance argue against the Dalai Lama's overtures to the Chinese. Abroad, the Tibetans enjoy the support of a growing number of Westerners and the sympathy of international opinion. It is true that no government in the world has recognized the Tibetan 'government-in-exile'. But the Dalai Lama meets a great many officials during his travels abroad, and the discreet yet enduring support he has received from a number of governments is a source of considerable irritation to China.

A ray of hope has appeared from the side of the Chinese dissidents who sought refuge in the West after the 4 June 1989 massacre on Tiananmen Square. The Federation for Democracy in China, based in Paris, insists that finding a satisfactory solution for the Tibetan people will be one of the priorities in a democratic China. Discussions with the entourage of the Dalai Lama are well under way. The award of the 1989 Nobel Peace Prize to the Dalai Lama served as a tremendous source of encouragement to the Tibetan people, particularly for those who were on the verge of losing hope in the possibility of achieving freedom for Tibet through non-violence. Another decisive event for the Tibetan side was China's loss of an important asset – the Panchen Lama, who died in peculiar circumstances in January 1989. For years, the Tibetan cleric had officially supported Peking's positions. In his last public statement, three days before his death, he unexpectedly declared that Tibet had lost more than it had gained from the arrival of the Chinese. The Dalai Lama refers to him as a 'freedom fighter'.

The Dalai Lama and non-violence

With the passing of the years, intentionally or not, the Dalai Lama has become a seasoned politician. He has a genuinely democratic outlook. Draped in the same purple and ochre robes that are worn by all Tibetan Buddhist monks, wearing glasses and a wrist-watch, there is nothing in his external appearance to reveal the exalted rank he holds in the Tibetan hierarchy. He has surrounded himself with Tibetan and Western political and legal advisors who are attuned to the subtleties of international diplomacy. Among them is Michael van Walt van Praag, an international lawyer who is the General Secretary of the Unrepresented Nations' and Peoples' Organization (UNPO) based in The Hague. A skilful tactician with optimism to spare, the Dalai Lama has managed to avoid traps laid by the Chinese to neutralize him since 1959. He has succeeded in devising meaningful, credible and resilient policies for a future free Tibet. The immense majority of Tibetans look upon him as their spiritual and temporal leader, and he has launched a far-reaching process to modernize the Tibetan community in exile and to lay the groundwork for an authentically democratic society in Tibet once the Chinese have left. The Dalai Lama is convinced that in the long run, justice will triumph in Tibet.

His message of peace has divided the exile community, but it has been well received all over the world. As a kind of Pope for Buddhists everywhere, he preaches compassion and non-violence, two fundamental precepts of the Dharma – the teaching of the Buddha. For the Dalai Lama, violence is always a sign of weakness, never of strength.

At a lunch at the European Parliament in Strasbourg, I asked the Dalai Lama to explain the reasons that impel him to believe in non-violence. After all, in our world only those who use violent means to attract attention seem to be taken seriously by governments. This was his reply:

'I know that some Tibetans are thinking about violence. But I tell them that they are wrong. Violence is immoral. If the Tibetans take the path of violence, the Chinese will resort to increasingly expeditious measures. Basically, I think violence is an inhuman act. It is unworthy of a human being. Instead, humans should cultivate the feeling of compassion that exists within each one of us. How can humans be so attracted to blood? I have always felt violence is unnatural. Furthermore, I feel that while it is certainly possible to achieve results by means of violence, that achievement will not be a lasting one. Very often, instead of eliminating one problem, violence creates more problems. Look at us: there are six million of us and over a thousand million of them! To plan on using violence would be stupid. When I explain this to young Tibetans, they sometimes start to cry. They can't contain their emotions. But they must accept the facts. Whether they like it or not, that is the reality.' To people who speak to him about liberation movements like the ones in Cambodia or in Afghanistan, the Dalai Lama points out that the use of arms has not produced the required result. Sometimes, with a great peal of laughter, he will add: 'Look! Even Yasser Arafat has come around to my position!'

In an autumn 1987 address to members of the US Congress, the Dalai Lama offered China the option of transforming Tibet into a demilitarized Zone of Peace. The 'Five-Point Peace Plan' he unveiled stated the different issues clearly: China was to cease stockpiling nuclear weapons and waste in Tibet; it was progressively to dismantle its military installations. The population transfer policy would have to be abandoned. The environment would be allowed to return to its natural state. The Chinese and the Tibetans would embark on 'earnest negotiations' on the future of Tibet. 'We wish to approach this subject in a reasonable and realistic way, in a spirit of frankness and conciliation and with a view to finding a solution that is in the long-term interest of all: the Tibetans, the Chinese, and all other people concerned', the Dalai Lama declared.

A few months later, he dropped a political bombshell that remains the focus of heated debates among Tibetan refugees. On 15 June 1988, the Dalai Lama was invited to address a group of European Parliamentarians in Strasbourg. For the first time ever, he implicitly renounced formal independence for Tibet; in exchange, he proposed that an 'association' between Tibet and China serve as the basis for negotiation. 'Every Tibetan hopes and prays for the full restoration of our nation's independence', said Tenzin Gyatso. 'I have thought for a long time on how to achieve a realistic solution to my nation's plight.' He proposed that 'the whole of Tibet known as Cholka-Sum (U-Tsang, Kham and Amdo) should become a self-governing democratic political entity founded on law by agreement of the people' existing 'in association with the People's Republic of China'. Within this framework, China could maintain responsibility for Tibet's foreign policy. It could also maintain a 'restricted number of military installations' pending the successful outcome of an international conference convened to negotiate neutral status for Tibet. Thereupon, Tibet would become a 'sanctuary of Peace'.

Were the Chinese government to accept this proposal, it could retain control over Tibet's foreign policy, but the Tibetan government would remain free to 'develop and maintain relations, through its own Foreign Affairs Bureau, in the fields of religion, commerce, education, culture, tourism, science, sports and other non-political activities'. The government of Tibet would be founded on a 'constitution or basic law' that would provide for 'a democratic system of government'. 'This means that the Government of Tibet will have the right to decide on all affairs relating to Tibet and the Tibetans', added the Dalai Lama. Under the terms of this agreement, the Tibetan government would be responsible for the protection of individual civil rights and freedoms, and it would adhere fully to the Universal Declaration of Human Rights. The Government of Tibet 'would be comprised of a popularly elected Chief Executive, a bi-cameral legislative branch and an independent judicial system'; its seat would be in Lhasa. To ratify the agreement between Tibet and China, a 'regional peace conference' would be convened to confirm Tibet's demilitarized status.

I questioned Lodi Gyaltsen Gyari, who was responsible at the time for the Tibetan government-in-exile's foreign relations, about the implications of the formal offer to relinquish foreign affairs to the Chinese government. To come to an agreement on a precise definition for the terms 'sovereignty' and 'suzerainty' is no easy matter, the Tibetan diplomat explained. These two concepts were unknown in Asia until they were introduced in the last century by the British. Even the Imperial Court of the Qing had no clear-cut definition for them. Would China be the suzerain state and Tibet its vassal? Or would the agreement allow China to claim sovereignty over Tibetan soil? That remains to be established in the course of the hoped-for negotiations. Would Tibet have a seat at the United Nations? 'The answer is simply no', replied Mr Gyari. The Tibetans would probably be compelled to hand over formally and publicly the sovereignty of the Land of Snow to the Chinese. Whatever the outcome, it goes without saying that the Chinese side can be expected to be adamant on that point. No ambiguity would be allowed to remain.

Sitting in his Dharamsala home, the Dalai Lama looked serene. He clarified what he meant by an 'association' of Tibet with China. 'Theoretically, the six million Tibetans may find it is in their interest to join forces with the more than one billion human beings in China. This I believe. If the Chinese side treats us as real brothers and sisters, on a totally equal basis, if they are willing to share our suffering as well as our happiness, there is no reason for us to insist on separation. For our young Tibetans, this is something difficult to accept. The experience of the last thirty years has been so excruciatingly painful, that when we Tibetans hear the word "Chinese" – you know, the Tibetan word *gyamee* – a very negative feeling is there. But I think that China will become an open society some day, a genuine democracy with freedom of speech and religious freedom. It will come. The truth is known abroad, but also in China and in Tibet. Communism is crumbling nowadays; dictatorships are being toppled. The call for human rights is making itself heard. The voice of freedom as well. We are human beings, we are only asking for more freedom, more democracy. We are not asking for a complete separation. What we are saying is: if you Chinese, you treat us with genuine friendship, if you take care of us, we will respond positively. But if you hit us, we will seek separation. If you treat us like true friends, we are prepared to stay with you. Whether we like it or not, we are neighbours and we must remain side by side. An appropriate solution will emerge from human contact between us. We have to meet and talk. We have to understand each other.'

Walking away from the interview with the Dalai Lama, I couldn't help wondering about the appropriateness of making such a major concession. Wouldn't relinquishing the principle of Tibetan independence make things rather easy for the Chinese? When all is said and done, they were the ones who played the part of the aggressors in Tibet. I found myself very much doubting China's willingness – under communist leadership or any other – to restrain itself in Tibet and abide strictly by the terms of an agreement – assuming an agreement would ever be forthcoming . . . Later on, having thought the matter over, it occurred to me that if it does not want to be wiped off the map, Tibet may have no choice but to compromise with China; this is the Middle Path advocated by the Dalai Lama. An 'association' with China would provide the Tibetan people with the breathing space required to heal their wounds, regenerate their strength and rediscover their identity. With no more Chinese settling on Tibetan soil and with freedom to organize their political affairs on their own, leaving aside foreign relations, and defence to some extent, Tibetans would basically have regained their freedom. After all, isn't that the main thing? If you were forced to choose between imminent, certain death and a slight chance of remaining alive, which would you prefer? Seen in this light, the Dalai Lama's moderation takes on the appearance of a wise formula that may ultimately provide the opening for peaceful coexistence between China and Tibet.

On 19 August 1991, having waited in vain for any positive response to his overtures from Peking, the Dalai Lama announced during a visit to Switzerland that he could no longer stand by his Strasbourg offer. 'Since the Chinese government has not expressed the wish to reply, I now consider my last proposal to be invalid.' This is not to say that he is advocating the violent option: 'I recognize that my 1988 proposal has failed, but I remain entirely committed to my general approach of non-violence. I believe that the authentic path towards a solution is based on dialogue and negotiation.' However, the Dalai Lama's entourage maintains that he would still be prepared to initiate discussions with Peking on the basis of the Strasbourg offer. Ultimately, the Dalai Lama's proposals are not entirely unlike the special status that China has promised to Hong Kong and Macao after they revert to Chinese jurisdiction, in July 1997 and December 1999 respectively. In the early 1980s, it was Deng Xiaoping himself who devised the formula known as 'one country, two systems' to arrive at a satisfactory solution to the questions of Hong Kong and Macao. After it returns to China, Hong Kong (a British colony since the Opium Wars were unleashed upon the Chinese by the Empire) will be known as a 'Special Administrative Region' governed by its own Basic Law. The Chinese government has formally undertaken to allow Hong Kong a broad measure of autonomy and to tolerate its capitalist system for at least fifty years after 1997. The Chinese flag will fly over Hong Kong and Peking will be allowed to post units of the People's Liberation Army. The PRC has already infiltrated all the business circles in the colony. The judiciary, however, is to be left as it is, and Hong Kong will allegedly be authorized to sign trade, cultural and sports-related agreements with the outside world. As one of the largest financial centres in the world, Hong Kong is to be allowed to retain its membership in the international organizations to which it belongs. The links between the Catholic Church and the Vatican are to remain intact. On Chinese soil, two radically different – not to say antagonistic – systems are supposedly going to coexist. The old Portuguese colony of Macao is to return to China under similar conditions. The Chinese authorities have promised not to touch the casinos and gaming rooms.

In the hopes of achieving the desired reunification of China, the same 'one country, two systems' status has been promised to the Nationalist government in Taiwan by the Chinese Communist government. In order to sweeten the pill for the Kuomintang, Peking has offered an additional concession: after returning to the embrace of the motherland, Taiwan would be allowed to keep its own army. Theoretically, the People's Republic and Taiwan are still at war, but on both sides of the straits the cannons are rusting. Hundreds of thousands of Taiwanese have visited the mainland since the ban was lifted in 1988. Behind a veil of secrecy, Chinese diplomats both Communist and Nationalist are busy negotiating an honourable way of saving face on both sides.

What about 'one country, two systems' for Tibet? The Dalai Lama looks upon the possibility with favour, but as we will see below, this is still out of the question for the present Chinese government.

A democratic Tibet

Since his departure into exile, the Dalai Lama has consistently spoken out in favour of democracy. To discredit his position, Peking has accused him of seeking to restore the old feudal system in Tibet. In fact, the Dalai Lama never misses a chance to imprint as forcefully as possible upon the mind of his people the need for a democratization of Tibetan society. It is a theme that crops up practically every time he addresses the public. He has his work cut out, for the religious beliefs and antiquated attitudes of the old society still hold sway in the people's mind. They are so devoted that it is not unusual for an older Tibetan to tremble with emotion and fold his hands with reverence when he catches a glimpse of the Dalai Lama in the distance. When 'His Holiness' holds a public audience in front of his Dharamsala home, endless queues start to form early in the morning for an individual blessing that will only last a second or two. Would any Tibetan dare contradict the Dalai Lama in public? Would any member of his government take the initiative to question openly a decision of his? Many Tibetans still equate criticizing the Dalai Lama with blasphemy, but the Dalai Lama has no time for such devotion. He wants no part of it. He works hard to uproot tradition. Almost every sector of Tibetan society requires an overhaul: the political system, the economy, the role of religion, the judiciary. For Tibet to survive, the status of the Dalai Lama himself will have to be reviewed, according to him. This process will be made easier by the spirit of Buddhism, which is based on tolerance. Buddhism adapts easily to the needs of our contemporary world. Its rules do not generally conflict with the rights and freedoms of the individual. In the annals of history, Buddhism has never caused religious wars, nor has anyone ever been killed in the name of the Buddha.

How can Tibetan society be made more democratic? What does the Dalai Lama have to say? 'In any human society, it is crucial that every individual be in a position to express freely his or her creativity. This can only take place in a democracy. Dictatorships and Communist regimes are anti-democratic by nature. Out of profound devotion to the Dalai Lama, Tibetans accept his choices and decisions instead of trusting their own judgment. This is why I feel we have to reflect about the status of the Dalai Lama. In China as well, but for different reasons, whenever a high cadre speaks, everybody has to agree with what he says. This is not a proper solution.'[1]

For the vast majority of Tibetans, the concept of democracy is a new one and a vaguely perceived one at that. When a hundred thousand

Tibetans fled into exile in 1959, were there even a dozen who knew the exact meaning of the word? Scattered all over India, Nepal, Europe and North America, the Tibetan diaspora has advanced some distance down that road in the intervening years. On 10 March 1963, the Dalai Lama and his entourage promulgated the first Tibetan Constitution. Subject to approval by the entire Tibetan population in a free Tibet, it sought to guarantee the fundamental rights of all Tibetans, including every citizen's right to vote, equality before the law and freedom of speech, assembly and religion. From 1960 onwards, all Tibetans in exile over the age of eighteen have enjoyed the right to vote in elections to designate representatives to the Assembly of Tibetan People's Deputies. Candidates must be over twenty-one. The Assembly meets in Dharamsala to discuss, amend or ratify any important decision affecting the future of the Tibetan people. A review of the 1963 Constitution was undertaken in 1992. A Charter of the Tibetans in Exile has now been adopted. As a result, Kashag (Cabinet) ministers are no longer appointed by the Dalai Lama; they are elected by the Assembly, now expanded to forty-six members, including representatives from exile communities overseas.

For Tibetans, voting is such an unfamiliar act that a sizeable number of government officials readily admit that until quite recently, they never bothered to participate in any of the elections. Additionally, not all Tibetans agree on the need for a prime minister, who as head of the government would be responsible for political affairs. Once relieved of this obligation, the Dalai Lama could concentrate more fully on spiritual matters of importance both to Tibetans and to Buddhists in general. The Dalai Lama has expressed a strong preference for this option, but for the Tibetan population, this would unacceptably undermine the status of their God-King. As for the Kashag, it remains too often nothing more than a sounding-board for the Dalai Lama's initiatives. Very seldom will the ministers make any decision in the absence of a preliminary consensus on the matter and without having at least requested the opinion of the Dalai Lama. None would dream of shouldering the responsibility. Last but not least, the Tibetan community in India is subject to Indian jurisdiction and cannot, therefore, set up an independent judiciary.

One day in Dharamsala, I asked Lodi Gyaltsen Gyari, now the Dalai Lama's special envoy to Washington, to describe the weak points of Tibetan society. He replied, 'People depend too much on the Dalai Lama. As he himself often says: "It is a great honour for me, but it is our nation's greatest weakness". Nobody wants to take any decisions. It's so much easier that way! At other times, when a decision has to be made, we make sure he participates in the decision-making process. Then it is easier to convince our people. If our fellow-Tibetans say the decision was not sound, we can always reply that it was the wish of the Dalai Lama.'

The Dalai Lama has repeatedly stated that he will completely give up his political activities and concentrate exclusively on the monastic life once an agreement is reached with China. Lodi Gyari emphasizes that it would be a great mistake to harbour any doubts about his intentions, for these are not empty words: he has weighed his decision very carefully. At the same time, the Dalai Lama's plan to retire creates an intimidating deadline for Tibetan society. For the first time in its history, it will have to take its fate into its own hands. 'We are in a very tight spot. At a time when the Dalai Lama's image and personality play such an important part in our Tibetan society, we lack a second tier in our administration. There is no one who could play a fraction of his role, nowadays. He has tried to compensate for this by setting up the Assembly and a Cabinet with executive powers. Today, Cabinet members are elected for a five-year term of office. When that term expires, they will require the approval of the Assembly for a second term and continued powers. This is a sign of progress, for only fifteen or twenty years ago such a limitation would not have been understood by the public.'

Lodi Gyari goes on: 'What is democracy for us? You know, sometimes I feel that if you have not had to fight for something, it is not the same. You French had to struggle for democracy. The word has important connotations for you, whereas we don't really understand democracy.' Lodi Gyari laughs as he describes the rather childlike attitude of the Tibetans who feel lost in the dark without a spiritual father to guide their footsteps. 'The Dalai Lama tells us we have to have democracy. Since it was he who said it, we have accepted the idea. But to be perfectly frank with you, I must confess that I had never voted until just recently. Although I myself was an elected member of the Assembly until not so long ago – I had never exercised my right to vote! Isn't that strange? You may wonder why. Well, psychologically, voting is not yet very important for us. I did go to vote the other day, for I felt that as a minister, I should at least set a good example! So that is why four days ago I went to deposit my voting paper in the ballot-box.'[2]

Another token of the ongoing process of democratization within the Tibetan society-in-exile: Tenzin Geyche Tethong, the Dalai Lama's secretary, says he is the last member of the government-in-exile who belongs to an aristocratic family. The same can be said for the children selected as the reincarnations of important Lamas. When the time came to 'find' the child who was the reincarnation of the Dalai Lama's Senior Tutor (who had died in Dharamsala in 1983) great hopes were being entertained by some of the wealthy families. Invoking a lack of familiarity with the complex divination procedures that must be performed in order to locate the child, Tenzin Geyche says with a wink that he personally took care to orient the search in the direction of the common people.

In order to find out more about the growing democratization of the

Tibetan community, I interviewed Nubpa Chodak Gyatso, who had presided over the Assembly of Tibetan People's Deputies in the 1980s. A man in his forties, wearing monk's robes, he received me in his office. Through the open windows, the deep booming of Tibetan trumpets from a nearby Dharamsala monastery intruded as he spoke. Historically, he emphasized, a form of democracy existed for centuries in the great monasteries. All important decisions were put to the vote before the assembled monks by a collegiate body composed of the high lamas and office-bearers. The office-bearers themselves were elected by the monks for a fixed period of time that varied from one monastery to another. Even before 1950, and despite the opposition of some monasteries that were reluctant to see new ideas taking hold in Tibet, the Dalai Lama had initiated reforms to make the social and political institutions more democratic. The arrival of the Chinese had put an end to those reforms. But, I asked, can one say that prior to 1950 the political and religious system in Tibet was non-democratic? He replied without a trace of hesitation: 'Yes, that's right. We are not trying to hide anything, you know.' And what is the situation in India today? The Dalai Lama remains the prime force uniting the Tibetans. The people's profound faith and trust in him is extraordinary.

This being so, any sudden or radical change could easily provoke the disintegration of Tibetan society. The first task is thus to prepare the Tibetans to be ready to face today's challenges on their own, without the help and guidance of their 'precious protector', the Dalai Lama. 'Nowadays, within the context of the Assembly, we are trying to educate the population, to instil a greater political awareness. This is exactly what the Dalai Lama wants.' Does the Kashag or the Assembly dare to take any decision running counter to the Dalai Lama's wishes? Nubpa Chodak Gyatso agrees that discussions with Tenzin Gyatso can be quite 'animated', when consultations with the Tibetan leader are felt to be required. But he cannot recall any occasion when either of the two bodies actually went so far as to oppose him.

For the Tibetan community (and this could apply to any society forced to live in exile) the apprenticeship of democracy has not been painless. In Dharamsala, vivid factional quarrels and personal animosities remain alive. They have been known to cause the operation of the government-in-exile to grind to a halt. Corruption has also surfaced, even within the close entourage of the Dalai Lama – to the joy of the authorities in Peking and Taipei, who never miss a chance to exploit rivalries among the Tibetan leadership. A painful yet comical episode in the long march towards democracy was the July 1991 election of the Kashag ministers – a first in Tibet's history. Seven ministers (Kalons) were to be elected, but the electors, the forty-six members of the expanded Assembly of Tibetan People's Deputies, indulged in so much intriguing and plotting in the corridors that after two rounds of balloting, they had only managed to agree on two of the candidates! It must be said that each candidate had to win 70 per cent of the votes. This was later reduced to 55 per cent, but produced no better results. The upshot: a month later, willy-nilly, the Dalai Lama had to appoint three more ministers. These difficulties in turn led to an amendment to the Charter being proposed and adopted in 1992, concerning elections. The five members of the Kashag resigned in January 1993, to pave the way for fresh elections under the new, unified system. Under the supervision of the new Election Commission, six candidates were chosen in the first round, and two who had tied for seventh place had to face a second round.

This shows that the seeds of democracy have been sown in fertile ground. The Dalai Lama's Strasbourg proposal was greeted with a loud chorus of protesting voices by the exile Tibetan communities in India, Europe, the USA and also inside Tibet. The strongest critics accused him of 'selling Tibet to the Chinese'. Other Tibetans were unhappy that such a momentous decision had been taken without first consulting the people. So many have rebelled against the idea of giving up Tibet's independence that it looks as if the storm is not about to blow over. The Dalai Lama is delighted with the uproar. His initiative having triggered off a tremendous debate within Tibetan society, he feels that the wheels of democracy are finally turning!

The advocates of terrorism

The members of the Dalai Lama's entourage admit that the vast majority of Tibetans are viscerally opposed to any agreement with China based on renouncing Tibetan sovereignty. What are the arguments of the most ardent opponents of the Strasbourg proposal and the options it contains? I started off by interviewing Tashi Namgyal, the General Secretary of the Tibetan Youth Congress. He invited me to his office at the Dharamsala headquarters of the organization, which claims to have over ten thousand active members worldwide. Here is what this former member of the Tibetan resistance had to say:

'Actually, we don't really believe this is a wise way of settling the Tibetan issue. Conceding defence and foreign affairs to the Chinese is the same as abdicating or relinquishing sovereignty over Tibet. We feel there should be no concessions on that score. In our opinion, we should fight to the bitter end until we regain our independence. This is what the Tibetan Youth Congress thinks, and this is what the Tibetans think. To talk to the Chinese is a fruitless exercise. What we have to do is fight for what is rightfully ours. We have to fight, not talk!

'The Chinese will not let go of Tibet easily, no doubt. But we will not easily lose our motivation. We may not be very many as compared to the Chinese, but we have determination on our side! And the yearning for freedom. Our fighting spirit will be passed on to future generations, although our aim is to regain independence in our own lifetime. We do not agree with the proposal of the Dalai Lama and we feel it is our duty to say so loud and clear.' Certain international jurists assert that handing over the conduct of foreign affairs to a third country does not necessarily imply abdicating national sovereignty. They are wrong: 'Control of its foreign relations is the backbone of a country. If you are not empowered to treat with foreign powers, if you have no diplomatic relations with them, what do you have? This would mean our country would have no status within the international community.'

Tibetans who are fighting must not lose hope, for history is replete with examples of countries that have regained their sovereignty. Some liberation movements waged a lonely struggle for long years in exile before their country was able to recover its independence. Furthermore, disintegration of the Soviet Union brought independence to its component republics; the ability of the three small Baltic States (Lithuania, Latvia and Estonia) to reassert their independence proves that no situation in history will eternally remain unchanged. Nor will China.

How many Tibetans reject the Dalai Lama's proposal and want to continue fighting for independence? Tashi Namgyal's forceful reply is 90 per cent – perhaps more. The leader of the Tibetan Youth Congress speaks curtly when discussing violence as a tool in the struggle: 'The Dalai Lama's proposal is bad. He says he is the Buddha of Compassion. Well, I'm not. The Dalai Lama wants happiness, not only for the Tibetan people, but for all beings. He talks about a world without borders and without passports, without police. He believes in that sort of thing. But we just can't see things in the same way. Let's be quite frank. We can't say: since the Dalai Lama doesn't hate the Chinese, we won't either. We simply cannot. On the contrary, we hate the Chinese. They invaded our country. Why should we let them sleep in peace?'

Are terror tactics a combat option in Tibet? Tashi Namgyal chooses his words carefully, but his attitude is unequivocal: terrorism is acceptable. 'We don't believe in terrorism. We don't believe in killing innocent people. Our motivation is shaped by our objective: the total independence of Tibet. If we kill Chinese, no one should accuse us of being terrorists; no Chinese who comes to Tibet is innocent. Everyone that comes is pursuing his own interest.' Would Tashi Namgyal support activists who targeted bombs at the Chinese in Tibet? 'Yes, with no hesitation. That would make things difficult for the Chinese. In this context any means are justified, absolutely. Look, if the occupation of Tibet by the Chinese is justified and the Chinese, as you know, use every method of torture against the Tibetans, then I can only reply "Yes". Every type of struggle against them is justified !' With a nervous laugh, the Tibetan leader adds that violence should be used only inside Tibet and directed exclusively against Chinese interests.

Even the Dalai Lama's younger brother sides with those who advocate violence to expel the Chinese from the Land of Snow. I went to his home in Dharamsala to discuss the matter with him. Tenzin Chogyal Rimpoche was surprisingly frank and outspoken. 'The situation is like this: someone has broken into another person's house without having been invited. That undesirable person should leave. That would solve the problem. As for the actual solution, it is no easy matter. It is extremely unlikely that the Chinese will simply move back out. Unless we use this [he gestures as though firing a gun]. The Dalai Lama has made the proposal with which you are familiar; he has manifested a compassionate attitude. He is peaceful, reasonable. He has put a great deal of himself in that initiative. He went as far as he could in the direction of the Chinese. But I don't think the Chinese are smart enough to see that. So, you see, we have to try to bring some pressure to bear on them, and the only pressure they recognize is violence. I am talking like a radical. I'm too old now to be a member of the Tibetan Youth Congress, but I still think we should do something. We will have to make blood flow. Imagine that we are playing cards: we need a handful of good cards to be able to play and to win, you know. The Dalai Lama makes overtures for peace. But we have to place a few trumps in his hand. Anyway, whatever the Dalai Lama does, as far as we are concerned, we have to wield the stick. Otherwise they will not understand.'

As the conversation progresses, the Dalai Lama's brother warms to his topic. He raises his voice. His serenity is ruffled: can any Tibetan remain calm when discussing this issue? He looks at me, lights a cigarette and continues in a dry tone: 'There are things we have to do without the knowledge of the Dalai Lama. He must not be told. He is above violence. But as you know, we live in a sad world. I hit you, you hit me, we both feel pain. That is what it takes to get the message across. It seems to me that the Chinese only understand the language of violence. Didn't they say that power comes out of the barrel of a gun? Very well then! Let us confront each other at that level! The problem is that we don't have any weapons. Will the Americans give us any?' Tenzin Chogyal bursts out laughing and sips his tea. The mood lightens. His wife, seated beside him, laughs heartily as well. 'Don't think the Chinese army is so very powerful, either. It can be overcome. The troops in today's army are not the Long March veterans, you know. These are no longer the men who fought in Korea. Those were highly motivated from the ideological point of view. This army has been routed and humiliated by the Vietnamese. The men lack morale. They don't believe in anything any more.'

We gradually turn to more sensitive dimensions of the Tibetan strategy. The Dalai Lama's Strasbourg proposal comes up again. Tenzin Chogyal has no doubts: this is the best conceivable way of getting the Chinese to sit down at the negotiating table. And then what? Could it serve as a springboard to full independence? The Dalai Lama's brother looks at me in silence, scratching his head. He is visibly debating how far he can go without doing a disservice to Tibetan diplomacy. He makes up his mind and says: 'Let us first of all achieve autonomy. Then we can throw out the Chinese! Just as Marcos was expelled from the Philippines and the British from India. We are thinking in terms of generations, the generations to come. This would be a start.'

Last but not least, I met with Phuntsog Wangyal, once the representative of the Dalai Lama in London and now Director of the Tibet Foundation in London. He is one of the three members of the ATPD who represent the Tibetans overseas. In his eyes, the Strasbourg proposal was a serious mistake, both in form and in substance. 'Personally, I disagree with everything that was proposed in that statement. Particularly the idea of living in association with China and entrusting our defence to the Chinese. Giving them any right to station Chinese soldiers in Tibet. That would be to settle for less than independence.'

It would be fanciful to expect China to abide by any agreement it might sign with the Tibetans: 'In fact, China has already passed the death sentence on us: the Tibetan nation must die. The only question that remains is whether it is to die quickly or slowly. That is why I think that whatever the cost, Tibetans must fight for full independence. I know it will be a very arduous struggle. But we can succeed, for history provides many examples of peoples who did succeed. Winning independence is not easy. Our warriors for peace will have to persevere for generations. We must continue.'

But how can a few million Tibetans hope to win the day against a billion Chinese and an army of three million men? 'The situation is changing in China. The international scene is also changing. Things are changing in the former Soviet Union. Things will also change in Tibet. More and more Tibetans and Chinese are becoming politically mature. The importance of religion may be waning but political awareness is growing instead, and this contributes to the changes. By that I mean that if we don't struggle for full independence, the people will gradually lose hope. We would be losing something without gaining anything for the Tibetans. I don't see how supporting the struggle for independence can harm the situation in Tibet in any way. I don't think that our accepting to become part of China will stop the Chinese from settling in our country in great numbers.'

Phuntsog Wangyal also feels that violence and terrorism are justified. There is not a trace of hesitation in his voice: 'I am not the type of person to say to the Tibetans: go ahead, go and fight! But if the people inside Tibet decide the best way is for each person to struggle individually for the country, they will have my unqualified support! And my admiration and dedication. And my prayers will go to them.' Even if they resort to terror tactics? 'Oh yes, definitely yes! Look, we have to be realistic. People always say terrorism is a very bad thing. Killing is very wrong. But nobody tries to find out why a person has been led to become a terrorist. What reasons impel him to resort to violence? You must ask yourself these questions! When the causes vanish, the violence will vanish as well. No one wants to get arrested. No one likes to be tortured. No one likes to get a bullet in his body! What are the reasons that incite these people to choose violence? It is the suffering that the Chinese inflict upon us! Let me tell you that the Chinese will not leave voluntarily. No colonial power has ever yielded on its own initiative without being unequivocally invited to go by the oppressed peoples themselves. However, with the rising generations in China, I have a little bit of hope. Our task is to make life difficult for them. If their position in the world becomes an uncomfortable one because of Tibet, they may change.'

I explain that official support for the Tibetan cause from the Western countries will be easier for governments to countenance if the Tibetan leadership in exile renounces violence. Phuntsog Wangyal is red with anger: 'International support? What a joke! I want to tell you something. People talk about international support. Have we used violence in Tibet since 1959? And where is the international support? There is none. And in 1950, what international support did we get? None at all! Zero! Today, unless we manage to attract attention to our Tibetan cause, if we remain non-violent, we will again get nothing. When Arafat kills and terrorizes, governments invite and welcome him. He has succeeded in obtaining assistance and sympathy for the Palestinian people. Kindly try to understand what I am saying: I am only putting the question of whether terrorism is heretical or not. Look at the mujahidin fighting in Afghanistan. When they come to London, they have dinner at 10 Downing Street. When the Dalai Lama visits, he talks about peace, love and compassion. So what happens: no one will see him. Why? Not because they think he is not a respectable person. Quite on the contrary, everybody admires him. But the Dalai Lama is harmless. He is not likely to cause any problems. So there is no need to worry about him.'

As for the veneration that is heaped on the Dalai Lama, it is high time for the Tibetans to wake up. 'They believe he sees everything: past, present and future. He is God and he can't make a mistake. I don't believe any of that. It is true that I am a Buddhist, but as far as I'm concerned, he is a man like everybody else. He has the qualities and the faults of a human. I often tell my countrymen that the Dalai Lama is getting old. We should be asking ourselves, is he or is he not a human manifestation of the Buddha? When he falls ill, no one asks that question, nor when he makes a mistake. These are questions that have to be raised. And when he makes a mistake, it is our duty to say so.'

When it comes to China's willingness to honour its promises, Phuntsog Wangyal smiles and suggests that being naive is foolish. China has displayed its deviousness on many occasions at the Tibetans' expense. Look at the example of the Seventeen-Point Agreement: the Chinese violated the spirit of the Agreement and reneged on every point from the first day onwards. Yet it was useful to them: it enabled them to buy time. The same would apply to any present-day compromise between the Tibetans and the Chinese. The main beneficiaries would again be the Chinese. On another level, Peking's open-door policy since 1979 as regards Tibet does not in any way imply that the Chinese have abandoned their goal of annihilating Tibet. 'In opening up Tibet, the Chinese are still doing their best to destroy the Tibetan culture and the Tibetan population. That hasn't changed. The only difference with the violent methods of the past is that now they could almost be saying to us: Hurry up and die, I'm going to kill you painlessly. In the end, the final result is the same, and that is not something we can accept.'

While I was in Dharamsala, the Tibetan Youth Congress held its Seventh General Body Meeting from 11 to 16 September 1989. It resolved to suspend the call for violence and armed struggle against the Chinese presence in Tibet. This was the largest meeting of young exiled Tibetans ever held, with delegates from all over India, Nepal, Bhutan, North America and Europe. Even before being awarded the Nobel Prize for Peace, the Dalai Lama had apparently managed to convince these impatient young people to renounce terrorism and the use of weapons in their struggle. But for how long?

On the other hand, the situation inside Tibet does not seem to favour moderation among the young. It is difficult to assess the strength of the few resistance movements that periodically come to the surface. Instead of armed resistance, useful methods seem to be civil disobedience, sabotage and isolated guerrilla attacks. The Tiger-Leopard Youth Association, one of the main resistance movements, recently declared its intention to give up non-violence if the international community continues to ignore the plight of Tibet. 'Our non-violent methods have been taken as a sign of weakness', it declared in a statement addressed to the Secretary-General of the United Nations. 'We are determined to regain our freedom, and the recent vote at the United Nations[3] clearly shows us that without bloodshed, sabotage and aggressive acts, we will not gain publicity, sympathy and support', the authors concluded. 'Hijacking and sabotage are tactics used by Palestinians, and still world bodies support them. Now we feel that if these acts of aggression bring results, why should we not do the same? The world believes in these acts.'[4]

Secretive Sino-Tibetan negotiations

Communist China claims to be ready to negotiate with the Dalai Lama. But apart from a few empty gestures, Chinese basic policy remains, visibly, very much the same as it was in the early 1980s. Peking is prepared to talk to the Dalai Lama about the details of his return 'to the mother-land', but not about finding a compromise solution to the status of Tibet. The policy with respect to the Dalai Lama was articulated in 1981. These are the five main points:

1. China has entered a new period of political stability and economic prosperity. The Dalai Lama and his followers should believe this. Otherwise, they can watch for a few more years.
2. There is no need for the Dalai Lama and his envoys to 'rehash the political issue'. The 1959 rebellion and the repression that followed should be forgotten.
3. The Chinese government 'sincerely welcomes the Dalai Lama and his followers' if they wish to return and settle in 'their motherland', China. China hopes the Dalai Lama will contribute to maintaining the unification of the country, particulary the unity between Han and Tibetan people.
4. 'After returning, the Dalai Lama may enjoy the same political treatment and living conditions as he had before 1959. He may be appointed Vice-Chairman of the National People's Congress (NPC). But 'it will not be necessary for him to hold any post in Tibet, because younger Tibetans have taken office and they are doing a very good job'. Of course, the Dalai Lama may visit Tibet often.
5. If he decides to return, the Dalai Lama may make a press statement. He will be received on arrival by a delegation of suitable ministerial rank.

These are the preconditions for any agreement with the leader of the Tibetan people. They remain unchanged in the early nineties and there is no reason to think that China is preparing to make any special concessions in the near future. Were the Dalai Lama to return from exile on these terms, he would be kowtowing to Peking; as a leader, he would become another 'Chinese chopstick', as the late Panchen Lama was derisively, and some would say unfairly, known. Just like the Panchen, he would be neutralized and kept in Peking, far from his people and bereft of his religious responsibilities. As for his promised political status, the post of Vice-Chairman of the NPC carries no decision-making power. The late Panchen Lama was Vice-Chairman for many years, but he never participated in any of the decisions made by the small handful of men that rule China. As he mournfully reminded the Tibet Committee of the NPC in 1987, 'it is not that we are not able to exercise power, it is that we have not been given any power'.[5]

It was he who announced a sensational piece of news on 4 April 1988 that seemed to indicate a softening of the Chinese position: upon his return, the Dalai Lama would be free to settle in Tibet if he wished to do so.[6] Many Western diplomats interpreted this gesture as a courageous decision on the part of the Chinese. It was not without its risks, for the Dalai Lama's return to the Potala would be met with tremendous enthusiasm among his people, and would unleash the energy of the Tibetans' boundless devotion, with unpredictable results. The situation could easily get out of control and provoke a repetition of the 1959 tragedy. It was impossible to obtain a clear confirmation of this offer from any member of the Chinese government. Seasoned observers speculated that the offer, made public one hour before the Dalai Lama landed in London for an important visit, was intended to place briefly a generous and conciliating patina on the Chinese government's position, to the detriment of the Dalai Lama's. Ten days later, with the Dalai Lama safely back in India and out of the limelight, Prime Minister Li Peng replied to an interviewer that the Dalai Lama's place of residence 'was not a very important matter'.

China's response to the Dalai Lama's overtures in Washington in September 1987 and in Strasbourg in June 1988 was to complain that his statements contained no genuinely new contributions; they were attempts to distort the present status of Tibet with the intention of legitimizing some type of 'semi-independence' or 'disguised independence'. In Peking's eyes, the Dalai Lama is bent on 'internationalizing' the Tibet issue. The Strasbourg proposal did however take the Chinese by surprise. It took them quite a while to reply: it was not until 23 September 1988 that the Chinese government formally offered to meet the Dalai Lama or his representatives 'whenever and wherever he preferred', in Hong Kong, in a Chinese embassy or elsewhere, subject to the condition that he 'sincerely wishes to improve his relations with the Chinese authorities and contribute to the preservation of unity between Hans and Tibetans'. Peking said 'everything is negotiable except Tibet's independence'.

At the same time, Chinese sources close to the government made it clear that Peking had not been taken in: any accord based on the Strasbourg proposal would place Tibet in a quasi-sovereign situation – under Chinese suzerainty, but virtually independent, somewhat like Bhutan, a country that enjoys independence although its foreign relations remain under Indian supervision. Under international law, China's relations with Tibet would belong in the category of relationships that can exist between two States when one State offers protection to the other, which accepts it. Therefore, the Dalai Lama's proposal was a 'trap' to be avoided by China, for what the Dalai Lama wanted was not 'one country, two systems' but 'two countries, two systems'.[7] Michael van Walt van Praag, one of the Dalai Lama's advisers, is quick to point out that an association with China would allow Tibet to recover its sovereignty; he emphasizes that in this type of relationship, the country that has decided to seek association with another power retains the option of terminating the relationship when it so desires.[8] An agreement of this type would mean that Tibet would be independent according to international law, but not in fact. Unfortunately, the Chinese government is likely to prefer the opposite, *de facto* independence rather than *de jure*.

Anyone who thought a giant step forward had been taken in the search for a compromise solution has been disappointed. In the opinion of many observers, China has not been acting in good faith, nor has it ever had any intention to really negotiate; basically, it has only been trying to buy time. Confronted with proposals that have won the Dalai Lama a reputation as a man of peace and conciliation, China has felt compelled to respond if only to avoid appearing on the international stage as the party that refuses to compromise. The theory has its merits. What does China need most? It needs time. For with the passing of time, Peking can reasonably expect the Tibetan problem to disappear.

In Peking, however, well-placed sources have hinted that prior to the massacre of 4 June 1989, the Chinese authorities were deeply divided on the Tibet issue. It seems that the moderates in Zhao Ziyang's camp were genuinely interested in securing a lasting arrangement with the Dalai Lama. Today, many moderates in Peking are waiting for Deng Xiaoping to pass away before they unveil their compromise proposals. One of China's greatest Tibet specialists is an enlightened moderate: Professor Wang Yao, the Director of the Tibet Department of the Central Institute for Minorities in Peking. 'I am only an academic and do not represent anyone in the government, but I love Tibet and I would like to serve as a bridge between the Dalai Lama and the Peking government', is what he says.[9] People in his position will have a important part to play when it comes to restoring trust and confidence between the Tibetan and the Chinese people. It is equally likely that the more orthodox clan was – and remains – uncompromisingly hostile to any notion involving political concessions regarding the status of Tibet and warmly supportive of the hardline option.

Be that as it may, the Peking massacre seems to have put paid to hopes of any imminent agreement between China and the Dalai Lama. He feels that it would have been unwise to seek a dialogue with a regime as thoroughly discredited as that of Li Peng. He waited in vain for a more moderate set of leaders in Peking to resume the interaction with China. A week after the imposition of martial law in Lhasa, Peking declared that 'the channels for a dialogue between the Dalai Lama and the central government remain open', so long as the Tibetan leader renounces Tibetan independence.[10] But this was manifestly a set piece of no great value. In September 1989, Ngapo Ngawang Jigme declared once more that China was willing to talk to the Dalai Lama and his representatives, but not to any member of the Kashag. His statement confirmed Peking's insistence on discussing the future status of the Dalai Lama rather than the future of Tibet itself.

While waiting for new reasons to hope for a Sino-Tibetan dialogue, what contacts have there been between the Dalai Lama and China?

Gyalo Thondup, the Dalai Lama's elder brother, has regularly visited Peking. The essence of discretion, he shuns the media and never publicizes his trips. He is known to have visited Peking in October 1987, July and November 1988, February and December 1989 and most recently, despite his 1991 election to a Kashag post, in the first week of June 1992. The only official channel for Sino-Tibetan contacts remains the Bureau of the Dalai Lama and the Chinese Embassy in New Delhi. Tashi Wangdi, elected minister in 1991, was for many years the Director of the Delhi Bureau. He also heads the Tibetan team appointed to conduct the hoped-for negotiations with China. He has met many times with Chinese diplomats in Delhi since 1979 and he outlined the substance of their periodical meetings.

'I met with them at least a dozen times between the announcement of the Strasbourg proposal in June 1988 and the Peking massacre of 4 June 1989. My counterpart was always the political counsellor of the Chinese Embassy. He is a very polite man. This is something I noticed on informal occasions as well, at receptions, for example. His job is to convey our explanations to his government and to tell us what his government wishes us to know. So whenever the Chinese had a message, he would call and we would set a time to meet. He was generally accompanied by two Tibetan interpreters and I would bring along one or two of my colleagues. He also speaks English, which we occasionally used instead. When the official portion of the meeting was over, we would sometimes have an informal discussion. I would then offer my personal opinion and he would very often give his own. But he never strayed much from the official position! He was very courteous and never lost his temper. Compared to the standards for Chinese diplomats only a few years ago, this constituted a striking departure from the norm. They would use very rough language with us. With the passing of the years, the embassy staff has become more polished. Now they listen to us. In the past, they would get irritated and interrupt our statements. They would openly display their anger. They wouldn't let us express our opinions. There seems to have been some change in their attitude. This must reflect what is going on in their government. But of course they remain circumspect and have very little to say about developments back home. We Tibetans who have been educated in India speak more freely and lack such inhibitions. As a result, they learn more about us than we do about them. As for the two Tibetan interpreters, we saw them from time to time outside the embassy. In their hearts they are Tibetans, but they have no freedom to say what they want.'

Have these contacts served any purpose? I wondered. The two parties definitely understand each other better now, I was told. Information passes back and forth between the Tibetans and the Chinese. But Tashi Wangdi is sceptical about China's willingness to negotiate. 'Either they are insincere, or opinions diverge too widely among themselves. The signs we have observed are very negative. Extremely negative. Sometimes, when we were having an informal discussion, they seemed to be saying that the Strasbourg proposal was reasonable and that negotiations should be initiated as soon as possible. They seemed to be saying that there was a possibility of some common ground there. My counterpart at the embassy would give me to understand that he thought negotiations should start. But the official reply to our overtures has been very negative, and this has been a great disappointment to me. The Dalai Lama has tried every possible approach. There has been no result. They continue to say the same thing over and over. They provide no opening at all for any progress.' This being the case, there are no plans for further approaches to the present regime, unless Peking manifests a new spirit. 'In the present situation, we see no need to knock on their door. When we feel the moment has come for us to contact them again, we will do so. Nowadays, everything indicates that such contacts would be pointless for the time being. They would lead us nowhere.'

When the Dalai Lama received the Nobel Prize for Peace in Oslo on 10 December 1989, his statement included a number of severe comments addressed to the Chinese regime. Here are some excerpts from his acceptance speech: 'In 1987, I made specific proposals in a Five-Point Peace Plan for the restoration of peace and human rights in Tibet ... Last year, I elaborated on that plan in Strasbourg, at the European Parliament. I believe the ideas I expressed on those occasions were both reasonable and realistic, although they have been criticized by some of my people as being too conciliatory. This is why I am very disappointed that China has rejected my proposals and has refused to initiate serious negotiations with the representatives I had appointed for that purpose. If the present Chinese leadership is not willing to discuss the suggestions we have made, which included important concessions, then we have the right to reconsider our position. What is at stake is not the fate of the Dalai Lama, as the Chinese government usually maintains. It is the future of the six million Tibetans; it is the Tibetans' right to self-determination, free from external domination and interference. Self-determination is not only a fundamental human right, it is the basis for the enjoyment of all other rights.

'Any relationship between Tibet and China will have to be based on the principle of equality, respect, trust and mutual benefit. It will also have to be based on the principle which the wise rulers of Tibet and of China laid down in a treaty as early as 823 AD, and carved on the pillar which still stands today in front of the Jokhang, Tibet's holiest shrine in Lhasa, which says that "Tibetans will live happily in the great land of Tibet and the Chinese will live happily in the great land of China". Most Tibetans are convinced that no satisfactory solution will be found until Tibet recovers full independence. The Chinese government's brutal attitude towards the Tibetans and towards its own people can only reinforce this view.'

The ups and downs of international solidarity

Can Tibet depend on international support in its efforts to hold its own against its large neighbour? It is hard to say. No country in the world has recognized the government-in-exile of the Dalai Lama. Over two hundred countries have established diplomatic relations with the People's Republic, implying recognition of Tibet as an integral part of China's territory. This applies to most of Western Europe and to the USA. The same can be said for the two dozen countries that recognize 'the other China', represented by the Kuomintang in Taiwan, which also considers that Tibet is an integral part of China. Inevitably, this creates a fearful handicap for the Dalai Lama and his Cabinet. Since they cannot be granted an official reception by high officials of Western governments, they have to settle for semi-official or private meetings. On occasion, the Dalai Lama has been made to wait in quite humiliating circumstances before being issued a visa to visit a country to which he has been invited. Sometimes the visa has unexpectedly been refused. Yet none of this has prevented him from tirelessly travelling all over the world. Since he fled into exile in 1959, he has visited some fifty countries. He has been to the USA, UK and France at least a dozen times since 1979. His peripatetic life has provided him with the opportunity to forge many and true friendships. In this fashion, he has gradually come to have a significant impact on foreign policy in a number of countries. With great perseverance, he has encouraged the activity of the pro-Tibetan lobbies that exert a growing influence in the Western democracies.

China has not been idly standing by, wringing its hands in the wings, for it holds a considerable number of trumps. China's embassies have brought the utmost diplomatic pressure to bear on the government of any country visited by the 'Tibetan Pope'. With the threat of immediate reprisals in the twin areas of trade and diplomacy, Peking has badgered local authorities not to open their doors to the Dalai Lama. Its rhetoric has acquired a familiar ring: 'We are firmly opposed to any organization or individual who supports the Dalai Lama's activities directed at sabotaging the unity of the motherland.'[11]

As the last big country in the Third World that is solvent, with international reserves in excess of 40 billion dollars, China remains an attractive market for Western companies. The Chinese market is still in the teething stage, but the business community is banking on miracles in the coming decades, as the economy matures.

When the initial threats fail to produced the desired effect, China will approach any public figures who are planning to meet with the Dalai Lama, in an attempt to discourage them. Chinese embassies exert considerable pressure on journalists who write about Tibet. If an article fails to find favour with the Chinese government, the embassy's press attaché will telephone the head office of the offending publication to complain or even threaten the editor. If the errant journalist refuses to change his ways and clings to his erroneous perception of the situation in Tibet, he will be told that since he is not a friend of China, further visits to China will be inappropriate. Deplorably, some journalists have been known to cave in.

Exerting pressure has enabled China to score some resounding victories. For decades, with this language, China was able to systematically obstruct any meeting between the Dalai Lama and officials belonging to governments other than the government of India. Until quite recently, the few who dared brave China's wrath were mainly Asian leaders: the King of Thailand in 1967, President Jayawardene of Sri Lanka in 1976, Prime Minister Zenko Suzuki of Japan in 1980 and Tunku Abdul Rahman of Malaysia and Adam Malik of Indonesia in 1982. In Europe, after meetings in 1973 with the Irish President and his Cabinet, no leader took the risk of displeasing the Chinese until 1986, when he was received by the Federal President of Austria.

The thin end of the wedge seems to have been an extremely discreet encounter between the Dalai Lama and Bernard Kouchner, then French Secretary of State for Humanitarian Affairs, in March 1989. Originally, the meeting was to have been kept secret. Bernard Kouchner slipped into the Hotel Meurice in Paris where the Dalai Lama had been lodged. To avoid leaks, he had not even informed his own aides in advance. Yet it was Kouchner himself who let the cat out of the bag two months later, in the course of a radio broadcast during which he called for an international mission to investigate the situation in Tibet.

Well before the Dalai Lama's arrival in France, Ambassador Zhou Jue had laid siege to the Quai d'Orsay, bitterly complaining that 'some people' wanted to 'sabotage the good relations between Peking and Paris'. He strongly 'advised' the French authorities to gag the Dalai Lama during his stay. After his French counterpart had unambiguously explained to him that France was playing host to a religious leader, His Excellency was most courteously shown the door. As for Secretary of State Kouchner's statements, it was made clear to the Chinese Embassy that while they did not necessarily reflect the position of the French government, they did reflect a general preoccupation among the French public.

Since then, the number of well-publicized encounters all over the world between the Dalai Lama and ministers, prime ministers and even presidents has multiplied exponentially, illustrating to what extent Tibet has become an international issue. Among the landmarks are his meetings with Presidents Salinas de Gortari of Mexico and Oscar Arias of Costa Rica in 1989; with former US President George Bush in April

1991 and most recently with President Clinton and Vice-President Gore in April 1993; with British Prime Minister John Major in December 1991; with Presidents Vaclav Havel of the Czech Republic and Vytautas Landsbergis of Lithuania, Bulgarian President Zhelyu Zhelev, President Richard von Weizsaecker of Germany, the King and Queen of Norway, Irish President Mary Robinson, Australian Prime Minister Paul Keating, Roland Dumas, French Minister of Foreign Affairs and Rene Felber, his Swiss counterpart. What is more, the Dalai Lama can rely on the support of a growing number of public figures and non-governmental organizations all over the world, including celebrities in the realms of politics, literature, the arts and sciences and many other fields. These include fellow Nobel prizewinners Elie Wiesel, Adolfo Perez Esquivel, Archbishop Desmond Tutu, Linus Pauling, Czeslaw Milosz, Wole Soyinka, and Octavio Paz; Danielle Mitterand, the wife of the French President; Heinrich Harrer, Yuri Orlov, actors such as Richard Gere, Harrison Ford, Liv Ullman, John Cleese, Stephane Audran and Isabelle Adjani; musicians such as Yehudi Menuhin, Philip Glass, Joan Baez, Peter Gabriel, Kate Bush, Paul McCartney and Joan Armatrading and photographer Henri Cartier-Bresson. Other names on this necessarily incomplete list would include Pope Jean-Paul II, Allen Ginsberg, the Spanish pop group Meccano, the historian Hugh Richardson, and a considerable number of Western parliamentarians such as Lord Ennals in the United Kingdom and Charles Rose and Claiborne Pell in the United States.

Several Western parliaments have extended very explicit support and recognition. The US Congress adopted a bold text on 23 May 1991 that declares Tibet (including the areas inhabited by ethnic Tibetans in the provinces of Sichuan, Yunnan, Gansu and Qinghai) an occupied country under the established principles of international law; and that 'Tibet's true representatives are the Dalai Lama and the Tibetan government-in-exile.' This is the first such recognition since China joined the United Nations in 1971. The resolution goes on to say that 'Tibet has maintained throughout its history a distinctive and sovereign national, cultural and religious identity separate from that of China and, except during periods of illegal Chinese occupation, has maintained a separate and sovereign political and territorial identity.'[12] The European Parliament's Tibet Intergroup has over a hundred members; some were part of the delegation that visited Lhasa in October 1991. Despite the best efforts of their hosts and minders, many were distinctly unimpressed with the living conditions of the Tibetans. In December 1992, the Parliament adopted a five-page resolution on Tibet that had been more than two years in preparation, along with a substantial report to its Political Affairs Committee by Socialist MEP Jannis Sakellariou. Several other Western European parliaments have set up committees or study groups on Tibet. In the UK, there is an All-Party Parliamentary Group for Tibet. In France, out of a total of 577 deputies to the *Assemblée Nationale*, the Tibet group boasts over a hundred members from every party except the extreme right wing and the Communists. The Supreme Council of Lithuania, the nation's parliament, adopted a declaration in 1992 in which it 'hold[s] His Holiness the Dalai Lama and the exiled Tibetan government as the true representatives of the nation of Tibet'. The declaration further expresses 'support for the legitimate aspirations of the Tibetan nation in international organizations and fora'.[13]

Sometimes, although quite rarely, Tenzin Gyatso has had reason to be somewhat less than pleased with the pronouncements of Western politicians who have publicly extended support to the Chinese position. Too often, their perspective has been narrowly economic. After all, a sympathetic public statement can work miracles during a difficult negotiation over a lucrative contract with the Chinese government. In other cases, there seems to have been a genuine lack of knowledge about events in Tibet. I would hesitate however to assume the latter when it comes to Bill Hayden, formerly Australian Minister of Foreign Affairs. On 22 July 1988 he declared that he could not accept the contents of the Dalai Lama's Strasbourg proposal, adding that information about repression in Tibet had been grossly exaggerated.[14] West German Chancellor Helmut Kohl has never spoken out against the initiatives of the Dalai Lama, but his controversial visit to Tibet in 1987, unintentionally or not, did contribute to legitimating the Chinese presence in Tibet. He was the first serving head of state or government to set foot in Tibet since 1950. I was in Peking at the time of Kohl's visit and I remember being told by a West German diplomat that his entire department had tried to discourage the Chancellor. The Federal Republic's ambassador to Peking avoided accompanying the Chancellor to Tibet by feigning a diplomatic illness.

At other times, it has been a government's turn to blush at a diplomatic fumble in China. Erik Derycke, Belgium's Secretary for Cooperation and Development, must have sorely regretted his plan to visit Tibet in March 1992 at the invitation of the Chinese government for the inauguration of an Alcatel-Bell telephone exchange; a gift from the Belgian taxpayer in the form of a 53-million-Belgian-Franc grant.[15] As soon as the public heard the news, the outcry compelled Mr Derycke to cancel his tour. Had he persevered, he would have been the first member of a European government to visit Tibet since the Tiananmen tragedy. There is one Italian official who always sides with the Chinese government on the Tibet issue: Gianni de Michelis. While serving as Minister of Foreign Affairs, he expressed hostility on several occasions towards Europeans who criticize Chinese policies in Tibet. As recently as March 1992, he inveighed against anyone who had the temerity to call upon the Chinese to leave Tibet. 'It is intolerable and arrogant to speak in this manner to a country of 1.2 billion inhabitants', he said.

'For the Chinese, the four million Tibetans are the same as the Basque minority in Spain ... yet we do not ask the Spanish to grant independence to the Basques nor do we call upon the UK to withdraw from Ulster because some of the inhabitants so desire', concluded Italy's chief diplomat.[16]

What is the position of the large international institutions on Tibet? In the 1950s, as we noted, only vague and muffled noises were heard at the United Nations. But the 1960 report on Tibet by the International Commission of Jurists, an organization with consultative status at the UN, contained much damning testimony and accused Peking of perpetrating genocide in Tibet. The ICJ sounded another warning in 1961, and three rather weak resolutions – quoted below – were adopted by the UN General Assembly in 1959, 1961 and 1965. Thereafter, very little if anything was heard from the international organizations. The silence became deafening after the People's Republic of China joined the United Nations in 1971 – prompting the UN High Commissioner for Refugees to decide suddenly that the nearly one hundred thousand Tibetan exiles in India were no longer refugees, and to withdraw all UN support and assistance in a matter of days.

In this sector as well, things have improved. Confronted with the reality of the bloody upheavals in Lhasa since 1987 and the June 1989 massacre on Tiananmen Square, even the most cautious organization can no longer turn a deaf ear. Aghast at Chinese police brutality against protesters in Lhasa in 1989, the European Parliament deplored the 'brutal repression' in Tibet.[17] The unprecedented condemnation constituted a major defeat for China's diplomacy. The response was not long in coming: almost instantaneously, Peking retorted that the vote had been an impudent initiative. A few days later in Peking, Martin Bangemann, Vice-President of the European Commission, called on Deputy Prime Minister Wu Xueqian to express the Community's distress at the loss of human lives and the hope that situations of this type would not recur. In knee-jerk response, China protested 'with intense indignation' against this 'flagrant interference' in its internal affairs. Replying in April 1992 to a request for information emanating from a French parliamentarian, Jacques Delors, the President of the European Commission, described the EC position on Tibet in the following terms: 'I am in a position to assure you that the commitment of the Community and its Member States in respect of human rights in general and their preoccupation concerning the situation in Tibet are clearly perceived by, and are well known to the Chinese authorities, who have been explicitly requested to show respect for the Tibetan people's freedom of opinion and to pursue the dialogue with the Dalai Lama.'

China experienced another stinging diplomatic rebuff in the aftermath of the Tiananmen massacre. For the very first time in the history of the United Nations a permanent member of the Security Council was called to task by the UN Sub-Commission on Human Rights at its August 1989 session in Geneva. Despite the high-powered pressures exerted by Chinese diplomats on the twenty-six experts who make up this body, they voted to condemn explicitly the savagery of the Chinese army. The power-play in the corridors was in vain, and the text was passed by fifteen votes to nine, with a number of abstentions. Once again, the government in Peking was reduced to expressing indignation at this unseemly interference in China's internal affairs. It went on to boast that the 'pressures of reactionary circles abroad' would never 'make the Chinese people yield'. But behind this screen of rather vapid jargon, the Chinese leadership was provoked to raging fury, according to well-placed Chinese sources. Quite understandably, for the adoption of the resolution, however mildly worded, cancelled out years of efforts in that very forum to burnish China's image as a respectable and democratic nation.

Even more significantly, with this resolution, the UN turned the page on twenty-five years of amnesia with respect to Chinese atrocities. Other than the three resolutions on violations in Tibet adopted soon after the Dalai Lama's departure into exile, whereby the General Assembly reiterated the 'Tibetan people's right to self-determination' and renewed its call for 'the cessation of all practices which deprive Tibetans of the human rights and fundamental freedoms which they have traditionally enjoyed', nothing had ever been said against China, not even at the height of the cultural revolution, when corpses floated down the Pearl River as far as Hong Kong. Two years later, on 23 August 1991, the Sub-Commission adopted another resolution, this time focusing explicitly on human rights in Tibet and expressing 'concern' about continuing violations 'which threaten the distinct cultural, religious and national identity of the Tibetan people'. As a permanent member of the Security Council since 1972, it had been easy for China to quell discordant voices and charm Western business circles. Now that the debate has been reopened at the United Nations, the fate of the Tibetan highlands will in all likelihood be influenced to a considerable extent by developments at the UN and other large multilateral institutions.

On 4 March 1992, the UN Commission on Human Rights, a highly politicized forum composed of fifty-three governments, voted to take 'no action' on a resolution criticizing Chinese policies in Tibet. At first sight, this outcome might look like a setback for the Dalai Lama and his followers, but it could also be considered a success in many ways. Never before had the question of Tibet been the focus of such intense lobbying and debate in Geneva. An examination of the voting pattern shows that a fair number of the twenty-seven governments that voted to protect China from investigation had good reason to fear international scrutiny on their own turf. The battle at the United Nations will be an uphill struggle, no doubt, but the omens are good. In March 1993, China invoked the same 'no action' stratagem at the Commission to avoid the passage of a resolution calling attention to violations throughout China. This time it was only supported by twenty-two governments.

International opinion is coming out in favour of the Tibetans. The Tibet Support Group in Norway was able to collect 200,000 signatures from sixty-eight countries on a petition addressed to the UN Secretary-General and handed over to the Human Rights Centre's New York office in March 1992. The high degree of mobilisation is demonstrated by the number of non-governmental organizations all over the world that have decided to support the Tibetan cause. I have counted over one hundred and fifty from France to Japan, via Eastern Europe, Latin America and Asia.

Gradually, the Tibetan cause seems to be making headway at other levels of the international community as well. In early December 1989, the Western European Union (WEU) criticized China's policies in Tibet. Its Parliamentary Assembly, which includes all the EC countries except Ireland, stated that 'the Chinese have been occupying Tibet for many years and deprive the Tibetan people of their human rights'. Peking responded with the now-familiar refrain that the text 'constituted gross interference in Chinese internal affairs and deeply offended the feelings of the Chinese people'.

The award of the 1989 Nobel Peace Prize to the Dalai Lama was a tremendous blow to the Chinese government's pride. Accepting the honour in December 1989 in Oslo, in the presence of the King and Queen of Norway, the Dalai Lama welcomed the prize 'with profound gratitude on behalf of the oppressed everywhere'. The Oslo jury's decision contributed to China's isolation during that period. What is more, the Nobel Prize provided tremendous encouragement to the Tibetan people at a crucial time. The news of the award was celebrated with dancing and screams of joy in the streets of Dharamsala. In Lhasa, it was welcomed with the same enthusiasm – whenever the Chinese police turned their backs. Reuters' Guy Dinmore was one of the few correspondents in Lhasa in October 1989. Taking advantage of a moment of distraction on the part of his official minders, a young Tibetan woman described the joy of the population: 'This news has made us so happy! We have been toasting the award and dancing and offering incense.' Another Tibetan commented: 'We are celebrating the event. The government is angry, but there is nothing they can do.'

The Peace Prize shored up the position of the Tibetans who reject violence and still believe in a peaceful solution. It also came as a warning to those who prefer another path: in a world saddled with myriad potential and declared conflicts, non-violence had finally won some recognition. Lastly, the prize came as a slap in the face for a faltering regime, a humiliation for the entire Chinese nation – no citizen of the PRC has ever been awarded a Nobel Prize in any field at all. What a blow to see the leader of the Tibetan barbarians walk away with the honour! It goes without saying that the government once more expressed its extreme indignation and profound regrets. The Oslo jury was accused of 'gross interference in [China's] internal affairs, which offends the national feelings of the Chinese people'. The *People's Daily* took this opportunity to refer to the Dalai Lama as a political gangster.[18]

The Nobel Prize enhanced the reputation of the Dalai Lama at the expense of China's prestige, and it conferred upon the Tibetan issue a respectability that has opened many doors and elicited strong support from many quarters. Yet while informal recognition and sympathy are growing, official diplomatic recognition from the Western governments is still pending. Objectively speaking, Peking can rely on a number of allies on this question. During the era of Sino-Soviet estrangement, the USSR maintained a certain level of contact with the exiles, going so far as to question the historical basis of China's sovereignty over Tibet. With the resumption of good relations between Moscow and Peking in 1989, the USSR expressed support for the Chinese presence in the Land of Snow. Boris Yeltsin's Russia has not taken a clearly defined position on this issue. This is not to say that Moscow is entirely indifferent. Two Soviet citizens were 'studying' in Dharamsala in 1989. One is a Buryat from Ulan Ude in southern Siberia, near Mongolia; he told me he was studying Tibetan Buddhism. The other had come to study traditional Tibetan medicine. Both carried USSR service passports.

India seems less willing than ever to support the Tibetan resistance. The Prime Minister of course announced that he was happy that the Nobel Prize had gone to the Dalai Lama, but in December 1988, locked into a delicate process of improving relations with China, Rajiv Gandhi travelled on official business to Peking only days after a protest march had been drowned in blood in Lhasa. He became the first Indian head of state to visit China since 1954. While his counterpart Li Peng voiced his admiration for the principled position of the Indian government on the question of Tibet, Rajiv Gandhi declared publicly that Tibet was an integral part of Chinese territory and that India 'would not allow the Tibetan separatists in India to indulge in political activities designed to break up China'.[19]

When it comes to its posture with respect to the Tibetans, Nepal enjoys even less latitude. Sandwiched between China and India, how can it even dream of annoying the Chinese? In 1974, 15,000 members of the Tibetan resistance were using the Mustang area as a base for incursions into Tibet, where they harried the Chinese army. This state of affairs lasted until Mao Tse-tung lost his temper and threatened the King of Nepal with fearful reprisals. From then on, the Nepalese government extended a precarious form of asylum only to resident Tibetan refugees. With little if any thought of human rights considerations, it did not hesitate to hand over incoming refugees to the Chinese border guards.

In 1988, as a warning, the Nepalese authorities returned a group of newly-arrived Tibetans to the Chinese police, at their request. The group of twenty-six men and boys, who had tried to visit the Nepalese Buddhist shrines before joining monasteries in India, had already spent almost a year in a Katmandu prison, where their only visitors were Chinese diplomats. 'We have good relationships with our neighbours and we do not want our soil to be used for hostile activities directed against these neighbours' said Foreign Minister Shailendra Kumar Upadhyaya in November 1988. The Dalai Lama's planned visit to Nepal in February 1991 was cancelled by the Nepalese government, which made no bones about the fact that it was yielding to pressure from Peking. The Dalai Lama has only visited Nepal once, towards the end of the seventies, when he went to Lumbini, known as the birthplace of the Buddha. One should not judge Nepal too harshly, for countries as 'civilized' as Japan have blithely handed over to the Peking authorities the new boat people, the Chinese who fled the mainland after Tiananmen.

Nevertheless, the Dalai Lama seems to be gaining ground in Asia, even among China's neighbours and friends. Despite the protests of the Thai Army and repeated warnings from Peking, the Tibetan leader visited Thailand in February 1993 in the context of a meeting with six other Nobel prizewinners in Bangkok, to protest about the detention of Burmese dissident Aung San Suu Kyi, still held under house arrest. A visit to Japan planned for the summer of 1993 was abruptly cancelled.

In Europe, there is growing pressure on the Chinese government relating to Tibet. In November 1992, a special session of the Permanent Peoples' Tribunal was held in Strasbourg to examine the question. The sentence declares that in 1950, the Chinese armed forces 'acted in breach of international law and continue to act in breach of the law by remaining in Tibet to this day, effectively as an occupying army'. For the Tribunal, the Tibetan people should freely exercise the right to self-determination and choose either independence or any type of association with China or with another State. The lengthy resolution adopted by the European Parliament in December 1992 calls for the 'immediate reversal of policies that encourage the mass transfer of Chinese to Tibet'; it 'urges the resumption of negotiations between the Tibetan government in exile and the Chinese authorities' and 'the consideration in these negotiations of genuine self-determination, and as a first step and sign of goodwill'; it recommends the incorporation of all Tibetan territories into 'a single administrative and political unit'. In January 1993, the British government publicly expressed its support for a dialogue with no preconditions between China and the Dalai Lama. Also in London, forty international lawyers and jurists met for a week in January to examine issues relating to self-determination and independence for Tibet, at the request of the UK All-Party Parliamentary Group for Tibet and the International Commission of Jurists. They took particular notice of the serious threat posed by the settlement of non-Tibetans from China in traditional Tibetan areas.

In a very recent development, an EC fact-finding mission to Tibet that seemed destined to be no more than a week's holiday for several Peking-based ambassadors and senior officials and their wives was suddenly transformed into the real thing when their capitals were alerted to the fact that three Tibetans had been detained in advance of the visit, on suspicion of planning to meet or hand information to the visiting European dignitaries. The eight ambassadors, one minister and two first secretaries (a diplomatic signal from France and the UK) were on the last leg of the trip by the time their staff managed to reach them with the news. The formal farewell banquet they had been scheduled to offer their expectant Chinese hosts was cancelled. Instead, a 'working dinner' served as the framework for a sober discussion of the situation and for requests that the authorities release the prisoners or allow diplomatic observers to attend their trial. 'It was a difficult trip', one diplomat was quoted as saying, 'there was no reassuring information about the human rights situation in Tibet.'[20]

On 24 May, one day after the departure of the delegation, the largest demonstration since 1989 swept through Lhasa. A small group of Tibetans marched along the main shopping streets to a government economic office, where they held a peaceful sit-in to protest against the severe inflation and punitive taxes on Tibetan businesses that have come in the wake of an unprecedented influx of Chinese settlers since Lhasa was declared a Special Economic Zone in 1992. The crowd grew to over 2,000 with the passing of the hours, and the slogans veered towards 'Chinese go home' and 'Free Tibet' as the Chinese security forces confronted them in full riot gear. The police dispersed the crowd with tear gas. Another demonstration occurred on the next day, again dispersed with no loss of life. But the tourists that remain in Lhasa report fear and tension on the rise and a number of Tibetans have been arrested.

Reporting on police action following these and a number of subsequent smaller acts of rebellion in the Tibetan capital, the *Sunday Times* of 30 May 1993 speculated that 'the crackdown had been delayed while Beijing awaited Washington's decision on China's most favoured nation trading relationship with America'.[21] In the event, when President Clinton announced the renewal for one year of China's MFN status, it was conditional on China making 'overall, significant progress' with respect to human rights, including 'protecting Tibet's distinctive religious and cultural heritage'. For the first time in decades, Tibet has reappeared on the agenda of bilateral US–China relations.[22] Three days later, on 1 June 1993, the EC communique issued by the Danish Presidency on behalf of the Community and its Member States expressed concern about the arrests and police action against the demonstrators and 'disquiet at the general human rights situation of the Tibetan people'; it urged the

Chinese authorities to engage in a dialogue without pre-conditions with the representatives of the Tibetan people.

The mysterious death of the Panchen Lama

'We declare with profound grief that the Great Wisdom Master, the Vajra-Holder, the Unequalled Tenth Panchen Erdini Losang Chinlie Lhunzub Qoigyi Gyancain entered the state of perfect rest at 8.16 pm on the twenty-first day of the twelfth month of the Earth Dragon Year of the Tibetan calendar, 28 January 1989 of the Gregorian calendar. The Great Master Panchen Lama was not only our religious leader. He was also a Vice-Chairman of the Chinese National People's Congress and the Honorary President of the Chinese Buddhist Association. He consistently observed a patriotic attitude, protecting the unity of the motherland and the interests of the people. He made magnificent contributions to political and religious affairs. In this way, he won the love, esteem and extreme veneration of the ordained and the lay people. We, the monks of Tashilhumpo, sincerely pray for a quick reincarnation of the Panchen Lama.

'The Democratic Management Committee of Tashilhumpo.

'29 January 1989.'[23]

On 28 January 1989, only a few days before his fifty-first birthday, the Tenth Panchen Lama suddenly passed away in truly extraordinary circumstances. Six days earlier, he had inaugurated the 'Great Stupa' of Tashilhumpo in Shigatse, before a crowd of five thousand of the faithful and in the presence of the highest-ranking Tibetan cadres. He had gone on to preside over the inhumation, according to Tantric rites, of the remains of the Fifth, Sixth, Seventh, Eighth and Ninth Panchen Lamas, whose tombs had been desecrated by the Red Guards during the cultural revolution. After destroying the former stupas, Mao's troops had dismembered the bodies and thrown them in a river. But the faithful had surreptitiously retrieved the remains and placed them in secret caches. 'I have just accomplished the most important mission in my life', he had announced in his deep, sonorous voice, after cutting the ribbon at the inauguration of the golden Great Stupa. A few days before, the Panchen Lama had arrived in Shigatse in an open Jeep, acclaimed by 30,000 Tibetans who lined the roads. On the way, he had ordered the official convoy to halt at the summit of a 16,500 foot pass, in order to pray at a small shrine. Dressed in his maroon and gold robes, he had danced with joy in front of the prayer flags. The Panchen Lama was happy – he was back in his country! On the day after the inauguration of the religious monument, he made a public statement that was extremely critical of the Chinese government. His mordant words will take their place in history as a sort of testament. Coming from the Panchen Lama, who served for most of his life as one of the most precious allies of China's policies in Tibet, his statement came as a particularly bitter blow to the Chinese government, unexpectedly betrayed by a most faithful helper. Here is the text of his statement as it appeared in the *China Daily*:[24]

'The price paid by Tibet for its development over the last thirty years has been higher than the gains, Bainqen (Panchen) Lama, the region's highest religious leader, said on Monday.

'Bainqen Lama, who came to Tibet for the grand opening of the newly established stupa, said since Liberation that region has witnessed considerable development in many fields. However, he said, "We have also paid a high price which is a mistake we should never repeat."

'The religious leader, who spent a year and eight months in prison during the "cultural revolution", said with regard to the situation in Tibet that the damage caused by the leftist mistakes was more harmful than that of rightist wrongdoings.

'Bainqen made his comments at a high level discussion between top Party and government leaders from Lhasa and five other autonomous areas in China.

'He told them that Tibet has had tremendous lessons as well as successful experiences. Most people in the leading positions had learned those lessons. Bainqen, who pointed out that he was a very frank person, said some had completely forgotten the tragedy and others had even begun to repeat the mistakes.

'Tibetan society, which went straight into socialism from the serf system, had not even reached its primary level of socialism. The emphasis in future work should be focused on correcting leftist mistakes, he said.

'Over the past several years, Bainqen said, the economic gap between Tibet and the coastal regions in China had enlarged. However, Tibet must try its best to take advantage of its rich resources and catch up with the economically advanced regions.

'Some people who are unfriendly or even hostile to Tibet have tried to destroy Han and Tibetan relationship by citing these economic differences, Bainqen said.'

Two years earlier, in his March 1987 statement to the Tibet Standing Committee of the National People's Congress, mentioned above, the Panchen Lama had also said, speaking about his comrades of the People's Liberation Army stationed in the Tibetan areas: 'We frequently say that great achievements were made with your sweat in the liberation and reformation of Tibet and that the people of Tibet will never forget this. This is an honest statement. However, you did make a great many mistakes, and these also in Tibet. These too, we will never forget.' Then, turning to the topic of persecution against Tibetans, he had reminded them that 'in Amdo and Kham, people were subjected to unspeakable atrocities. People were shot in groups of ten or twenty. I know that it is not good to speak about these things. But such actions have left deep wounds in the minds of the people'. Concerning Qinghai (Amdo), '[I]f there was a film made on all the atrocities perpetrated in Qinghai province, it would shock the viewers. In Golok area, many people were killed and their dead bodies were rolled down the hill into a big ditch. The soldiers told the family members and relatives of the dead people that they should all celebrate since the rebels had been wiped out. They were even forced to dance on the dead bodies. Soon after, they were also massacred with machine-guns.'[25]

If one is to believe the official statement, the Panchen Lama suffered an acute heart attack on 28 January at 4.30 am, in his room at Shigatse. A medical team immediately administered oxygen as well as a vasodilator, a sedative and a drug to regulate his heartbeat. Four hours later, the Panchen suffered a second attack and lost consciousness. An electrocardiogram revealed ventricular fibrillation. The doctors gave him cardiotonic injections, a cardiac massage and put him on a respirator. By the evening, specialists sent from Peking arrived at his bedside. One of them was Liu Yuanxu, Deputy Director of Peking Hospital. But they laboured in vain and the Panchen Lama's heart stopped beating at 8.16 pm.[26] Some of the exiled Tibetans to whom I have spoken are convinced he was assassinated by the Chinese. Others believe that he had himself decided when he would die, as only the greatest masters are able to do. They feel that he had decided to die in his town, in his monastery. He had decided to rest for all time in the stupa he had just inaugurated, alongside his illustrious predecessors. On the eve of his death, his entourage relates, a biting wind had buffeted Shigatse, blowing the yellow sand up into the sky – a omen of the Panchen Lama's disappearance.

While there is no possibility of confirming or disproving the different theories, the heart attack seems to be the most likely one. The Panchen Lama had become extremely fat after his rehabilitation. The visit to Shigatse had been very tiring, and he had spent much of his time blessing the countless faithful. The Dalai Lama mourned the passing of a 'freedom-fighter'. Peking was stunned. The Chinese government expressed sorrow at the death of a 'great patriot' and 'devoted friend of the Chinese Communist Party'. A cynical obituary for someone who from 1964 to 1978 had spent exactly nine years and eight months of his life in a cell at Peking's Number One Prison or in a labour camp, followed by house arrest in Peking. For some time, he was even thought to be dead. One day he suddenly reappeared and made a humiliating self-criticism, admitting that, 'for a while, I rejected the banner of patriotism and I made mistakes. Guided by Chairman Mao's revolutionary line, I have corrected my mistakes.'

During his time in detention, the Party's solicitude for his well-being extended to finding him a wife, Li Jie, the daughter of General Dong

Qiwu. In breach of his vows as a celibate monk, they married and had a daughter, Renji Wangmu, in 1983. A married Panchen Lama would lose all credibility with the Tibetans, thought the Chinese leadership, for monks of the Yellow Hat school are expected to remain celibate. They were wrong. Most of the faithful took no notice, just as they ignored his penchant for lavish food and drink in a luxurious residence in Peking. After the Panchen Lama's death, his wife – almost twenty years his junior – broke the government-imposed silence for the first time.

She allowed herself to be interviewed by Lu Kang, a well-known Hong Kong journalist who had travelled to Peking to see her. The marriage had not been arranged by the Party; it had been the wish of the Panchen Lama himself, she said. After Deng Xiaoping had blessed the union, the wedding had been held at the Ethnic Minority Culture Palace (*Wenhua Minzugong*) in the spring of 1978. A few days after the Panchen Lama passed away, the Chinese authorities arranged for a commemorative ceremony to be held at the People's Palace in Peking, attended by all the leadership, from Deng Xiaoping downwards. But Li Jie was not invited. This inconvenient wife was unwelcome. She rebelled against the decision and popular rumour had it that she intended to set herself on fire in Tiananmen Square in protest. She told Lu Kang, 'if a lama marries, he is not breaking any monastic rule. Many Living Buddhas are married. The Dalai Lama's elder brother and his youngest brother are both married.'

There is some truth in this, since two of the Dalai Lama's brothers, both supposed to be reincarnate lamas, have abandoned their ordination and married. Thubten Jigme Norbu, the eldest brother, was the head lama of Takster monastery in Amdo and he has taught for many years at State University in Indiana; the youngest is Tenzin Chogyal, Ngari Rinpoche. He is married and lives in India with his wife and two children. Li Jie wonders: 'Why after living as man and wife for ten years without breaking any monastic rules should we have to hide that fact after his death?' Li Jie's Tibetan name is Dechen Wangmo. She often accompanied the Panchen Lama when he visited Tibet. 'Many Tibetans called me "Mother of Tibet", when we travelled around', she added.[27]

The Panchen Lama's entire career is tied to the history of the Kuomintang and the Chinese Communist Party. The Ninth Panchen Lama reincarnation had died in 1937. Born in February 1938 to a peasant family in Qinghai, Goinbo Cedan was three in 1941 when he was recognized as a reincarnation of the lineage of the First Panchen Lama, who had lived in the fifteenth century. Some monks and lamas of the Yellow Hat school were manipulated by the Kuomintang into recognizing him as the reincarnation; Lhasa was forced to accept this particular candidate. In 1949, the Chinese Communists inherited him and used him as a valuable rival to the Dalai Lama. As we saw earlier, the child was said to have sent a telegram congratulating Mao Tse-tung on the proclamation of the People's Republic of China on 1 October 1949. He was eleven at the time. When he was sixteen, he was officially received by Mao Tse-tung, then made a member of the National Committee of the Chinese People's Political Consultative Conference. The rest of the sad story is by now familiar.

The Panchen Lama's death has created an unprecedented situation: the necessity to hunt for the reincarnation of a high Tibetan official in a Communist country! Ever since 1959, Peking has obstinately refused to recognize the reincarnations of high lamas who pass away. From the point of view of Party ideology, the lama tradition is seen as a harmful relic of feudal times. Another problem: for the search to be valid and acceptable to the Tibetans, it must be carried out under the close supervision of the Dalai Lama. Wasting no time, Peking's official media, somewhat incongruously led by the *People's Daily*, announced to the Chinese and Tibetan public the extraordinary news that the late Panchen Lama was going to reincarnate as a baby and that the search would soon get underway. This was the official start of the procedure to find the reincarnation of a Living Buddha in an atheistic Communist country! In Shigatse, the seven hundred monks of Tashilhumpo prayed for the return of the Panchen Lama.

In keeping with tradition, Tibetan specialists started embalming the Panchen's body. The first stage of the complex process of mummification took five days. Peking raised no obstacles. On the contrary, the Tibet Regional Committee of the Chinese Communist Party organized a car pool with official vehicles to convey the 1,200 pounds of medicinal herbs required for the rites. Strictly speaking, since the Panchen Lama had posthumously become a 'Great Patriot' of the People's Republic, he should have been laid to rest in Babaoshan with the majority of the heroes of the Chinese Revolution, Communist or otherwise. The regime produced another twist to the rules to allay the anger of the Tibetans: the Panchen Lama's remains were enshrined in the stupa he himself had consecrated a few days earlier. His embalmed body lies next to those of his predecessors. A remarkable symbol of epic proportions! After spending most of his life as a tool of the Chinese, in death the Panchen Lama has eluded their grip, in order to rest at Tashilhumpo, the traditional seat of the Panchen lineage.

By December 1993, the search for his reincarnation had still not produced any candidates. It is hard to imagine Communist Party cadres indulging in prayer or divination, but for the Chinese government, the temptation is likely to be too strong. It will be hard-pressed to refrain from trying to control the selection of the child. How can the Party fail to try to mould a new personality that will fully support its views? This is what is implied by the Chinese government's declarations. On 25 August 1989, the State Council, China's highest government body, gave its blessing to a group of Tashilhumpo lamas and monks appointed to search for and recognize the Panchen's reincarnation. The Abbot of Tashilhumpo and leader of the group, Xiaja Qiangba Chilie in Chinese (Jhadral Jampa Trinley in Tibetan), reportedly said that in virtue of 'recognized historical practices' and in keeping with the Constitution of the PRC, the search for the reincarnation could be carried out exclusively within the country. The final decision would require the approval of the State Council. The Dalai Lama and his entourage have said that for Peking to choose the reincarnation is unacceptable, and they point out that the future Panchen Lama may well be discovered outside Tibet. The race is on.

A dialogue with the Federation for Democracy in China

Does Tibet stand a chance if China adopts democracy some day? The Dalai Lama and his closest aides are confident that it does. Recent developments seem to support their view. Chinese dissidents who sought refuge in France and in the USA have displayed a constructive attitude towards Tibet and its leader. The Federation for Democracy in China (FDC) has taken a courageous stand, bearing in mind that Tibet is one of the most sensitive issues it has to confront. The risks are real – a single mis-step, just one wrong word, and the leadership in Peking will immediately turn it to advantage. If the FDC supports the principle of independence for Tibet, it will be easy for Peking to discredit the movement in the eyes of the many Chinese to whom this is pure treason, but if its members refuse to consider the possibility, it will tarnish their halo as enlightened reformers, at least in the West.

The exiled Chinese dissidents started reflecting on the question of Tibet as soon as they arrived in the West. In July 1989, barely a month after Tiananmen, Yan Jiaqi, a well-known member of the FDC leadership, had already decided on a line of action: China should become a Federation and negotiations with the Dalai Lama would be necessary. When the founding Assembly for the Federation for Democracy in China was held in September, Zhao Ziyang's trusted aide took one step more by declaring that the struggle of the Tibetans since 1959 was to be seen as a struggle for human rights: 'The Tibetan uprisings of 1959 and 1989 against the Communist Chinese were not counter-revolutionary and we must do justice to the situation.'[28] After being elected President of the FDC, it was Yan Jiaqi who warmly congratulated the Dalai Lama as soon as he was awarded the Nobel Peace Prize. He went on to express his respect for the Dalai Lama's 'brave struggle for the restoration of justice and human rights'.

The dialogue between the Tibetans and the Chinese in exile officially began on the afternoon of 12 October 1989, at the Paris headquarters of the FDC. The initial meeting was sheltered from prying eyes, and no foreigners were in attendance. Only six people were present. On the Tibetan side were Kelsang Gyaltsen, the Dalai Lama's representative in Europe, Ugen Nubpa, for the Tibetans in France and Phuntsok Takla, one of the two surviving members of the delegation that signed the Seventeen-Point Agreement in Peking in 1951. The Chinese side was represented by Yan Jiaqi, Wan Runnan (former chairman of the privately-owned Stone computer company in China) and another FDC official, Lin Qiling. To secure the best chances of success for the negotiations, the parties quite understandably decided to maintain strict confidentiality as an essential prerequisite for progress. The Dalai Lama met Yan Jiaqi in Paris on 4 December 1989. They agreed that the meeting had been of historical importance and decided that their representatives should pursue the dialogue to enhance mutual understanding and explore areas for cooperation. Peking lost no time in branding Yan Jiaqi a criminal and a traitor and berated him for conniving with the Dalai Lama to 'split the motherland'.

On a day when I knew Yan Jiaqi would be attending a talk about China at the Paris Institute for Political Studies, I went to ask him a few questions about his approach to the Tibetan issue. He looked a little nervous but agreed to reply, with the understanding that his words were his own and should in no case be taken as the position of the Federation for Democracy in China. Here are the main points we covered:

— Yan Jiaqi, do you share the opinion of the Panchen Lama, who stated that Tibet had lost more than it had gained since the arrival of the Chinese army in 1950?
— 'I agree with his perspective. In forty years, there have been good sides to the Chinese Communist Party but naturally also bad sides. On the bad side, the Communist Party compelled the Tibetans to adopt its single-party system. On the good side, it must be said that the Chinese government has contributed to the economic development of Tibet. Among the negative points, we must mention the denial of religious and cultural freedom to the Tibetan people.'

I ventured to ask the most burning question right away: in general terms, is Tibet part of China or not? Yan Jiaqi looked at me, and replied after a second's hesitation.

— 'Yes, Tibet is part of China.'
— Since when, exactly? I asked.
— 'That is a matter for historians. I haven't done any thorough research on that point. If I had ... I am not a Tibet specialist. Personally, I am a researcher, a scientist. You can see that my knowledge about Tibet is not enough. However, as regards the events that occurred in Tibet in 1959 and in 1989, they are to be placed on a par with the Peking massacre

of 4 June 1989. All of this has aroused an interest about Tibet among the Chinese people.'

I pursued the issue: if you believe Tibet is part of China, how do you see the right of all people to self-determination? Is that not one of the pillars of democracy? How do you respond to Tibetans fighting for the total independence of Tibet?

— 'I think that attitude of some Tibetans is natural. It is necessary to look at the question of Taiwan at the same time. There are also people in Taiwan who want independence. There is a movement for independence. But for Taiwan as well as for Tibet, there is ultimately no chance of independence. In Taiwan's case, the reason is that the people of Taiwan have seen the Chinese Communist Party at work and fear that there will be no hope of freedom after reunification. Another reason is that the Kuomintang, whether prior to 1949 or after it arrived on the island, has never been too keen on freedom either. Over the past few years, Taiwan has experienced an opening and a measure of democratization. But in the end, whether it is the Kuomintang or the Communist Party, these are not systems that recognize the people's right to be free. That is why there is a market for ideas of independence. As for Tibet, before 1949 and even well before that time, China attached little importance to its culture, religious beliefs and socio-economic development. Out of this situation, the need for self-determination was born for some people. I think the phenomenon is a natural one.

'But I think that if China becomes a genuine democracy, if the government in Peking is really democratic and guarantees a high level of authentic autonomy in Tibet, the trend towards self-determination will grow weaker. As a result, I think there will no longer be any danger of agitation for independence. The Dalai Lama himself has a position that I think is a very good one. He says that the scope of autonomy has to be widened in Tibet, including freedom of belief and opinion, even as regards the political system in Tibet. It seems to me that within that context, with Tibet as part of China its defence would be assured by the central government, along with its foreign relations. All other matters would be the province of the Tibetan government alone. I think that in this way, the desire for independence would grow less. It is therefore not a problem of self-determination. Tibet does possess that right. It may claim it. The same applies to Taiwan. Look at Hawaii: if some people start saying "we want our independence", we cannot say that the desire for independence in itself is a mistake. The question is, will the people of Hawaii be able to attain that independence?'

As I continued to press him on the topic, Yan Jiaqi replied without making any difficulties, but I sensed some irritation.

— In a democratic China, would the Tibetan people be free to organize a referendum to determine whether they wanted independence or not?
— 'If you are asking whether they have the right – every part of the world, every country has that right. That right belongs to every people. But for Tibet, I believe independence is impossible. As far as I'm concerned, as a Chinese from Jiangsu, I think independence would be a disaster for the Tibetan people as well as for China as a whole. But if we are speaking about rights, then the Tibetan people, the overseas Tibetans [the exiles] have the right to express those views. The right to self-determination is an inalienable right. If China denies it to the Tibetan people, they will claim it with redoubled force. The same applies to Taiwan. But I think that in China, whether in Taiwan or in Tibet, independence is not attainable. Let us take the example of Hainan island [off South China]. It is also a distinct region. Do the inhabitants of Hainan have the right to demand self-determination? Yes. But in reality, it is unimaginable that the people of Hainan would start calling for independence and wanting to found a 'Hainan Country' [*Hainan Guo*]. The same goes for Tibet. To resolve this issue, four conditions must be met:

1. We have to arrive at a correct judgment concerning people who were condemned as counter-revolutionaries in 1959 and 1989. We must recognize that these events are part of the Tibetan people's struggle for their rights.
2. Freedom of belief and the protection of Tibet's culture must be guaranteed. This must be guaranteed by the Constitution and by legislation.
3. How Tibet will be governed must be decided by the Tibetans themselves. It is not representatives from Shanghai and Peking or Shanxi and Sichuan who should make decisions that will later be imposed in Tibet. Tibet must be free to choose its type of government. This must be provided for in the Chinese Constitution.
4. Tibet is part of China but it must become part of a federated system. A federal system will settle the problem of Tibet. In this manner, Shanghai, Peking, Sichuan, Shanxi and Jiangsu will all be part of the federation, under the authority of a federal government. The freedom of the federal government will be limited in turn.

'If this comes to pass, I don't think Tibet will become an independent country. If it does, it will be a disaster for them. I think the Dalai Lama himself is not in favour of independence. When he expressed such views, he did so to protest against the Communist Party.'
— Would this solution be identical to the status of Hong Kong after 1997?
— 'No. It's not the same thing. The government and the parliament in Hong Kong will not be elected by universal suffrage. Whereas for Tibet,

I feel we can study a political system from another perspective. It will resemble neither Hong Kong's system nor Taiwan's, nor the systems for Peking and Shanghai. For a start, it would not be subject to the authority of the Chinese National People's Congress.'

— What about reconsidering Tibet's borders to account for the previously Tibetan areas that are now situated in the Chinese provinces of Gansu, Qinghai and Sichuan?

— 'This is something to be examined within the context of a federation. A federation like the West German Federal Republic or the United States. Tibet's borders would be defined through negotiations among the Chinese people, including the Tibetan people. The solution of this problem does not depend on what I may say. It is a question that concerns all of China. I know there are many Tibetan-populated areas in Qinghai and in Sichuan.'

— But since 1950, a considerable number of Han settlers have moved to Tibet. In 1980, Hu Yaobang visited Tibet and criticized that method. Do you agree?

— 'I agree with that criticism. He went to Tibet and saw the situation for himself. It does not benefit the Han nation or the Tibetan nation. If the people had moved of their own free will, and if they had been accepted by the Tibetans, then I would have said it was all right. But coercion was applied. As I see it, these migratory currents must occur on a voluntary basis. If they wanted to, Tibetans could also settle in inland China. The Hans could go to Tibet. Any type of compulsion will only provoke a disaster.'

— If I understand correctly, the Hans should return home?

— 'All of this must be on a voluntary basis. If they were free to do so, many Hans would undoubtedly return inland, but their departure would also create problems for the Tibetans. For Tibet's economic construction requires all the nationalities to work together, whether they be Tibetans, Hans or Mongolians. I think the Dalai Lama agrees with this way of looking at things. It is essential that no form of compulsion be applied. In a federal system, Tibet could freely decide on its own how to proceed with its development as regards education, cultural affairs, the economy. The Tibetans themselves could decide to invite Hans or Mongolians or other nationalities such as [China's] Koreans. Everything is possible! Even foreigners such as yourself, for instance, who are a friend of the Tibetan people, you could go to help them.'

— But the Tibetans have been duped so often by Chinese promises. Why should they ever believe you again?

— 'The reason for such doubts is very simple: China is not democratic. Even its Constitution is without practical significance, and calling Tibet an "Autonomous Region" doesn't mean Tibet is really autonomous. It is in no position to exercise the rights it supposedly enjoys by virtue of its autonomous status. All of this must change. Later on, it will not be

a question of being an "Autonomous Region" but a part of a federation.'
— But just compare the two: if you look at the Han nation, with such
a large population, and the Tibetan nation, so weak, what hope is there
that the Chinese Han will respect the Tibetans?
— 'There is hope. For what I have told you today is not the product of
my imagination. I am sure that the average Chinese agrees with me.
Including the Han. But if we start talking about independence for Tibet, virtually no one will agree. Among the Han, even the common
people would not agree. This is a very important fact. If we say "independence for Tibet", another problem immediately arises. By definition,
it will not be possible to find a solution to that problem. It would be a
very serious problem. So it is necessary to think about a federation in
order to find a solution to the question of Tibet. After the Communist
Party relinquishes its position and the 1989 movement is rehabilitated,
the Dalai Lama will return to China. Then we can jointly examine how
to set up such a federation.'
— But just think of the emotional impact of his return to Tibet. What
if a huge number of people, led by the Dalai Lama, were to clamour
suddenly for Tibetan independence? Would you call in the army to crush
the rebellion, as in 1959?
— 'I don't think the Dalai Lama could behave in that way. I trust him.
It is true that some Tibetans do think like that. But that is a natural
phenomenon. I feel that if the enlightened Tibetans, including the Dalai
Lama, return there, we will also return to China some day. On that day,
Tibet will become truly autonomous. It is true that the question of Tibet
will not be easy to resolve. But the Dalai Lama's government-in-exile
has already thought a great deal about that question. To arrive at a
solution, many negotiating sessions will be required. Many meetings. Only
then will we reach a satisfactory solution, for the good of the Tibetan
people and for the good of China as a whole.'
— What if the democratization of power were to cause China to lapse
once more into chaos, wouldn't the Tibetans again have to suffer the
consequences? How can we be sure what the future will bring?
— 'Listen, I think that would be unlikely. China has already suffered
such a lot. Additionally, we do not represent the Communist Party. We
do not have to pay for them. Furthermore, the people inside China hope
for democratization and expect it. They would not tolerate a repetition
of the upheavals of the past. In general terms, without democratization,
there is no future for China. Democracy is Tibet's future and it is China's
future. On that topic, we agree entirely with the Dalai Lama's entourage. We would not allow such a situation to recur. We would not tolerate a return to the situation that prevailed in China between 1949 and
1989.'
— If you succeed, will you allow Tibet to have a multi-party system?

— 'Of course. A multi-party system is necessary. But does Tibet need political parties? It will be up to the Tibetans to decide.'

— What if there were a party in favour of independence?

— 'Such a situation may indeed occur. Then it will be up to the Dalai Lama to examine the question. But let me say once more that in a democratic China, a party that stood for Tibetan independence would be allowed to exist. It would not be banned. But think carefully about the four points I mentioned in connection with the settlement of the question of Tibet. The day the Dalai Lama returns to China, there is no doubt he will be welcome. No one will be against him. The Tibetans have suffered so much. He will be welcome for all the Tibetans and for all the Chinese. All of China will welcome him!'

Yan Jiaqi's moderate tone is encouraging. Coming from a close adviser of the former chief of the Chinese Communist Party, this language may seem the stuff of dreams. If only Zhao Ziyang were to return to power some day and permanently neutralize all the hardliners who miss the good old Maoist days . . . Does this scenario belong in a kind of political science-fiction? Not necessarily. The laws of nature are inflexible: the next few years will take their toll of the remaining members of China's gerontocracy. Following which, it is inconceivable that China would still cling to the extreme positions adopted after June 1989, especially in the light of the rapid liberalization that took place in the former USSR and the Eastern European countries. The new policy of dialogue articulated by the Taiwan government is another very encouraging sign for the Tibetans. Should we expect peace in Tibet soon? Not so soon. For even were the most favourable options to materialize, a sizeable obstacle will remain on the road to any reconciliation, and that is Chinese nationalism. At critical junctures in their history, never has the clarion call of nationalism failed to stir the Chinese people – quite a normal state of affairs.

So how will it be possible to convince a quarter of the human race that six million Tibetans need a place in the sun of their own? How will they to be made to understand that those Tibetans have every right to live in a different way? How can the emotions be ruled out of the debate between the Chinese and the Tibetans, so they can talk without killing each other? Even the Hong Kong Chinese take a hardline attitude on the Tibetan issue. One of my Hong Kong friends immediately flies into a rage whenever I mention the Dalai Lama. In his opinion, just one look at the Dalai Lama's face is enough to tell that he is a crook!

I can remember the outcry that followed an article published in the Hong Kong monthly *Cheng Ming* in November 1987. Written by a Chinese woman whom I know and who signs her work Ming Lei, the article presented a number of critical remarks from the Western media concerning the repression that followed the rioting on 1 October 1987 in Lhasa. Ming Lei had ventured to write that, 'generally, people in China do not have any knowledge in depth about Tibet and refer to it only in disparaging terms. Westerners, however, are interested in its religion.' Quoting an article in the press, she added that 'history shows that Tibetans don't oppose the Communists, as Taiwan claims, but all Chinese governments whatsoever'. In conclusion, she said that, 'it cannot be said that in the past Tibet used to be part of China's territory'.

This was sacrilege. The editors of *Cheng Ming* were swamped by indignant letters from their readers. Several were published, including one signed by Zhen Feixiong, which began with, 'Is Ming Lei really Chinese?' Unable to fathom that a Chinese would dare to write such heresy, he opted for an international plot to split China, an old leitmotif that the Chinese Communist government brings out from time to time. Another reader, Bu Pingren, spoke out for Ming Lei, saying that merely quoting what the foreigners were saying did not make her into a foreigner herself. That same reader added that in Switzerland where he lives and where there is a large exile Tibetan community, he had not met a single Tibetan who thought of himself as Chinese.

Since 1989, the Sino-Tibetan dialogue has flourished in exile. There have been a number of meetings between the Chinese dissidents and the Dalai Lama or his people. The first Sino-Tibetan conference, held in New York at Columbia University in September 1991, brought together a fair number of Tibetan and Chinese academics and researchers in exile. Another conference entitled 'Sino-Tibetan relations, future prospects' was held near Washington DC on 5 and 6 October 1992, with the participation of several dozen respected Chinese and Tibetans. The first delegation of Chinese dissidents visited Dharamsala in July 1992 to meet with the Dalai Lama and officials of the Tibetan administration in exile. They were accompanied by Jigme Ngapo, whose father, Ngapo Ngawang Jigme, is China's number-one Tibetan collaborator. Last but not least, a growing number of Chinese in exile or overseas Chinese are now bold enough to express publicly their opinions about the Tibet issue. Fang Lizhi has said on several occasions that the question of Tibetan independence is for the Tibetan people themselves to decide, and that the Chinese will have to respect that decision. Mei Yangzhong, another Chinese dissident who belongs to the Federation for Democracy in China, feels that the Dalai Lama and his followers have 'a good chance' of gaining independence for Tibet some day. 'My research has shown me that the Tibetans are definitely different from the Chinese and that they are a people in their own right. I placed a great deal of emphasis on that point during a conference I gave in Japan. Since then, the FDC has been carrying out much research on the separate identity of the Tibetans. The Tibetans have the legitimate right to decide about their own future', he declared.[29]

The famous author and Chinese Communist Party veteran Wang Ruowang, expelled from the Party in 1987 and now living in the USA, has taken a stand in support of the principle of self-determination for the Tibetans. 'The Tibetans have an inalienable right to independence if that is what they want. When a genuinely democratic regime is in power in Peking, there will certainly be negotiations between the Han (Chinese) and the Tibetans. We could offer membership in a future Federation with China to the Tibetans. But if they decline, no one can deny them their fundamental right to self-determination', he commented in November 1992 in Paris.

As for myself, it has not been easy to write about Tibet. I am and will remain an observer. This is a comfortable position, since I have no reprisals to fear from either side, but it is also quite sensitive, owing to the acutely controversial nature of the issue. I am in a position to step back as much as required to arrive at the most serene perspective possible on the Tibetan tragedy, something which is out of the question for a Chinese or a Tibetan.

However, as I wrote, I was constantly aware that some people might continue to feel justified in accusing me of belonging to 'foreign imperialist circles' whose sole aim is to split China the better to dominate it. As we all know, slander always leaves some trace behind. It also occurred to me that when the book was finally published, some of my Chinese and Tibetan friends might not be satisfied. Some Chinese friends might think, however wrongly, that I had fallen prey to the 'anti-Chinese' Tibetan camp. The Tibetans might be annoyed by my uncompromising depiction of the old Tibetan society and think I am in sympathy with the idea of a non-independent Tibet. But when all is said and done, I have no regrets. I am gambling on their intelligence, and I nourish the hope that despite the complexity of the problem and the tremendous antagonism involved, one day we shall witness the triumph of reason. Let us hope that when that day comes, there will still be a Tibet left to enjoy it.

Notes

1. Statement of the Dalai Lama to the opening ceremony of the General Body meeting of the Tibetan Youth Congress in Dharamsala, on 11 September 1989.

2. These words date back to 1988, when Lodi Gyaltsen Gyari was serving as 'minister for foreign affairs'.

3. This is a reference to the failure of the Spring 1992 session of the UN Commission on Human Rights to condemn Chinese policies in Tibet.

4. *Tibet Information Network*, 16 May 1992.

5. Panchen Lama's address to the TAR Standing Committee of the National People's Congress, Peking, 28 March 1987.

6. *Renmin Ribao*, 5 April 1988.

7. *Liaowang* (Perspectives), Hong Kong, 22 August 1988.

8. *The Status of Tibet*, op. cit.

9. *Hong Kong Standard*, 10 May 1990.

10. Press conference of Yuan Mu, Chinese government spokesman on 14 March 1989 in Peking.

11. Li Zhaoxing, spokesman for the Chinese Ministry of Foreign Affairs, at a press conference on 16 June 1988.

12. US Congress Foreign Relations Authorization Act, Fiscal Years 1992 and 1993, 3 October 1991.

13. *Tibet Press Watch*, International Campaign for Tibet, April 1992, pp. 4 and 5.

14. *South China Morning Post*, 23 July 1988.

15. *La Libre Belgique*, 28–29 March 1992.

16. Reuters, 18 March 1992.

17. Resolution adopted in Strasbourg on 16 March 1989 by the European Parliament.

18. *Renmin Ribao*, 11 October 1989.

19. *Xinhua*, 19 December 1988.

20. 'Red Face for China: European Envoys Cancel Tibet Banquet', *International Herald Tribune*, 24 May 1993.

21. 'Chinese tighten grip on rebellious Lhasa', *Sunday Times*, 30 May 1993, London.

22. 'Clinton Conditions MFN on Preservation of Tibetan Culture', International Campaign for Tibet, 28 May 1993, Washington DC.

23. *Xinhua*, 29 January 1989.

24. *China Daily*, 25 January 1989, on the front page.

25. Panchen Lama, op. cit.

26. *Xinhua*, 29 January 1989.

27. Interview by Lu Kang in the Hong Kong monthly *Baixing*, No. 189, April 1989.

28. *World Journal* (in Chinese), New York, 21 September 1989.

29. *Actualités Tibétaines*, Vol.III No.2, Summer 1992, pp. 8 and 9.

Appendix

1. The Seventeen-Point Agreement, 1951

The agreement of the Central People's Government and the Local Government of Tibet on measures for the peaceful liberation of Tibet, 23 May 1951

The Tibetan nationality is one of the nationalities with a long history within the boundaries of China and, like many other nationalities, it has done its glorious duty in the course of the creation and development of the great motherland. But over the last hundred years and more, imperialist forces penetrated into China, and in consequence, also penetrated into the Tibetan region and carried out all kinds of deceptions and provocations. Like previous reactionary Governments, the KMT [Guomindang] reactionary government continued to carry out a policy of oppression and sowing dissension among the nationalities, causing division and disunity among the Tibetan people. The Local Government of Tibet did not oppose imperialist deception and provocations, but adopted an unpatriotic attitude towards the great motherland. Under such conditions, the Tibetan nationality and people were plunged into the depths of enslavement and suffering. In 1949, basic victory was achieved on a nation-wide scale in the Chinese people's war of liberation; the common domestic enemy of all nationalities – the KMT reactionary government – was overthrown; and the common foreign enemy of all nationalities – the aggressive imperialist forces – was driven out. On this basis, the founding of the People's Republic of China and of the Central People's Government was announced. In accordance with the Common Programme passed by the Chinese People's Political Consultative Conference, the Central People's Government declared that all nationalities within the boundaries of the People's Republic of China are equal, and that they shall establish unity and mutual aid and oppose imperialism and their own public enemies, so that the People's Republic of China may become one big family of fraternity and cooperation, composed of all its nationalities. Within this big family of nationalities of the People's Republic of China, national regional autonomy is to be exercised in areas where national minorities are concentrated, and all national minorities are to have freedom to develop their spoken and written languages and to preserve or reform their customs, habits, and religious beliefs, and the Central People's Government will assist all national minorities to develop their political, economic, cultural, and educational construction work. Since then, all nationalities within the country, with the exception of those in the areas of Tibet and Taiwan, have gained liberation. Under the unified leadership of the Central People's Government and the direct leadership of the higher levels of People's Governments, all national minorities have fully enjoyed the right of national equality and have exercised, or are exercising, national regional autonomy. In order that the influences of aggressive imperialist forces in Tibet may be successfully eliminated, the unification of the territory and sovereignty of the People's Republic of China accomplished, and national defence safeguarded; in order that the Tibetan nationality and people may be freed and return to the big family of the People's Republic of China to enjoy the same rights of national equality as all other nationalities in the country and develop their political, economic, cultural, and educational work, the Central People's Government, when it ordered the People's Liberation Army to march into Tibet, notified the local government of Tibet to send delegates to the Central Authorities to hold talks for the conclusion of an agreement on measures for the peaceful liberation of Tibet. At the latter part of April 1951, the delegates with full powers from the Local Government of Tibet arrived in Peking. The Central People's Government appointed representatives with full powers to conduct talks on a friendly basis with the delegates of the Local Government of Tibet. The result of the talks is that both parties have agreed to establish this agreement and ensure that it be carried into effect.

1. The Tibetan people shall be united and drive out the imperialist aggressive forces from Tibet; that the Tibetan people shall return to the big family of the motherland – the People's Republic of China.

2. The Local Government of Tibet shall actively assist the People's Liberation Army to enter Tibet and consolidate the national defences.

3. In accordance with the policy towards nationalities laid down in the Common Programme of the Chinese People's Political Consultative Conference, the Tibetan people have the right of exercising national regional autonomy under the unified leadership of the Central People's Government.

4. The Central Authorities will not alter the existing political system in Tibet. The Central Authorities also will not alter the established status, functions and powers of the Dalai Lama. Officials of various ranks shall hold office as usual.

5. The established status, functions, and powers of the Panchen Ngoerhtehni shall be maintained.

6. By the established status, functions and powers of the Dalai Lama and of the Panchen Ngoerhtehni is meant the status, functions and powers of the 13th Dalai Lama and of the 9th Panchen Ngoerhtehni when they were in friendly and amicable relations with each other.

7. The policy of freedom of religious belief laid down in the Common Programme of the Chinese People's Political Consultative Conference will be protected. The Central Authorities will not effect any change in the income of the monasteries.

8. The Tibetan troops will be reorganised step by step into the People's Liberation Army, and become part of the national defence forces of the Central People's Government.

9. The spoken and written language and school education of the Tibetan nationality will be developed step by step in accordance with the actual conditions in Tibet.

10. Tibetan agriculture, livestock raising, industry and commerce will be developed step by step, and the people's livelihood shall be improved step by step in accordance with the actual conditions in Tibet.

11. In matters related to various reforms in Tibet, there will be no compulsion on the part of the Central Authorities. The Local Government of Tibet should carry out reforms of its own accord, and when the people raise demands for reform, they must be settled through consultation with the leading personnel of Tibet.

12. In so far as former pro-imperialist and pro-KMT officials resolutely sever relations with imperialism and the KMT and do not engage in sabotage or resistance, they may continue to hold office irrespective of their past.

13. The People's Liberation Army entering Tibet will abide by the above-mentioned policies and will also be fair in all buying and selling and will not arbitrarily take even a needle or a thread from the people.

14. The Central People's Government will handle all external affairs of the area of Tibet; and there will be peaceful co-existence with neighbouring countries and the establishment and development of fair commercial and trading relations with them on the basis of equality, mutual benefit and mutual respect for territory and sovereignty.

15. In order to ensure the implementation of this agreement, the Central People's Government will set up a military and administrative committee and a military area headquarters in Tibet, and apart from the personnel sent there by the Central People's Govern-

ment it will absorb as many local Tibetan personnel as possible to take part in the work. Local Tibetan personnel taking part in the military and administrative committee may include patriotic elements from the Local Government of Tibet, various district and various principal monasteries; the namelist is to be prepared after consultation between the representatives designated by the Central People's Government and various quarters concerned, and is to be submitted to the Central People's Government for approval.

16. Funds needed by the military and administrative committee, the military area headquarters and the People's Liberation Army entering Tibet will be provided by the Central People's Government. The Local Government of Tibet should assist the People's Liberation Army in the purchases and transportation of food, fodder, and other daily necessities.

17. This agreement shall come into force immediately after signatures and seals are affixed to it.

Signed and sealed by delegates of the Central People's Government with full powers:

Chief Delegate: Li Wei-han (Chairman of the Commission of Nationalities Affairs);
Delegates: Chang Ching-wu, Chang Kuo-hua, Sun Chih-yuan.
Delegates with full powers of the Local Government of Tibet:
Chief Delegate: Kaloon Ngabou Ngawang Jigme (Nhabo Shape)
Delegates: Dzasak Khemey Sonam Wangdi, Khentrung Thuptan, Tenthar, Khenchung
    Thupten Lekmuun Rimshi, Samposey Tenzin Thundup

2. Five-Point Peace Plan for Tibet,
21 September 1987

The world is increasingly interdependent, so that lasting peace – national, regional, and global – can only be achieved if we think in terms of broader interest rather than parochial needs. At this time, it is crucial that all of us, the strong and the weak, contribute in our own way. I speak to you today as the leader of the Tibetan people and as Buddhist monk devoted to the principles of a religion based on love and compassion. Above all, I am here as a human being who is destined to share this planet with you and all others as brothers and sisters. As the world grows smaller, we need each other more than in the past. This is true in all parts of the world, including the continent I come from.

At present in Asia, as elsewhere, tensions are high. There are open conflicts in the Middle East, Southeast Asia, and in my own country, Tibet. To a large extent, these problems are symptoms of the underlying tensions that exist among the area's great powers. In order to resolve regional conflicts, an approach is required that takes into account the interests of all relevant countries and peoples, large and small. Unless comprehensive solutions are formulated, that take into account the aspirations of the people most directly concerned, piecemeal or merely expedient measures will only create new problems.

The Tibetan people are eager to contribute to regional and world peace, and I believe they are in a unique position to do so. Traditionally, Tibetans are a peace loving and nonviolent people. Since Buddhism was introduced to Tibet over one thousand years ago, Tibetans have practised non-violence with respect to all forms of life. This attitude has also been extended to our country's international relations. Tibet's highly strategic position in the heart of Asia, separating the continent's great powers – India, China and the USSR – has throughout history endowed it with an essential role in the maintenance of peace and stability. This is precisely why, in the past, Asia's empires went to great lengths to keep one another out of Tibet. Tibet's value as an independent buffer state was integral to the region's stability.

When the newly formed People's Republic of China invaded Tibet in 1949/50, it created a new source of conflict. This was highlighted when, following the Tibetan national uprising against the Chinese and my flight to India in 1959, tensions between China and India escalated into the border war in 1962. Today large numbers of troops are again massed on both sides of the Himalayan border and tension is once more dangerously high.

The real issue, of course, is not the Indo-Tibetan border demarcation. It is China's illegal occupation of Tibet, which has given it direct access to the Indian sub-continent. The Chinese authorities have attempted to confuse the issue by claiming that Tibet has always been a part of China. This is untrue. Tibet was a fully independent state when the People's Liberation Army invaded the country in 1949/50.

Since Tibetan emperors unified Tibet, over a thousand years ago, our country was able to maintain its independence until the middle of this century. At times Tibet extended its influence over neighbouring countries and peoples and, in other periods, came itself under the influence of powerful foreign rulers – the Mongol Khans, the Gorkhas of Nepal, the Manchu Emperors and the British in India.

It is, of course, not uncommon for states to be subjected to foreign influence or interference. Although so-called satellite relationships are perhaps the clearest examples of this, most major powers exert influence over less powerful allies or neighbours. As the most authoritative legal studies have shown, in Tibet's case, the country's occasional subjection to foreign influence never entailed a loss of independence. And there can be no doubt that when Peking's communist armies entered Tibet, Tibet was in all respects an independent state.

China's aggression, condemned by virtually all nations of the free world, was a flagrant violation of international law. As China's military occupation of Tibet continues, the world should remember that though Tibetans have lost their freedom, under international law Tibet today is still an independent state under illegal occupation.

It is not my purpose to enter into a political/legal discussion here concerning Tibet's status. I just wish to emphasize the obvious and undisputed fact that we Tibetans are a distinct people with our own culture, language, religion and history. But for China's occupation, Tibet would still, today, fulfil its natural role as a buffer state maintaining and promoting peace in Asia.

It is my sincere desire, as well as that of the Tibetan people, to restore to Tibet her invaluable role, by converting the entire country comprising the three Provinces of U-Tsang, Kham and Amdo – once more into a place of stability, peace, and harmony. In the best of Buddhist tradition, Tibet would extend its services and hospitality to all who further the cause of world peace and the well-being of mankind and the natural environment we share.

Despite the holocaust inflicted upon our people in the past decades of occupation, I have always striven to find a solution through direct and honest discussions with the Chinese. In 1982, following the change of leadership in China and the establishment of direct contacts with the government in Peking, I sent my representatives to Peking to open talks concerning the future of my country and people.

We entered the dialogue with a sincere and positive attitude and with a willingness to take into account the legitimate needs of the People's Republic of China. I hoped that this attitude would be reciprocated and that a solution could eventually be found which would satisfy and safeguard the aspirations and interests of both parties. Unfortunately, China has consistently responded to our efforts in a defensive manner, as though our detailing of Tibet's very real difficulties was criticism for its own sake.

To our even greater dismay, the Chinese government misused the opportunity for a genuine dialogue. Instead of addressing the real issues facing the six million Tibetan people, China has attempted to reduce the question of Tibet to a discussion of my own personal status.

It is against this background and in response to the tremendous support and encouragement I have been given by you and other persons during this trip, that I wish today to clarify the principal issues and to propose, in a spirit of openness and conciliation, a first step towards a lasting solution. I hope this may contribute to a future of friendship and cooperation with all of our neighbours, including the Chinese people.

This peace plan contains five basic components:

1. Transformation of the whole of Tibet into a zone of peace;

2. Abandonment of China's population transfer policy which threatens the very existence of the Tibetans as a people;

3. Respect for the Tibetan people's fundamental human rights and democratic freedoms;

4. Restoration and protection of Tibet's natural environment and the abandonment of
China's use of Tibet for the production and use of nuclear weapons and dumping of nuclear
waste;

5. Commencement of earnest negotiations on the future status of Tibet and of relations between the Tibetan and Chinese peoples.

Let me explain these five components.

1. I propose that the whole of Tibet, including the eastern provinces of Kham and
Amdo, be transformed into a zone of 'Ahimsa', a Hindi term used to mean a state of
peace and non-violence.

The establishment of such a peace zone would be in keeping with Tibet's historical
role as a peaceful and neutral Buddhist nation and buffer state separating the continent's
great powers. It would also be in keeping with Nepal's proposal to proclaim Nepal a peace
zone and with China's declared support for such a proclamation. The peace zone proposed by Nepal would have a much greater impact if it were to include Tibet and neighbouring areas.

The establishment of a peace zone in Tibet would require the withdrawal of Chinese
troops and military installations from the country, which would enable India also to
withdraw troops and military installations from the Himalayan regions bordering Tibet.
This would be achieved under an international agreement which would satisfy China's
legitimate security needs and build trust among the Tibetan, Indian, Chinese and other
peoples of the region. This is in everyone's best interest, particularly that of China and
India, as it would enhance their security, while reducing the economic burden of maintaining high troop concentrations on the disputed Himalayan border.

Historically, relations between China and India were never strained. It was only when
Chinese armies marched into Tibet, creating for the first time a common border, that
tensions arose between these two powers, ultimately leading to the 1962 war. Since then
numerous dangerous incidents have continued to occur. A restoration of good relations
between the world's two most populous countries would be greatly facilitated if they were
separated – as they were throughout history – by a large and friendly buffer region.

To improve relations between the Tibetan people and the Chinese, the first requirement is the creation of trust. After the holocaust of the last decades in which over one
million Tibetans – one-sixth of the population – lost their lives and at least as many lin-
gered in prison camps because of their religious beliefs and love of freedom, only a withdrawal of Chinese troops could start a genuine process of reconciliation. The vast occupation
force in Tibet is a daily reminder to the Tibetans of the oppression and suffering they
have all experienced. A troop withdrawal would be an essential signal that in future a
meaningful relationship might be established with the Chinese, based on friendship and
trust.

2. The population transfer of Chinese into Tibet, which the government in Peking
pursues in order to force a 'final solution' to the Tibetan problem by reducing the Tibetan
population to an insignificant and disenfranchised minority in Tibet itself, must be stopped.

The massive transfer of Chinese civilians into Tibet in violation of the Fourth Geneva
Convention (1949) threatens the very existence of the Tibetans as a distinct people. In the
eastern parts of our country, the Chinese now greatly outnumber Tibetans. In the Amdo
province, for example, where I was born, there are, according to Chinese statistics, 2.5
million Chinese and only 750,000 Tibetans. Even in the so-called Tibet Autonomous Region
(i.e., central and western Tibet), Chinese government sources now confirm that Chinese
outnumber Tibetans.

The Chinese population transfer policy is not new. It has been systematically applied
to other areas before. Earlier in this century, the Manchus were a distinct race with their

own culture and traditions. Today only two to three million Manchurians are left in Manchuria, where 75 million Chinese have settled. In Eastern Turkestan, which the Chinese now call Sinkiang, the Chinese population has grown from 200,000 in 1949 to 7 million, more than half of the total population of 13 million. In the wake of the Chinese colonization of Inner Mongolia, Chinese number 8.5 million, Mongols 2.5 million.

Today in the whole of Tibet, 7.5 million Chinese settlers have already been sent, outnumbering the Tibetan population of 6 million. In central and western Tibet, now referred to by the Chinese as the 'Tibet Autonomous Region', Chinese sources admit the 1.9 million Tibetans already constitute a minority of the region's population. These numbers do not take the estimated 300,000–500,000 troops in Tibet into account – 250,000 of them in the so-called Tibet Autonomous Region.

For the Tibetans to survive as a people, it is imperative that the population transfer is stopped and Chinese settlers return to China. Otherwise, Tibetans will soon be no more than a tourist attraction and relic of a noble past.

3. Fundamental human rights and democratic freedoms must be respected in Tibet. The Tibetan people must once again be free to develop culturally, intellectually, economically and spiritually and to exercise basic democratic freedoms.

Human rights violations in Tibet are among the most serious in the world. Discrimination is practised in Tibet under a policy of 'apartheid' which the Chinese call 'segregation and assimilation'. Tibetans are, at best, second class citizens in their own country. Deprived of all basic democratic rights and freedoms, they exist under a colonial administration in which all real power is wielded by Chinese officials of the Communist Party and the army.

Although the Chinese government allows Tibetans to rebuild some Buddhist monasteries and to worship in them, it still forbids serious study and teaching of religion. Only a small number of people, approved by the Communist Party, are permitted to join the monasteries.

While Tibetans in exile exercise their democratic rights under a constitution promulgated by me in 1963, thousands of our countrymen suffer in prisons and labour camps in Tibet for their religious or political convictions.

4. Serious efforts must be made to restore the natural environment in Tibet. Tibet should not be used for the production of nuclear weapons and the dumping of nuclear waste.

Tibetans have a great respect for all forms of life. This inherent feeling is enhanced by the Buddhist faith, which prohibits the harming of all sentient beings, whether human or animal. Prior to the Chinese invasion, Tibet was an unspoiled wilderness sanctuary in a unique natural environment. Sadly, in the past decades the wildlife and the forests of Tibet have been almost totally destroyed by the Chinese. The effects on Tibet's delicate environment have been devastating. What little is left must be protected and efforts must be made to restore the environment to its balanced state.

China uses Tibet for the production of nuclear weapons and may also have started dumping nuclear waste in Tibet. Not only does China plan to dispose of its own nuclear waste but also that of other countries, who have already agreed to pay Peking to dispose of their toxic materials.

The dangers this presents are obvious. Not only living generations, but future generations are threatened by China's lack of concern for Tibet's unique and delicate environment.

5. Negotiations on the future status of Tibet and the relationship between the Tibetan and Chinese peoples should be started in earnest.

We wish to approach this subject in a reasonable and realistic way, in a spirit of frankness and conciliation and with a view to finding a solution that is in the long-term interest of all: the Tibetans, the Chinese, and all other peoples concerned. Tibetans and Chinese are distinct peoples, each with their own country, history, culture, language and way of life. Differences among peoples must be recognized and respected. They need not, however, form obstacles to genuine co-operation where this is to the mutual benefit of both peoples. It is my sincere belief that if the concerned parties were to meet and discuss their future with an open mind and a sincere desire to find a satisfactory and just solution, a breakthrough could be achieved. We must all exert ourselves to be reasonable and wise, and to meet in a spirit of frankness and understanding.

Let me end on a personal note. I wish to thank you for the concern and support which you and so many of your colleagues and fellow citizens have expressed for the plight of oppressed people everywhere. The fact that you have publicly shown your sympathy for us Tibetans has already had a positive impact on the lives of our people inside Tibet. I ask for your continued support in this critical time in our country's history.

Thank you.

3. The Strasbourg Proposal: framework for Sino-Tibetan negotiations

We are living today in a very interdependent world. One nation's problems can no longer be solved by itself. Without a sense of universal responsibility our very survival is in danger. I have, therefore, always believed in the need for better understanding, closer co-operation and greater respect among the various nations of the world. The European Parliament is an inspiring example. Out of the chaos of war, those who were once enemies have, in a single generation, learned to co-exist and to co-operate. I am, therefore, particularly pleased and honoured to address the gathering at the European Parliament.

As you know, my own country – Tibet – is undergoing a very difficult period. The Tibetans – particularly those who live under Chinese occupation – yearn for freedom and justice and a self-determined future, so that they are able to fully preserve their unique identity and live in peace with their neighbours.

For over a thousand years we Tibetans have adhered to spiritual and environmental values in order to maintain the delicate balance of life across the high plateau on which we live. Inspired by the Buddha's message of non-violence and compassion and protected by our mountains, we sought to respect every form of life and to abandon war as an instrument of national policy.

Our history, dating back more than two thousand years, has been one of independence. At no time, since the founding of our nation in 127 BC, have we Tibetans conceded our sovereignty to a foreign power. As with all nations, Tibet experienced periods in which our neighbours – Mongol, Manchu, Chinese, British and the Gorkhas of Nepal sought to establish influence over us. These eras have been brief and the Tibetan people have never accepted them as constituting a loss of our national sovereignty. In fact, there have been occasions when Tibetan rulers conquered vast areas of China and other neighbouring states. This, however, does not mean that we Tibetans can lay claim to these territories.

In 1949 the People's Republic of China forcibly invaded Tibet. Since that time Tibet has endured the darkest period in its history. More than a million of our people have died as a result of the occupation. Thousands of monasteries were reduced to ruins. A generation has grown up deprived of education, economic opportunity and a sense of its own national character. Though the current Chinese leadership has implemented certain reforms, it is also promoting a massive population transfer onto the Tibetan plateau. This policy has already reduced the six million Tibetans to a minority. Speaking for all Tibetans, I must sadly inform you, our tragedy continues.

I have always urged my people not to resort to violence in their efforts to redress their suffering. Yet I believe all people have the moral right to peacefully protest injustice. Unfortunately, the demonstrations in Tibet have been violently suppressed by the Chinese police and military. I will continue to counsel for non-violence, but unless China forsakes the brutal methods it employs, Tibetans cannot be responsible for a further deterioration in the situation.

Every Tibetan hopes and prays for the full restoration of our nation's independence. Thousands of our people have sacrificed their lives and our whole nation has suffered in this struggle. Even in recent months, Tibetans have bravely sacrificed their lives to achieve this precious goal. On the other hand, the Chinese totally fail to recognize the Tibetan people's aspirations and continue to pursue a policy of brutal suppression.

I have thought for a long time on how to achieve a realistic solution to my nation's plight. My cabinet and I solicited the opinions of many friends and concerned persons. As a result, on September 21, 1987, at the Congressional Human Rights Caucus in Washington, DC, I announced a Five-Point Peace Plan for Tibet. In it I called for the conversion of Tibet into a zone of peace, a sanctuary in which humanity and nature can live together in harmony. I also called for respect for human rights and democratic ideals, environmental protection, and a halt to the Chinese population transfer into Tibet.

The fifth point of the Peace Plan called for earnest negotiations between the Tibetans and the Chinese. We have, therefore, taken the initiative to formulate some thoughts which, we hope, may serve as a basis for resolving the issue of Tibet. I would like to take this opportunity to inform the distinguished gathering here of the main points of our thinking.

The whole of Tibet known as Cholka-Sum (U-Tsang, Kham and Amdo) should become a self-governing democratic political entity founded on law by agreement of the people for the common good of themselves and their environment, in association with the People's Republic of China.

The Government of the People's Republic of China could remain responsible for Tibet's foreign policy. The Government of Tibet should, however, develop and maintain relations, through its own Foreign Affairs Bureau, in the fields of commerce, education, culture, religion, tourism, science, sports and other non-political activities. Tibet should join international organizations concerned with such activities.

The Government of Tibet should be founded on a constitution or basic law. The basic law should provide for a democratic system of government entrusted with the task of ensuring economic equality, social justice and protection of the environment. This means that the Government of Tibet will have the right to decide on all affairs relating to Tibet and the Tibetans.

As individual freedom is the real source and potential of any society's development, the Government of Tibet would seek to ensure this freedom by full adherence to the Universal Declaration of Human Rights including the rights to speech, assembly, and religion. Because religion constitutes the source of Tibet's national identity, and spiritual values lie at the very heart of Tibet's rich culture, it would be the special duty of the Government of Tibet to safeguard and develop its practice.

The government should be composed of a popularly elected Chief Executive, a bicameral legislative branch, and an independent judicial system. Its seat should be in Lhasa.

The social and economic system of Tibet should be determined in accordance with the wishes of the Tibetan people, bearing in mind especially the need to raise the standard of living of the entire population.

The Government of Tibet would pass strict laws to protect wildlife and plant life. The exploitation of natural resources would be carefully regulated. The manufacture, testing and stockpiling of nuclear weapons and other armaments must be prohibited, as well as the use of nuclear power and other technologies which produce hazardous waste. It would be the Government of Tibet's goal to transform Tibet into our planet's largest natural preserve.

A regional peace conference should be called to ensure that Tibet becomes a genuine sanctuary of peace through demilitarization. Until such a peace conference can be convened and demilitarization and neutralization achieved, China could have the right to maintain a restricted number of military installations in Tibet. These must be solely for defence purposes.

In order to create an atmosphere of trust conducive to fruitful negotiations, the Chinese Government should cease its human rights violations in Tibet and abandon its policy of transferring Chinese to Tibet.

These are the thoughts we have in mind. I am aware that many Tibetans will be disappointed by the moderate stand they represent. Undoubtedly, there will be much discussion in the coming months within our own community, both in Tibet and in exile. This, however, is an essential and invaluable part of any process of change. I believe these thoughts represent the most realistic means by which to re-establish Tibet's separate identity and restore the fundamental rights of the Tibetan people while accommodating China's own interests. I would like to emphasize, however, that whatever the outcome of the negotiations with the Chinese may be, the Tibetan people themselves must be the ultimate deciding authority. Therefore, any proposal will contain a comprehensive procedural plan to ascertain the wishes of the Tibetan people in a nationwide referendum

I would like to take this opportunity to state that I do not wish to take any active part in the Government of Tibet. Nevertheless, I will continue to work as much as I can for the well-being and happiness of the Tibetan people as long as it is necessary.

We are ready to present a proposal to the Government of the People's Republic of China based on the thoughts I have presented. A negotiating team representing the Tibetan government has been selected. We are prepared to meet with the Chinese to discuss details of such a proposal aimed at achieving an equitable solution.

We are encouraged by the keen interest being shown in our situation by a growing number of governments and political leaders, including former President Jimmy Carter of the United States. We are encouraged by the recent changes in China which have brought about about a new group of leadership, more pragmatic and liberal.

We urge the Chinese Government and leadership to give serious and substantive consideration to the ideas I have described. Only dialogue and a willingness to look with honesty and clarity at the reality of Tibet can lead to a viable solution. We wish to conduct discussions with the Chinese Government bearing in mind the larger interests of humanity. Our proposal will therefore be made in a spirit of conciliation and we hope that the Chinese will respond accordingly.

My country's unique history and profound spiritual heritage render it ideally suited for fulfilling the role of a sanctuary of peace at the heart of Asia. Its historic status as a neutral buffer state, contributing to the stability of the entire continent, can be restored. Peace and security for Asia as well as for the world at large can be enhanced. In the future, Tibet need no longer be an occupied land, oppressed by force, unproductive and scarred by suffering. It can become a free haven where humanity and nature live in harmonious balance; a creative model for the resolution of tensions afflicting many areas throughout the world.

The Chinese leadership needs to realize that colonial rule over occupied territories is today anachronistic. A genuine union or association can only come about voluntarily, when there is satisfactory benefit to all the parties concerned. The European Community is a clear example of this. On the other hand, even one country or community can break into two or more entities when there is a lack of trust or benefit, and when force is used as the principal means of rule.

I would like to end by making a special appeal to the honourable members of the European Parliament and through them to their respective constituencies to extend their support to our efforts. A resolution of the Tibetan problem within the framework that we propose will not only be for the mutual benefit of the Tibetan and Chinese people but will also contribute to regional and global peace and stability. I thank you for providing me with the opportunity to share my thoughts with you.

(Speech by H.H. the Dalai Lama at the European Parliament, Strasbourg, 15 June 1988)

4. The Panchen Lama speaks, 28 March 1987

Introductory note

Ever since the Chinese invasion of Tibet in 1949, there have been hundreds of demonstrations and protests against their illegal occupation of Tibet, the inhuman treatment meted out to Tibetans and the systematic destruction of Tibet's cultural heritage. But unlike other demonstrations, the one on 27 September 1987 received unprecedented international publicity because it was witnessed by a large number of foreigners who were present in Lhasa at the time. As usual, the Chinese authorities not only suppressed the demonstration ruthlessly, but blamed the whole incident on a 'handful of splittists instigated from outside'.

Six months before the demonstration, the Panchen Rinpoche and other senior Tibetan officials gave a full and frank account of the situation in Tibet in a meeting of the Sub-Committee of the National People's Congress in Peking. In his speech, the Panchen Rinpoche gave a graphic and horrifying account of the massacres, mass graves, atrocities, the destruction of Tibet's culture and her natural environment, population transfer, and continued negligence of the economic development of Tibet by Chinese rulers. He also warned of very serious consequences if the wrongs done to the people of Tibet were not corrected.

The Chinese government did nothing except to circulate a Chinese translation of the transcript of the speech as a 'secret document' among the top Chinese Communist Party members.

Whenever we raised these issues with the Chinese government we were told that we had no right to do so and they dismissed our legitimate concerns as mere propaganda activities by 'a handful of splittists' and 'reactionaries'.

The Panchen Rinpoche spoke about the 'Seventy-Thousand-Character Petition' he had submitted to the Chinese government in the early 1960s, long before the Cultural Revolution, complaining about the deteriorating situation in Tibet. For this he suffered nine years and eight months of imprisonment, much of which was in solitary confinement. He was tortured and humiliated during the detention.

At this 1987 meeting, the Panchen Rinpoche also expressed his anguish over the continued ill-treatment of Tibetans, and warned that there is growing discontent in Tibet.

On 6 March 1989 the Chinese authorities formally imposed Martial Law in Tibet. Although it was officially lifted after more than a year, the Australian Parliamentary Human Rights Delegation which visited Tibet and China in July this year reported that in Tibet the 'martial law continues to exist in all but name'.

It is well known that the Panchen Rinpoche made another scathing attack on Chinese policy in Tibet during his visit to Tibet in January 1989. A few days later he died unexpectedly under mysterious circumstances. The truth behind his tragic death and the controversies surrounding the search for his reincarnation remain in question.

Recently the Chinese government published a 'White Paper' on Human Rights in China. In order to expose the falsehoods of the claims made in this 'White Paper', we have decided to publish this document. The Chinese government cannot dismiss this official transcript as propaganda by the 'splittists and foreign agents' since this document was circulated by themselves. They must answer these very serious charges. Today, the onus is on the Chinese themselves to answer for their policies in Tibet.

November 1991

Tashi Wangdi, Kalon,
Department of Information and International Relations,
Central Tibetan Administration of HH the Dalai Lama,
Gangchen Kyishong, Dharamsala (H.P.), India

Text

The following is the text of the Panchen Lama's Address to the 'TAR' Standing Committee meeting of the National People's Congress held in Peking on 28 March 1987.

The government's work report and other related matters presented by Prime Minister Zhao Ziyang was received with great appreciation by everyone, and I fully support that.

It is good to speak on all aspects of our country. The policy directions charted by the 3rd Meeting of the 11th Session of the CPC Central Committee were appropriate to the reality of our country. I have no doubt that these will help improve our efficiency and ensure good results. The work report deals with these in detail. I am certain that they will even help us to become a truly modern, powerful, democratic and socialist country. The report contains clear guidelines and directives which should help the government in implementing its policies. These were good ideas which should help the government in formulating its policies. I also appreciate his brief reference to the conditions of different nationalities in China.

Ours is a country of many nationalities. Apart from the Chinese, there are 55 nationalities, which are in the minority. The leftist trend before, and especially after the time of the Cultural Revolution, has caused the minorities to suffer in many ways. Just recently, a story, entitled 'Pasang and Her Relatives', was intentionally published in a journal to ridicule the Tibetans. Last year our representatives from Tibet raised their objection to this story when it was a film-script. We even asked Vice-Chairman Ngabo Ngawang Jigme to express our misgiving about this story to the concerned departments. However, there has been no response. Instead, the film was awarded a first prize. Another film of this nature, entitled 'Compassion Without Mercy', was also given an award. Things like this have been done to other nationalities as well.

In November, last year, a ten-point legal document was circulated with an instruction that we should study it. But this document was silent on the subject of the regional autonomy of minority areas. During the 20th Session of the Standing Committee of the National People's Congress, we asked the law department how such an important matter was left out of this document. The response was that the study of the laws relating to the government of autonomous regions should be left to the respective minority nationalities.

I strongly objected to this by stating that it should be studied also by the Chinese and especially by the officials, who are in a position to implement it. 'It is not that we are not able to exercise power, but that we have not been given any power. A servant is naked not because he does not want to wear clothes, but because his master has not given him any clothes', I said.

Finally, some changes were made, which were announced in the *People's Daily*. There have been many other instances where problems relating to the minority nationalities were completely ignored. This was the reason why I pointed out the drawbacks of the government in a joint session of the sub-committee of the 20th NPC Standing Committee Meeting. I had no objection to the importance attached to Hong Kong and Taiwan. But we did not like the way we were pushed aside and totally ignored.

At the time of the liberation, Mao Tsedong and Chou Enlai proceeded in consultation with concerned nationalities. But what has become of the status of nationalities since then is something I cannot understand. I hope everybody will try to understand it.

Although the minority nationalities constitute only about six per cent of the Chinese population, they own 64 per cent of Chinese territory. Therefore, it is in the interest of China to ensure that there is peace and stability in these regions.

In the State Planning Commission's report, there were many proposals for poverty alleviation in many areas. But the proposals did not say a word on the minority regions. Raising this point in the Standing Committee meetings, I said, 'There is nothing wrong in you becoming prosperous first. We will wear threadbare garments and beg for food. But does that do you proud?' I am no expert on the subject of economic development. But that does not mean that I am a complete novice. I am certain that if the transport and communications facilities in Tibet were developed and if its energy resources were tapped, we should be able to recover the capital investment within two to three years. We are aware of the economic hardship of the nation. We also know that the nation does not have enough capital resources to invest in all important projects. However, there is nothing wrong with making this kind of decision as a matter of policy.

As I said earlier, the leftist policies implemented in the minority regions during the last more than two decades have been very detrimental. The effects of these policies are being felt in Tibet even today. Good as the present policy of liberalization is, the Tibetans are apprehensive that it might not last long.

During my visit to Kham last year, I noticed a great deal of devastation caused by large-scale and indiscriminate deforestation. I saw huge landslides caused by this. Industries with the potential to generate high revenue are closed down in minority regions. To take an example, there was a cigarette factory in Taklo-Tron, Yunnan, which could be very profitable. But this factory had to be closed down because of a shortage of trained manpower and the poor quality cigarettes it produced. This despite the fact that it was using high quality raw materials. The industries in Shanghai, on the other hand, do not use high quality raw materials, but they have trained personnel and the best possible technology, resulting in high quality goods and profit.

Special attention should be paid to the minority areas. Industries in minority regions should also be given state help. It so happens that the government starts paying attention only when the industries in these regions are on the verge of bankruptcy. This is either due to lack of concern or a deliberate attempt to put more burden on the people of these regions. When Comrade Hu Yaobang visited Tibet in 1980, he decided to repatriate all the useless Chinese personnel from Tibet. We consider this a wise decision. We definitely need skilled and capable personnel. But what is the point of having useless personnel? I do not believe that all Chinese are competent. There are both competent and incompetent people among the Chinese.

The expense of keeping one Chinese in Tibet is equal to that of four in China. Why should Tibet spend its money to feed them? Instead, we should think carefully on how best the money can be used for the development of Tibet. Tibet has suffered greatly because of the policy of sending a large number of useless people. The Chinese population in Tibet started with a few thousand and today it has multiplied manifold. That is the reason why many old Chinese personnel who worked very hard in the initial period are left without any career now. Today, the Chinese personnel come to Tibet accompanied by their families. They are like the American mercenaries. They fight and die for money. This is ridiculous.

Tibetans are the legitimate masters of Tibet. The wishes and feelings of the people of Tibet must be respected. It is widely believed that Wu Jinhua is going to be replaced. I have been instructed to submit an honest report on him. My report is that he is one of the best officials in Tibet. Amongst other things, he has successfully implemented the nationalities, religions, and United Front policies. Since economic development is our overriding priority at the moment, we must take a long-term view. We cannot ignore the problems of minority nationalities. Economic development and minority issues must be given equal importance.

A few schools have been established in Tibet. But the quality of education in these schools is very poor. The schools in 16 provinces in China have started Tibetan classes, which naturally demonstrates the government's concern for our people. But this also leads to some problems. First of all, the students are selected on a merit basis which adversely affects the schools in Tibet. It is also a drain on Tibet's resources as Tibet has to spend a considerable sum of money for them. Secondly, since most of these students are from primary schools, they are separated from their own culture and home at a very early age. Gradually, they will be alienated from their own parents, people and country. What's more, the kind of education they receive in China is not at all appropriate to their needs. I noticed in some schools in Yunnan province that although Tibetan is on the school syllabus, the students don't get to learn much of it. The parents want their children to get a job and stay with them at home after finishing the middle school. This shows that they do not want them to be far away from home.

Last year, I said during a visit to Kham area that the Chinese have very powerful wings and are well-versed in the technology of flying. 'They can fly within China and over the Indian Ocean. They can even fly to overseas countries for education. However, only about 30 per cent of them will return home to help the nation. We minority nationality peoples, if given the opportunity to study abroad, can also fly back home. Tibet and other regions of China spend an enormous amount of money on the education of these Chinese students. But if they don't come back after completing their education, then what is the use of spending so much money on them?' I raised this point even in the Standing Committee meetings. There should be a system by which future students to overseas countries should be made to sign a bond promising to serve the nation for a certain period of time. If they don't return, they should reimburse the entire expenses the state has incurred on their education. Even the students from Tibet should be subjected to the same rule.

Now consider the educational disparity between the Tibetan and Chinese students. Whereas the Chinese students must get an aggregate of 250 points to pass their examinations, the Tibetans need to earn only 190 points. But the number of Chinese students passing the examinations is much higher than that of Tibetans. This is because of the language barrier suffered by the Tibetans. I have personally experienced this. Although I can speak Chinese, I frequently make big mistakes. This is because Chinese is not my mother tongue. I can never hope to compete with the Chinese as far as the Chinese language is concerned. To make matters worse, the Tibetan students who have been sent to other provinces find it difficult to acclimatize to the weather, water, food, and so on and so forth. This causes many of them to fall ill, thus affecting their education. When the parents come to know about this, the only way for them to get to see their children is to fly from Tibet. Some students take leave from the school to go home and meet their parents in Tibet. This obviously is a big financial drain on the concerned families.

Last year, some schools in Shanghai and other areas bought vehicles in the name of schools in Tibet, but which were actually used for their own construction work. The authorities, later on, found out about this racket and set the matter right. But it never became public knowledge since everybody conspired to hush it up. Anyway, things have improved slightly since then. Nevertheless, we must make sure that this kind of practice is never repeated.

The government is soon organizing a meeting to discuss education in Tibet. This meeting intends to encourage an in-depth discussion of the education system in Tibet. I feel that educational facilities for Tibetans must be based in Tibet. The utmost efforts must be made to establish all levels of schools in Tibet. When the students finish their upper-middle school, they should be sent for higher education depending on their aptitude and the needs of the region. By this time, they will have a basic knowledge of Tibetan language and a strong sense of affinity to their region which, in turn, will motivate them to give their best to the region. This arrangement, I think, will be a big improvement. I think it is very important for people of every nationality to learn and use their own language. The Central Government has frequently talked about the importance of learning and using the Tibetan language in Tibet. But it has done nothing to ensure its implementation.

The government has announced four modernization plans. I am no expert on science, but I believe in the Buddhist principle of compassion. It is important that we learn from the developed countries. But what we must learn from them is their technological know-how and scientific way of management. Whoever has the higher standard of living has the best system. I have not thought much on this point. The Japanese way of life is rather complicated. They have a very highly developed educational system to teach culture, science and technology. If a new book is published anywhere in the world, within 30 days one can read it in their language. In Tibet we have very deplorable translation facilities, especially when it comes to the European languages. It is much worse than in Eastern Turkestan or Inner Mongolia. Last year, when I went abroad for a visit, I could not find anyone capable of translating between Tibetan and English. Therefore, I had to use a Chinese translator and speak in Chinese. This must have given a very bad impression to the outsiders. This fact proves how poor is the standard of education in Tibet.

In the whole of the Tibet Autonomous Region, no one has been able to translate physics books into Tibetan. What are the authorities in TAR doing? In Qinghai, they have translated everything, whatever the quality. They are also willing to help the TAR. But the authorities of the TAR have not responded even to this gesture. These officials, in effect, are trying to neglect the Tibetan language completely. This is really a very sad thing. Vice-Chairman Ngabo Ngawang Jigme is scheduled to visit Tibet this year. I am wondering if you can find a way to enact a law for the development of the Tibetan language. If such a thing is done, I can assure you that things will improve even within the next two or three years. Ninety-five per cent of the Tibetans do not speak or understand Chinese. The use of the Chinese language for administrative work in Tibet is aimed only at making things convenient for Chinese officials. Can't you see that using Tibetan for administrative work will greatly help the Tibetan masses? Some people complain that I talk too much. Maybe, yes. But many people have expressed similar discontent. So angry was Ngabo Ngawang Jigme with the situation, as I have outlined just now, that he banged his fist on the table during a meeting last year. I hope everyone will think seriously over this matter. Development of the Tibetan language is no small matter. It is directly related to politics.

You, Dorjee Tseten [head of the Institute of Tibetology in Peking and former chairman of 'TAR People's Government'] and others! How can the people who are not well-versed in the Tibetan language and culture hope to do research on Tibetan studies? Many people have told me that there are serious complaints against the Institute of Tibetology, especially against the recruitment system there. In short, there are many things to be done with regard to Tibet work. It is my request that the TAR Party Committee and the TAR People's Government should carefully study the administrative functioning in Tibet and make concerted efforts for improvement.

I also hope that the Central Government will take more interest in the political situation in Tibet and come up with greater economic support for the region. Tibet today has a very big burden. We, the TAR representatives at the National People's Congress, have made some suggestions. In the middle-level offices, the old and infirm officials have now been replaced by young and qualified staff. Nevertheless, there are many among them who still have not got over their leftist hangover, and are guilty of atrocities during the Cultural Revolution. Some of these people have been given promotions despite strong objections among the people. The Central Government has decided not to repeat the policies of the Cultural Revolution. The promotion of these people was based on a campaign called 'Repenting for the Past Mistakes and Willing to Change' which was launched only in Tibet. This movement did not originate from the Central Government. But there is no knowing who launched this campaign.

These are not examples of just a few isolated cases in Tibet. Therefore, Tibet should be treated as a special region and special political and economic policies should be formulated for this region. And, these policies must be implemented till Tibet's acute economic problems are redressed and till its people are satisfied.

What Ringzin Wangyal said regarding the handling of unrest in Tibet was quite true. In 1959 there were rebellions in Tibet. Forces were despatched to quell the disorder, which was a right decision and should not be gainsaid. However, a lot of innocent people were also persecuted. Many mistakes were made in the way the crack-down operations were mounted. The authorities did not make any distinction between those guilty and not guilty of participation in the disturbances. People were arrested and jailed indiscriminately. There were no interrogations. On sight Tibetans were taken to jail and beaten. Things like this are still commonplace in Tibet. We should consider this as a serious matter. We should examine and investigate these practices and bring the guilty to book. This is the way by which we will be able to assuage people's resentment. Isn't this what we are here to discuss?

Ngabo Ngawang Jigme (Vice Chairman of National People's Congress and Chairman of 'TAR People's Congress'): *That is right.*

In the past I was punished for submitting the 70,000-character petition. I had clearly mentioned these facts in that petition. In fact, I said the same thing as Ngabo about the way senior officials of the former local government of Tibet functioned. They had a well-established structure and legal system. The aristocrats, who were members of the government, were banished, wearing a white chuba (Tibetan garment) and riding a red ox, if they failed to carry out the instruction of the government. What would you do if this sort of thing happened to you? A career is important to everyone.

In the Seventeen-Point Agreement, it was emphatically stated that there would be no change in the power of the Tibetan local government until the introduction of democratic reforms. The same promise was made to the Tashi Lhunpo monastic authorities. However, what happened later could be summed up by this dictum: 'Criticizing the old system from the perspective of a new ideology'. This kind of practice is not very ethical. A scientist must arrive at his decision according to whatever is proved right scientifically. The Tibetan aristocrats had served the government for generations. They were deeply devoted to the Dalai Lama and turned to him for refuge both in this and the next life. In the same way, the masses have deep respect and devotion. This is an undeniable fact. Later on, however, the aristocrats were accused of being the leaders of the rebellions and persecuted. This, I think, was an absolutely wrong thing to do. I had clearly recorded these facts in my petition. Of course, I was criticized and punished for this. But truth is timeless. It always remains the same. Undoubtedly, there were mistakes in my petition. But I have never been wrong in speaking up. The mistakes in the content of my petition are mistakes, both today and in the past. But there should be a clear dividing line spelling out where I went wrong and where I was right.

Talking about Lhoka, first the Khampa guerrillas were based there. But when the Dalai Lama passed through there, people happily donated butter, barley flour and other provisions without being asked. This was, of course, a spontaneous gesture of love by the people. Later on, the people who served them were treated as active members of the resistance. How can you do such a thing? This is something that everyone should know. Speaking about myself, those days whenever I passed by, people would show love and devotion to me. Now should this be construed as a politically motivated act? Amongst other things, they showed respect to me because they were religious-minded and it is a Tibetan custom. Due care and consideration must be shown to customs and traditions that are special to Tibet.

Quelling the rebellions and introducing reforms was right in principle. But there was a strong leftist tinge to the way these were done. Such things should not happen again and they must be rectified. During the last three decades of communist rule, there have been many good things done and many bad things also. These were considered in the 6th meeting of the 11th National Congress of CPC, and were publicized internationally. Owning up to our mistakes will not damage the Party's image; rather it would help build it. Speaking about the former comrades in the Tibet Military Command Centre and the Chengdu Military Command Centre, some comrades told me that they should not have done what they did. This was a healthy attitude. We frequently say that great achievements were made with your sweat in the liberation and reformation of Tibet and that the people of Tibet will never forget this. This is an honest statement. However, you did make a great deal of mistakes, and these also in Tibet. These too, we will never forget. What I am saying is for the purpose of rectifying these mistakes. If we can do this, we can make progress. I am saying this with the best of intentions.

I will tell you a more personal story at this point. The Government of the Kashang spearheaded the rebellion. Those of us at the Labrangs (Monastic institutions) were not a party to any agitation. In the beginning, we were told great things about peaceful reforms and policies of fraternal relations. However, when the reforms were undertaken, people belonging to our establishment were subjected to untold sufferings. This filled people with disgust and disbelief. Most of the members of the local Tibetan government fled from Tibet. A handful, who stayed back, were praised and appointed to government jobs as shining examples of a progressive element. Our people who stayed back in solidarity with China were subjected to unthinkable sufferings. Being in Lhasa, as I was at that time,

I did not suffer so much. But all my family members were subjected to 'Thamzing' (Public Struggle Sessions).

There was one women, a wife of one of my staff, who was also arrested. One day, when she was called into the interrogation chamber, she muttered, 'This man called Panchen has caused me so much suffering that I will die of depression.' This utterance led the authorities into believing that she would say something incriminating about me. This was a much-awaited chance for the authorities to take up punitive measures against me. They immediately called the scribes to record her testimony. Then she went on, 'We made a big mistake by following this man called Panchen and not participating in the fight against the Chinese. If he had led us in rebellion against the Chinese, our condition today would be much better than this. Because, initially, we would have killed as many Chinese as possible and then fled to India, which would have been easy since India is near our village. But this man told us to be progressive and patriotic. And this is what we get for following his advice. Now it is not possible for us to flee to India. Our people, both men and women, are being persecuted here. We are experiencing hell on earth.'

Ringzing Wangyl, you said that those who have stayed back in Tibet are better off than those who fled. This is true. Speaking about my personal experience, in 1979, when the five-man delegation sent by the Dalai Lama came to Tibet, my father had to go to Tibet for some personal work. But no one cared for him. He was not even allowed to enter into the TAR territory and had to wait in the rain. On the other hand, each of the Dalai Lama's delegation had the service of a chauffeured car. They were even offered the service of a translator and security guards. Actually, in old Tibet my father was much higher in rank than those delegation members. There were only two people with the rank of 'Gung'. One was the Dalai Lama's father and the other was my father. However, my father had to suffer this humiliating treatment because he was a progressive element. I am saying this not because I want to settle old scores, but to advise you to see to it that all factors are taken into consideration when we implement our policies.

If there was a film made on all the atrocities perpetrated in Qinghai province, it would shock the viewers. In Golok area, many people were killed and their dead bodies were rolled down the hill into a big ditch. The soldiers told the family members and relatives of the dead people that they should all celebrate since the rebels had been wiped out. They were even forced to dance on the dead bodies. Soon after, they were also massacred with machine-guns. They were all buried there.

Actually, the rebellions did not occur in all these areas. In Kham, of course, there were rebellions in many places. In Jharoong Parpo and Mili, both in Amdo, the nomads collected their guns and gave them over to the Chinese authorities. They were praised and garlanded during a special function. After the function, they were driven to their villages where they were immediately arrested and imprisoned for a long time. There were some very old people among them. In Amdo and Kham, people were subjected to unspeakable atrocities. People were shot in groups of ten or twenty. I know that it is not good to speak about these things. But such actions have left deep wounds in the minds of the people. There are some officials who always leave behind a bad legacy. What is the purpose of doing this? The guilty must, of course, be punished. But what is the use of leaving behind a bad legacy? People who persist in doing this are really stupid. But there are some who consider these people very wise and capable. Comrade Wu Jinhua has a plan to investigate the methods and mistakes made by some of the officials in putting down the Tibetan rebellion. I feel this investigation needs to be done with the utmost diligence.

Dorjee Tseten (Present head of the Institute of Tibetology in Peking and former chairman of 'TAR People's Government'): *In my opinion, three serious mistakes were made at that time. a) People were arrested indiscriminately; b) In terms of region, there were very severe and wide-scale atrocities against people in Chamdo, Nagchu and Lho-Dzong; c) Every member of the old, local government, who had attended the meeting, were arrested irrespective of whether they participated in the rebellion.*

Even Sampho would have attended the meeting if people had not hurled stones at him. The officials had to attend the meeting. They had been ordered to do so. It is not justified to say this is tantamount to participating in the rebellion. This is completely illogical.

Dorjee Tseten: The three mistakes I pointed out earlier are very serious. At that time, the order was: 'Since the senior Chiang Kai-shek fled to Taiwan, the junior Chiang Kai-sheks must be finished off.'

Mao Tsedong said clearly in his speech that he would not only kill the senior Chiang Kai-shek, but also the junior ones. Although I, the senior Panchen, managed to survive, many junior Panchens were killed and tortured in prisons.

Dorjee Tseten: At that time there was an official saying which goes thus: 'Unless the middle-level leaders are finished off, the people will never be able to raise their heads.' I mean people were persecuted irrespective of whether they had participated in the rebellion. This shows that the leftist tendency was strong in Tibet right from the beginning. After Comrade Wang Tai-ho was disgraced in 1959, a nation-wide campaign was launched to oppose the rightist elements. This was how the seeds of leftist elements were sown. The seeds even started flowering at that time. Personally speaking, we have also made mistakes. But in 1959, a large number of Chinese cadres were sent to Tibet. At that time, the leftist influence became firmly rooted in Tibet. Those cadres immediately started the commune system, long before the democratic reforms were completed. In my view, the commune system in Tibet was planned long before. These matters need to be carefully analysed. Perhaps the armed forces did not understand everything.

Ngabo Ngawang Jigme: I have no knowledge that the armed forces misunderstood anything. When we were having the 4th meeting of the 6th session, last year, Dren Minyin (a high-ranking military official) came to my house and asked me what the participants of the meeting thought about the crack-down operation in 1959. I said there was no particular opinion, only that the scale of the operation was too big. Dren Minyin, in reply, asked me, 'Didn't the Panchen say that it was a correct step?' Dren Minchin said that he had read this in the news digest. That was the first time I realized that the armed forces did not have a clear idea. In reality, it was not wrong to suppress the rebellion. Only the scale of atrocities was too high.

In Qinghai, for example, there are between one to three or four thousand villages and towns, each having between three to four thousand families with four to five thousand people. From each town and village, about 800 to 1,000 people were imprisoned. Out of this, at least 300 to 400 people of them died in prison. This means almost half of the prison population perished. Last year, we discovered that only a handful of people had participated in the rebellion. Most of these people were completely innocent. In my 70,000-character petition, I mentioned that about five per cent of the population had been imprisoned. According to my information at that time, it was between 10 to 15 per cent. But I did not have the courage to state such a huge figure. I would have died under Thamzing (Public Struggle Session) if I had stated the real figure. These are serious matters as far as Tibet is concerned. If we pay only lip service to these kinds of mistakes and do nothing to redress them, there will be equally serious consequences. People may not like what I am saying. But I am saying this out of my love for the motherland.

When I was in East Turkestan, I told the cadres there, 'Your works will be put to test if there is a foreign invasion of East Turkestan. What people say in meetings is all lies. We should not believe in them. You will be thought to have done a good job here if the people of East Turkestan rise up in support of the PLA in the event of a Soviet invasion of this province. Here, I will cite two examples from history. Lenin said that the triumph of the October Revolution in Russia showed that their work with the masses had been good. Stalin did not do good works for the masses. As a result the peoples of minority republics did not support the Russian army in defending the Soviet Union against the Nazi invasion. We have seen films on the Vietnam war. The people belonging to minority races welcomed the PLA, showed them ways and gave them water only because the minority groups were fed up with their regime, which favoured the Ching majority race against all the others. The people of the Ching race were very cruel. If others did not submit to them, they would shoot down people of even fifty or sixty years old. We should learn from these historical facts.

In 1964, when I was called to Beijing, some leaders told me, 'You are turning against the motherland. Are you trying to start a secessionist rebellion? Even if the whole of the Tibetan population is armed, it will only make over 3 million people. We are not scared of this.' On hearing this, I felt very sad and realized how it is to be without freedom. First of all, I have never harboured such a thought. Secondly, even if I wanted to launch a secessionist movement, how can I enlist the support of the whole population of Tibet? Who would dare do it under the prevailing situation? Even if someone did, he would be exterminated immediately.

The rebellion in Tibet was started by a few who had no sense of timing and were completely ignorant of politics and military strategy. If you really want to fight a war, you have to have a sense of timing. You should be sufficiently powerful. You should know your own might and that of your enemy. Without these elements, you cannot hope to win a war. You cannot fight a war with a few outdated rifles. The rebels of that time were ridiculously naive. However, if something like that happened in the event of a foreign invasion, then it would be a serious matter for our nation.

That is why it is essential to think about the welfare of the minority nationalities during peacetime. We should make sure that the people of these nationalities are happy as part of the motherland. If this happens, they will be happy to work with the Chinese people in developing the nation. On the other hand, if you hold the attitude that you will always rule and suppress the minority nationalities, then there will be serious problems in the future. The examples I gave earlier are relevant here. It is essential to think about war as this possibility looms large nowadays. Of course, we have the power to prevent it. What would we do if a war breaks out now? The PLA was successful in the 1962 Sino-Indian border conflict, mainly because the Tibetans provided the logistic service with their backs and pack animals. These days some people are talking about a possible war with India, which is unlikely. However, should it break out, it is questionable whether the Tibetans would support the war effort as they did in 1962. Some of our comrades are hesitant to implement the new policies. These people have no sense of military strategy. They also have no knowledge of politics. If there were disturbance in Tibet, the government would call an emergency meeting and order Ngabo and me to tackle the situation. We would, of course, be happy to do whatever we could. But if nothing is done for the people all the time, how could we hope to help the government when there is trouble?

I always speak very rudely. But it is only for the good of the nation. I have nothing to gain personally from it. Personally, I am quite happy. I feel that I am the happiest man in China. Therefore, you should think in broad terms. What are we gaining from the leftist practices in Tibet? Those with leftist ideology are suppressing everything. When Comrade Hu Yaobang was disgraced recently, the leftist officials exploded fire crackers and drank in celebration. They commented that the stalwart supporter of the Tibetan people had been defeated. They also said that We Jinhua, Panchen, and Ngabo would not be able to return to Tibet. Why can't we be allowed to return to our homeland? But, as it turned out, they celebrated a bit too early. These are the people who are trying to drive a wedge between the Tibetans and the Chinese. We are the members of one family. How dare they say that the Tibetan supporter had been defeated?

I would request everyone to think carefully and work for the welfare of the Tibetan people. Tibet always faces financial problems. We also have a problem of air transportation. With great difficulty, we managed to buy two passenger aeroplanes. But due to many problems they are not flown. Prime Minister Chou Enlai helped us in many ways. He laid on an oil pipeline to Tibet. But now the government is increasing the price of oil, once again. If this happens, our transport facilities will come to a standstill. We are guilty of several things. The government has approved a large budget for Tibet. But where has the money gone? Isn't it true that the bulk of the money has been misappropriated by the officials and technicians. This is the reason why many projects could not be implemented. We must do something to help the people in Tibet since they are dependent solely on whatever they can earn with their physical labour.

Ngabo: Tibet manufactures almost nothing. Industry is almost non-existent. Farm produce is the only thing Tibet produces.

There are so many things we are unable to do, because we do not have the capability. There is not much attention given to the study and use of the Tibetan language. If Tibet is the most religious region, it goes without saying that the study and use of the Tibetan language should be promoted. But many wrong things have been done. In 1958, when I was in Qinghai, I heard that an official document stated this policy: 'First the rebellion should be suppressed. Then in launching the campaign to prevent future rebellion, a clear nationality and religious policy decision should be taken.' In retrospect, we should have thought how such a policy could be formulated for the future. Although there may be peace and stability today, many minor disturbances will occur. But it is good to think about the entire problem. There is at the moment racial harmony, peace and stability. But we should not be satisfied with this. What are we going to do if there are disturbances in the future? Although the government has not been able to come up with enough money for the nationalities' affairs, the liberalization policy provided some assurances of flexibility for the minority nationalities.

5. CIA report: The integration of Tibet: China's progress and problems

Introductory note

A highly critical report by the United States Central Intelligence Agency found that Tibet was an independent country and that the occupation measures of the Chinese government has made Tibetans 'second class' citizens. The detailed 22 page report, written in the late 1970s, says that there will be 'no welcome mat for Chinese settlers for years to come' and that Chinese attitudes towards Tibetans are characterized by 'superiority' and 'ridicule of the Tibetans'.

The declassified report was obtained from the CIA through the Freedom of Information Act.

The report is much more critical of Chinese policies in Tibet than the annual State Department human rights reports issued to the public during the late 1970s. Relations between Beijing and Washington were good at the time, and conclusions reached by the CIA report were not translated into policy or statements by the Administration. The report represents one of the most critical assessments of Tibet made by a government agency since the warming of relations between Washington and Beijing. The report throws light on the discrepancy between what the US Government knew what was going on in Tibet and what it was saying to the US public.

Chinese settlement in Tibet linked to local food production

The report is significant in that it focuses on the Chinese population transfer, a subject which the US State Department does not recognize as a significant issue, and is not mentioned in recent State Department human rights reports. The major impediment to Chinese migration to Tibet is said to be limited arable land to produce an adequate food supply for the Chinese settlers. According to the report the first officially designated 'permanent settlers' were moved to Tibet in 1976 and the Chinese population probably did not exceed an estimated 200,000 at that time.

Only in recent years, with major funding from the United Nations World Food Programme, has the Chinese government started to substantially increase agricultural production in order to feed the growing number of Chinese settlers. The World Food Program project may be the largest international development project in the Tibet Autonomous Region and is seen as mainly designed for Chinese needs. The marginal increase in agricultural production by the late 1970s 'neither benefited the majority of Tibetans nor came close to restoring the barley production–consumption balance that has existed for hundreds of years', the report said.

Chinese settlers are characterized as a crucial link to the economic and political absorption and integration of Tibet into the Chinese state, according to the report. The report also surveyed the transportation network, concentrating mostly on plans to link

Lhasa by rail to China. Those plans, which are still periodically mentioned by planners, would pose a very real threat to what remains of Tibet's autonomous identity.

Report contradicts China's claim to Tibet

Tibet had a historical 'legacy of independence' despite attempts by Chinese dynasties to assert some degree of administrative control over Tibet, says the report. The relationship between Tibet is said to be 'more religious in nature than political'. The report calls the Chinese takeover an 'invasion' and 'occupation' that left the 'politically unsophisticated' Tibetan government 'no alternative' to signing the controversial 1951 agreement with Beijing.

The report also contradicts the repeated Chinese claims that Tibet's government was cruel and feudal. While it says that 'all land' belonged to the government and was parcelled out to monasteries, noble families and commoners in return for services, there existed a dual form of government which acted as a system of checks and balances. The report said that while Tibet was 'not Shangri-la', the 'unique system worked' because 'population growth was stable, everyone had a functional place in the system and food production met the people's needs'.

Future prospects

The report concludes that the 'key' to the future settlement of Tibet by large numbers of Chinese is the completion of the rail link between Qinghai (Amdo) and Lhasa, and increasing local agricultural production. While the Chinese are in control, their situation is 'uneasy' and compliance with Chinese authority is 'only under threat'.

International Campaign for Tibet
Washington D.C.

Summary

Tibet has proved the most difficult of all China's frontier regions for Peking to bring under full control. The problem has been caused by a mix of cultural, historical, and physical factors that, though of lessened significance today than in the past, still hinder and restrict Chinese actions. They include:

A culture based on religion (Tibetan Buddhism) whose influence permeates every aspect of Tibetan life. The attempt by Peking to eradicate religion and its practices has been a major factor in the prolonged overt and covert Tibetan resistance to Chinese rule.

Historically, Tibet has been independent, a fact recognized by the 1959 investigation of Tibet's legal status by the International Commission of Jurists. This legacy of independence and strong feelings of a Tibetan national identity have contributed to the Tibetan resistance potential.

The physical isolation of Tibet, a major reason why Tibet has escaped dominance by China or any other power, is still a problem but has been largely overcome through the building of roads, several airfields, and a recently completed petroleum products pipeline.

The lack of arable land and adequate food supply in Tibet has made it impossible to move in large numbers of Chinese settlers – the tactic successfully used in other frontier regions such as Sinkiang and Inner Mongolia to consolidate control.

In spite of these difficulties, which have been compounded by the need to militarily secure Tibet's borders, Peking has finally reached the point where true administrative integration is at hand: collectivization of the countryside has been completed; the road net and other transport links are adequate; and the first batch of Chinese designated as 'permanent settlers' (less than 1,000) have arrived.

Nevertheless, obstacles remain and the key to the total integration of Tibet is the completion of the Tsinghai-Tibet railroad, which is at least a decade away from completion. Until then, Chinese progress will continue to be governed by the logistics capacity of the roads and by the limited ability to increase food production to meet growing food demands.

Chronology of events in Tibet 1950–1976

1950 Chinese troops invaded eastern Tibet.
1951 Lhasa and Peking signed a 17-point agreement for the 'liberation of Tibet'; Chinese army established headquarters in Lhasa and garrisons in main centers of population.
1954 Roads from Tsinghai and Szechwan were open to limited traffic.
1957 Peking announced that reforms in Tibet postponed until 1962.
1959 Tibetans revolted in Lhasa and Dalai Lama fled to India; Chinese abrogated the 1951 agreement and replaced the local government, headed by the Panchen Lama, with the Preparatory Committee for the Autonomous Region of Tibet. Reforms postponed for a second time, or to 1965.
1960 Sinkiang–Tibet road completed in western Tibet.
1962 Border war with India.
1964 Panchen Lama deposed.
1965 Autonomous region of Tibet established; basic road network in Tibet completed.
1973 Plan for construction of the Tsinghai–Tibet railroad revived.
1974 China claims that Tibet is self-sufficient in grain production.
1975 Establishment of agricultural and nomadic communes completed in Tibet.
1976 First permanent settlers arrive in Tibet; pipeline laid.

Discussion

Introduction

In 1976 nearly a thousand Han Chinese entered Tibet[1] and were ordered to 'settle permanently' in rural areas. Although the number involved is small, the significance of the event is far greater. When couples with the establishment of communes throughout the countryside and the continuing efforts to upgrade Tibet's transport links, it signifies that Peking may be on the verge of achieving an ancient Chinese ambition – the complete absorption and integration of Tibet with China. Questions raised by these events include:

— What changes have been made that allow Chinese settlers to enter Tibet?
— Are there environmental limitations to the numbers of Han settlers that can be absorbed?
— Is the transportation network and its logistics capabilities adequate to accommodate increasing numbers of settlers?
— Do problems remain that will continue to make difficult the realization of Chinese objectives in Tibet?

These questions relate to a complex series of relationships that have influenced past and present developments in Tibet. Key factors are the physical isolation of Lhasa and other Tibetan-populated centers from Chinese-settled areas, the harsh Tibetan environment, the strategic location of Tibet, and its long and disputed border with India.

Background

Tibet is a unique region whose distinctiveness stems from a physical environment of high mountains and plateaus, a long history of independence and isolation, and a culture dominated by religion. Ethnically, the Tibetan homeland comprises the present Tibetan Autonomous Region (TAR) and an area equally as large but administratively subdivided among several provinces – all of Tsinghai, the western portion of Szechwan, and smaller adjacent areas in northwestern Yunnan and southwestern Kansu.

Historically, the most important factors affecting the political relationship between Tibet and China have been the great distances that separate the two countries and the severe environmental character of Tibet and its contiguous areas – a region known as the Tibetan Highlands. High passes 4,000 meters and upwards had to be crossed to enter Tibet; the average caravan distance of 2,000 kilometers between Chinese settled areas and Lhasa meant 3 months of travel. Until the Chinese occupation in 1952, Tibet remained largely untouched by the 20th century – a political and cultural relic evoking interest from explorers and adventurers but of cursory political interest to the outside world.

Devotion to religion was the pervasive force in traditional Tibet, providing a bond that unified diverse groups and a means to implement and institutionalize political control. Buddhism, introduced into Tibet from India and Nepal by several religious teachers during the 7th century AD, gradually became established as the dominant religion, although fragmented into several different sects. The ascendancy of the Gelungpa (Yellow Hat) sect during the 15th and 16th centuries was highlighted by the evolution of the Dalai Lama as spiritual leader of all Tibetan Buddhists.[2] By the mid-17th century the powerful 5th Dalai Lama took both religious and temporal affairs in his own hands; church and state became interchangeable, and all political, economic, and other matters were subordinate to the needs and interests of religion.[3] This unique system worked. Little privation existed in Tibet because population growth was stable, everyone had a functional place in the system, and food production met the people's needs.

Traditional Tibet, however, was not Shangri-la. In addition to its harsh environment, the country was plagued with political intrigue, power struggles among the monasteries were common, and civil war and invasion threatened from time to time. Despite frequent internal turmoil and attempts by expansive Chinese dynasties to assert some degree of administrative control over the country, Tibet retained a separate political identity throughout most of its history.

Tibet and surrounding areas of Tibetan population have always presented a political problem for Chinese leaders. Chinese frontier policies traditionally were adapted to the conditions and characteristics of each major frontier region. In the case of Tibet, the primary Chinese concern historically has been that Tibet would be used as a base area by other countries or groups hostile to China. During the 17th and 18th centuries, Manchu leaders worried that the bond of Tibetan Buddhism would find political expression with a union between Tibet and the many Mongol groups spread across the entire northern and northwestern frontiers of China. As this threat faded, new fears were aroused during the late 19th and 20th centuries that Great Britain, Russia, or, later, the Government of India would gain a political or economic foothold in Tibet and with it pose a threat to Chinese hegemony of this region.

In general, the historic relationship between China and Tibet was more religious in nature than political: the emperor assumed the role of patron or protector of religion and the Dalai Lama the priest or religious mentor of the Chinese emperor. Some degree of political control was exercised sporadically during the 18th and 19th centuries by Manchu China, resulting from appeals by Tibet for military assistance against foreign invaders or to quell internal revolts, but all vestiges of a Chinese presence were ended when the Lhasa government evicted a Chinese garrison in 1910–11. Tibet had equal representation at the tripartite (China, Tibet, and Britain) Simla Conference in 1914 whose primary objective was to partition Tibet into Inner Tibet (Tsinghai and Szechwan east of the Yangtze) where chiinese sovereignty would be recognized, and Outer Tibet (the present TAR) which would be autonomous. When the legal status of Tibet came under scrutiny in 1959, the International Commission of Jurists, under the auspices of the United Nations General Assembly, concluded that Tibet was in independent state, at least from 1913 to 1950.

The Chinese takeover

Chinese troops moved into the Tibetan borderlands in the fall of 1950 – an action viewed by Peking as the reassertion of a centuries-old policy that Tibet was an integral part of

China. The Lhasa government, however, considered it open aggression and dispatched an urgent appeal to the United Nations protesting the invasion and requesting assistance. The appeal was tabled before it reached the General Assembly, an action that left the politically unsophisticated Lhasa government no alternative but to sign a 17-point agreement in May 1951. The terms gave Peking control of Tibet's foreign relations and responsibility for its defense and permitted entry of the People's Liberation Army (PLA) into Tibet and the establishment of the PLA headquarters in Lhasa. The agreement also assured the entegrity of the political and religious structure of Tibet, the Dalai Lama's authority, and the right of the people to exercise national regional autonomy as defined by Peking. To carry out the latter provision, the Chinese established in May 1955 a Preparatory Committee for the Autonomous Region of Tibet with the Dalai Lama as chairman.

A quarter-century of Chinese rule in Tibet has been marked by periods of repression and interludes of liberalization and internal rebellion and revolt. Despite the uneven course of Chinese administration and the varying degree of political control imposed on Tibet by Peking, communist goals of the socialization and integration of Tibet have remained unchanged – though the timetable has been frequently readjusted (see chronology).

Early attempts by the Chinese to introduce land reform and the preliminary stages of agricultural collectivation and to restrict religious activities were met with much resistance. These threats to such basic Tibetan institutions provided the spark that led to outright revolt by some Tibetan groups – particularly in eastern Tibet. Despite a Chinese announcement in 1957 that 'reforms would be postponed, tensions heightened and the revolt widened, culminating in 1959 with the flight of the Dalai Lama and his entourage to India. This provided Peking with the justification to deal harshly with Tibetan power groups. The 1951 Sino-Tibet agreement was abrogated; uncooperative Tibetan officials, nobles, and monastic personnel were arrested and their property confiscated; and the local government was dissolved and replaced with the Preparatory Committee headed by the Panchen Lama. Because of continued unrest and the urgent need not to disrupt agricultural production, the Chinese postponed reforms for 5 years for a second time in 1960–61. The Chinese extended their efforts to control the Tibetans by initiating a program of 'educating the masses', intensifying the training of receptive adult Tibetans as cadres, and sending large numbers of Tibetan children to China for schooling.

The last remnants of the Tibetan government were swept away in 1964 when the Panchen Lama was arrested – and subsequently disappeared – after publicly supporting the exiled Dalai Lama and the independence of Tibet, and Chinese officials assumed the major administrative posts. With the inauguration of the Tibetan Autonomous Region in 1965, the Chinese began a forceful program of suppression, disassembling the remains of the religious structure, purging many of the Tibetan collaborators and ineffective Chinese officials, and establishing communes 'on an experimental basis' – that is, establishing them by force in selected areas. The arrival of the Cultural Revolution in Tibet served as a catalyst for carrying out the program, but continued Tibetan obduracy and the poor food supply situation again necessitated the temporary relaxation of controls. Although occasional reports of Tibetan resistance continued, the overall situation had in Peking's view been resolved sufficiently to complete the formation of communes in 1974–75 and to extend Chinese domination throughout Tibet.

Population of Tibet

It has been alleged that Peking has moved millions of Chinese into Tibet since 1950. The PRC, in fact, has imposed restrictions on the numbers of Chinese to a size that can adequately be supplied with food and other necessities by road. Although population figures for Tibet are ambiguous, the Chinese segment probably does not exceed 13 per cent of the total population of 1.8 million.

No official census of the population in Tibet – either before or after 1950 – has ever been made. The earliest estimate of the number of Tibetans with some basis for reliability was a figure of 3.9 million computed from records of a head tax collected in an area roughly equivalent to the present TAR by the Lhasa government in 1915.

The official 1953 census gave an estimated figure of 1.3 million for the area of the present TAR and a total Tibetan population figure of 'over' 3 million. The bulk of the 2 million claimed to be outside the TAR were located in Tsinghai and western Szechwan. The Chinese continued to carry the rounded 1.3 million figure for Tibet until 1974 when the estimate was revised upward to 1.4 million. Since 1951 both Chinese civilian and military personnel – particularly retired servicemen – have been moved into Tibet but none of the official estimates indicated the number of Han Chinese in the total population.

The most recent population figures for Tibet were obtained by Robert L. Bartley (a member of the Schlesinger group) from Chinese officials during his trip there in 1976. According to these estimates, the population comprised 1.7 million Tibetans and 125,000 Han Chinese for a total population of 1.8 million. An identical total was given to Dr Han Su-yin during a 1975 visit, though the number of Tibetans (1.6 million) and Han Chinese (200,000) varied from the breakdown provided to Bartley. In turn, the figure of 1.8 million is higher by 400,000 than the official 1974 estimate of 1.4 million for the total population. The 400,000 figure would represent natural increase, Tibetans not counted previously, and additional Han Chinese entering Tibet.

The first Han Chinese designated publicly by Peking as 'permanent settlers' began entering Tibet in early 1976. By yearend some 780 had arrived or were en route. The majority of the new settlers were to become farmers; the remainder were to be placed where needed regardless of their particular skills.

Economic development

Transportation and agriculture are the only segments of the Tibetan economy developed to any extent by the Chinese. Industry is of local significance and consists of such small-scale enterprises as machinery repair and maintenance, production of farm tools, woollen textiles, and numerous small coal mines. Geological surveys have revealed fairly extensive mineral deposits which have not been worked, and the search for petroleum has been pushed but without result.

Transportation

Roads Road transport has been the key to Chinese control of Tibet. The major approach roads, which are included by the Chinese as part of the total network of Tibet, extend from Sinkiang, Tsinghai, and Szechwan and share the burden of supplying Tibet. Within the region the road network connects the few urban centers and all but three of the 71 hsien seats. Numerous branch and feeder roads lead to and support border posts and installations along the Himalayan frontier.

Since 1965 when the road network in Tibet was basically completed, the Chinese have directed their attention to upgrading existing roads. An official announcement in January 1973 on road statistics (the first in 10 years) indicated that of a total network of 15,800 kilometers (km), only 800 km had been added since the completion of the network. Since then about 8 km of roadbed have been rebuilt for every new kilometer added, road surfaces and drainage have been improved, and wooden and bailey-type bridges replaced with concrete structures. The upgrading of the road net, which should continue for some time, is concentrated in central and southern Tibet and on the main approach roads – particularly on the Tsinghai–Tibet road.

Airfields The Chinese have been less successful in establishing air transport links in Tibet because of the high altitude, terrain limitations on runway length, and lack of adequate fuel supplies. Although three airfields have been built, and an additional one is under construction, only the airfield at Kung-ka is operational. It is located some 70 km south of Lhasa and used only on an irregularly scheduled basis.

Petroleum products pipeline The Chinese have recently completed a pipeline to Lhasa which will alleviate the chronic shortages of petroleum products in Tibet. It is estimated that 2 months operation of the pipeline – when it is operational – will provide enough fuel to meet annual requirement for several years.

Railroad   Tibet is the only region of China not connected by rail with the remainder of the country. Peking has always considered extension of its rail network to Lhasa vital to the total integration and future settlement of Tibet but construction has been delayed by several reverses in the economy and the discovery of an extensive layer of permafrost on the Tsinghai–Tibet plateau. Recently, however, the Chinese have revived plans to build the railroad to Lhasa but its completion is at least a decade away.

Food supply and agriculture

Food supply has been a serious and continuous problem for the Chinese in Tibet. Prior to Chinese occupation, Tibet grew enough food for its own needs – but little more. Barley, the principal grain grown in Tibet, is not a favored item in Chinese cuisine nor is the locally grown rice. The result has been that much of the foodstuffs required for the PLA and Chinese civilian personnel have had to be transported long distances by truck from China.

From the Chinese point of view, conditions improved after 1959–60 when much of the best agricultural land was confiscated, thereby providing the means to introduce organizational and agricultural modernization changes designed to increase food output. Since 1960 agricultural production has increased, though not to the extent of dispensing with food imports from China or of reaching self-sufficiency in grain production – a feat Peking claimed was achieved in 1974.

Grain production   The production of grain has been increasing in Tibet, but the rate of increase appears to have been sufficient only to keep pace with the growth in the Tibetan population. (It is estimated that total grain production in 1974 was 370,000 tons and was increased to 450,000 tons in 1976.) Although barley remains as the staple grain (almost entirely for native Tibetans), recent emphasis on crop diversification has led to increases in other grains, particularly winter wheat. Increased output of wheat and other crops has permitted the Chinese to ease somewhat their reliance on food imports – specifically vegetables, some oil-bearing crops, and grain. Nevertheless, the Chinese still import substantial amounts of rice and processed grain from China.

Methods of increasing production   The Chinese have achieved increased agricultural production through modernization of existing Tibetan agricultural techniques. Irrigation systems have been extended and water pumps installed; wooden plows have been replaced by metal ones; the amount of organic fertilizer used – compost, river mud, human and animal waste – has been boosted; and Chinese supervision of the grain harvest has helped guarantee that state grain quotas are met. The Chinese also have shipped in a token number of tractors and other mechanized equipment. Use of the equipment is confined to larger valleys with extensive flat land and hindered by shortages of fuel, lack of adequate maintenance facilities, and the need to import spare parts.

The Chinese have had a measure of success in developing higher-yield, cold-resistant seed, growing varieties of vegetables suitable for the Chinese diet, and introducing plants new to the Tibetan region. The new plants, grown mainly on experimental plots, include winter wheat, sugar beets, soybeans, peanuts, tea, tobacco, cotton, and ramie. Winter wheat, first introduced in the Lhasa Valley in 1959, has been slowly extended to other regions north and east of Lhasa and into southern Tibet; acreage has been increased to more than 690,000 mou (46,000 hectares) by 1975–76. Winter wheat has been the most successful – or has had the most effort expended on it – of all the new plants.

Land limitations   All of the best arable land in Tibet consists of flat land in river valleys below 4,300 meters. The Chinese estimated the cultivated area at 3 million mou or 200,000 hectares (ha) in 1960, considerably less than 1 percent of the total land area of Tibet. Since then the cultivated area has been expanded to over 250,000 ha through cultivation of marginal, often less productive land: fallow fields have been b_ght into production, some grazing land has been added; swamp areas in the Lhasa_ley have been drained and reclaimed; and narrow strips of land that delimit Tibet_fields have been eliminated.

Because the most productive land is presently cultiva_ expansion is limited to higher elevations where the growing season is very short a_where improved irrigation and additional fertilizer are no guarantees of increased pr_ction. Several publicized attempts to expand production into higher elevations have f_d. Despite claims of bumper barley harvests above 4,300 meters, the short growing _son produced immature grain useful only for fodder. The Chinese have had more s_ess in those high altitude areas where it is possible to grow hardy root vegetables th_mature in a few weeks or months.

Outlook settlement

The key to the future settlement of Tib_ by large numbers of Han Chinese is the completion – possibly in the late 1980s –_the Tsinghai–Tibet railroad. Until then:

Settlement will have to proceed _wly and the number of Chinese settlers entering Tibet annually probably will be n_more than 1,000 or so.

The Chinese will need to con_ue their restrictions on the size of the Chinese population to that which can be suppl_ by road because local agricultural production is unlikely to meet the needs of the Chi_se in Tibet. Dependence on the road network to supply Tibet will continue for some _ars and is the reason why the Chinese place a high priority on improving the access r_ds to Tibet and the network within the country.

The Chinese have inc_ased agricultural production. Output, however, is still insufficient to dispense with im_orts of foodstuffs from China. Moreover, the increases achieved by the Chinese have n_ther benefited the majority of Tibetans nor come close to restoring the barley produ_ion–consumption balance that had existed for hundreds of years. Most good arable la_d is now under cultivation and expansion into less favored areas will require sizable inv_tments in labor and other resources for reclamation. Furthermore, the poorer environm_ntal conditions in these areas will limit increases in production.

Although th_ Chinese are now in complete control of Tibet, their situation is uneasy. Chinese contr_l probably is harsher than in other areas populated by sizable minorities. The majorit_ of Tibetans stubbornly cling to their belief in the Dalai Lama and in their religion de_pite Chinese declaration that it is treasonable and punishable by imprisonment or d_ath. Compliance with Chinese authority and collectivism policies is only under threat of less food and excessive hard labor. The Tibetans distrust the Tibetan cadres becaus_ of their duplicity even though, on occasion, the cadres act as a buffer between them and the Chinese. A problem created by the Chinese is the growing political awareness and feeling of national identity among the Tibetan youths trained in China, an atmosphere as intolerable to the Chinese as the religious one. The youths – and the Tibetan cadres – resent their 'second class' status and the denial of decisionmaking powers to them by the Chinese.

The most pervasive feeling among Tibetans, however, is one of resentment toward Han chauvinism, which is expressed at all levels. This Chinese attitude of superiority and their ridicule of the Tibetans were evident to members of the Schlesinger party that visited Lhasa in 1976. The visitors noted also that the division of Lhasa into discrete Tibetan and Chinese sections gave the impression of an occupied area.

Although organized resistance to the Chinese has disappeared or gone underground, overt sporadic resistance occasionally flares up. Given the traditional feelings of mutual antipathy, deepened by the revolt and Chinese occupation measures, there will be no welcome mat in Tibet for Chinese settlers yet to come.

Notes

1. Tibet, where it is used in this paper, refers to the Tibetan Autonomous Region (TAR).
2. The Dalai Lama is believed to be a reincarnation of previous Dalai Lamas and is

selected when a child by complicated ritual. The idea of reincarnation took hold about 1475; and the title of Dalai Lama was created some 100 years later by a Mongol prince, Altan Khan, and conferred on Sonam Gyatso, a high abbot of the Gelungpa sect. The present Dalai Lama, now in exile in india, is the Fourteenth.

3. The Tibetan government consisted of two parallel authorities headed by the Dalai Lama, who commanded in essence two separate civil services of specially trained monks and an equal number of hereditary lay nobles. This dual lay–monk structure existed at all levels of government and acted as a system of checks and balances. The dualism extended into the social structure where a hierarchy of upper and lower levels existed among the nobles and commoners and among the religious community in clearly defined gradations. All land belonged to the government and was parceled out to the monasteries, noble families, and commoners in return for services in the form of administration, education, production of food, and other services.

6. US Congressional Declaration: China's illegal control of Tibet, 1991

It is the sense of the Congress that:

1. Tibet, including those areas incorporated into the Chinese provinces of Sichuan, Yunnan, Gansu, and Quinghai, is an occupied country under the established principles of international law;

2. Tibet's true representatives are the Dalai Lama and the Tibetan Government in exile as recognized by the Tibetan people;

3. Tibet has maintained throughout its history a distinctive and sovereign national, cultural, and religious identity separate from that of China and, except during periods of illegal Chinese occupation, has maintained a separate and sovereign political and territorial identity;

4. historical evidence of this separate identity may be found in Chinese archival documents and traditional dynastic histories, in United States recognition of Tibetan neutrality during World War II, and in the fact that a number of countries including the United States, Mongolia, Bhutan, Sikkim, Nepal, India, Japan, Great Britain, and Russia recognized Tibet as an independent nation or dealt with Tibet independently of any Chinese government;

5. in 1949–1950, China launched an armed invasion of Tibet in contravention of international law;

6. it is the policy of the United States to oppose aggression and other illegal uses of force by one country against the sovereignty of another as a manner of acquiring territory, and to condemn violations of international law, including the illegal occupation of one country by another; and

7. numerous United States declarations since the Chinese invasion have recognized Tibet's right to self-determination and the illegality of China's occupation of Tibet.

List of Relevant Organizations

Argentina

Friends of Tibetan Culture, Pasco Colon 1131 2nd 11, (1063) Buenos Aires; Tel: (54-1) 782 1722.

Australia

The Office of Tibet, 3 Weld Street, Yarralumla, ACT 2600, Canberra; Tel: (61-6) 285 4046; Fax: (61-6) 282 4301.
Australia Tibet Council, National Office, PO Box 1236, Chatswood NSW 2057.
Australian Campaign for Tibet, 27/51 Musgrave Street, Yarralumla ACT 2600.
Australian Tibet Society, PO Box 39, Gordon, NSW 2072; Tel: (61-2) 371 4239; Fax: (61-2) 628 3292.
Freedom in Tibet Association, 50A Swaine Avenue, Rose Park, South Australia 5062; Tel: (8) 333 2334.
Tibetan Friendship Group, PO Box 39, Gordon, NSW 2072.
Tibet Information Service, PO Box 87, Ivanhoe, 3079 Victoria; Tel: (3) 499 7347; Fax: (3) 663 4484.
Tibet Welfare Group, PO Box 618, Hawthorn 3122, Victoria.
Tibetan Community Association, 4 Libya Cres., Allambie Heights, NSW 2100.
Tibetan Community Association, 60 Parkers Rd, Parkdale, Victoria 3095.

Belgium

Tibet Support Group Belgium, BP 56, B-1170 Bruxelles 17; Tel: (32-2) 673 0398.

Brazil

Tibetan Friends of Brazil, R. Leoncio de Carvalho 99, Paraiso, 04003 Sao Paulo-SP; Tel: (55-11) 262 6493.

Bulgaria

Bulgaria-Tibet, 5 Chandor Petioffi Street, 1606 Sofia; Tel. & fax: (359-2) 650 084.

Canada

Canada-Tibet Committee (CTC)-Montreal (National Office), 4675 Coolbrook Ave., Montreal, Quebec H3X 2K7; Tel: (1-514) 487 0665.

CTC-Ottawa, 1046 Riviera Drive, Ottawa, Ontario K1K oN8; Tel: (613) 748 7469.

CTC-Toronto, PO Box 62, 260 Adelaide St. East, Toronto, Ontario M5A 1NO; Tel: (416) 298 0464.

CTC-Saskatoon, Grosvenor Part, Postal Outlet, PO Box 21021, Saskatoon, Saskatchewan S7H 5N9; Tel: (306) 373 9321.

CTC-Calgary, 572 Strathcona Dr S.W., Calgary, Alberta T3H 1K5; Tel: (403) 246 8366.

CTC-Edmonton, 10257-95 Street, Edmonton, Alberta T5H 2B3; Tel: (403) 429 3679.

CTC-Vancouver, Station F, PO Box 65851, Vancouver, B.C. V5N 5L3; Tel: (604) 253 8490.

CTC-Victoria, 582 Cedar Crest Drive, Victoria, B.C. V9C 1M3; Tel: (604) 478 0754.

Canada-Tibet Friendship Society, PO Box 6588, Station A, Toronto, Ontario M5W 1X4.

Gaden Relief Projects, 637 Christie St., Toronto, Ontario M6G 3E6; Tel: (416) 651 3849.

Mitra, Palden McLennan, 142 Spadina, Apt. 2, Ottawa, Ontario K1Y 2C3; Tel: (613) 761 9249.

Chile

Humberto Barahona B, Drigung Kagylu Ling, PO Box 3249, Santiago; Tel: (56-2) 221 2614.

Costa Rica

Tibetan-Costa Rican Cultural Association, PO Box 2820, 1000 San Jose; Tel: (50-6) 23 90 95.

Czech Republic

Friends of Tibet, Pelhrimovska 5, 140 Prague 4; Tel: 42-2-692-0738.

Denmark

Danish Tibetan Cultural Society, Store Sohoj, Horsholm Kongevej, DK 2970 Horsholm; Tel: 0045 42 862027; Fax: 0045 42 817 097.

Tibetan Community in Denmark, Landelandsvery 47 ATV Frederiksbjerg.

Tibet Support Group Denmark, Finsenvej 8F 2TV, DK-2000 KBHN F.; Tel: (45-31) 860 168.

France

Bureau du Tibet, 28 rue Sorbier, 75020 Paris; Tel: (33-1) 43 58 47 03, 43 58 65 43; Fax: 44 62 97 39.

La Maison du Tibet, 36 rue Mauconseil, 75001 Paris; Tel: (33-1) 40 39 01 96; Fax: 40 39 02 57.

Comité de Soutien au Peuple au Peuple Tibétain, 1 rue St Vincent, Château d'Agnou, 78580 Maule.

France-Tibet, 48 Quai le Gallo, 92100 Boulogne-Billancourt.

Germany

Tibet Initiative Deutschland, Postfach 2531, D-5300 Bonn 1; Tel: (49-2152) 8632; Fax: (49-282) 261 620.

Tibet Information Service, Florastr. 22, D-4018 Langenfeld; Tel: (49-2173) 75151; Fax: (49-228) 485450.

Hong Kong

Asia Pacific Forum for Tibet, PO Box 98650, T.S.T. Kowloon; Tel: (852-3) 721-1974; Fax: (852-3) 721-2942.

Friends of Tibet, Hong Kong, 203 Wing Ting Building, 7-9 Wellington Street, Central Hong Kong; Tel: (852-5) 230-3501; Fax: (852-5) 868-4479.

Hungary

Office of Tibet, Varosmavor u. 23,1. em 2, 1122 Budapest XII; Tel: (36-1) 1551152, Fax: 155 1152.

India

Bureau of H.H. The Dalai Lama, 10 Ring Road, Lajpat Nagar IV, New Delhi 110 024; Tel: (91-11) 647 3386; Fax: 646 1914.

Department of Information and International Relations, Central Tibetan Secretariat, Gangchen Kyishong, Dharamsala 176 219; Tel: (91-1892) 2457; Fax: 4357.

Himalayan Committee for Action on Tibet, Ladakh Buddhist Vihar, Bela Road, New Delhi 110054; Tel: (91-11) 252 0455.

Indian Committee for Action on Tibet, F-18 Nizamuddin West, New Delhi 110013; Tel: (91-11) 618 923.

Indo-Tibetan Friendship Society, K 11/28 Lajpat Nagar, New Delhi 110024; Tel: (91-11) 683 3745.

Private Office of H.H. The Dalai Lama, Thekchen Choeling, PO McLeod Ganj, Dharamsala 176 219; Tel: (91-1892) 2759; Fax: 4213.

Tibetan Women's Association, Bhagsunath Road, PO McLeod Ganj, Dharamsala 176 219; Tel: (91-1892) 2527.

Tibetan Youth Congress, PO McLeod Ganj, Dharamsala 176 219.

Ireland

Tibet Support Group Ireland, 15 Cherry Court, Killiney, Co. Dublin; Tel: (35-31) 2821702; Fax: 2821702.

Italy

Associazione Italia-Tibet, Via Bronzino, 14, Milano 20133.
Casa del Tibet, c/o Dr. Stefano Dallari, Via Che Guevara 55, Reggio Emilia 42100.

Japan

The Office of Tibet in Japan, Celebrity Plaza, Shinjuku Bldg. (3F) 1-36-14 Shinjuku, Shinjuku-ku, Tokyo 160; Tel: (81-3) 3353-4094; Fax: 3225-8013.
Tibetan Snow Lion Friendship Society, Dotemachi Marutamachi Sagura, Komano-cho 554-3, Kamigyoo-ku, 602 Kyoto; Tel: (75) 256 0859.
Tibet Culture Center, Room 607, 3-28-1 Nishi-Gotanda, Shinagawa-Ku, Tokyo 141; Tel: (81-3) 3767-0518; Fax: (81-3) 3490-7868.

Mexico

Casa Tibet Mexico, Orizaba 93a, Col Roma, Mexico DF 067000; Tel: (52-5) 514 6580.

Nepal

Office of the Representative, Gadhen Khangsar, PO Box 310, Lazimpat, Kathmandu; Tel: (977-1) 419 240; Fax: 411 660.

Netherlands

Tibet Support Group Holland, Postbus 1756, 1000 BT Amsterdam.

New Zealand

Friends of Tibet, PO Box 66-002, Beach Haven, Auckland 10; Tel. & fax: (64-9) 483 7275.
Tibetan Children Relief Society, 1 Lifford Pl, Mt. Roskill, Auckland 4.

Norway

Tibetan Community in Norway, Otto Rugesvei 84A, 1345 Osteras.

Poland

Friends of Tibet, Adam Koziel, ul. Solec 109 AM/14, 00-382 Warsaw.

Free Tibet, ul. Nad Wilkowice 24, 43-365 Wilkoska; Fax: 48-302-1050.

Russian Federation

Office of Tibet, 49 Ostozhenka Street, Moscow 119 034; Tel: (7-095) 318 3190; Fax: 248 0264.

Sweden

Tibetan Community in Sweden, Bastuve.53es Court, 138 00 Stockholm-Alta.
Swedish Tibet Committee, Sjalagrardsgatan 2 D/3 o.g., S-11623 Stockholm; Tel: (46-8) 204 114; Fax: (46-8) 201 187.

Switzerland

Tibet Office, 10 Waffenplatzstrasse, 8002 Zurich; Tel: (41-1) 201 3336; Fax: 202 2160.
Bureau for UN Affairs, 13 rue de l'Ancien-Port, 1202 Geneva; Tel: (41-22) 738 7940; Fax: 738 7941.
Comité de Soutien au Peuple Tibétain, C.P. 2204, 1211 Geneva 2; Tel: (41-22) 733 7762; Fax: 734 4712.
Tibetan Folklore Association in Switzerland, c/o Tashi Tsering Takang, Himmeristr. 56, 8052 Zurich; Tel: (41-1) 302 2249.
Tibetan Refugee Educational Effort-Tree, c/o Phillip & Lill Sturgeon, Postfach 43, 3920 Zermatt; Tel: (41-28) 67 15 38.
Tibet Support Group Switzerland, Entrebois 57, 1018 Lausanne; Tel: (41-21) 36 92 75.
Tibetfreunde, Postfach, Kramgasse, CH-3000, Bern 8.

United Kingdom

All Party Parliamentary Group for Tibet, c/o Dr Norman Godman, House of Commons, Westminster, London SW1A 0AA; Tel: 071 586 7372.
Appropriate Technology for Tibetans, 6 Rockhall Rd., London NW2 6DT; Tel: 081 452 2820.
Campaign Free Tibet, 12 Stoughton Close, Kennington, London SE11.
Help Tibet, PO Box 138, Barnes, London SW13 9RN; Tel: 081 748 8784.
Office of Tibet, Linburn House, 342 Kilburn High Road, London NW6 2QJ; Tel: 071 328 8422; Fax: 372 5449.
Tharpa Publications, 15 Bendemeer Road, London SW15 1JX.
The Tibetan Charitable Trust, 129 Hamilton Terrace, London NW8 9QJ; Tel: 071 624 3921.
Tibetan Community in Britain, 13 St. Giles Court, Ealing, London W13 9QA; Tel: 081 567 7882.
Tibetan Information Network, 7 Beck Road, London E8 4RE; Tel: 081 533 5458; Fax: 985 4751.
Tibet Foundation. Phuntsong Wangyal. 10 Bloomsbury Way, London WC1A 2SH; Tel: 071 379 0634; Fax: 379 0465.

Tibet Image Bank, 36 Constantine Road, London NW3 2NG; Tel: 071 485 7382.

Tibet Society, Olympia Bridge Quay, Russell Road (Westside), Kensington, London W14 8YL; Tel: 071 603 7764.

Tibet Support Group UK, 9 Islington Green, London N1 2XH; Tel: 071 359 7573; Fax: 405 3814.

Wisdom Publications, 402 Hoe Street, London E17 9AA; Tel: 081 520 5588.

United States

The Office of Tibet, 241 East 32nd St., New York, NY 10016; Tel: (1-212) 213 5010; Fax: 779-9245.

Tibet House, 241 East 32nd St., New York, NY 10016; Tel: (1-212) 213 5592; Fax: 213 6408/5010.

International Campaign for Tibet, 1518 K Street, N.W. Suite 410, Washington D.C. 20005; Tel: (1-202), 628-4123; Fax: 347 6825.

American Himalayan Foundation, 909 Montgomery St., Suite 400, San Francisco, CA 94133; Tel: (415) 434 1111; Fax: (415) 434 3130.

Bay Area Friends of Tibet, 347 Dolores St., Suite 206, San Francisco, CA 94110; Tel: (415) 241 9197; Fax: (415) 626 0865.

Capital Area Friends of Tibet, 1518 K Street, NW, Suite 410, Washington, D.C. 20005; Tel: (202) 628 4123; Fax: (202) 347 6825.

Center for Cultural Survival, 11 Divinity Avenue, Cambridge, MA 02138; Tel: (617) 496 8786; Fax: (617) 496 8787.

Friends of Tibet, 6611 Clayton Road, Suite 200, St. Louis, MO 63117; Tel: (314) 862 8770.

Friends of Tibetan Women's Association, 1667 Las Caneas Rd., Santa Barbara, CA 93105; Tel: (805) 962 1190.

Institute for Asian Democracy, 1518 K St., N.W., Washington, D.C. 20005; Tel: (202)

International Fund for the Development of Tibet, PO Box 2169, Cambridge, MA 02238.

Mendocino Coast Tibet Support Group, PO Box 1158, Mendocino, CA 95460; Tel: (707) 961 1137; Fax: (707) 964 6543.

Midwest Tibet Association, PO Box 55051, Madison, WI 53705; Tel: (608) 233 2703.

Pioneer Valley Friends of Tibet, 57 North Prospect St., Amherst, MA 01002; Tel: (413) 253 5074.

Project Tibet, 403 Canyon Road, Santa Fe, NM 87501; Tel: (505) 982 3002; Fax: (505) 988 4142.

Rigpa Dorje Foundation, 328 N. Sycamore Ave., Los Angeles, CA 90036.

Sacharuna Foundation, PO Box 130, The Plains, VA 22171.

Sarnath Project, The Padmasambhava Society, Box 6036, West Palm Beach, FL 33405.

The Tibet Fund (Inc.), 241 E. 32nd St., New York, NY 10016; Tel: (212) 213 5010; Fax: (212) 779 9245.

Tibet-Net Inc., 7002 Boulevard East, Apt. 7C, Guttenberg, NJ 07093; Tel: (201) 662 7752; (201) 249 2502.

Tibetan Cultural Center, PO Box 2581, Bloomington, IN 47402; Tel: (812) 855 8222.

Tibetan Cultural Study Center, 316 Center Street, Old Town, ME 04468; Tel: (207) 827 6212.

Tibetan Cultural Institute, 61 Grove Street, #4A, New York, NY 10014; Tel: (212) 989 1829.

Tibetan and Buddhist Studies Society, Earl Hall, Columbia University, New York, NY 10027; Tel: (212) 854 5154; (212) 854 3218.

Tibetan Health and Education Fund, 1162 Adams Street, Denver, CO 80206; Tel: (303) 393 7466.

Tibetan Nuns Project, PO Box 40542, San Francisco, CA 94140; Tel: (804) 295 5533.

Tibetan Refugee Sponsorship Fund, PO Box 7604, Missoula, MT 59807; Tel: (406) 542 2110.

Tibetan Rights Campaign, PO Box 31966, Seattle, WA 98103; Tel: (206) 562 0265.

U.S. Tibet Committee, Inc., 241 E. 32nd St., New York, NY 10016; Tel: (212) 213 5010; Fax: (212) 779 9245.

Venezuela

Rafael F. Ortiz P., Apartado 60.961, Zone Postal 1060-A, Caracas; Tel: (58-2) 462 6713.

Bibliography

1 History, reference books and travellers' accounts

Ackerly, John and Blake Kerr, *The Suppression of a People: Accounts of Torture and Imprisonment in Tibet*, November 1989.

Avedon, John F., *In Exile from the Land of Snow*, Wisdom Publications, London, 1985.

Amnesty International, *Torture and Ill-Treatment of Tibetan Prisoners*, London, 1989.

Amnesty International, *People's Republic of China, Recent Reports on Political Prisoners and Prisoners of Conscience in Tibet*, October 1991.

Amnesty International, *China, Repression in Tibet from 1987 to 1992*, London, May 1992.

Asia Watch, *Prison Labor in China*, April 1991.

Aten, *Un Cavalier dans la neige, un vieux guerrier Khampa*, Jean Maisonneuve, Paris, 1981.

Barber, Noel, *The Flight of the Dalai Lama*, Hodder & Stoughton, London, 1960.

Bass, Catriona, *Inside the Treasure House*, Gollancz.

Bell, Sir Charles, *Tibet Past and Present*, Clarendon Press, Oxford, 1968.

Bell, Sir Charles, 'China and Tibet', *Journal of the Central Asian Society*, London, 1949.

Bonavia, David and Magnus Bartlett, *Tibet*, The Vendome Press, New York, 1981.

Bonin, Charles-Eudes, *Les Royaumes des Neiges, Etats Himalayens*, A. Colin, Paris, 1911.

Butterfield, Fox, *China, Alive in the Bitter Sea*, Bantam Books, New York, 1982.

Bushell, S.W., 'The Early History of Tibet, From Chinese Sources', *The Journal of the Royal Asiatic Society*, London, 1880.

Caroe, Sir Olaf, 'Tibet and the Chinese People's Republic', *Journal of the Central Asian Society*, London, 1960.

Dalai Lama, His Holiness the Fourteenth, *Freedom in Exile*, Gollancz, London, 1990; HarperCollins, London, 1990.

Dalai Lama, Tenzin Gyatso, *My Country and my People*, Snow Lion, Ithaca, 1988.

David-Neel, Alexandra, *Voyage d'une Parisienne à Lhassa*, Plon, Paris, 1927.

David-Neel, Alexandra, *Le Vieux Tibet Face à la Chine Nouvelle*, Plon, Paris, 1953.

David-Neel, Alexandra, *A l'Ouest Barbare de la Vaste Chine*, Plon, Paris, 1947.

David-Neel, Alexandra, *Mystiques et Magiciens du Tibet*, Plon, Paris, 1929.

David-Neel, Alexandra, *Grand Tibet au Pays des Brigands Gentilshommes*, Plon, Paris, 1933.

Dhondup, K., *The Water-horse and Other Years*, Library of Tibetan Works and Archives (LTWA), Dharamsala, 1985.

Dhondup, K., *The Water-bird and Other Years*, LTWA, Dharamsala, 1986.

Donnet, Pierre-Antoine, Privat, and Ribes, *Tibet, des Journalistes Témoignent*, Editions L'Harmattan, Paris, 1992.

Edgar, J.H., *The Great Open Land, Journal of the West China Border, 1930–34*, Shanghai.

Edou, Gérome and René Vernadet, *Les Chevaux du Vent*, Editions Shambala, 1988.

Gold, Peter, *Tibetan Reflections: Life in a Tibetan Refugee Community*, Wisdom Publications, London, 1984.

Goldstein, Melvyn H., *A History of Modern Tibet, 1913–1951*, University of California, 1989.

Goodman, M.H., *The Last Dalai Lama, A Biography*, Sidgwick & Jackson, London, 1986.

Gopal, Ram, *India–China–Tibet Triangle*, Lucknow, 1964.

Graham, David, *An Expedition to the China-Tibetan Border*, Shanghai, 1937.

Guillermaz, Jacques, *Le Parti Communiste au Pouvoir*, Payot, Paris, 1972.

Hadfield, J., *A Winter in Tibet*, Impact, London, 1988.

Han Suyin, *Lhasa, the Open City*, Triad Panther Books, London, 1979.

Harrer, Heinrich, *Seven Years in Tibet*, Paladin Books, London, 1988.

Harrer, Heinrich, *Return to Tibet*, Penguin Books, London, 1987.

Hopkirk, Peter, *Trespassers on the Roof of the World*, John Murray, London, 1982.

International Campaign for Tibet, *The Long March, Chinese Settlers and Chinese Policies in Eastern Tibet*, Washington, September 1991.

International Campaign for Tibet, *Nuclear Tibet*, Washington, April 1993

International Commission of Jurists, *The Question of Tibet and the Rule of Law*, Geneva, 1959.

International Commission of Jurists, *Tibet and the Chinese People's Republic: A Report to the International Commission of Jurists*, Geneva, 1960.

Jagou, Fabienne, 'Tibet Langue de Bois, 10 Ans de Chroniques Tibétains du Journal Chinois *Le Quotidien du Peuple* de 1980 à 1989', academic paper, Paris, 1991.

Jamatel, Maurice (trans.), *Histoire de la Pacification du Tibet sous le Regne de l'Empéreur Kien-Long*, Ernest Leroux, Paris, 1882.

Kelly, Petra and Aiello Bastian, *The Anguish of Tibet*, Parallax, 1991.

Kimura, Hisao, *Japanese Agent in Tibet*, Serindia, London, 1990.

Lang, Nicolas, *Le Colonialisme Chinoise au Tibet*, Est-Ouest, Paris, 1962.

Leroy, Gilbert, *Le Rire Jaune*, Editions L'Harmattan, Collection Partir Là-bas, Paris, 1988.

Leys, Simon, *Ombres Chinoises*, Christian Bourgois, Paris, 1974.

Levenson, Claude B., *Le Chemin de Lhassa*, Lieu Commun, Paris, 1985.

Levenson, Claude B., *The Dalai Lama: A Biography*, Allen & Unwin, London, 1988.

Levenson, Claude B., *Ainsi Parle le Dalai-Lama*, Editions Balland, Paris, 1991.

Levenson, Claude B., *L'An Prochain à Lhassa*, Editions Balland, Paris, 1993.

Lhamo, Rinchen, *We Tibetans*, Potala Books, New York, 1985.

Maraini, Fosco, *Tibet Secret*, Editions Arthaud, Paris, 1990.

Mitter, J.P., *Betrayal of Tibet*, Allied Publishers, India, 1964.

Moraes, Frank, *The Revolt in Tibet*, Sterling Publishers, Delhi, 1959.

Musée de l'Homme, *Voyages dans les Marches Tibétaines*, Paris, 1990.

Norbu, Dawa, *Red Star Over Tibet*, Sterling Publishers, Delhi, 1987.

Norbu, Jamyang, *Warriors of Tibet*, Wisdom Publications, London, 1986.

Norbu, Thubten Jigme, *Tibet is my Country*, Wisdom Publications, London, 1986.

Norbu, Thubten Jigme and Colin Turnbull, *Tibet, its History, Religion and People*, Penguin Books, London, 1969.

Patterson, George, *Tibet in Revolt*, Faber & Faber, London 1960.

Patterson, George, *Requiem for Tibet*, Faber & Faber, London, 1990.

Peissel, Michel, *Les Cavaliers du Kham*, Robert Laffont, Paris, 1972.

Pemba, Tsewang, *Tibet, l'an du Dragon*, Maisonneuve & Larose, Paris, 1975.

Richardson, Hugh E., *A Short History of Tibet*, Dutton, New York, 1962

Richardson, Hugh E., *Tibet and its History*, Oxford University Press, London, 1962.

Richardson, H.E. (ed.), *Adventures of a Tibetan Fighting Monk*, The Tamarind Press, Bangkok, 1986.

Sen, Chanakya (ed.), *Tibet Disappears: A documentary history of Tibet's international status*, Asian Publishing House, Bombay, Calcutta, New Delhi, 1960.

Seymour, James D., *Human Rights and Tibet, the Many Layers of Contradictions*, Columbia University Press, New York, 1991.

Shakabpa, Tsepon W.D., *Tibet, a Political History*, Potala Publications, New York, 1988.

Société des Missions Etrangères de Paris, *Trente Ans aux Portes du Thibet Interdit 1908–1938*, Maison de Nazareth, Hong Kong, 1939.

Stein, R.A., *Tibetan Civilization*, Stanford University Press, Stanford, 1972.

Stoddard, H., *Le Mendiant de L'Amdo*, Société d'Ethnographie, Paris, 1985.

Taring, Rinchen Dolma, *Daughter of Tibet*, John Murray, London, 1970, Repr. Allied Publishers, Delhi, 1983.

Templé, Erwan, *Bibliographie du Tibet, Tome 1 – Bouddhisme*, Editions Tibet Diffusion, 1992.

Thondup, K., *Tibet in Turmoil, a Pictorial Account*, Nihon Kogyo Shinbun, Tokyo, 1983.

Tibet Information Network and Asia Watch, *Political Prisoners in Tibet*, London, February 1992.

Tibet Information Network and Lawasia, *Defying the Dragon*, London, March 1991.

Tieh-Tseng, Li, *The Historical Status of Tibet*, King's Crown Press, New York, 1956.

Trungpa, Chogyam, *Born in Tibet*, George Allen & Unwin, London, 1966.

Vernier-Palliez, C. and B. Auger, *Le Dalai Lama, La Presence et L'Exil*, Editions Lattès-Filipacchi, Paris, 1991.

Vigniel, Corinne, *The Shift from 'Merciless Repression' to the 'Comprehensive Management of Public Security' in the Tibetan Autonomous Region*, SOAS, London University, 1991.

van Walt van Praag, Michael C., *The Status of Tibet*, Westview Press, Colorado, 1987.

van Walt van Praag, Michael C., *Population Transfer and the Survival of the Tibetan Identity*, The U.S. Tibet Committee, New York, 1986.

Wang, Xiaoping and Bai Nanfeng, *The Poverty of Plenty*, Macmillan, London, 1991.

Yudon Yuthok, Dorje, *House of the Turquoise Roof*, Snow Lion, 1990.

2 Official Chinese publications

Changhao, Xi, and Gao Yuanmei, *Tibet Leaps Forward*, Foreign Languages Press, Peking, 1977.

Epstein, Israel, *Tibet transformed*, New World Press, Peking, 1983.

Epstein, Israel, *From Opium War to Liberation*, Joint Publishing Co., Hong Kong, 1980.

Kaiming, Su, *Modern China, A Topical History*, New World Press, Peking, 1985.

Questions and Answers about China's National Minorities, New World Press, Peking, 1985.

Tibet Today and Yesterday, Beijing Information, Peking, 1984.

Tibet, a General Survey (vols. 1 to 10, entitled 'Why Tibet is an integral part of China', 'Origin of the so-called "independence" of Tibet and the truth about this matter' 'The Dalai Lama and the the "17-Point Agreement"', 'Tibet, the Last Shangri-La?', 'The Tibetan people's right to autonomy', 'The Population of Tibet, facts and figures', 'New developments in Tibetan culture', 'Freedom of religious belief', 'Tibet, Big changes in 40 Years' and 'A Watershed in the Evolution of Tibet's History'. New Star Editions, Peking, 1991.

100 Questions about Tibet, Beijing Review, Peking, 1989.

Furen, Wang and Suo Wenqing, *Highlights of Tibetan History*, New World Press, Peking, 1984.

Tibetans about Tibet, China Reconstructs, Peking, 1988.

Tibet, A General Survey, New World Press, Peking, 1988.

Tibet: Myth vs. Reality, Beijing Review Publications, Peking, 1988.

Great Changes in Tibet, Foreign Languages Press, Peking, 1972.

Tibet: No Longer Medieval, Foreign Language Press, Peking, 1981.

Tibet Today, Foreign Language Press, Peking, 1974.

Zhongguo Shaoshu Minzu, Guojia Minzu Weiyanhui Xinhua Shudian, Peking, 1981.

Laizi Xizang de Baodao, Zhongguo Jianshi Zazhishe, Peking, 1983.

China's Tibet, quarterly, Minzu (Nationalities') Press, Peking.

3 Publications of the Tibetan government-in-exile

Andrugtsang, Gompo Tashi, *Four Rivers, Six Ranges, A true account of Khampa resistance to Chinese in Tibet*, The Information Office of H.H. the Dalai Lama, Dharamsala, 1973.

Choedon, Dhondub, *Life in the Red Flag People's Commune*, The Information Office of H.H. the Dalai Lama, Dharamsala, 1978.

Chopel, Norbu, *Folk Culture of Tibet*, Library of Tibetan Works & Archives, Dharamsala, 1983.

Gashi, Tsering Dorje, *New Tibet*, The Information Office of H.H. the Dalai Lama, Dharamsala, 1980.

Paljor, Kunsang, *Tibet, the Undying Flame*, The Information Office of H.H. the Dalai Lama, Dharamsala, 1977.

Trulku, Ribhur, *The Search for Jowo Mikyoe Dorjee*, The Office of Information & International Relations, Dharamsala, 1988.

Tibet in the United Nations, 1950–1961, The Bureau of H.H. the Dalai Lama, New Delhi.

Tibet Under Chinese Communist Rule, a compilation of Refugee Statements, 1958-1975, The Information Office of H.H. the Dalai Lama, Dharamsala, 1976.

From Liberation to Liberalisation, The Information Office of H.H. the Dalai Lama, Dharamsala, 1982.

Glimpses of Tibet Today, The Information Office of H.H. the Dalai Lama, Dharamsala, 1978.

Tibetans in Exile, The Information Office of H.H. the Dalai Lama, Dharamsala, 1981.

Tibet, A Land of Snows Rich in Precious Stones and Mineral Resources, Research and Analysis Centre, Department of Security, Dharamsala, 1991.

Tibet: Environment and Development Issues 1992, Department of Information & International Relations, Dharamsala, 1992.

4 Magazines and periodicals

Tibet Information Network, news updates by fax or post, Tel: 081-533 5458, Fax: 081-985 4751.

Tibetan Review, monthly, Editor: Tsering Wangyal, S.O.S. Hostel, Sector 14 Extn, Rohini, Delhi 110 085.

Tibet Press Watch, an international selection of noteworthy articles, International Campaign for Tibet, Washington D.C.

Tibetan Bulletin, bi-monthly, the Official Journal of the Tibetan Government-in-Exile, Department of Information and International Relations, Dharmsala.

Lungta, two issues a year, in English and in French, published by Comité de Soutien Au Peuple Tibétain, Switzerland.

Nouvelles Tibétaines, monthly, by Maongpa, Dip Tse Chok Ling, McLeod Ganj, Dharmsala 176 219.

Index